Studies in Nietzsche and the Judaeo-Christian Tradition

"If the previous course of Western thought is, in a decisive sense, summed up and culminates in Nietzsche's thought, it follows that a reckoning with Nietzsche is a reckoning with Western thought."

Heidegger, *Nietzsche*

"The most serious Christians have always been well disposed toward me."

Nietzsche, *Ecce Homo*

Studies in Nietzsche and the Judaeo-Christian Tradition

EDITED BY

JAMES C. O'FLAHERTY,

TIMOTHY F. SELLNER AND

ROBERT M. HELM

UNC Studies in the Germanic Languages and Literatures
Number 103

Copyright © 1985

This work is licensed under a Creative Commons CC BY-NC-ND license.
To view a copy of the license, visit http://creativecommons.org/licenses.

Suggested citation: O'Flaherty, James C., Timothy F. Sellner, and Robert M. Helms, editors. *Studies in Nietzsche and the Judaeo-Christian Tradition.* Chapel Hill: University of North Carolina Press, 1985. DOI: https://doi.org/10.5149/9781469656557_OFlaherty

Library of Congress Cataloging-in-Publication Data
Names: O'Flaherty, James C., Sellner, Timothy F., and Helm, Robert M., editors.
Title: Studies in Nietzsche and the Judaeo-Christian tradition / edited by James C. O'Flaherty, Timothy F. Sellner, and Robert M. Helm.
Other titles: University of North Carolina Studies in the Germanic Languages and Literatures ; no. 103.
Description: Chapel Hill : University of North Carolina Press, [1985] Series: University of North Carolina Studies in the Germanic Languages and Literatures. | Includes bibliographical references and index.
Identifiers: LCCN 84011963 | ISBN 978-1-4696-5654-0 (pbk: alk. paper) | ISBN 978-1-4696-5655-7 (ebook)
Subjects: Nietzsche, Friedrich Wilhelm, 1844-1900 — Religion. | Religion — History — 19th century.
Classification: LCC B3318.R4 S88 1985 | DCC 193

Chapter VI is a slightly modified English translation of "Dionysos gegen den Gekreuzigten: Nietzsches Verständnis des Apostels Paulus," originally published in *Zeitschrift für Religion und Geistesgeschichte* © 1974 Verlag E.J. Brill. Republished by permission of Koninklijke Brill NV, Leiden, Netherlands.

Chapter XVI is an English translation from *Nietzsche, critique des valeurs chrétiennes* by Georges Goedert (Paris: Editions Beauchesne, 1977), and is reprinted here by permission of the publisher.

Chapter XVII consists of an excerpt from *Does God Exist? An Answer for Today* by Hans Küng, translated by Edward Quinn (New York: Doubleday, 1980) and is reprinted here by permission of Hans Küng.

Chapter XVIII consists of an excerpt from *Church Dogmatics* ©Karl Barth, edited by G.W. Bromiley and T.F. Torrence, 1960, *Church Dogmatics: Vol. 3 Part 2*, T. & T. Clark, an imprint of Bloomsbury Publishing Plc.

UNC | COLLEGE OF ARTS AND SCIENCES
Germanic and Slavic Languages and Literatures

From 1949 to 2004, UNC Press and the UNC Department of Germanic & Slavic Languages and Literatures published the UNC Studies in the Germanic Languages and Literatures series. Monographs, anthologies, and critical editions in the series covered an array of topics including medieval and modern literature, theater, linguistics, philology, onomastics, and the history of ideas. Through the generous support of the National Endowment for the Humanities and the Andrew W. Mellon Foundation, books in the series have been reissued in new paperback and open access digital editions. For a complete list of books visit www.uncpress.org.

Contents

Introduction *James C. O'Flaherty*	3
I. Nietzsche: Critic in the Grand Style *Eugen Biser*	16
II. The Case against Apolitical Morality: Nietzsche's Interpretation of the Jewish Instinct *Harry Neumann*	29
III. Nietzsche and the Old Testament *Israel Eldad*	47
IV. Morality and Deity in Nietzsche's Concept of Biblical Religion *Charles Lewis*	69
V. The Critical Imitator of Jesus: A Contribution to the Interpretation of Nietzsche on the Basis of a Comparison *Eugen Biser*	86
VI. Dionysus versus the Crucified One: Nietzsche's Understanding of the Apostle Paul *Jörg Salaquarda*	100
VII. *Amor dei* and *Amor fati*: Spinoza and Nietzsche *Joan Stambaugh*	130
VIII. Nietzsche and Luther: A Testimony to Germanophilia *Max L. Baeumer*	143
IX. "The Only Logical Christian": Nietzsche's Critique of Pascal *Brendan Donnellan*	161
X. Lessing and Nietzsche: Views on Christianity *Diana Behler*	177
XI. Nietzsche, Heine, and the Otherness of the Jew *Sander L. Gilman*	206
XII. Nietzsche and Kierkegaard *Gerd-Günther Grau*	226

XIII. Language and the Critique of Language in Nietzsche 252
Josef Simon

XIV. The Intuitive Mode of Reason in *Zarathustra* 274
James C. O'Flaherty

XV. Jesus, Christianity, and Superhumanity 295
Bernd Magnus

XVI. The Dionysian Theodicy 319
Georges Goedert

XVII. Nietzsche: What Christians and Non-Christians Can Learn 341
Hans Küng

XVIII. Humanity without the Fellow-Man: Nietzsche's Superman and Christian Morality 353
Karl Barth

Contributors 375

Index 379

Acknowledgments

The editors wish to express their gratitude to Wake Forest University for the grant that has made possible the publication of this volume. They also wish to express their appreciation to Mrs. Mary C. Reid, secretary of the German Department, for her efficiency and considerable patience not only in the typing of the manuscript but also in all matters pertaining to the project. Permission to reprint articles in the volume as individual chapters granted by the following publishers is acknowledged: Verlag E. J. Brill (chap. VI, in translation); Editions Beauchesne (chap. XVI, in translation); Doubleday and Co. (chap. XVII); T. & T. Clark, Limited (chap. XVIII).

Key to Abbreviations

Individual works by Nietzsche:

GT   *Die Geburt der Tragödie (The Birth of Tragedy)*
U   *Unzeitgemäße Betrachtungen (Untimely Meditations* or *Thoughts out of Season)*
MA   *Menschliches, Allzumenschliches (Human, All-Too-Human)*
S   *Der Wanderer und sein Schatten (The Wanderer and His Shadow)*
M   *Morgenröte (The Dawn* or *The Dawn of Day)*
FW   *Die fröhliche Wissenschaft (The Gay Science* or *The Joyful Wisdom)*
Z   *Also sprach Zarathustra (Thus Spoke Zarathustra)*
J   *Jenseits von Gut und Böse (Beyond Good and Evil)*
GM   *Zur Genealogie der Moral (On the Genealogy of Morals)*
G   *Die Götzen-Dämmerung (The Twilight of the Idols)*
A   *Der Antichrist (The Antichrist)*
WM   *Der Wille zur Macht (The Will to Power)*

Editions of Nietzsche's works:

GOE   *Werke: Großoktavausgabe*, ed. Elisabeth Förster-Nietzsche et al. (Leipzig: Naumann, 1894–1904), 15 vols.; 2nd ed. (1901–13), 19 vols., indicated by: GOA(2). Vol. XX, published as a partial index to 2nd ed. (Leipzig, 1926).
MusA *Gesammelte Werke: Musarionausgabe*, ed. Richard Oehler, Max Oehler, and F. C. Würzbach (Munich: Musarion Verlag, 1920–29).
HKG   *Werke und Briefe: Historisch-Kritische Gesamtausgabe*, ed. under supervision of the "Stiftung Nietzsche-Archiv" (Munich: Beck, 1933–42), 9 vols.
K   *Sämtliche Werke in zwölf Bänden*, ed. Alfred Bäumler (Stuttgart: Kröner, 1964–65). The twelve vols. are reprints of Nos. 70–78, 82–83, and 170 in *Kröners Taschenausgabe* series, and are identified by the series number in italics, followed by the page number, e.g.: *70*, 48; *71*, 49; etc. The last vol. (*170*) is Richard Oehler's index to the previous vols.

W *Werke in drei Bänden*, ed. Karl Schlechta (Munich: Carl Hanser, 1954–56; 1966). *Nietzsche Index* to foregoing (Munich, 1965).

WKG *Werke: Kritische Gesamtausgabe*, ed. Giorgio Colli and Mazzino Montinari (Berlin: de Gruyter, 1967 ff.), about 30 vols. planned.

KSA *Sämtliche Werke: Kritische Studienausgabe*, ed. Giorgio Colli and Mazzino Montinari (Berlin: de Gruyter, 1980).

GB *Gesammelte Briefe*, 5 vols. in 6 (Leipzig: Insel, 1902–9). Volume V consists of two separately bound parts, designated V/1 and V/2.

Studies in Nietzsche and the Judaeo-Christian Tradition

Introduction

James C. O'Flaherty

"No one has equaled him [Nietzsche] in the acuteness, depth, and radicalness of his thought: not Feuerbach, not Marx and not even Freud; at most, Pascal."

—Hans Küng

The present volume is a sequel to the earlier *Studies in Nietzsche and the Classical Tradition* published by the University of North Carolina Press.[1] The positive reception of that volume, which necessitated a second edition, encouraged the editors to publish a second volume along the lines of the first but on an even more important subject. For, despite the great significance for Nietzsche of the classical tradition and his own preference for the Greek over the Christian ideal in all areas of life, the overriding concern of his writings is, on the one hand, to unmask what he conceived to be the decadence of both Judaism and Christianity—especially the latter—and, on the other hand, to supplant those faiths with the doctrines proclaimed in *Also sprach Zarathustra*. The purpose of the present volume is to present studies that deal with crucial aspects of his thought concerning the dominant religions of the West. Although there exists a vast body of literature on the subject of Nietzsche and Christianity, most of it is in German or other languages,[2] and much of it is either out-of-date or too tendentious to be considered serious scholarship. Further, since

---

1. James C. O'Flaherty, Timothy F. Sellner, and Robert M. Helm, eds., *Studies in Nietzsche and the Classical Tradition*, University of North Carolina Studies in the Germanic Languages and Literatures, no. 85 (Chapel Hill: University of North Carolina Press, 1976; 2nd ed., 1979).

2. See *International Nietzsche Bibliography*, ed. Herbert W. Reichert and Karl Schlechta, University of North Carolina Studies in Comparative Literature, no. 45 (Chapel Hill: University of North Carolina Press, 1968); and *Nietzsche Studien*, ed. Ernst Behler, Mazzino Montinari, Wolfgang Müller-Lauter, and Heinz Wenzel (Berlin: de Gruyter, 1972–). See Peter Köster, "Nietzsche Kritik und Nietzsche-Rezeption in der Theologie des 20. Jahrhunderts," *Nietzsche Studien*, 10/11 (1981–82), 615–85, not only for an excellent overview of its subject, but also for an indication of the areas where more research needs to be done.

World War II there has been a general tendency in all Nietzsche research to scant this important subject. The essays presented here are offered not only for their intrinsic worth but also as a potential stimulus for further research in the field. With the recent publication of the historical-critical edition of Nietzsche's complete works and correspondence by Giorgio Colli and Mazzino Montinari a firm basis has been provided for a more adequate understanding of Nietzsche's thought.

Nietzsche's relationship to Judaism and Christianity is exceedingly paradoxical. Claiming to be the most radical critic of those faiths the world has ever known—a claim few would be inclined to dispute—he has nevertheless evoked from many of their best representatives admiration not only for his honesty and courage, but also for his genius as a critic of religion and for his uncanny skill at ferreting out the alien and secular elements that so often masquerade under the cloak of the accepted faiths. On this latter point he makes common cause with those sincere Jewish and Christian believers who deplore the all-too-easy accommodation of their respective faiths to secular culture. One should, however, make no mistake about Nietzsche's intentions. As he most emphatically declares in *Ecce Homo*: "Above all do not mistake me!"—which means that he wanted always to be known as the implacable foe of Christianity.

Strangely, however, the spirit of Nietzsche's criticism of Christianity is one that, far from immediately and irretrievably alienating the sincere believer, may, and often does, attract and hold his deepest attention. In spite of the acerbity of Nietzsche's language and the harshness of his judgments, one senses in his assaults a spirit quite different from that of most other severe critics of Christianity of whatever rank—for example, a Voltaire, an H. L. Mencken, or a Gore Vidal. The empty cynicism and at times outright malevolence that so often characterize the animadversions of critics are lacking. Perhaps Nietzsche's different, if quite vehement, spirit stems from his conviction that one is ennobled by the choice of a worthy enemy. In fact, he goes so far in *Ecce Homo* as to say that for him to attack an individual Christian was "a sign of benevolence" (*Wohlwollen*). Be that as it may, it is certainly true that, with the possible exception of David Friedrich Strauß, he chose adversaries whom he respected, often deeply. There is even evidence that his attitude toward the Apostle Paul was not entirely negative. Perhaps it was the underlying respect for his antagonists, like that of the true athlete for his rival, or of the genuinely chivalric warrior for his foe, that has caused many adherents of the faiths he has attacked to feel a special affinity for him. In any event, it is true that a number of striking paradoxes emerge in connection with Nietzsche's view of Judaism and Christianity.

A brief enumeration of such paradoxes suffices to confirm the challenge they pose for an understanding of Nietzsche's thought. First, there is the singular fact that although Nietzsche has often been regarded—and still is by some—as a major source of anti-Semitism, it is above all the Jews who have figured most prominently in furthering his reputation. Thus, it was the eminent Danish Jewish scholar Georg Brandes who first launched the wider reputation and stimulated the serious study of Nietzsche by giving public lectures on him in 1888. Sigmund Freud was not at all reluctant to admit that Nietzsche had anticipated many of his own basic ideas, and his admiration for the German philosopher clearly shines through his references to him. Chaim Weizmann, the pioneering Zionist and first President of Israel, had been an enthusiastic reader of Nietzsche in his youth, an enthusiasm that he never repudiated. Martin Buber, without doubt the greatest Jewish philosopher of the twentieth century, once translated the first part of *Also sprach Zarathustra* into Polish, and he remained in creative dialogue with Nietzsche's atheism throughout his entire career. The Russian philosopher Lev Shestov, who was deeply appreciative of both his Jewish heritage and Christianity, could say sincerely but with consummate, if unintentional, irony: "Nietzsche has shown us the way. We must seek that which is *higher* than compassion, higher than the 'good'; we must seek God."[3]

After World War II, when Nietzsche's reputation was at its lowest ebb in this century, it was the Jewish scholars Karl Löwith and Walter Kaufmann who, before the epoch-making appearance of Heidegger's two-volume study of Nietzsche's philosophy, were in the vanguard of the attempt to recover his reputation as a seminal philosopher and to give the lie to the notion that he was simply a fascist ideologist.[4] The names of other important, but lesser-known, Jewish thinkers and scholars who, adopting a positive attitude toward him, have contributed to a better understanding of his thought might very well be added to the list. Responsible scholars have long known and stressed that Nietzsche abominated anti-Semitism. Nevertheless, there are those who, with obdurate perversity, continue to associate him with anti-Semitism—indeed, at times, anti-Semitism of

---

3. Lev Shestov, *In Job's Balances: On the Sources of Eternal Truths*, trans. C. Coventry and C. A. Macartney (Athens, Ohio: Ohio University Press, 1976), pp. xi–xii.

4. Cf. Rudolf Augstein, *Der Spiegel*, 8 June 1981, pp. 150–84, where Nietzsche is presented simply as the theoretician of Hitlerism.

the most virulent sort.⁵ In the present collection the contribution of Israel Eldad is an emphatic reminder of the continuing affinity of certain Jewish intellectuals for Nietzsche. A lecturer on the Bible at the University of Haifa, Eldad has translated seven volumes of Nietzsche's works, as well as Walter Kaufmann's major work on him, into Hebrew.

Even more paradoxical than the Jewish reception of Nietzsche is that of leading Christian thinkers, for Christianity was far more the target of his attacks than was Judaism. Yet it is precisely among certain Christian theologians, philosophers, and scholars that we find either an appreciative or, in some important cases, a creative encounter with his thought. His remark in *Ecce Homo* that "the most serious Christians have always been well disposed toward me" is not wide of the mark. The articles by Karl Barth and Eugen Biser in the present collection speak for themselves. But it is impressive to note that Christian leaders of the nineteenth and twentieth centuries like Vladimir Soloviev, Nicholas Berdyaev, Adolf Harnack, Ernst Troeltsch, Albert Schweitzer, Dietrich Bonhoeffer, William Ernest Hocking, and Paul Tillich were all appreciative of and influenced by Nietzsche in varying degrees. Especially instructive is the impact of Nietzsche on that quintessential American philosopher, William Ernest Hocking. Recalling his student days in Berlin, Hocking wrote: "And then, oddly enough, I got a good deal from that scapegrace, Nietzsche. . . . I found this reckless player-with-lightning [in *Also sprach Zarathustra*] strangely refreshing. I couldn't digest his condemnation of Die Mitleidigen but I saw what he meant by saying that 'it is the will of all great love, the beloved to *create*; and all creators are *hard*.' So I changed his 'Wille zur Macht'—to the 'will to suffer in creation'. . . ."⁶ Albert Schweitzer, whose ethical philosophy is the antithesis of Nietzsche's, could nevertheless praise him for his affirmation of life and for holding that "individual morality comes before social morality."⁷

Of all those named the most impressive is Bonhoeffer, not only because of his careful and lifelong study of Nietzsche, but because of his martyrdom at the hands of the Nazis. Eberhard Bethge, his

---

5. Cf. W. A. Carto's "Publisher's Foreword," in his reprint of H. L. Mencken's translation of *The Antichrist* (Torrance, California: The Noontide Press, 1980), p. ix, where he speaks of "the myth of the 'Holocaust.'"

6. Quoted by Leroy S. Rouner, *Within Human Experience: The Philosophy of William Ernest Hocking* (Cambridge, Mass.: Harvard University Press, 1969), p. 157.

7. Albert Schweitzer, *Civilization and Ethics*, quoted by Henry Clark, *The Ethical Mysticism of Albert Schweitzer* (Boston: Beacon Press, 1962), p. 25.

friend and biographer, writes: "Bonhoeffer read all of Nietzsche very carefully, and Nietzsche's tremendous plea for the earth and for loyalty to its creatures never left his mind."[8] The sincerity of any professing Christian whose faith has never been tested by the fires of martyrdom may always be brought into question by the skeptic. In the case of Bonhoeffer, however, there can be no question. Nietzsche's influence combined with that of the Greek myth of the giant Antaeus, "who was undefeatable as long as he had his feet on the ground,"[9] to render Bonhoeffer most sensitive to the need to oppose with all his resources the clear and present danger of Nazism in his day.

If we view the essays in the present collection from the standpoint of Nietzsche's mode of reasoning as it emerges in them, we shall find that he employs reason in two major ways: as intuitive and as abstract reason. The terms "intuitive reason" and "abstract reason" are defined and treated in detail in my essay, "The Intuitive Mode of Reason in *Zarathustra*." It will suffice to say here that intuitive reason tends to express itself in metaphorical or poetic language; abstract reason, on the other hand, must express itself in prose or in its extension as logical or mathematical symbolism. Nietzsche's philosophical prose is, of course, *characterized* by logic, but is not *dominated* by it, as would be the case with a rigorously discursive thinker. Nietzsche was no irrationalist, despite the opinion of a Georg Lukács. He simply uses reason to decry the excessive use of reason. This fact results from his conviction that the higher the degree of abstraction, the emptier the concept. His use of logical or abstract reason in the prose writings is generally critical or analytic; his use of analogical or intuitive reasoning in the poetic writings is generally divinatory or prophetic. That he philosophizes in the two distinct literary genres is not simply a stylistic matter, but has to do with two discrete modes of thought.

In surveying the following essays briefly from the perspectives indicated, I do not desire thereby to see them more narrowly than they ought to be or to force them into the framework suggested by the argument of my essay. It is simply *one* helpful way among others of looking at them by way of introduction. For even a cursory glance at the essays reveals their considerable variety and richness, and also the fact that they may be viewed profitably from a number of perspectives.

8. Eberhard Bethge, "The Challenge of Dietrich Bonhoeffer's Life and Theology," in Ronald G. Smith, *The World Come of Age* (Philadelphia: Fortress Press, 1967), p. 27.
9. Ibid., p. 76.

First we may note that Joan Stambaugh's comparison of Spinoza's idea of *amor dei* with Nietzsche's idea of *amor fati* highlights in a special way the contrast between the two kinds of reason with which we are concerned here. For despite important substantive agreements between the two thinkers, Nietzsche's method of reasoning appears in strong contrast to Spinoza's highly abstract method. While there is a rationalistic or critical aspect of Nietzsche's discussion of *amor fati* (e.g., the difference between "Turkish" and "Russian" fatalism), his mode of reasoning is there primarily intuitive. For it is the intuiting soul of the individual, symbolized above all by Zarathustra's "azure bell," that divines the meaning of the world as well as of the self. As Stambaugh well says, "this poetic 'imagery' for the soul is about as far removed from the Cartesian *res cogitans* as possible; the soul is not a separate substantial thinking thing. . . ."

In the following group of essays we find Nietzsche employing chiefly critical or analytic reason for an explication of his ideas. The approaches he adopts are various, and reflect his reaction to the subject matter he is treating, but they all fall for our purposes chiefly under the rubric of "critical reason." In his introductory essay, "Nietzsche: Critic in the Grand Style," Eugen Biser writes that "Nietzsche exercises his role as a critic with differing intensity." He thereupon mentions individual works, describing each differently according to the spirit in which it was written. Thus, one was written with "élan," another "with vehemence," and still another "with the gestures of an evangelist." One was written "aggressively," another "with analytic rigor." Again, Nietzsche writes "in uninhibited and tendentious fashion." These changes of mood underlying his criticism are not surprising when we note with Biser that "Nietzsche does not merely criticize; he lives and exists critically." This is one of the important reasons there exists "a pressing need for a Nietzschean hermeneutics."

In his second essay, "The Critical Imitator of Jesus," Biser argues that Nietzsche can be understood properly only by seeing his imitation of Christ as crucial and as the archetype for his relation to the numerous and varied figures with whom he compared himself, for they too do not escape his criticism. Nietzsche's relation to Jesus results in a sort of independent dependence on Him, issuing in "existential disquietude." The dependent aspect of the relationship results in Nietzsche's imitation of Jesus, the independent aspect in his criticism, which is both positive and negative.

In "The Case against Apolitical Morality: Nietzsche's Interpretation of the Jewish Instinct," Harry Neumann argues that Nietzsche believed the Jews had never really given up their Messianic hope and hence were always instinctively political. The adoption of (apolitical) monotheism in the diaspora was only a means of finally returning, with the restoration of the Temple, to the henotheistic *Volksgott* or tribal God. Nietzsche's critique of what he saw as the unfortunate transformation of Judaism is also aimed at the Christians. Nietzsche saw himself as an outsider, and in this regard he could identify with the Jews. However, as Sander L. Gilman emphasizes in "Nietzsche, Heine, and the Otherness of the Jew," he was not born an outsider like the Jews of the diaspora but, rather, chose the role of outsider. Nietzsche saw the Jews in a favorable light when they were the object of anti-Semitism, and in an unfavorable light when he recognized in them many of the characteristics of German Christians.

It is ironic that Nietzsche, the philosopher, did not publish his most rigorously philosophical writings, but relegated them to his *Nachlaß*, or unpublished notebooks. In his "Language and the Critique of Language in Nietzsche" Josef Simon has systematically elaborated Nietzsche's epistemology as it emerges from his philosophy of language. Here Nietzsche, the critic, is most analytical, for we find him using the criticism of language quite logically to decry abstract or discursive reason. We see clearly from this study that Nietzsche actually stands in the tradition of nominalism, which, among other and secular predecessors, also includes important Scholastic theologians. In my study "The Intuitive Mode of Reason in *Zarathustra*," insights and practices of Nietzsche's are appealed to, but the conceptual framework is, in the main, derived from the language philosophy of Johann Georg Hamann; there is, as far as their epistemological critique of language is concerned, general agreement between the two, despite their antithetical views of Christianity.

In his exhaustively documented study, "Dionysus versus the Crucified One: Nietzsche's Understanding of the Apostle Paul," Jörg Salaquarda shows that Nietzsche's criticism of Paul is not *entirely* negative as many commentators have held, but that Nietzsche could at times appreciate Paul as "a great man" or as a "Dionysian revaluator," to whom he himself bore a "dialectical resemblance." Salaquarda is of course demonstrating Nietzsche's critical powers at their strongest and most hostile in the polemics against Paul, but he also invokes a kind of Hegelian dialectic as *implicit* in Nietzsche's late philosophy. Thus, Rome represents for Nietzsche the thesis, Pauline Christianity the antithesis. The synthesis—which lies in the future—would not be "a *mere* return to the 'master morality'" of the Romans, but is to be "a forward movement in which the experience that humanity has made on its way to the present is to be overcome and yet preserved." Salaquarda's suggestion here removes Nietzsche's thought from the sphere of critical reason to that of speculative reason, the latter certainly a tendency of the late Nietzsche. Nevertheless, Nietzsche's speculative thought moves generally in the realm of intuitive—not discursive—reason.

Pascal was perhaps the Christian whom Nietzsche most admired, and one whom, as he wrote to Georg Brandes, "I almost love, since he has enlightened me infinitely." Brendan Donnellan has shown in his essay, " 'The Only Logical Christian': Nietzsche's Critique of Pascal," that both thinkers manifest that incorruptible will to truth which is one of the finest fruits of Christianity. In the case of Pascal it led to a recognition that Christianity and science cannot be reconciled except through faith; in Nietzsche's case it led to a final rejection of Christianity; but confrontation with Pascal led him to adopt a stringently rationalistic stance and to attack his adversary with telling logic, as in the case of his critique of Pascal's idea of self-hate.

The theme of the intellectual honesty of the true Christian and its ultimate destructiveness for faith is seen in a different light in Gerd-Günther Grau's essay, "Nietzsche and Kierkegaard." Both thinkers recognize that the fact that the Second Coming of Christ, the Parousia expected by the early church, did not take place posed, and continues to pose, a serious dilemma for the believer: he must either give up his faith, or acknowledge the "unfulfilled divine intervention" while somehow retaining his faith. Nietzsche followed the first course; Kierkegaard, through the "leap of faith," the second. Nevertheless, the problem remained to plague Kierkegaard's personal development, for the expected divine intervention in connection with his engagement to Regine Olsen failed to materialize. If Pascal's problem with Christianity was essentially intellectual, Kierkegaard's problem was historical in the sense that man, like Job, receives from God no satisfactory answers to his questions. Grau has shown that Nietzsche's and Kierkegaard's critiques of historical Christianity generally coincide; only their conclusions are radically different.

Charles Lewis offers, in the essay "Morality and Deity in Nietzsche's Concept of Biblical Religion," a metacritique of Nietzsche's critique of biblical religion. Apart from the question of whether God exists or not, Nietzsche failed to discern the difference between the biblical and postbiblical conceptions of deity: the former is rooted in an attitude of worship that cannot be adequately understood in terms of the moral and psychological categories of Nietzsche's account. It is argued that the God of Nietzsche's critique is the highest

Good of a new, essentially moral religion—a religion whose God, demythologized through the influence of Western philosophy, must be *worthy* of worship. The biblical God, rightly seen, is not the moral ideal of this new religion and hence cannot be understood as a creature of the *ressentiment* of inferior human beings that is directed toward their superiors.

If Nietzsche's speculative thought is generally expressed in terms of intuitive reason in his more poetic writings, Georges Goedert's study "The Dionysian Theodicy" is a reminder that this is not the whole story, for he has garnered the arguments for Nietzsche's "theodicy" (Dionysus, the god of *this* world, is the god to be justified) from Nietzsche's philosophical prose writings as well as from *Zarathustra*. One must remember, however, that Nietzsche relegated (as he wrote to Franz Overbeck) his major prose works prior to *Zarathustra* to the status of a mere "commentary" before the fact. Goedert throws light on an important aspect of Nietzsche's thought that is often overlooked. He shows that Nietzsche did not desire the destruction of Christianity, rather its preservation: "in the end, the superman justifies Christian values. . . . Dionysus ends by rallying to his cause the Crucified One." Thus, the pessimism and decadence of Christianity provide the counterforce necessary to maintain the vitality of Dionysus. In such a way "Nietzsche at the same time says yes and no to Christianity."

Max L. Baeumer traces Nietzsche's radical change from an "ardent admirer to a deadly enemy of Martin Luther" by a thorough documentation of his comments on the Reformer. In Nietzsche's changing view of Luther we have a striking example of how formidable his critical powers could be, in whatever direction they might be turned. In his early phase, Nietzsche eloquently defends Luther as a bearer of the Dionysian spirit. In his later phase, however, he condemns Luther as a "barbarian," and sees him together with the Reformation as the force that fomented not only a peasant revolt in the literal, historical sense, but also a peasant revolt of the spirit that permeated all levels of German society. It was this spirit that, to a great extent, aborted the Renaissance in Germany. Baeumer summarizes: "Nietzsche is . . . not interested in Luther the writer, the theologian and religious reformer, unless he can use these aspects of his work for his own purpose of praising or condemning German nationalism." In "Nietzsche and the Old Testament" Israel Eldad casts Nietzsche in the role of a literary critic who can value the Old Testament above the New. This is true because of the former's "absolute 'Yes' to life." Nietzsche admired the "heroic personalities" of the Old Testament, "patriarchs, kings, and prophets struggling against the ruling priestly establishment."

In "Lessing and Nietzsche: Views on Christianity," Diana Behler underscores the dialectical nature of Nietzsche's critical thought. In regard to his fundamental antithesis, "Christ and Christianity—Dionysus and Winckelmann's Greece," Behler cautions, however, that the antithesis is by no means absolute, for both Christ and Dionysus are linked in their "demands for symbolic, rather than literal comprehension." Further, it was Nietzsche's view that "Christianity may have spoiled the glorious spontaneity of heathen Greek culture, but it simultaneously preserved it and transmitted it to us. . . ." This critical subtlety Nietzsche shared with Lessing, despite their differing views of the role of reason in the evolution of true humanity. In her comparison of Lessing and Nietzsche, Behler stresses that both thinkers interpret their religious heritage in the interest of their speculations. Both want a new Bible: Lessing foresees an extension of the biblical revelation, Nietzsche envisions a clear break with it and with all forms of transcendence.

It is worth noting, in our present context, that Spinoza and Lessing share a common approach in their speculative writings. Although the former is more rigorously logical than the latter, both view mathematical exactitude and clarity as the model for veridical thinking, even in areas remote from mathematics. Since both have much to say about God, man, and nature in the Judaeo-Christian heritage, their basic presuppositions are to be taken seriously. Nietzsche's principal speculative method provides, as we have already noted in the case of Spinoza, a striking contrast to that of certain rationalistic thinkers.

The studies we have considered to this point have dealt, for the most part, with Nietzsche's critical thought concerning Judaism and Christianity. In the remaining essays, those by Bernd Magnus, Hans Küng, and Karl Barth, Nietzsche's divinatory or prophetic role comes to the fore. The first half of Magnus's essay "Jesus, Christianity, and Superhumanity" is devoted to Nietzsche's critique of the Christian religion; the second half is concerned with the explication of the idea of the superman. Despite the fact that Magnus is not, on the whole, interpreting *Zarathustra* directly, he is doing so *indirectly* in citing other passages from Nietzsche's self-styled prose "commentaries" on that work as well as the commentaries of others. Thus, it is not amiss to say that here the concern is primarily with Nietzsche's intuitive speculation, especially as it appears in *Zarathustra*. Magnus rejects the "ideal type" theory of the superman in favor of an existential theory. The *Übermensch* is one who becomes "aware of what is worthy of infinity" in his life, and wills its eternal recurrence, even though that would also entail pain and suffering. One might find a parallel to this selectivity or judging the worth of an experience (though Magnus does not) in Jesus' admonition to seek first the kingdom of God whereby all other things will be added or, again, in the parables of the kingdom, the pearl of great price, the treasure hidden in a field, and others. If these "existential" sayings are true parallels to Nietzsche's thought one should not be surprised, for it would be simply another way in which Jesus' example comes into play.

Hans Küng deals with Nietzsche's two uses of reason in his article "Nietzsche: What Christians and Non-Christians Can Learn." Concerning Nietzsche's critique of Christianity he writes: "If Christianity *were* as Nietzsche saw it, then it could be and would have to be rejected today...." According to Küng, this misunderstanding nevertheless raises searching questions about the Church, the priesthood, and the idea of God. He sees in Nietzsche's contrast of historical Christianity with the religion of Jesus "a provocation for Christians which can be salutary." If Christians must be radically critical of Nietzsche's version of historical Christianity (not only of his underlying assumptions, but also of his knowledge and scholarship), non-Christians must be equally radical in their criticism of his speculations regarding the superman. Neither the weakling (allegedly promulgated as an ideal by Christianity) nor the superman provides a genuine model for the realization of true humanity. Not only do Nietzsche's ideas bear heavy responsibility for the advent of Nazism, but they continue today to spawn relativism and nihilism in morals, the justification of war, and even such neo-Nazi ideas as the manipulation of genes through microbiology.

The most consistent treatment of Nietzsche's intuitive speculation in our collection is Karl Barth's essay, "Humanity without the Fellow-Man: Nietzsche's Superman and Christian Morality." In an excursus at the beginning of his discussion, Barth adopts, with remarkable empathy, the standpoint of one who sees all of reality in terms of his own subjectivity, and he points out what "a powerful radius" the "I am" can have. Barth sees Nietzsche as having lived out and expressed, "in azure isolation," the secret of German Idealism: that it was really humanity without the fellow-man. "Nietzsche was the prophet of that humanity.... He did not merely reveal its secret; he blabbed it out." None of the German philosophical idealists—Kant, Fichte, Schelling, Hegel—had had the genuine courage of his deeply held convictions. As for Goethe, Barth suspects that he was "personally a far more obstinate pagan than Nietzsche." Like Magnus, Barth cautions against interpreting Nietzsche as the principal source of Nazism; he sees the latter rather as a confluence of ideas and impulses that were rife in the German culture of the last two hundred years.

Of the eighteen articles included, thirteen were written expressly for the present volume; five are reprints, though one has been revised by the author for inclusion here. Five articles have been translated from German, one from French, and one from Hebrew.

It should be mentioned here that the late Walter Kaufmann had agreed to give a lecture at Wake Forest University on 4 November 1980, which was to have been the introductory essay for this volume, but fate intervened. That his lecture would, characteristically, have raised some penetrating questions about the assumption of the editors that there *is* such a thing as a "Judaeo-Christian tradition"[10] and not simply two discrete traditions, is quite probable. In any event the absence of his reflections on our theme is highly regrettable, as is indeed the great loss to Nietzsche scholarship in general that has resulted from his untimely death. It is further regrettable that the untimely death of a colleague at Wake Forest University—James Steintrager, a leading Bentham scholar—also deprived the present project of a valuable contribution: his essay was to have been a comparative study of Jeremy Bentham's and Nietzsche's views of Christianity.

If Nietzsche's agonistic striving constantly demands a vigorous opponent against which to measure its strength, there is ample evidence, if the testimony of certain academics is to be trusted, that both Judaism and Christianity, far from being moribund, can continue to offer the required resistance. It was S. S. Prawer who originally suggested, in his review of *Studies in Nietzsche and the Classical Tradition*, the desirability of such a companion volume as the present one on the grounds that it "would bring out more clearly . . . the fundamental wickedness of this sensitive, intelligent, perceptive, poetic, suffering man."[11] And Henry Hatfield wrote, a few years ago: "Looking back on many years of interest in German Hellenism, I find it surprising that the one figure who emerges as authentic from all

---

10. Since the term is generally accepted, no attempt has been made to define "Judaeo-Christian tradition." If one were to venture a definition, some interesting questions would arise. For example, how would Islam, which owes so much to Judaism, be related to that faith or indeed to Christianity?

11. S. S. Prawer, "Nietzsche and the Greeks," *Times Literary Supplement*, 18 November 1977, p. 1346.

the welter of myths is precisely Jesus Christ." It would be absurd, he maintains further, to claim that the gods of Greece, whether Winckelmannian, Goethean, or Nietzschean, are "even remotely as real as Jesus Christ. This is not a matter of religious belief; it is simply an observable fact, evident in the texts of the great German writers. . . ."[12] One might argue that, in a profound sense, Nietzsche, the self-styled "Antichrist," is himself, *nolens volens*, now part and parcel of the Judaeo-Christian heritage—for his work is forever wedded to that which he would destroy and supplant. On the other hand, most of his readers will probably prefer to take him at his word and see his doctrines simply as a radical alternative to both Judaism and Christianity.

That Nietzsche's feelings toward Christianity always remained mixed is attested by the fact that as late as 1881 he wrote to Peter Gast that he considered it really "the best version of ideal life" that he had ever known, adding: "I have followed it from my childhood on into many nooks and crannies, and believe in my heart that I have never harbored base feelings toward it. After all, I am the descendant of whole generations of Christian ministers."[13] Whether the ultimate result of his efforts will have a positive or a negative meaning for his great adversary remains to be seen.

12. Henry Hatfield, *Clashing Myths in German Literature: From Heine to Rilke* (Cambridge, Mass.: Harvard University Press, 1974), p. 189.
13. Nietzsche to Peter Gast, 21 July 1881, *Briefwechsel*, ed. Giorgio Colli and Mazzino Montinari, III-1, (Berlin/New York: de Gruyter, 1981), 109.

I. Nietzsche:
Critic in the Grand Style

Eugen Biser
(Translated by Timothy F. Sellner)

I. Some Preliminary Hermeneutic Considerations

Nietzsche probably never expressed his (inconsistent) position more neatly and succinctly than with the sentences from his *Genealogy of Morals* that proclaim the man of the future: "this bell-stroke of noon and the great decision who makes the will free again and gives man back his hopes, this Antichrist and Antinihilist, this victor over God and nothingness."[1] For what sounds more critical, revolutionary, or destructive than this postulate, which speaks of the victory over God and, in doing so, secretly takes up the fight against the essence of being, against the central sun of the archetypes gathered in the Platonic heaven of ideas? And where on earth is there a more positive goal than the vanquishing of nothingness, and with it that epochal destiny which Nietzsche sought to diagnose, render obsolete, and dispense with under the catchword "nihilism"?[2]

Nevertheless Nietzsche does not lay claim to this postulate expressly for himself. Rather, he links it up with the figure of the uniquely authoritative Zarathustra, with whom he plays through the entire drama of role interchange, beginning with the noon of life, when the "friend Zarathustra came, the guest of guests,"[3] through the phase of identification, in which he speaks of his "son" Zarathustra,[4] to the stage of crisis and rejection, in which a "terrible antago-

---

1. GM, II, sec. 24. All translations from the German are by Timothy F. Sellner.
2. See also the prefatory remark in *The Will to Power*, in which Nietzsche designates himself as the first complete nihilist in Europe, "who nonetheless has even lived nihilism to its conclusion—who has put it behind him and beneath him" (WM, sec. 3).
3. J, "Aftersong. From High Mountains."
4. According to the collection *Nietzsche in seinen Briefen*, ed. Alfred Bäumler (Stuttgart: Kröner, 1932), p. 366, Nietzsche spoke in a letter addressed to his sister (April 1885) of his "son Zarathustra," if only as an indication of his incipient dissociation, which then (to judge by a note from the spring of 1885) culminated in the resolve: "I wish to speak, and no longer [as] Zarathustra."

nism" against the entire imagery of Zarathustra takes possession of him.[5]

Such evidence in itself should be sufficient to demonstrate the pressing need for a Nietzschean hermeneutics.[6] For not only does Nietzsche love the play with disguises and interchanged roles, which he carries to extremes at the conclusion of his *Zarathustra*, there is hardly a single position that he takes without abandoning it again after a time, or even, as is not infrequently the case, exchanging it for its opposite. And it is more than simply a kind of artistic skirmishing in the foreground of his thinking when he makes reference to stylistic differences in his writings and reminds us that in dealing with him (for whom nothing is so hateful as the attitude of the doctrinaire) we must always be mindful of backgrounds and omissions, or even of the converse of these—that is, of polemic overstatements and tendentious crudities. For in the final analysis, as we are told in one of his key statements on the theory of language, it is not so much a matter of what is expressly stated as of the music behind the words, of the passion behind the music, and above all of the person behind the passion who represents the true goal of our understanding.[7]

In our attempt to define more precisely Nietzsche's position as a critic, it is sufficient to keep the hermeneutic background in mind to the extent that we derive the sense of the word "criticism" not so much from Nietzsche's domain in the history of ideas as from the context of his own life. An important reference point for this notion is provided by his expression "the victor over God and nothingness." On the one hand, it corresponds precisely to the self-evaluation of Nietzsche that in *Ecce Homo* differentiates the "Yes-saying" part of his life's task from its "No-saying, No-doing" half.[8] On the other hand, the assignment of a role to the Zarathustra figure with now greater, now lesser importance is made understandable by the fact that Nietzsche exercises his role as a critic with differing intensity: full of *élan* in the *Untimely Meditations*; with anger in *Human, All-Too-Human*; with vehemence in *The Dawn*; with consummate skill in *The Gay Science*; emphatically, with the gestures of an evangelist, in *Zarathustra*; aggressively in *The Twilight of the Idols*; with analytic rigor in *On the*

---

5. In the opinion of Hans M. Wolff, *Friedrich Nietzsche. Der Weg zum Nichts* (Bern: Francke, 1956), p. 204.

6. For further discussion of this point, see my article "Das Desiderat einer Nietzsche-Hermeneutik," *Nietzsche Studien*, 9 (1980), 1–37.

7. *Nachlaß* (*Die Unschuld des Werdens*, I), sec. 508.

8. *Ecce Homo*, "Why I Write Such Good Books": Beyond Good and Evil, sec. 1.

Genealogy of Morals; in uninhibited and tendentious fashion in *The Antichrist.*

Naturally we cannot ascribe Nietzsche's role interchange with Zarathustra simply to his use of differing styles in his critical activity. Moreover, it never reaches the point where he becomes bored with criticism, neither in *Zarathustra,* which up to the very end either openly or secretly thrives on antithesis, nor in his (long prepared yet never completed) principal work, which, to judge by the material collected in his *Nachlaß,* would have possessed a strong critical strain despite its bias toward systematics. In fact, his relationship to Zarathustra makes it clear that criticism for Nietzsche—just as for the "victor over God and nothingness"—is not only an instrument for analysis, but also, and to a far greater extent, a path to the discovery of himself. Nietzsche does not merely criticize; he lives and exists critically. And the significance of this is that while Nietzsche, like Zarathustra, doubtless often utilizes his critical possibilities instrumentally, he also makes ever more conscious use of them in an existential way. This gives his criticism a quality that raises it above other comparable forms of criticism, even if the difference, as a rule, is only perceived in terms of atmosphere. We can see this most clearly by juxtaposing Nietzsche with his model Heine, whom he both admired and imitated at significant points in his life:[9] for precisely where Heine launches into irony and persiflage, Nietzsche remains measured and austere, so that the seriousness of his existential perplexity is constantly perceptible in the midst of his critical encounter.[10]

Yet such a vigorous coupling of criticism with his own existence also brings about a more intense relationship with the particular object being criticized than is normally the case, especially when it is of a higher dignity, as with culture and religion. For the loftier the object, the greater the role it plays in connection with the process of self-discovery in the critic.

But what, in fact, are the objects of Nietzsche's critical interest?

---

9. Nietzsche repeatedly expressed his high esteem for Heine, who, as he assures us as late as *Ecce Homo*, conveyed to him "the highest conception of the lyric poet" ("Why I Am So Clever," sec. 4); the fact that he used Heine in addition as a source and model, however, was first shown by Henri de Lubac in his work *Die Tragödie des Humanismus ohne Gott* (Salzburg: Miller, 1950), pp. 336ff.

10. The hypothesis formulated by de Lubac, with which I express my complete agreement in my article "Nietzsches Kritik des christlichen Gottesbegriffs und ihre theologischen Konsequenzen" (*Philosophisches Jahrbuch*, 78 [1971], 34–65, 295–305), can only be confirmed by means of word indices and the comparison of motifs, because Nietzsche is silent concerning his definitive "sources" and the extant remains of his library do not contain Heine's essay "On Religion and Philosophy in Germany" (1834).

II. Preferred Areas of Critical Inquiry

Nietzsche never consciously sought out the objects of his criticism; rather, they were presented to him by the world in which he lived. Thus in every case his critical interest changes to the extent that his life changes and broadens. It has been established on the evidence of his youthful poems that his critical sense was first enkindled by the religious beliefs of that pietistically tinged Christianity which, together with the demands of bourgeois morality, determined the atmosphere in the house of his parents. To the degree that he grows away from the circle of his childhood and as a *fugitivus errans* traverses the landscape of European culture and civilization, he then directs his critical sense toward those fields through which he has previously passed. That his relationship to them is chiefly critical could perhaps be explained by his own impression that he had never found the possibility for setting down roots, had never found a place of domicile and security. It is this impression that later for him—as it had earlier for Franz Schubert[11]—consolidated itself into the figure of the "wanderer" who sees himself cast about in the great "desert" of a lifeless, disenchanted, and debased landscape, moving from loneliness to loneliness, accompanied only by that inescapable "dog," his pain.[12] With the clear-sightedness of the renouncer he conceives of these illusions, which constantly shift the "desert" as if it were a stage set, and which maintain the measured pace of culture in order to simulate life in this landscape of death, as the mere surrogate of that which they claim to be. However, since Nietzsche retains as the single indispensable conclusion from Christian morality the will "to intellectual purity at any price,"[13] his critical task is presented to him almost of itself; for now, as he states in his preface to *The Twilight of the Idols*, it is a matter of "examining," with the hammer of philosophical criticism, the empty "idols" concerning their content, by which he means convicting them of their deception.[14]

From this point on, Nietzsche's criticism is concentrated on four areas which, as pseudoforms of that which they claim to be, are especially suspicious to him: education, culture, morality, and religion—the latter being for him, in spite of several allusions to the Parseeism with which he came into contact through the figure of Zarathustra, synonymous with Christianity. Within this "target qua-

---

11. See my article "Abschied und Ankunft. Religiöse Momente im Werk Franz Schuberts," *Beiträge zur pädagogischen Arbeit*, 23 (1979), 16–28.
12. MA, II/II: *The Wanderer and His Shadow*.
13. GM, III, sec. 27 (in reference to sec. 357 of FW).
14. G, foreword of 30 September 1888.

ternity," moreover, there exists a relationship of gradation and subordination, since education for Nietzsche is a derivative of culture in the same sense that morality appears as a generalizing preformation of Christianity. Accordingly, in many cases his criticism of education is in fact directed at the phenomena of culture, just as, conversely, the most penetrating thrust of his criticism of morality is doubtless aimed at Christianity.

The fact that Nietzsche's relationship to education and culture—whose enthusiastic advocate he had been in the beginning—became increasingly more critical is tied in a fundamental way to his relationship to truth, a relationship that appears more and more strained in each of his successive creative periods. Characteristic of this is the early study "On Truth and Lie in an Extra-Moral Sense" (1873), which speaks of a nature that keeps "almost everything" of her secrets from mankind:

> She threw away the key; and woe to that fateful curiosity that might sometime be able to peer through a keyhole out and down from the chamber of consciousness, and would then suspect that the thing resting on all the mercilessness, greed, insatiability, and murderousness in life is man himself, in the indifference of his ignorance, dreaming, as it were, on the back of a tiger. From where in all the world do we get the drive for truth amid such a constellation?[15]

From this time on, even from this early phase of his thought, truth for Nietzsche is nothing more than a pragmatic "peace treaty," a linguistic regulator that invents universally binding designations for things in order to facilitate our orientation in the darkness of the unknowable. Accordingly, as he states in the continuation of his study, truth is nothing more than a "movable army of metaphors, metonymies, and anthropomorphisms; in short, a summation of human relations," which appeared to people as fixed and binding through long usage, and were no longer perceived in terms of their illusional nature.[16] From this perspectivistic fragmentation of truth we can trace a direct line in Nietzsche's middle period to the note in the *Nachlaß* that no longer views in "truth" anything more than "an opinion of various errors regarding each other."[17] Man, however, is that certain kind of being which cannot exist without this constella-

---

15. "On Truth and Lie in an Extra-Moral Sense," sec. 1.
16. Ibid.
17. *Nachlaß* (WM), sec. 595.

tion of errors;[18] for the average man shrinks back just as much from the "terrible basic text *homo natura*" recorded within him as from the chaotic sight of the world seen without illusion.[19] In order to tolerate the abyss of his own self, man produces for himself the "flattering overpainting" of his humanistic self-analysis; to come to grips with the chaos that is the "world," he creates culture and education.

Thus Nietzsche already sees in his first attack on German education—which he began with his lecture series "On the Future of Our Educational Institutions" (1872)—two antagonistic drives at work: "on the one hand, the drive toward the greatest possible broadening of education, on the other, the drive toward a lessening and weakening of the same."[20] Moreover, the tension in this relationship is scarcely alleviated by the fact that at the conclusion of the fifth lecture he looks for the educational woes he has just described to be overcome by a "preestablished harmony between the leader and the led." It is not without reason that he assures us in *Ecce Homo* that his first attack was intended for the German educational system, which he looked upon "even then with ruthless disdain."[21] Accordingly, whoever takes this questionable educational path is threatened by the "untragic death" resulting from being "crushed by a statue."[22] In the same sense Zarathustra also warns his disciples and admirers: "Be careful that you are not crushed to death by a falling statue!"[23]

Much more dramatic in nature is Nietzsche's critical encounter with the "glittering phantom" culture, for the reason that for some time the genius of "higher culture" seemed for Nietzsche to be embodied in the figure of Richard Wagner. Just as it was through Wagner that Nietzsche's fascination at first expressed itself in the hope for a renewed culture of the future, so the disappointment that Wagner later brought about took the form of an ever more radical criticism of culture. To be sure, Nietzsche holds on to an idealized understanding of culture up to the very end: like a pyramid, the dominant image "culture" rises up from a "strongly and healthily consolidated mediocrity"[24]—to use the language of one of his later works. Yet at the same time he realizes that it is with culture as it is with the "glorious dream-birth of the Olympic gods": only with their help

18. Ibid., sec. 493.
19. J, VII, sec. 230; FW, III, sec. 109.
20. From the planned introduction (1871).
21. *Ecce Homo*, "Why I Write Such Good Books": The Untimely Ones, sec. 1.
22. "On the Future of Our Educational Institutions," third lecture (1872).
23. Z, I, "Of the Bestowing Virtue," sec. 3.
24. A, sec. 57.

did the Greeks learn to bear "the terrors and abominations of existence."[25] In view of this schism between greatness and illusion, Nietzsche sees culture caught in the undertow of nihilism, so that he only is able to make the single prognosis: "Our whole European culture has for a long time now moved in a torture of tension which increased from century to century as if bent on catastrophe: like a stream flowing toward its end, which no longer pays heed to its direction and is afraid to reflect, to deliberate."[26]

Nietzsche's criticism of morality and religion—the latter for the most part synonymous with Christianity—appears, on the other hand, as a kind of exaggerated counterpart to that of culture and education. Here also a clear downward slope prevails, which becomes especially apparent when we consider the conception of morality that underlies *On the Genealogy of Morals*. It is appropriate to begin with this work, because Nietzsche always considered it his business to inquire after the origin of moral judgments and value determinations.[27] The answer, which obtrudes itself upon Nietzsche after his attempt to decipher the "hieroglyphic text of the past of human morality," is radically pessimistic: it is the will to nothingness, the disgust with life, the revolt against the most basic presuppositions of life. Moreover, this will to nothingness must be considered the foremost requirement for moral judgments.[28] For this reason it is morality itself that has to be held primarily responsible "if the greatest power and splendor in the type man is never attained."[29] For morality is not merely that sublimated form of life "that itself cuts into life";[30] rather, with his notions of moral value man has created for himself an ideal counterworld and world-behind-this-world that condemns him to an existence of continuous self-estrangement.[31] Thus morality is for Nietzsche, as he explains in *Ecce Homo*, the "Circe of humanity,"[32] which seduces us to a total

25. GT, sec. 3.
26. Nachlaß (WM), sec. 2.
27. See, for example, MA, II/II, sec. 57; FW, IV, sec. 335; Nachlaß (*Die Unschuld des Werdens*, II), sec. 875 (outline of a plan for the Second Book from 1886).
28. GM, Preface, sec. 7; III, sec. 28.
29. Ibid., Preface, sec. 6.
30. Z, II, "On the Famous Wise Men"; IV, "The Leech."
31. Wolff (*Friedrich Nietzsche. Der Weg zum Nichts*, p. 250) finds "this decisive thought of the work" expressed chiefly in the third lecture, "Was bedeuten asketische Ideale?" which according to him has its origin in the belatedly added fifth book of FW, "We Fearless Ones."
32. *Ecce Homo*, "Why I Write Such Good Books," sec. 5.

suppression of the feeling for life; it is the renunciation of the will to existence, or, more succinctly, "a sickness."[33]

Nietzsche is convinced that morality in and of itself has as little to do with religion as has the latter with morality; nevertheless the "two descendants of the Jewish religion"—Christianity and Islam—are "essentially moral religions."[34] Consequently in both religions, and especially in Christianity, it is primarily that denial of life expressed as the essence of the divine which must be opposed; and "in fact," according to a note in the *Nachlaß*, "only the moral God has been refuted."[35] This fragment, composed in the form of a dialogue, is emphatic in its expression: "You call it the self-disintegration of God: but it is only his moulting: he is shedding his moral skin! And you shall see him again soon, beyond good and evil."[36]

This passage signifies an important retreat in Nietzsche's thinking, insofar as in it his criticism of morality and religion is in accord with his criticism of Christianity. For he sees Christianity too, like "all great things," as involved in an "act of self-overcoming." He reasons: "After Christian veracity has come to one conclusion after another, it will come finally to its most severe conclusion, its conclusion against itself." Thus Christianity will perish from its own "training in truth," or, to speak concretely, from its morality.[37] The prospect of this "great drama in a hundred acts which is reserved for the next two centuries in Europe" hardly hinders Nietzsche, however, from keeping an eye open for additional strategies for destruction.[38] He proceeds here in precisely the same manner as with his criticism of morality and religion. The alleged "self-destruction" of God, which represents for him but an early instance of the differentiation between morality and religiosity, is merely additional stimulus for him in carrying out the work of the destruction of the Christian belief in God. At the same time, he reaches the point where his struggle against morality—and especially against the "ascetic ideal"—shifts definitively to criticism of religion.

Nietzsche may have received strong encouragement for this plan in the thesis put forth by Heinrich Heine in his essay "On Religion

33. *Nachlaß* (WM), secs. 11, 273.
34. Ibid., sec. 146.
35. *Nachlaß* (*Die Unschuld des Werdens*, II), sec. 994.
36. Ibid., sec. 949.
37. GM, III, sec. 27.
38. See further my Nietzsche article in *Religionskritik von der Aufklärung bis zur Gegenwart*, ed. Karl von Weger (Freiburg im Breisgau: Herder, 1979), pp. 241–47.

and Philosophy in Germany" (1834), namely, that Kant in his attack on the traditional proofs of the existence of God had been able to refute only the cosmological and physico-theological arguments, but not the ontological argument, which had been present long before Anselm of Canterbury in Augustine's treatise *De libero arbitrio*.[39] Since Nietzsche has no hope of proceeding farther than Kant on the path of analysis or speculation, he hits upon the colossal idea of defeating the Christian belief in God with its own weapons. Thus in *The Gay Science* he tells the parable of the "madman" who seeks to bring about a change in belief after the fashion and style of the parables of Jesus—only in the opposite direction.[40] Accordingly, he has this "madman"—a counterpart to the "fool" in Anselm's argument in the *Proslogion*—appear with a lantern in his hand among the godless in the marketplace, so that after he had bewildered them with his question "Whither has God gone?" he could shout his "God is dead" in their faces.[41] The God who saw everything and by means of his all-seeing gaze had shown himself to be the last moral court of appeal for man, this God, according to the words of the "ugliest man" in the masquerading procession at the end of *Zarathustra*, had to "die." And his reason: "Man cannot bear to have such a witness alive."[42]

III. The Contours of the Criticism

If this passage through the fields of Nietzsche's criticism teaches us anything, it is the continuous escalation of his critical intent. This escalation reveals itself explicitly in the fact that as his involvement as a critic increases, his readiness to form alternatives, or even to permit them, clearly diminishes. For no matter how mercilessly Nietzsche took the German educational establishment to task, his reference to the repressive character of the existing educational system was motivated by the desire to bring about a change for the better—although we must view as questionable that incoherency which in this particular instance caused him to speak in terms of

---

39. For further discussion, see my article "Nietzsches Kritik des christlichen Gottesbegriffs und ihre theologischen Konsequenzen" (above, n. 10).

40. For further discussion, see my *Theologische Sprachtheorie und Hermeneutik* (Munich: Kösel, 1970), pp. 441–69, and *Die Gleichnisse Jesu* (Munich: Kösel, 1965).

41. See also my investigation *"Gott ist tot": Nietzsches Destruktion des christlichen Bewußtseins* (Munich: Kösel, 1962).

42. Z, IV, "The Ugliest Man."

"leaders and followers."[43] Moreover, within the context of his criticism of culture he has no hesitation, at the end of his critical undertaking, about offering himself as an alternative: "And in all seriousness, no one before me knew the right way, the way upwards; it is only beginning with me that there are again hopes, tasks, prescriptible paths of culture—I am their joyful herald."[44]

Finally, with the transition to the criticism of morality and religion, a more far-reaching change takes place. It is as if his critical will were taking the entire task upon itself. Yet this impression is not merely accidental. Just as we saw with the exorbitant utterance from *Ecce Homo*, when Nietzsche is dealing with the most significant subjects it is a question of the identification of critic with criticism. But it is precisely because Nietzsche now "fills out" the entire field of critical encounter with his person that new alternatives become possible; however, these no longer lie in the realm of emotionally neutral counterpositions, but rather in the center of Nietzsche's own will to existence. A direct line can be traced from the claim to be opening up new paths through himself, to the self-proclamation of the herald of madness in which Nietzsche designates himself as the "successor to the dead God" who did not dare to carry his own private egotism so far as to be able to forego for its sake the creation of the new—Dionysian—world.[45] If we add to this the appellations of the herald of madness in which Nietzsche alternately refers to himself as "Dionysus" or as "The Crucified One," we find confirmation for the growing tendency of Nietzsche in his deranged state to identify himself with that which had previously been the target of his severest polemic. Moreover, he now constitutes the alternative himself by elevating that which he had previously passionately denied to the level of content within his own—shattering—existence.

Even if we merely illuminate the context to this extent, the criticism practiced by Nietzsche gains, at least in its excessive forms, a new and quite unexpected aspect. There, where he utters his most decisive No, we suddenly find traces of a covert or overt affirmation. Thus in its extreme intensity his criticism becomes, in a figurative sense, a receptacle whose contours let us see the criticized object as if it were in a hollow mold. This opens up the possibility of what is at first a completely unsuspected interpretation, for the intensity of

---

43. "On the Future of Our Educational Institutions," fifth lecture.
44. *Ecce Homo*, "Why I Write Such Good Books": Twilight of the Idols, sec. 2.
45. See, for example, the first part of his letter of 6 January 1889 to Jakob Burckhardt.

Nietzsche's criticism is not merely a measuring stick for that which he perceived as the main content of the "No-saying, No-doing half" of his life's task,[46] nor does it merely show us what challenged the capacity of his critical faculties to react in any given case. Nietzsche's criticism rather, at least in its excessive forms, is intended to be understood and interpreted as a dialectical reflection of its targets. This interpretation would—in Nietzsche's own words—be only halfway complete if we were merely to see in it his critical genius, the passion of his power to negate, and the intensity of his destructive will, for such a view would fail to perceive the background Yes in his foreground No. And with that it would perhaps overlook precisely that quality on which Nietzsche himself, with his avowed feeling for allusions and inexpressible connotations, presumably would have placed the greatest value.

If we do not wish to forfeit this quality, then Nietzsche's criticism, notwithstanding our estimation of its critical-negative approach, must be interpreted "reconstructively." It also becomes necessary to recognize once again in its "hollow mold" the outline of the object of his negation. And not merely in order to do full justice to Nietzsche's critical method. Rather, we must acknowledge the fact that his criticism also possesses heuristic functions, for Nietzsche's criticism is as sensitive as it is severe. No matter how blindly—or filled with blind rage—it lashes out in its severity, in its sensitiveness it is often imbued with an astounding clear-sightedness. As a consequence, Nietzsche in using this critical approach feels his way forward from a position far in advance of that possible with an affirmative approach to his subject. This cognitive quality has to be taken into account in connection especially with his criticism of religion, for in spite of all his passion and the relentlessness of his negation, it is precisely here that he not infrequently succeeds in gaining insights and perceptions that encroach upon the limits of theological understanding. To cite but two examples: Who would have been capable of developing an understanding of the parable, at a time when theological interpretation was for the most part entangled in the concept of allegory, that could have vied with that documented in his own parable of the "madman"?[47] And who, after Nicholas of Cusa, would

---

46. *Ecce Homo*, "Why I Write Such Good Books": Beyond Good and Evil, sec. 1.

47. See further the assessment by Adolf Jülicher in his monumental work *Die Gleichnisreden Jesu* (Tübingen: Mohr, 1910); also my study *"Gott ist tot": Nietzsches Destruktion des christlichen Bewußtseins* (above, n. 41), which is continued in *Die Gleichnisse Jesu* (above, n. 40).

have emphasized once again the motif of the "allseeing God" with such vehemence?[48]

One final factor, however, carries more weight than all these heuristic references. For in the existential encounter that at times drives Nietzsche the critic of religion almost to the point of identification it becomes apparent that the "material" of religion cannot be treated as if it were of neutral value, as an object among objects, but only in relation to a personal state of inner disquietude. It was not without good reason that Rudolf Bultmann compared the cognitive situation that arises when we deal with religious subject matter with that involved in the investigation of microphysical processes, in which the observing subject comes into play as a factor by himself constituting an object.[49] But here he was merely repeating on a theoretical level what Jean Paul long before had declared to be the "intention" he was pursuing with the "vision of terror" in his "Speech of the Dead Christ":

> I also intend with my writing to strike fear into the heart of a few Masters of Arts, either now lecturing or who have lectured in the past; for truly these people, now that they have been elevated from the status of building-slaves in the construction of dikes and the shoring up of excavations for critical philosophy to that of paid workers, ponder the existence of God as cold-bloodedly and cold-heartedly as if we were talking about the existence of the kraken or the unicorn.[50]

That, however, is the language of an affirmative mode of thought that has religious experience on its side. In Nietzsche, on the other hand, a voice is raised that concurs in this experience—but from the point of view of criticism. And he underscores this concurrence with his most suggestive metaphors. After the "madman" has proclaimed

---

48. In this sense, the chapter of *Zarathustra* entitled "The Ugliest Man" has to be seen and evaluated in terms of Cusa's *De visione Dei*. The conclusion of my article "Nietzsches Kritik des christlichen Gottesbegriffs und ihre theologischen Konsequenzen" (above, n. 10) points out further such cross-references.

49. In his article "Zum Problem der Entmythologisierung" Bultmann emphasizes that modern science has come by means of Heisenberg's Uncertainty Principle to recognize that "the object being observed is already disfigured or modified in some way by the observer himself" (*Glauben und Verstehen. Gesammelte Aufsätze*, vol. 4 [Tübingen: Mohr, 1965], 129).

50. Johann Paul Friedrich Richter, "Rede des toten Christus vom Weltgebäude herab, daß kein Gott sei," in *Siebenkäs*, erstes Blumenstück; also Walther Rehm, *Jean Paul—Dostojewski. Eine Studie zur dichterischen Gestaltung des Unglaubens* (Göttingen: Vandenhoeck & Ruprecht, 1962), pp. 5–53.

his terrible tidings of the death of God, he impresses his stunned audience with the consequences of this "greatest of modern events" by asking them: "What did we do when we unchained this earth from her sun? Whither is it moving now? Whither are we moving? Away from all suns? Are we not falling continually? And backwards, sideways, forwards, to every side?"[51]

No one has ever spoken more suggestively of the loss resulting from the "death of God." In these questions is revealed the experience of that criticism which had been working its way up to this "death." But in doing so it has already left its critical function far behind. To appreciate fully the significance of this we must follow it into another realm.

51. FW, III, sec. 125.

II. The Case against Apolitical Morality: Nietzsche's Interpretation of the Jewish Instinct

Harry Neumann

"How can one today still concede so much to the naiveté of Christian theologians that one joins them in decreeing that the development of the notion of God, from 'God of Israel,' from a political god (*Volksgott*) to the Christian God constitutes progress?"

—The Antichrist

Although Nietzsche welcomed the modern Jew's eagerness to end his nomadic existence, the eternal wandering of the *galut*, he believed that it arose from the weakening of the Jewish instinct.*[1] The willingness to find a home in Europe, especially in Germany, followed upon Napoleonic destruction of the ghettos in which the exiled Jews had continued to await the messiah who would restore their political integrity by rebuilding their ancestral Temple on its ancestral site in Jerusalem and by reestablishing the prescribed tribal sacrifices in it; until that messianic restoration they chose to live in ghettos segregated from the (moral-political) abomination of gentile life. Millennia of persecution could not deprive what Shylock still called "our sacred nation" of its messianic zeal. Nietzsche considered it the goal of the Jewish instinct. By calling it an instinct he intentionally abstracted from Jewish piety. Instincts are shared by all animals—they do not distinguish men from beasts—yet Nietzsche perceived instinct as central to human life: "Every mistake in every sense is a consequence of degeneration of instinct, of the degeneration of the will: one could almost define what is bad in this way. Everything good is instinct."[2]

---

*The research for this paper was assisted by a grant from the Earhart Foundation and the John Brown Cook Association for Freedom.

1. J, sec. 251. Translations from Nietzsche are those of the author.
2. G, "The Four Great Errors," sec. 2; FW, sec. 11; Z, I, "On the Despisers of the Body"; A, sec. 6.

Proper instincts are acquired through millennia of brutal, tyrannic imposition of a morality that then becomes self-evident to those so educated: "Everything good is inherited: what is not inherited is imperfect, is a mere beginning."[3] The main human problem is to attain "the perfected autonomy of instinct—this presupposition of every mastery, of every kind of perfection in the art of life."[4] Nietzsche prized the Jewish instinct as a more developed form of this mastery than that possessed by other European peoples.[5] Characteristically Nietzsche finds this instinct's most revealing aspect in the unconditional obedience to parents: "To honor father and mother and even in the depths of the soul to be obedient to their will."[6] Like most modern men, he abstracts, as he must, from the most essential element of Judaism, its piety. He discovers Judaism's core in the human experience central to it, not in the divine commandment that calls forth that experience.

Nietzsche believed that the Jews originally worshiped their exclusive tribal gods, and particularly their chief war god, whose main job was insurance of victory over enemies. The existence of those gods was disproved in the only way gods could be disproved in that radically political world: by military defeat and the subsequent destruction of their temples.[7] Prior to such catastrophe, the worth of one's gods appeared self-evident, subject to doubt only by madmen or fools. To its devotees, this piety had nothing to do with faith or belief. It informed a way of life in which the main concern—the piety that unified the nation—was experienced as self-evident truth. This political piety left no room for the serious philosophic or scientific questions that became possible only with its discreditation by defeat and the destruction of its temples. All moralities or religions informed by this disestablishment naturally are experienced as faith in something questionable, something open to philosophic-scientific inquiry.

Once the certainties of the old tribal or civic piety are lost, politics no longer can escape "the police supervision of doubt," however desperately partisans may cling to the self-evidence of some pious truth.[8] Most men dread the rootless, aimless lives forced upon them

---

3. G, "Skirmishes of an Untimely Man," secs. 47 and 39; J, secs. 188, 229–30, 264; GM, II.
4. A, secs. 57–59.
5. M, sec. 205; J, sec. 251.
6. Z, I, "On the Thousand and One Goals."
7. A, sec. 25; FW, sec. 136.
8. FW, sec. 344.

by the discrediting of tribal-civic piety. This dread was responsible for the Jewish denial that destruction of their temple disproved the existence of their gods; instead, they claimed that their defeat and enslavement were god's way of testing or punishing them. In time that same god would empower the messiah to reestablish their tribal sacrifices in their temple. However, a god capable of effecting this miraculous resurrection no longer could be merely concerned with his own people. "Formerly he had only his own people (*Volk*), his chosen people. Then he, just as his people, went wandering into foreign places . . . that great cosmopolitan."[9] He became the one god of all men; the tribal piety of victorious Judaism was transformed into the monotheism of defeated Judaism:

> A people that still believes in itself, still has its own god. In him it reverses the conditions by means of which it is victorious, its virtues. . . . Such a god must know how to help and harm, must be able to be a friend and an enemy—one admired both his good and his terrifying qualities. The *antinatural* castration of a god to a god merely of good qualities would be undesirable here. . . . What would be the use of a god who was not even alive to the delightful *ardeurs* of victory and annihilation of enemies? . . . To be sure, when a people is destroyed; when it feels the irrevocable disappearance of its faith in its future, its hope for its freedom . . . then its god becomes a god for everyone, becomes a private person, a cosmopolitan. Formerly he represented a people (*Volk*), the strength of a people, everything aggressive and thirsty for power in the soul of a people: now he is merely the good god.[10]

Although victorious Judaism had one main war-god, it acknowledged that other peoples had their gods and it itself had various lesser gods.[11] This polytheism was a luxury that defeated Judaism no longer could afford: what was desperately required was an omnipotent god who could create *ex nihilo*, transforming ultimate political annihilation and degradation into salvation. Since this god could not be limited by anything outside himself, he must be the one omnipotent god. Beside him there is only the nothingness out of which he creates whatever he wills. Nietzsche interpreted that nothingness as the cosmic reflection of the emptiness experienced by Jews when defeat discredited their ancestral gods, the guarantors of their politi-

---

9. A, sec. 17.
10. Ibid., sec. 16.
11. FW, sec. 143; Baruch Spinoza, *Theological-Political Treatise*, 2, 15, 17.

cal integrity who defined their morality. In their radically political world that emptiness meant slavery or suicide.[12] However, Jewish invention of omnipotent monotheism permitted them to interpret the ultimate degradation, the destruction of their Temple in Jerusalem, as divine providence.

This desperate invention sprang from "the deepest political instinct (*Volks-Instinkt*), the toughest will to live that ever existed on earth."[13] That will's toughness sprang from the realization that life is nothing for men deprived of their political integrity: "If I forget thee, O Jerusalem!"[14]

In the rebirth demanded by that tenacious will to live, the Jewish mission no longer could be what it most wanted to be, that is, deeply tribal. Now it was compelled to be global, since divine omnipotence must control the whole universe—otherwise it could not bring the Jews back to Jerusalem, transmuting defeat into victory. Obviously this new piety could be held only by blind, desperate faith in *ex nihilo* creation. Prior to the destruction of their Temple, Jews had experienced no need for such faith. In their old polytheism, military virtue corresponded to the role played in monotheistic Judaism by the will to believe. The main work of the warriors was also the main work of their gods: the destruction of enemies. Only with defeat did peaceful priests seem better than the warriors celebrated by the old warrior piety, for the omnipotent god valued humility and meekness over manly pride. The priests who interpreted that deity's will naturally were preferred to the now defeated warriors.[15]

Written by those priests, the Bible, from Nietzsche's point of view, is the record not of what actually happened, but of what omnipotent monotheism needed in order to transform defeat into victory.[16] After the defeat of one's tribal or civic gods, the alternative to this falsification of one's past is political suicide or slavery; confronted with this alternative the Jews, according to Nietzsche, chose a life grounded in lies. Nietzsche interprets this preference as the ground of all subsequent politics, a politics separated from religion: "The Jews created that miracle of an inversion of values thanks to which life on earth

12. FW, sec. 136.
13. A, sec. 27.
14. Ps. 137.
15. A, secs. 16–17; cf. Spinoza, *Theological-Political Treatise*, 17: "After its destruction and reestablishment, the Jewish state was a mere shadow of the first state, for the high priests had usurped the rights of the tribal military commanders."
16. A, secs. 26–27, 54–58; J, sec. 38; WM, sec. 481.

has acquired a new and dangerous charm for a few millennia. . . . The slave-rebellion in morality begins with them."[17]

Nietzsche's Jesus drew the radically apolitical consequences of the discrediting of the old polytheism. Open to everything because nothing is foreign to him, he has lost the capacity to experience the distinction at the heart of serious politics, the distinction between friends and enemies, between his own and what is hostile to it.[18] Only Israel's original warrior piety justified that distinction by which serious politics stands or falls.

For Jesus, no enemies—and therefore no politics—exist because military defeat has deprived his people of the pious ties that made them a people, not a group of random, independent individuals. Jesus' radical lack of discrimination precludes awareness of any crucial distinctions between man and man and even between god and man, heaven and earth: the kingdom of heaven is here and now within oneself as soon as one becomes alive to the consequences of military defeat for the old political piety. Nietzsche's Jesus refuses to discriminate between slave and freeman, male and female, Jew and gentile, wisdom and ignorance, life and death, noble and base:

> The glad tidings are precisely that opposites no longer exist; the kingdom of heaven belongs to the children; the faith that makes itself heard here is no faith obtained through struggle—it is here, it exists from the beginning; it is, as it were, an infantilism that has retreated into the spiritual . . . a retarded puberty caused by degeneration. . . . This kind of faith is not angry, does not condemn, does not defend itself: it does not bring "the sword"—it cannot even imagine how it might one day be divisive. It does not prove itself, either by miracle or by reward and promise or even "by scripture": it itself is in every moment its own miracle, reward, proof, its "kingdom of god." . . . It stands outside all religion, history, science, all experience of the world, all knowledge, all politics, all psychology, all books, all art—its knowledge is pure foolishness precisely about the existence of such things. . . . Such a teaching cannot contradict. It cannot even grasp that other teachings exist or can exist.[19]

17. J, sec. 195.
18. Cf. Carl Schmitt, *The Concept of the Political*, ed. and trans. George Schwab (New Brunswick, N.J.: Rutgers University Press, 1976), pp. 27–36, 53–55, 69–105; WM, sec. 218; Z, II, "On Immaculate Perception"; Plato *Republic* 335B–336A.
19. A, sec. 32.

In a passage suppressed by his sister, Nietzsche describes Jesus as an idiot—using the word in its ancient meaning, according to which an idiot (*idiotēs*) is a private person, a man with no tribal or civic gods, and therefore no politics, of his own.[20] Such people—mere human beings or persons—seemed slavish or infantile on the ancient polytheism's radically political horizon. To escape this idiotic fate the Jews interpreted it as a temporary divine punishment, which would be terminated when their messiah restored their political integrity by rebuilding their ancestral Temple on its ancestral site in Jerusalem. In opposition to Jesus, the Jews did not see their recourse to monotheism as an end in itself: it was a means to restore their warrior piety. Unable to bear the thought of perpetual enslavement, they invented an omnipotent redeemer. Yet if this redeemer exists, nothing can exist outside him: omnipotence cannot be limited. Jesus' infantilism was incapable of experiencing anything as foreign or hostile to its kingdom of god. Only their old warrior gods, not their new omnipotent *deus ex machina*, could justify the Jews' political life, their continued concern with themselves as a people opposed potentially or actually to other peoples.

Since the monotheism needed to restore the old political polytheism reduces everything, including that polytheism, to nothing, it *cannot* restore the old warrior piety. Under monotheism, nothing is more than a toy to be willfully created or destroyed by divine omnipotence. Nothing is serious because politics no longer is serious. Apparently, omnipotent monotheism can do anything except create a world in which warring political gods can be taken seriously; at best, such a creation would be childish amusement.[21]

Contrary to Nietzsche's Jesus, his Paul loathed the idiotic consequences of the discrediting of his people's tribal piety. In a monotheistic world, the only choice is between political suicide and some form of infantilism. According to Nietzsche, Paul wanted revenge against the victorious enemies who had forced this absurd choice upon his people. Indeed, he wanted to make everything political or victorious seem ungodly, and thus he originated the contemporary democratic usage of "political" as a term of reproach. Nietzsche interpreted him as the originator of the most powerful expression of

---

20. A, secs. 29–31; cf. Spinoza, *Theological-Political Treatise*, 19: "The Christian religion was not taught at first by kings but by private persons. . . . among the Hebrews things were very differently arranged: for their church began at the same time as their dominion, and Moses, their monarch, taught religion to the people, arranged their sacred rites and chose their priests" (tr. Elwes).

21. Z, I, "On the Three Metamorphoses"; Schmitt (above, n. 18), pp. 53 and 98.

the spirit of revenge (*Geist der Rache*), the drive that informs all human or cosmopolitan, as distinct from political, thought.[22] Paul realized that the destruction of polytheism could not eliminate the political passions whose goals that polytheism had sanctified. Those passions, especially the need to escape the infantilism fostered by monotheism, want vengeance against a world that degrades them to mere superstition or "racism."

To gain that revenge, Paul consciously falsified the meaning of Jesus' life:[23] he created Christianity according to which military victory, political greatness, was hellish. Thus he dragged his victorious enemies down to the hell into which defeat had cast his people. Paul shared Jesus' insight that Jewish messianic dreams were negated by the monotheism needed to actualize them. However, his determination to avenge the defeat responsible for monotheism precluded Jesus' infantile harmony with it. For Paul, monotheistic devaluation of politics was a way to vengeance, not a way of life.

Some Christian or post-Christian form of monotheism, and with it the death of serious politics, has triumphed everywhere during the last two millennia. If isolated pockets of warrior piety exist today its adherents are pitied as "backward" or "underdeveloped" peoples, that is, people whose "sexist," "chauvinist," or "racist" prejudices require replacement by Christian or pacifist ideals. The Jews, and only the Jews, never were reconciled to this replacement; they remained aware of the terrifying emptiness of apolitical, cosmopolitan solutions. Nietzsche believed that the Jewish instinct constituted by this awareness prevented wholehearted acceptance of any religious or secularized monotheism. For the Jews, monotheism never was more than a means to return to polytheism's serious (political) world.

Prior to what Nietzsche diagnosed as the dying of their radically political instincts, the Jews insisted upon living in ghettos segregated from the emptiness, the lack of seriousness, of Christian-cosmopolitan regimes. Unlike contemporary opponents of "segregation" or "discrimination" who denounce their ghettos, the Jews demanded ghetto segregation so long as their yearning for political regeneration had not lost its pious flame.

Nietzsche knew that the Jewish instinct always had been in danger of losing itself to monotheism's apolitical orientation. Both "rational" persuasion and horrible persecution joined to weaken that instinct's desperate clinging to its impossible goal. The weakening by persua-

22. A, sec. 58; WM, sec. 765; Z, II, "On Child and Marriage"; FW, secs. 359–70; "An Spinoza," MusA, XX, 129.
23. A, secs. 40–49.

sion was never very successful until after the American and Napoleonic "liberation" of the ghettos; however, Nietzsche insisted that it already had been responsible for the falsification of Jewish history in most of the Old Testament and all of the New Testament.[24] Since the destruction of the Temple, Judaism's hallmark has been the conflict between this alien tendency to interpret it as essentially apolitical and cosmopolitan and the Jewish instinct's subordination of monotheism to the restoration of its old warrior piety. That alien, "rationalist" tendency to reject the depth of instinct linking Jews to their ancient polytheism never was stronger or more persuasive than in Spinoza, the last Jewish philosopher.

Nietzsche noted that Spinoza advised abandonment of the Jewish instinct precisely because monotheistic omnipotence cannot be limited by any morality, especially by the warrior piety that it was invented to restore: "How can Spinoza's position, his denial and rejection of all morality, be understood? It was a consequence of his theodicy!"[25] Spinoza defended omnipotent freedom's monotheism against limitation by any political—and therefore exclusive—piety.[26] More knowledgeable about Judaism than most modern Jews (and gentiles), he identified it heart and soul with tribal, not cosmopolitan, piety.[27] Moreover, he agreed with the Jews that morality or politics (which the Jews, like all pre-Christians, did not distinguish) is possible only in a polytheist world of warring political gods, not in a monotheist world of brotherly love:

> [Jesus' words] were spoken to men who were oppressed, who lived in a corrupt commonwealth on the brink of ruin, where justice was utterly neglected. The Christian doctrine inculcated just before the destruction of Jerusalem was also taught by Jeremiah before the first destruction of Jerusalem. . . . However, Moses, who did not write in times of oppression but—mark this— founded a well-ordered regime . . . ordained that an eye be given for an eye. . . . Jesus' and Jeremiah's teaching concerning submission to injuries is only valid in places where justice is neglected . . . not in a well-ordered regime.[28]

24. Ibid., secs. 25–27; GM, III, sec. 22.
25. WM, sec. 410.
26. GM, II, sec. 15; Spinoza, *Theological-Political Treatise*, 16; *Political Treatise*, 2; Leo Strauss, *Spinoza's Critique of Religion*, trans. E. M. Sinclair (New York: Schocken, 1965), pp. 231–38, 302 (n. 302).
27. Spinoza, *Theological-Political Treatise*, 3, 5, 7, 12, 17–19; A, secs. 17, 25; Strauss (above, n. 26), p. 18.
28. Spinoza, *Theological-Political Treatise*, 7; cf. ibid., 17: "The love of the Jews for their own country was not only patriotism, but also piety, and was cherished and

Although Spinoza agreed that genuine morality was possible only in the world of the old Jewish warrior piety, the dread of monotheism's infantilism was weak or nonexistent in his soul. This weakness is responsible for the lack of depth discerned by Nietzsche in Spinoza and in all men unable to grasp why clinging desperately to Jewish messianic hopes, however impossible their realization, reveals a rare awareness of *the* human problem, rare at least in regimes founded on cosmopolitan (apolitical) principles. Nietzsche interpreted Jesus' infantilism as the radicalization of this shallowness.

Spinoza knew that serious political-moral cares were possible only under the ancestral Jewish piety. Consequently he also knew that the Jewish instinct, a political will *par excellence*, required subordination of all life to its warrior piety. This piety necessarily hated scientific-philosophic cosmopolitanism for the same reason that it hated Christianity, the pacifist way of Jesus' infantilism.[29] Spinoza's attachment to his form of (scientific) cosmopolitanism was responsible for his attempt to liberalize, that is, depoliticize, Judaism. The heart of his liberalization has been elimination of the Jew's instinctual yearning for regeneration of his ancestral gods who were discredited by destruction of their Temple in Jerusalem.[30] Like all contemporary "liberation" movements, Spinoza's liberalism insisted that there was private, apolitical morality as well as political morality; indeed, Spinoza and those "liberators" teach the primacy of private—individual—rights over political duties.

Spinoza never could persuade genuine (orthodox) Jews to aban-

---

nurtured by daily rites till, like their hatred of other nations, it passed into their nature.... Thus the heart of the Jews was strengthened to bear all things for their country with extraordinary constancy and bravery.... Never so long as Jerusalem stood could they endure to remain under foreign domination.... Poverty was nowhere more endurable than in a country where duty to one's fellow-citizen was practiced with the utmost piety.... Thus Jews were nowhere so well off as in their own country; outside its limits they met with nothing but loss and disgrace."

29. Ibid., 11 (end).

30. Ibid., Preface: "The law revealed by god to Moses was merely the law of the individual Hebrew republic and therefore was binding on none but Hebrews, and not even on Hebrews after the downfall of their nation." Cf. ibid., 19: "After the destruction of the Hebrew dominion, revealed religion ceased to have the force of law; for as soon as the Jews were forced to transfer their allegiance to the king of Babylon, their kingdom of God and divine right ceased to exist." See also ibid., 12, where Spinoza notes the Bible's prudent silence on "what became of the Ark of the Covenant, for there is no doubt that it was destroyed together with the Temple; yet there was nothing which the Jews considered more sacred or held in greater reverence.... We [Christians or philosophers] must not say that the word of god suffered in like manner, else we shall be like the Jews, who said that the Temple which would then be the Temple of god had perished in the flames."

don their messianic fervor and, therefore, their ghettos. The alternative was too degrading for their radically political yearning. The centrality of that yearning links (orthodox) Judaism with Socratic-Platonic thought, however implausible this linkage may seem to most "platonic" scholars. Like the mission of Nietzsche's chief enemy, Socrates (or Plato), "the mission of the Jews always was to bring a people to reason." In the decisive sense, as Nietzsche realized, this mission is more Socratic than Nietzschean. But Socrates both needed and fought the warrior piety for whose restoration Jews alone always longed; he saw that this piety (in his case, his ancestral Athenian polytheism) gave his philosophy its direction and its seriousness.

The heart of Nietzsche's opposition to modern classical scholarship is his awareness of its blindness to Socrates' deep need for the Athenian piety that condemned him to death. Lacking, as moderns do, the narrow political piety provided by birth into pre-Christian regimes, modern scholars cannot be alive to Socrates' debt to what Nietzsche called his herd instinct.[31]

Nietzsche rightly notes that the herd instinct always provides herd members with one central care, however differently that care may be interpreted in different bestial or human herds. That care concerns the right way of life, how best to live—in short, the moral-political care. Generally this care is informed by the regnant orthodoxy (instinct) of one's particular herd. Socrates turned that care into a question whose answer was not self-evident (as it usually is to champions of the going orthodoxy), and spent his life trying unsuccessfully to answer that question. In this crucial sense, his life served his (Athenian) herd instinct by trying to answer its main question. Nietzsche insisted that all pre-Nietzschean thought served the instinct of the thinker's herd: the conscious or unconscious aim of "the famous wise men" was to answer the main question of their respective herds, the question of how best to live. The heart of pre-Nietzschean thought was political (and therefore moral or religious).

The primacy of politics and the political question cannot be established by any philosophic-scientific inquiry. Rather, it is revealed by the same herd instinct that inspires the faith that men live in a world that exists independently of their experience of it. No rational inquiry can show that the so-called "external" world exists indepen-

---

31. Z, II, "On the Famous Wise Men"; Harry Neumann, "The Beginning of Wisdom" (to be published) and his review of Bernd Magnus's *Nietzsche's Existential Imperative* in *The Independent Journal of Philosophy*, 3 (1979), 139–41.

dently of one's experience—or, for that matter, that one's "internal" self possesses this independent reality.

Socrates saw that the herd instinct that reveals an independently existing world and self is not democratic: it presents a (aristocratic) hierarchy of concerns or questions, primarily the moral-political question. Denial of this question's priority means denial of the whole political (or herd-instinct) orientation, including the faith that one's "internal" self and the "external" world exist independently of one's experience.

That apolitical denial of the herd-instinct orientation is at the heart of Nietzsche's nihilism. The nihilist denies that anything (this table, that tree, his self, the law of contradiction,[32] and so forth) is anything but his experiences, mere impressions as Hume called them. There is nothing "in" things (or "behind" or "above" them) that gives them a reality apart from immediate experience—whether this experience be that of a fish, an infant, or a Socrates.[33] The herd-instinct faith in such an existence (apart from experience) is a faith in "beings," things that exist in themselves, as opposed to what might be called mere "things" (or nothings) without any intrinsic being.[34] Nihilists recognize only things or nothings but no beings. The first (and last) sentence of Stirner's *The Ego and Its Own* summarizes the nihilist, and therefore apolitical, core of Stirner and Nietzsche: "I have based my reality on nothing" ("Ich hab' mein Sach' auf Nichts gestellt").

Aware that he himself was radically nihilist, indeed "Europe's first perfect nihilist," Nietzsche insisted that truth led to despair, not to messianic redemption or to happiness: "Those who really have looked into the heart (*Wesen*) of things—they are the knowers. . . . Knowledge kills action, action needs the veil of illusion. . . . Real knowledge, insight into the horrible truth, outweighs any motive for action."[35] Realization of the horrible (because radically apolitical) truth destroys life, a life grounded in the illusions of common (or political) sense, the instincts of one's herd: "Not doubt but *certainty* drives men insane. . . . We all fear the truth."[36] Nietzsche invented

32. WM, secs. 507, 515–16; Martin Heidegger, *Nietzsche* (Pfullingen: Neske, 1961), I, 508–616.
33. WM, secs. 556, 481; FW, sec. 57; Spinoza, *Theological-Political Treatise*, 16.
34. Plato *Republic* 511D; Aristotle *Physics* 193a1–10.
35. GT, sec. 7 (end); WM, Preface (sec. 3) and sec. 25; Heidegger (above, n. 32), I, 436–37; II, 281–83.
36. *Ecce Homo*, "Why I Am So Clever," sec. 4; WM, sec. 598; Z, IV, "On Science" and "The Shadow"; Heidegger (above, n. 32), I, 531 and 581.

the superman, his version of Israel's messiah, to appease the same fear of truth's radically idiotic horror that compelled the Jews to live on messianic hope.[37]

Nietzsche interpreted both Socratic questioning and Jesus' infantilism as consistent efforts to appease that politically inspired fear of truth. Socratic questioning is political at heart because it is informed by the priority of the herd instinct's main concern. The Socratic questioner understands himself as enslaved to the herd whose instincts give meaning and direction to his questioning.

Nietzsche commanded a rare insight into the deeply political orientation of the Socratic enterprise. In terms of the cave image in Plato's *Republic* (511D–517C), nobody, including Socratic philosophers, ever really leaves the cave to look directly at the sun, the idea of the good. The Socratic's relation to that real, self-subsisting good is guaranteed by his faith or trust in its reality, a faith inspired by his herd instinct. The instincts of his herd teach every herd member that his chief concern is securing what is good for him. Insofar as he remains a pious herd member and not a questioning, Socratic one, he wholeheartedly accepts some form (there sometimes are opposing forms) of his regime's regnant orthodoxy about what is good for him. Far more than modern "liberated" Jews, Nietzsche knew that Judaism's messianic longing—its deepest stratum—is for a regime in which Jews again can be pious herd members in this sense.

Although Socratic herd members question the goodness of their herd's political orthodoxies, they never forget what they owe to their herd: it is responsible for their fundamental conviction, the faith that the question of the good life is the crucial question and, consequently, that political philosophy is not one "field" or "discipline" among many. For the same reason politics is central and not one human activity among many. To demote it to one of many essentially equal human or "cultural" activities is to reduce the question (or care) at the core of serious politics, the question of how best to live, to a question of "ethics" (or political or moral science) among other equally important questions of "cultural fields" such as science, humanities, stamp-collecting, or religion. On a Socratic horizon, *nihilism is precisely this apolitical demotion*, not the throwing of bombs or the assertion that nothing exists or the denial of external and internal reality—for these more sensational things are mere consequences of that demotion. Both require membership in a sacred political, and therefore noncosmopolitan, community. The hallmark of such a

---

37. Above, n. 31.

community is the identity of politics, religion, and morality in it. There can be no Aristotelian division of moral and philosophic virtue or modern opposition between private and public or political morality. Such divisions or oppositions presuppose that men have a life—often their most important life—apart from the sacred ties of birth linking them to their tribes or cities. The necessary, if not sufficient, condition of being either Socratic or Jewish is membership in a community whose warrior piety precludes these divisions or oppositions.

Without the faith inspired by one's herd instinct, men (and beasts) are nihilist. Socrates owed his escape from nihilism to his rootedness in the Athenian herd whose goodness he questioned and who finally killed him for that questioning. In this sense his worst enemy (the Athenians who killed him) was also his best friend.

Socratic thought resembles the original Jewish political piety for which birth, familial-political rootedness, determines whether one is divine or human or a mixture of both. Contrast this emphasis on birth with Genesis (3:22) where God, agreeing with the serpent, complains that Adam has "become as one of us" (gods) because Adam's disobedience made him knowledgeable about good and evil. Here being or becoming a god has nothing to do with birth. Divinity's core is the apolitical, immoral resolve to defy the authority ("god") dominant in one's herd. The resultant knowledge is not of some moral truth or reality outside of one's own will, as Socrates, on the basis of his herd-instinct faith, believed the true good is. Socrates questioned the claim that the Athenian gods constituted that ultimate, independently existing source of morality; he did not question the Athenian faith that such a source, the idea of the good as he called it, existed even if it were impossible to grasp adequately.

Genesis' "knowledge of good and evil" is in reality the radically apolitical will to be free and independent, to recognize no moral authority outside of one's own nihilist will, a will limited quite literally by nothing. No wonder that the apotheosis of this apolitical willfulness is the biblical god's creation of all reality out of nothing.

Because he is nihilist will, Genesis' God constitutes rejection of politics and political privilege, the privileges of birth common to Socrates and his pious Athenian accusers. He has no parents, no family or herd out of which he was born. No herd-instinct faith guides his creation *ex nihilo*. He must create and think *ex nihilo* because he experienced no birth or, perhaps, as Mephisto in Goethe's *Faust* suggests, he is born *ex nihilo*, "that great cosmopolitan" of Nietzsche's *Antichrist* (sec. 17). His omnipotent cosmopolitanism can do anything except what the defeated Jews, in their desperation, required of him: restoration of their ancestral polytheism in their Jerusalem Temple—the earthly not the heavenly Jerusalem!

Anybody can become a biblical god as God and the serpent define divinity in Genesis (3:22). It has nothing to do with birth, with being born into an exclusive sacred tribe or city. The sole prerequisite is nihilist liberation from such exclusive ties and from the "racist," "sexist," and "chauvinist" "prejudices" created by the bellicose gods sanctifying those ties. This biblical divinity liberates men from more than the piety into which Socrates was born and whose worth he questioned. Genesis' God negates the very possibility of Socratic questioning. Nietzsche rightly insisted that Socrates' thought, his radically political philosophy, is rooted in faith in the instincts of his Athenian herd. That thought is meaningless if those instincts are illusory. Consequently the job of Socratic or political philosophy in any herd is twofold: (1) to investigate the validity of that particular herd's answer to the question of the good life, but also (2) to protect the instincts of the herd against nihilist rejection of their validity. The second requirement would make Socrates champion the this-worldly Jewish messianic enterprise against Christianity's merely heavenly Jerusalem; for the same reason, it sparks Nietzsche's ultimate preference for Christianity over Judaism.

Nietzsche noted that modern intellectuals, whether humanists or scientists, usually are democratic and egalitarian, opposed to discriminatory, aristocratic emphasis on the privileges of birth. In this spirit Hitler once complained that the Kaiser was born with the Iron Cross around his neck, while ordinary soldiers had to risk their lives to earn it. Similar complaints often are leveled against England's queen. Such rejections of the rights of birth would eliminate not only Prussian kaisers and English queens, but all Socratic (nonnihilist) thought. They would reduce life to an apolitical reality in which nothing has a being of its own and, most importantly, in which no moral limits exist except by tyrannic fiat. For one learns of those limits by birth, by being born into a particular (noncosmopolitan) herd whose instincts supply the faith that they exist. Just as not everyone could become a god of Greek mythology (as distinct from Genesis's God), so not everyone can become Socratic. In both cases the prerequisite is birth, being piously rooted in the instincts of one's particular herd. Precisely this particular, political rootedness is undermined in modern regimes informed by Christian or post-Christian (humanitarian) cosmopolitanism. Yet this essential particularity is the most Socratic aspect of the Platonic problem of participation, the question of the relation of particulars to universals or ideas.

Radically political, the Platonic problem of participation cannot seriously arise in the souls of citizens of modern regimes in which the legitimacy of politics' exclusive ties is derived from universal ties or rights (the rights of man, for example). (Orthodox) Jews always have prayed for a messiah to redeem them from the apolitical nihilism of these (gentile) regimes. This messianic yearning made them alive to the Socratic-Platonic problem of participation as the central question of human life and not merely as an academic problem in so-called "platonic" scholarship.

For Socrates, even a man's loftiest metaphysical-theological flights remain bound to the instincts of his particular herd: science or philosophy is always herd philosophy. Refusal to acknowledge this political enslavement as the necessary condition of one's investigations is nihilist. Far from nullifying inquiries into being or the universe, the philosopher's dependence upon the instincts of his herd, his common or political sense, reveals the only nonnihilist way to maintain those inquiries. Socrates did not renounce nonnihilist metaphysics or science when he insisted upon political philosophy's priority. Socratic emphasis on the moral-political cares of one's herd, his radically political approach to life, is meant to rescue life from conscious, but more often unconscious, nihilism. Nietzsche has just this rescue mission in mind when he observes that "we all fear the truth."[38]

The Socratic rescue mission is fueled by that fear of truth. Nietzsche sees execution of the same mission as the job of Israel's messiah, whose success would restore the necessary condition of Socratic philosophy: rootedness in a tribe or city whose piety sanctifies *only* that rootedness. In this crucial—but usually overlooked—sense, an "unenlightened" ancient Israeli or Zulu warrior was more Socratic than a Jesus, a Spinoza, a Marx, or a Nietzsche.

Genuinely Jewish hopes always were for a messianic redemption in which Jews again could be seriously political and would not be degraded to the apolitical level of ancient, medieval, or modern "individualists." On their horizon, Jesus' crucifixion was a scandal pre-

---

38. Above, n. 36. Nietzsche does not exempt himself from this fear, which drove him to attempt the transcendence of nihilism or moral emptiness. Put differently, Nietzsche still yearned to be a philosopher, a lover of truth, although as "Europe's first perfect nihilist" he realized how unrealistic the love of (as opposed to fear of or indifference to) truth was: WM, Preface (sec. 3) and sec. 25; Heidegger (above, n. 32), I, 436–37; II, 281–83.

cisely because it pointed to an other-worldly, cosmopolitan redemption of Jews as individuals and not to the political redemption to be effected by Israel's messiah.[39] Worship of a crucified "messiah" sanctified the split that Israel's messiah was meant to eliminate: the split between private and public, conscience and society, political morality and private morality. More decisively, it sanctified the priority of private or apolitical morality or religion, thus degrading war and politics to—at best—necessary evils.

Socrates would agree with Nietzsche that in regimes in which this priority (of the private or apolitical) determines morality "the mission of the Jews always is to bring a people to reason." However, Nietzsche knew that Socratic (political) reason is not Nietzschean (apolitical) reason. Socratic reason can exist seriously only in men rooted by birth in a warrior piety no longer available in modern regimes. In these regimes the strongest link to Socratic thought would be something akin to messianic Judaism's impossible yearning, the homesickness for an exclusively political regeneration.[40]

The reason to which Judaism forces men, if they can be made alive to its real message, is a harsh, unwelcome ordeal for both Jews and gentiles: it is nothing less than the question of whether life is worth living after the discrediting of polytheism's warrior orientation. Would not suicide have been better for the Jews (and for all pre-Christian peoples) after their Temple was destroyed? Little more than the power of the subhuman craving for mere life at any price, a passion shared by all beasts, militates against suicide, when the sole living choice is between impossible messianic hopes (Jews) and some infantile "life-style" (gentiles). It surely is no accident that this craving's power is apotheosized in Spinoza's omnipotent god whose hegemony means the natural right to self-preservation of anything powerful enough to maintain itself, however infantile it may be.[41]

39. 1 Cor. 1:23; Gal. 4:24–36, 3:26–28; Luke 14:26; Matt. 12:47–48. Consider Ps. 137 and 1 Kings 21:3.

40. *Martin Heidegger zum 80. Geburtstag von seiner Heimatstadt Meßkirch* (Frankfurt am Main: Klostermann, 1969).

41. GM, II, sec. 15; WM, sec. 410; FW, sec. 349; Strauss (above, n. 26), pp. 231–38; Spinoza, *Theological-Political Treatise*, 16: "For instance, fish are determined by nature to swim and the big ones to eat the smaller ones and therefore fish enjoy the water and big ones eat smaller ones with supreme natural right. For it is certain that nature has supreme right to do anything she can; in other words, her right is co-extensive with her power. The power of nature is the power of god, which has supreme right over all things. . . . It is the supreme law and right of nature that every individual should strive to preserve itself as it is without regard to anything but itself; therefore this supreme law and right belongs to every individual. . . . We do not here acknowledge

The Jews have two important days of mourning: one generally known, the other unknown, to gentiles. The aim of Yom Kippur, the individual asking his omnipotent god to forgive his sins, is readily intelligible to gentiles; Tishah b'Ab (the ninth of Ab) is not, for it is a day of national, not personal, mourning, a day when Jews mourn the catastrophe that compelled them either to die politically or to live on impossible hopes. On that day dirges are sung mourning the destruction of the Temple in Jerusalem. If monotheism by its very nature cannot restore serious politics, Tishah b'Ab actually is a day of mourning for the destruction of the Jewish people. Nor is its message of doom limited to Jews! In a world dominated by the nihilism responsible for monotheism, Tishah b'Ab is a bitter reminder to non-Jews that their life, too, lost its seriousness, that is, its political core, with the destruction of the old polytheistic world.

Since nothing goes more against the grain than Tishah b'Ab's message, it does not receive the publicity among gentiles that is accorded to Yom Kippur. That message is given by Zarathustra's prophet or truth-sayer (*Wahrsager*), "the proclaimer of the great weariness": "Everything is empty, all is the same. . . . To be sure we have harvested, but why did all fruit turn rotten and brown for us? . . . Verily we have become too weary even to die; so we are still awake and continue to live—in tombs! . . . Nothing is worthwhile, the world is without meaning, knowledge strangles."[42]

Zarathustra's truth-sayer also gives the reason for his nihilism: "Everything was." That is, genuine politics, which alone makes life serious and not infantile "fun," once was—in ancient, polytheistic regimes; it no longer exists in modern, post-Christian regimes where politics is derived from individual will, government from the consent of the governed. The pacifist goal of such regimes can only be something akin to a Marxist classless society in which politics and the state wither away. Once that occurs, individuals will be free to live as they—as individuals and not as citizens—please. On this apolitical horizon the individual's arbitrary whim determines whether to live seriously or playfully, since, "apart from whim or 'taste,' nothing in this world is inherently 'choiceworthy.' "[43]

---

any difference between men and other individual natural entities nor . . . between fools, idiots and sane men. Whatsoever any individual does by the laws of its nature, it has a supreme right to do."

42. Z, II, "The Soothsayer"; IV, "The Cry of Distress"; Strauss (above, n. 26), pp. 10–11.
43. Z, II, "On Those Who Are Sublime"; WM, sec. 481.

Aware that modern "liberation" movements spark this elimination of politics and therefore of seriousness, Nietzsche could not but honor the tenacity with which messianic Judaism had clung to its dream of political regeneration in spite of refutation (by apolitical reasoners) and persecution. It was the quixotic last stand of politics in an essentially apolitical and therefore infantile world. Prior to what Nietzsche rightly diagnosed as the modern decay of the Jewish instinct, nothing could compel Jews not to grieve on Tishah b'Ab for what they had lost; nor could anything reconcile them to the finality of that loss. Life is hopeless both for them and for Socratic (political) philosophers, if truth is on the side of Zarathustra's truth-sayer rather than with Israel's messiah. Nietzsche's rejection of that warrior messiah and his attack on Socrates both spring from the same roots or apolitical lack of roots.

Nietzsche knew that this lack of roots precludes thoughtfulness (as distinct from mere cleverness). Serious thought, that is, Socratic or political philosophy, is impossible in modern regimes for the same reason that it is impossible in the God and serpent of Genesis. No wonder that Nietzsche saw the highest form of life, the superman's, as something akin to child's play, an activity recalling the infantilism ascribed by him to Christianity's messiah.[44]

44. Z, I, "On the Three Metamorphoses"; and the descriptions of the last man in Z, Preface, sec. 5, and of Jesus in A, secs. 29–35.

III. Nietzsche and the Old Testament

Israel Eldad
(Translated by Yisrael Medad)

Dedicated to the memory
of Walter Kaufmann

A Value Judgment

The dedication of this article to Walter Kaufmann is more than an expression of my friendship and personal sorrow upon his death; certainly he would have dealt with the subject better than I. Actually, the dedication is part of the subject at hand, and I think it well to begin by relating something that I remember about him. During his stay in Jerusalem, a city he loved, I inquired of him in Kantian style while he was visiting with me (for I was then working on my Hebrew translation of Nietzsche): *Wie ist Dionysos in Jerusalem möglich?*—How can Dionysus be possible in Jerusalem? He seemed pleased by the question and his reply the next day was a poem whose theme was "And David was leaping and dancing before the Lord" (2 Sam. 6:14).

Here in one sweep we have three elements: Kaufmann's poetic soul, which was full of enthusiasm for Nietzsche; the living Bible; and one of the keys to Nietzsche's own love for the Old Testament. In fact, this key is provided by Nietzsche himself: "All honor to the Old Testament! I find in it great human beings, a heroic landscape, and something of the very rarest quality in the world, the incomparable naiveté of the *strong heart*; what is more, I find a people."[1]

This respect for the Old Testament is highlighted further when compared with Nietzsche's negation of most of the personalities in the New Testament, for it is clear that personalities or situations of a Dionysian character are absent from the New Testament. Nietzsche, in truth, does not mention this biblical episode of David's wild

---

1. GM, III, sec. 22; *Basic Writings of Nietzsche*, ed. and trans. Walter Kaufmann (New York: The Modern Library, 1966), p. 580.

dance before the Ark of the Lord. Incidentally, the language there is more explicit and stronger in that it stresses not the Ark but that he danced before the Lord himself, even though the subject there is the transporting of the Ark to Jerusalem. Yet the example chosen by Kaufmann to illustrate the possible connection between Dionysus and Jerusalem is concise in the extreme, as it usually is with expressionists. Ancient Greek culture had, as is known, a decisive effect on the thought of Nietzsche, which lends added significance to the clash with the culture of Israel, a clash quite surprising in its modernity.

The accepted historiography—and this too with a large measure of help from Jewish thinkers—always stressed the polarization between Judaism and Hellenism: on the one hand strict ethical monotheism, and on the other agnostic polytheism and creative philosophy. Nietzsche, however, as a philosopher of culture who opened gates to a new value scale, freed himself from such platitudes of thinking and unveiled new and surprising vistas.

It is obvious that Nietzsche possessed a profound knowledge of the New Testament and profited greatly from the deep Protestant tradition of his family. Yet there is no sharp division between the Old and New Testaments. The New is in no way an absolute negation of the Old, for already in the Old are to be found the roots of Christianity, for instance in the account of the separating of man from nature. Christianity, especially the Pauline version, inherited from Judaism the very concept of sin, the "revolt of the slaves," and the priestly rule. All these, according to Nietzsche's outlook, do not apply to the personality of Jesus himself. At times it seems that the idea of the Jews' being "guilty" of Christianity is accepted by Nietzsche not in conjunction with the heroes of the Old Testament, but as a postbiblical link. It was the Exile that forced the Jews to develop an unnatural Judaism, the fruit of which is Christianity.

In this sense one can find the discerning distinction between the terms "Israel" and "the Jews" or "Judaism." The first usually merits a positive response, whereas the latter is treated in a negative fashion. "Usually," I note, for, from a historical-psychological standpoint and apart from a religious value system, Nietzsche is astonished at the will to survive and the strength of life of the Jews throughout their exilic history, and especially in their state of dispersion. It is as if this strength of will atones for their "sin" toward mankind's history: "Jewish" morality.

And yet, it does not escape the eyes of a man of truth such as Nietzsche that the Old Testament already contains the possibilities for the religious-moral development that he negates, just as he negates the morality that denies nature, even if it is clear to him that it was only Christianity that drew the final conclusions from these possibilities and brought them to a total denial of life, whereas Judaism—and this is its glory and the secret of its survival—did not follow this path to the end.

> The history of Israel is invaluable as the typical history of all *denaturing* of natural values. I indicate five points. Originally, especially at the times of the kings, Israel also stood in the right, that is, the natural, relationship to all things. Its Yahweh was the expression of a consciousness of power, of joy in oneself, of hope for oneself: through him victory and welfare was expected; through him nature was trusted to give what the people needed—above all, rain. Yahweh is the god of Israel and therefore the god of justice: the logic of every people that is in power and has a good conscience. In the festival cult these two sides of the self-affirmation of a people find expression: they are grateful for the great destinies which raised them to the top; they are grateful in relation to the annual cycle of the seasons and to all good fortune in stock farming and agriculture. This state of affairs long remained the ideal, even after it had been done away with in melancholy fashion: anarchy within, the Assyrian without. The people, however, clung to the vision, as the highest desirability, of a king who is a good soldier and severe judge: above all, that typical prophet (that is, critic and satirist of the moment), Isaiah.[2]

An almost Dionysian description, at least in the later implication when Nietzsche's "wildness" was already restrained by the Apollonian element. The use in this instance of the name of the Divinity, Yahweh, rather than the plain "God," is an indication of Nietzsche's intention: this is His personal name, or in other words, the reality of Israel's god, His real sense. This is a living god of a people, an expression of its natural needs and of its soul. The morality of this god, too, is harnessed to Israel's life-needs as well as to its will to power, its need to know how to hate its enemies—who, of course, are Yahweh's enemies—and how to rejoice in its victories. All of Nietzsche's admiration for the Old Testament stems from the affirmation of life, the saying of "yes" to life, in which its religion is subordinated to this affirmation of life and its god is patterned on man and this life. The

---

2. A, sec. 25; *The Portable Nietzsche*, ed. and trans. Walter Kaufmann (New York: Viking, 1954), p. 594.

strength of this life is so great in the Old Testament that Nietzsche is not above setting it as an example even for the Greeks who are without doubt in his opinion—even in the Apollonian view, without mentioning the hedonistic outlook—a sure example and symbol of the affirmation of life: "The Jews, being a people which, like the Greeks, and even to a greater degree than the Greeks, loved and still love life, had not cultivated that idea ['life after death'] to any great extent."[3] Even the Greeks could learn from the heroism of the Patriarchs, says the admirer of Greece—that Greece which was itself an epitomization of heroic figures.

The resemblance between the later fate of Greek culture and that of Judaism, to Nietzsche's mind, is self-evident, and even more so if Hellenization is seen to be an almost inexorable process. There is, therefore, a resemblance between the passage from youth to decadence in Hellas and that same passage in Judaism or, to be exact, in the Old Testament itself. Socrates and Plato are the watershed of Greek culture. All that preceded them was youthful, naive, strong, and healthy, even the thought of the earlier philosophers. From that time onwards—decadence. The watershed in the Old Testament is the struggle of the prophets against the kings: "The appearance of the Greek philosophers from Socrates onwards is a symptom of decadence.... Plato is just as ungrateful to Pericles, Homer, tragedy, rhetoric, *as the prophets were to David and Saul*."[4]

As a classical philologist, Nietzsche naturally concerns himself with the particulars of the Greek stagnation, its "decadence," to a greater degree than he does with the Old Testament, more so because in the former there is spread before him—and his critical soul —an aspect of Christianity that is the continuation and extreme extension of the decadence that began in Judaism. It was as if two streams of decadence met within Christianity: on the part of religion, the "gloomy religio-moral pathos," and on the part of philosophy, the "Platonic slandering of the senses"; in either case, a negation of naturalism even unto the negation of life. The line of comparison is drawn out until it is established that "when Socrates and Plato took up the cause of virtue and justice, they were *Jews*."[5]

Therefore, David dancing before God is perhaps indeed Dionysian, just as is his resemblance to Pericles—whom Plato attacks—

---

3. M, sec. 72; *The Complete Works of Friedrich Nietzsche*, ed. Oscar Levy, 18 vols. (Edinburgh and London: T. N. Foulis, 1909–13), IX, 74.

4. WM, sec. 427 (my emphasis added); *The Will to Power*, trans. Walter Kaufmann and R. J. Hollingdale, ed. Walter Kaufmann (New York: Random House, 1968), p. 231.

5. WM, sec. 429; ibid., p. 234.

when David makes war and establishes a great kingdom. The presence of these figures in the Old Testament, full of life, full of vividness, and even imbued with a sense of humor, is what endeared the book to Nietzsche over the gloom of the New Testament that could not include a dancing David. Dance itself is even one of the signs of recognition of the true God: "a god prefers to stay beyond everything bourgeois and rational . . . between ourselves, also beyond good and evil. . . . Zarathustra goes so far as to confess: 'I would only believe in a God who could dance.' "[6]

The Old Testament David, of course, is not divine, just as Nietzsche in *The Will to Power* is not yet Dionysus to the extent that he would become in the last months of his creative work. What holds Nietzsche's attention is the similitude between the above expression of Nietzsche's and the dancing David, which lies beyond the bourgeois. Michal's despising of David's dancing expresses the situation well, and even though she is Saul's daughter, the stern moral spirit of Samuel is present and becomes even more evident in Nathan's indictment of David's involvement with Bathsheba—another event characterized as Dionysian (in the words "*also* beyond good and evil," as noted above). Incidentally, the Old Testament does not consider that it was his act with Bathsheba that was sinful, but rather his act directed toward Uriah.

What happened with the history of the Old Testament, which appears heroic to Nietzsche (and in the early parts of which Yahweh, the God of the Old Testament, is heroic), is not simple and clear-cut, just as Nietzsche's views of Socrates and Plato are complex and contradictory. In the first instance, as pointed out above, he sees the prophets in much the same way as he does Socrates and Plato, branding them as destroyers of the naturalness of ancient Israel. On the other hand, Socrates merits high admiration, along with the prophets of Israel, if only for having struggled against the establishment in the form of the priesthood.

"These had a fine sense of smell who, in the past, were called prophets."[7] There is no contradiction here. Rather, the similarity in Nietzsche's view of Socrates and the prophets stems from the same process of evaluation. Socrates is the fighter against accepted norms and goes forward, nobly and calmly, to his death as a result of his struggle. The essence of Socratism is the rule of moral values over all other values, and this is exactly what characterizes the prophets. The

---

6. WM, sec. 1038; ibid., pp. 534–35.
7. "Die Unschuld des Werdens," sec. 1047; K, 83, 371.

heroic aspect in this is not damaged by the content of their struggle—neither in the case of Socrates nor in that of the prophets—which Nietzsche rejects as a contradiction of nature.

While it is Socrates, as befits a philosopher, who upholds *knowledge*, from which morals stem, the prophets of Israel rank God as primary, for it is He who commands morality ("God has been made a Jew"). In a deeper sense (as in *The Will to Power*), what benefits the herd is that which speaks through God's will or the metaphysical imperative of knowledge. For our purposes, though, nothing more is needed than the empirical and conscious level: the prophecy in the Old Testament created a new world of values. The prophecy is, in a sense, a continuous correction of the establishment; that is its positive aspect, for it struggles and suffers ("the prophet is naturally alone") and is heroic. Nietzsche, thereby, stands before three decisive factors—the Old Testament prophets, the pre-Pauline Jesus, and Socrates—in a dual relationship of admiration for their personalities but rejection of their theories, and especially of the conclusions drawn from them. These conclusions include, in Judaism, the assumption of the slaves' morality as the fruit of the Exile; in Christianity, the Pauline church; and in Hellenism, the Platonic decadence in the world of simplistic "ideals" that affected Christianity as well.

This dual nature of Nietzsche's relationship to Judaism and the Old Testament was expressed in his summing up of "What Europe owes the Jews!":

> Many things, good and bad, and above all one thing of the nature both of the best and the worst, the grand style in morality, the fearfulness and majesty of infinite demands, of infinite significations, the whole Romanticism and sublimity of moral questionableness—and consequently just the most attractive, ensnaring and exquisite element in those iridescences and allurements to life, in the aftersheen of which the sky of our European culture, its evening sky, now glows—perhaps glows out. For this, we artists among the spectators and philosophers are—grateful to the Jews.[8]

In spite of the fact that the subject at hand is the Jews and Nietzsche goes on to hint at their power to assume control of Europe if they so desire, even suggesting an admiration for their propensity—as a result of the loss of the Jewish instinct—to assimilate into European culture, it is clear that he is describing not the later Jewish characteristics but the intensity of life exhibited by them as an imprint from the Old Testament.

8. J, sec. 250; *Complete Works*, XII, 206–7.

In the Jewish "Old Testament," the book of divine justice, there
are men, things, and sayings on such an immense scale, that
Greek and Indian literature has nothing to compare with it. One
stands with fear and reverence before those stupendous remains
of what man was formerly, . . .—the taste for the Old Testament is
a touchstone with respect to "great" and "small." . . . To have
bound up this New Testament (a kind of *rococo* of taste in every respect) along with the Old Testament into one book, as the "Bible,"
as "The Book in Itself," is perhaps the greatest audacity and "sin
against the Spirit" which literary Europe has upon its conscience.[9]

In other places Nietzsche terms the act of the joining together of
the two portions of the Bible "an act of barbarity." As one who, like
Schopenhauer, was a devotee of music, which he considered the
highest expression of man's soul and the soul's contributions, he
writes in *Nietzsche contra Wagner*: "It was only in Händel's music that
the best in Luther and in those like him found its voice, the Judaeo-
heroic trait which gave the Reformation a touch of greatness—the
Old Testament, *not* the New, become music."[10]

Nietzsche makes a distinction between the Old Testament of the
"older" parts and that of the "later" sections, a distinction that stems
from his firm contrast between two philosophies: the one that says
"yes" to life and the one that says "no."

What an affirmative Aryan religion, the product of the ruling
class, looks like: the law-book of Manu. (The deification of the
feeling of power in Brahma: interesting that it arose among the
warrior caste and was only transferred to the priests.) What an affirmative Semitic religion, the product of a ruling class, looks like:
the law-book of Mohammed, the older parts of the Old Testament.
(Mohammedanism, as a religion for men, is deeply contemptuous
of the sentimentality and mendaciousness of Christianity—which
it feels to be a woman's religion.) What a negative Semitic religion,
the product of an oppressed class, looks like: the New Testament
(—in Indian-Aryan terms: a chandala religion). What a negative
Aryan religion looks like, grown up among the ruling orders: Buddhism. It is quite in order that we possess no religion of oppressed
Aryan races, for that is a contradiction: a master-race is either on
top or it is destroyed.[11]

---

9. Ibid., sec. 52; ibid., p. 71.
10. *Nietzsche contra Wagner*, "Eine Musik ohne Zukunft"; *Complete Works*, VIII, 63–64.
11. WM, sec. 145; *The Will to Power*, p. 93.

Here we have the distinction between Aryans and Semites and, it is unnecessary to add, without the two connotations that were attached to the terms as a result of National Socialism. The difference between the healthy and sick foundations (in order not to be misled by using the phrase "between good and evil") runs through the Aryans as it does through the Semites. The primary and decisive mode of measurement is the saying of "yes" or "no" to life. It is at this point that the Old Testament, but only in its older parts, finds its place among the "yes"-sayers.

In biblical scholarship, especially that of the Christian school combined with the popular evolutionism of the nineteenth century, there most certainly was a distinction between the older and later layers as seen from the idealistic-spiritual viewpoint. The assignment of value was in terms of a development from the primitive to the sublime, and thus monotheism reaches its climax in the days of the Second Temple. However, what is presumed by Christian Bible study to be progression is termed decadence by Nietzsche. The more the Old Testament and the God of Israel assume spiritualization and, more importantly, moralization (*Moralin* in his words), the more they lose their original power. "In itself, religion has nothing to do with morality: but both descendants of the Jewish religion are essentially moralistic."[12] Thus, the Old Testament in its essence and original form was not a moral code. What developed from it later, by virtue of the prophets and the weakness of the priests who turned morality into an instrument of state, was two daughter-religions whose essence derived from that which was either implicit in it or arbitrarily imputed to it—at the least, a deception almost from the start. I say "almost," for Nietzsche attempts to represent Jesus as standing above good and evil, above morality, a sacred anarchist. Paul is, as is known, the greatest deceiver, according to Nietzsche, but this deceit is only a continuation of that begun in the Old Testament. The same Israelite deity described above (see p. 49), God, is in almost Dionysian fashion a deception on the part of the priests. Isaiah, the "typical prophet," still considers as an outstanding king one who is a valiant soldier and bound to justice.

The concept of justice remains in its naturalness as a servant of the self-confidence of the people. But a tragedy occurred as a result of the Assyrian destruction or that of Babylon, which was the beginning of the Exile. The priests attempted to explain the tragedy with the help of a "sleight of exegesis" and rejected the natural causa-

---

12. Ibid., sec. 146; ibid.

tion in favor of the discovery of a "nature-contradicting cause." In the stead of a helping god there appears a demanding god, and this is the source of the weakening of the necessary conditions. "Sin" is thus a central concept in the morality of Judaism and, in consequence, of Christianity. "The concept of God is falsified . . . the priest uses the name of God in vain."

> In the hands of the Jewish priests the great age in the history of Israel became an age of decay; the Exile, the long misfortune, was transformed into an eternal punishment. . . . depending on their own requirements, they made either wretchedly meek or sleek prigs or "godless ones" out of the powerful, often very bold, figures in the history of Israel; they simplified the psychology of every great event by reducing it to the idiotic formula, "obedience or disobedience to God." . . . the priest lives on sins, it is essential that people "sin." Supreme principle: "God forgives those who repent"—in plain language: "those who submit to the priest."[13]

This is the effect, according to Nietzsche, that the Exile had on the Old Testament in its early form. Classical prophecy is not especially dealt with by Nietzsche and does not merit the same penetrating psychological analysis as does the priesthood. Incidentally, the priesthood, ruling in the court of sacred falsehood, is not the creation of Judaism or of the Old Testament in its later parts; that same law-book of Manu the Aryan which Nietzsche places alongside the life-assertive religions of the Aryan race itself is responsible for the sacred falsehood, for it is but an instrument of the will to priestly power. The law-book of Manu is based on the sacred falsehood: "we may therefore hold the best-endowed and most reflective species of man responsible for the most fundamental lie that has ever been told. . . . Aryan influence has corrupted all the world."[14]

In the Old Testament, the heroic prophets struggle with the falsification of life and, above all, against the corrupt priesthood. Hosea's lament that "the sin-offering of my people do they eat and for their iniquity each one's soul longs" (Hos. 4:8) reflects concisely the development that Nietzsche describes in his criticism of the priesthood (although he himself does not quote this stinging verse pointing to the vested interests of the priests and their own role in the sins of the people). Undoubtedly, it is not easy to distinguish between, on the one hand, the prophets—including that typical prophet Isaiah,

---

13. A, sec. 26; *The Portable Nietzsche*, pp. 596–98.
14. WM, sec. 145; *The Will to Power*, p. 92.

struggling on behalf of the God of Israel, the Lord of Hosts, and reproving the corruption—and, on the other, those who demand justice and morality in the purest sense, not necessarily as instruments of nature. Moreover, the distinction that Nietzsche does draw between the Old Testament in its early parts and its later form—as if it were a priestly forgery—cannot be established unless one wishes to slice through the entire Scriptures, to dissect them completely. For example, the sons of Eli represent the priestly corruption in that early portion. Samuel speaks out against this: "Behold, to obey is better than to sacrifice, to hearken than the fat of rams" (1 Sam. 15:22). But what will Nietzsche do when the same Samuel opposes the monarchy and Saul, or afterwards, for example in the case of Nathan versus David—is this to him like Plato railing against Pericles? And in a deeper sense still, even Moses, the first of the prophets and the lawgiver, formulates a value-system of obedience to God; it is unimportant whether this is the original Moses or the product of the later priests. Nietzsche does not engage in a scientific analysis of the sources. Moses, as he appears, takes the people out of Egypt while also constructing a constitution in fine detail that assures the rights, and sacrificial offerings, of the priests, the "holy parasites."[15] "God's will," as it were, was transferred to the priests via revelation—in order to permit the assumption of authority over the people—and is expressed in the "Holy Scriptures" that from now on are made into a "desecration of nature."[16]

If, nevertheless, these "Holy Scriptures" never stopped being "the most powerful book"[17] (and in another place, in a more mocking manner, "the greatest German book"), this is due to the heroic figures therein (the patriarchs and kings). But no less credit is due the prophets despite certain reservations of Nietzsche's in connection with the prophetic morality. These prophets are prophets of wrath, and by their example the people of Israel fashion their God: "The Jews, again, took a different view of anger from that held by us, and sanctified it: hence they have placed the sombre majesty of the wrathful man at an elevation so high that a European cannot conceive it. They moulded their wrathful and holy Jehovah after the images of their wrathful and holy prophets. Compared with them, all the Europeans who have exhibited the greatest wrath are, so to speak, only second-hand creatures."[18] It is obvious that Nietzsche is

15. A, sec. 26; *The Portable Nietzsche*, p. 597.
16. Ibid.
17. MA, I, sec. 475; *The Portable Nietzsche*, p. 62.
18. M, sec. 38; *Complete Works*, IX, 44.

still relating in this instance to the early parts of the Old Testament that he admires, even though he is speaking of Jews and is not precise regarding the term "Israel." And "holy wrath" is in this case a term of praise and not of disapproval. This admiration for the prophets of Israel is expressed most astutely—as is usual for him—in a comparison with the Christian "inheritors" of that prophecy. He quotes from Luke 6:23, "For in the like manner did their fathers unto the prophets," and bursts forth in the style that marks his later writings: "Impertinent rabble! They compare themselves with the prophets, no less."[19]

This dark and angry horizon of Israel's God is a dialectical necessity for the revelation of the religion of love and grace. This surely belongs to the internal contradictions within Nietzsche himself, whether he "explains" or is excited by the appearance of the "light" out of this deep biblical gloom:

> A man such as Jesus was not possible except on the Jewish horizon—I mean a horizon over which continually hangs the dark and exalted storm cloud of a wrathful Yahweh . . . the sudden breaking-through, quite rare, of a single ray of light from out of the dark, perpetual night-day, only here could they feel it as a miraculous deed of "love," a ray of light of grace of which they were unworthy. Only here could Jesus have dreamt dreams of the rainbow and the heavenly ladder.[20]

The emphasis here is, of course, on Jesus. Thus, the "*single* ray of light": for it was Christianity and its church, and especially Paul, that quickly ruined the purity of the love and grace. Further, not all the Jewish people felt the need for this ray of grace, since not all felt the distress in such an acute way.[21] For this is the advantage of the Old Testament, in theory, over the New and the practice in the daily life of the people. In other words, the heavenly ladder of Jesus' dream is but the upper portion of Jacob's ladder when Jacob-Israel remained earthbound, if only in exile.

Nietzsche saw well the factor that differentiated the New from the Old Testament: the difference between "thou shalt love thy neighbor as thyself" (which did not overly impress him since, among other things, man can hate himself) and "love thine enemy." *Nature is driven out of morality* by this and it is a crime against life. The will to

---
19. A, sec. 45; *The Portable Nietzsche*, p. 624.
20. FW, sec. 137.
21. Ibid., sec. 128.

life of the Jewish people seemingly prevented the execution of the final conclusions of the concept of sin that they created and nourished for the world. Like the chandala, Christianity spread itself among the nations and races and lost all trace and symbol of nationality. The Old Testament conceptualization of a jealous and vengeful God and of the commandment "thou shalt have no other gods before me" (other than the one who took them out of Egypt) preserved the survival of the Jewish nation, since "God himself was a Jew" and "a nation that yet believes in itself has its own God."[22]

"What importance is there to a God that knows no revenge, jealousy, scorn, guile, and violence?" This jealousy, in addition to its being a national value for a people jealous of its own God, is also a general cultural asset that protects against the veneration of man. Nietzsche, who envisions a "superman," cannot bear this jealousy which truly evolves from the command "there shall be no other gods before me,"[23] and which in the end leads him—whether because of his experimental thought process in general or because of the differences of the periods—to see the prohibition of "thou shalt have no" as one of the most barbaric threats to the culture of man.

This contradiction in the different evaluations of the idea-content of the Old Testament finds its solution in the distinction between Nietzsche's descriptive analysis and his admiration for religion, morality, and human culture overall. Therefore, his criticism of the biblical law of morality as being a revolt of slaves, a revolt of the rabble element of society against the aristocracy—all aristocracy—and therefore antinature, does not contradict his positive approach to the revolt as revolt. The first tablets should have been shattered; the very act of the smashing of the old idols by the Old Testament was heroic. Moreover, on a deeper level—fundamentally, and not merely on the simple telling-of-the-story level—Yahweh, the Hebrew God of Hosts, grants land, a way of life, and nature to his people. And prior to the onset of the Exile, the Jewish religion never ceased being a religion of nature. All culture is the placing of the tablets and commands upon the collective public so as to harness and restrain its urges. Every Dionysus requires an Apollo. It is not enough for every prophet to rage against the establishment, for he himself must become a lawgiver. A prophet is not a nihilist or anarchist, nor is he decadent. This is the difference between a healthy morality, which fixes "do" and "do not" commandments because the life-will guides it, and

22. A, sec. 16.
23. MA, II/I, sec. 186.

Christian morality, which in its entirety is antisocial, antinature, and turns God into an opponent of life.[24] The Old Testament established new values, but these values still served life. Nietzsche, as is known, did not champion a "return to nature" in the style of Rousseau,[25] but he did demand a return to the body, "up into the high, free, even terrible nature and naturalness."[26]

As a result of this, the Greeks are Nietzsche's standard-bearers, not on the basis of two or three mentions of the "blond beast" taken out of context, but on the basis of restraint. "Before oneself too, one must not 'let oneself go.'"[27] This is the essence of the sanctity of life according to the Old Testament, including that introduction to all moral commandments: "Holy shall you be for holy am I your God" (Lev. 19:3). Neither death nor any antinatural act is enjoined in those commandments, but actually self-restraint on behalf of a more beautiful life. Not in vain does Nietzsche repeatedly make this surprising linkage between Jews and Greeks, as pointed out at the beginning of this chapter. Moreover, European civilization owes the Jews a debt for struggling on behalf of an occidentalization: "if Christianity has done everything to orientalize the Occident, Judaism has helped significantly to occidentalize it again and again: in a certain sense this means as much as making Europe's task and history a continuation of the Greek."[28]

The words "again and again" imply a constancy of this people in keeping alive a spirituality without escaping into nothingness, escaping to the metaphysical from the physical. These words were preceded by others of appreciation for the Jewish people who gave the world the greatest book and life-directed laws (that is, the Old Testament), the most noble of men (Jesus, who, from various Nietzschean sources, is not a Christian in the Pauline sense, nor was he the sole and only Christian), and the purest scholar of all (Spinoza: "Deus sive Natura"—"God or Nature"—this is the opening of his *Law of Ethics*).

Nietzsche's positive outlook on the Old Testament—as well as occasionally on the idea of the "Bible" encompassing both books, the Old and the New—is a result of three factors: first, his forefathers' Protestantism; second, a literary sense that gained more satisfaction

---

24. G, "Morality as Anti-Nature," sec. 5.
25. Ibid., "Skirmishes of an Untimely Man," sec. 48.
26. Ibid.; *The Portable Nietzsche*, p. 552.
27. Ibid., sec. 47; ibid., p. 551.
28. MA, I, sec. 475; ibid., p. 63.

from the Old than the New, finding in it a work closer to the epic Greek spirit, with more positive figures; and third, his general inclination to prefer the "ancient" over the "modern," just as he preferred the "ancient philosophy" of Greece—the pre-Socratic—over the "new."

However, it cannot be denied that most of Nietzsche's appreciative remarks for the Old Testament, despite his critique of its idealistic-moral-religious content, flowed from the ever-growing outpouring of opposition, revealed and concealed, to Christianity in theory and in practice, except for the character of Jesus himself. It is to ridicule Christianity, in a certain sense, that he repeatedly raises the positive elements in the Old Testament. In like manner, he does not hesitate to accuse Christianity of acts of forgery committed against the Old Testament. It is here that he castigates the Protestants more sharply than he does the Catholics because of their greater use of, and reliance on, the Old Testament:

> What are we to expect of the after-effects of a religion that enacted during the centuries of its foundation that unheard-of philological farce about the Old Testament? I refer to the attempt to pull away the Old Testament from under the feet of the Jews—with the claim that it contains nothing but Christian doctrines and *belongs* to the Christians as the *true* Israel, while the Jews had merely usurped it. And now the Christians yielded to a rage of interpretation and interpolation, which could not possibly have been accompanied by a good conscience. However much the Jewish scholars protested, everywhere in the Old Testament there were supposed to be references to Christ and only to Christ, and particularly his cross. Wherever any piece of wood, a switch, a ladder, a twig, a tree, a willow or a staff is mentioned, this was supposed to indicate a prophecy of the wood on the cross. . . . Has anybody who claimed this ever believed it?[29]

Due to his intellectual integrity, Nietzsche did not permit himself to distinguish between biblical Judaism and Talmudic Judaism or, more explicitly, between the Judaism up to Jesus' time—whose goal was his coming—and the Judaism after Jesus, which was superfluous and stubborn. The concept of sin before God, which is the central iniquity of ancient priestly Judaism, is frequently to be found in the Old Testament, although without the extreme metaphysical conclusions that resulted in the New Testament with Paul in the fore-

---

29. M, sec. 84; ibid., pp. 80–81.

front. Judaism still maintained as a religion a degree of naturalness for the benefit of the people. The obedience to divine command was a necessity for survival for Israel, and this remained unchanged even after Jewish societal fabric had been altered. "The Jews tried to prevail after they had lost two of their castes, that of the warrior and that of the peasant."[30]

The healthy God, the God of the people, He is Yahweh whose name is special and unpronounceable and He is, understandably, a function of the health and naturalness of ancient Jewish society (and Nietzsche uses the term "Hebrews" in addition to "Israel"). The Exile, which did not automatically bring about assimilation and complete collapse—as it did in the case of other ethnic groups who left their lands and, with that, their gods and cultures—that Exile caused and brought about the critical spiritual turning point in Judaism, thus permitting the nation to continue to exist. Moreover, this nation created a historic precedent. This Judaism became possible, and perhaps had to be possible, due to the loss of political independence and, afterwards, the probable loss of a state-political ability that had become redundant.

> This was also the case with the earliest Christian community . . . whose presupposition is the absolutely unpolitical Jewish society. Christianity could only grow in the soil of Judaism, i.e., amidst a people that had already renounced politics and lived a kind of parasitic existence within the Roman order of things. Christianity is a step further on: one is even more free to "emasculate" oneself—circumstances permit it.
>
> One drives nature out of morality when one says "love your enemies": for then the natural "Thou shalt love thy neighbor and hate thy enemy" in the law (in instinct) has become meaningless.[31]

Nietzsche knows just how much this goes against the spirit of the Old Testament that establishes the attribution of character to God: "I will be an enemy to your enemies," God says, "and an adversary to your adversaries" (Exo. 23:22). This, of course, is conditional upon the upholding of the commandments of the Torah, but the religio-spiritual basis is still that of the God of peasants and warriors for that chapter and, in fact, deals with the conquest of the Land of Israel from the Canaanites and the smashing of their idols.

30. WM, sec. 184; *The Will to Power*, p. 111.
31. Ibid., sec. 204; ibid., p. 120.

Nietzsche explains how this people, close to the earth and almost Dionysian, changed into an exiled people, creating new moral values for the world and in the process destroying not only the Canaanite idols but also those of the naturalist world arbitrated by Christianity.

Despite the Jews' falling into sin or, in other words, despite most sections of the Old Testament, Nietzsche does not hold back his respect for them even in their exile. First of all because they did not submit completely to the consequences of their uprooting but preserved their national existence in the worst of conditions, and second, because they continued to contribute to mankind's culture even after the Old Testament basis had been completed: they participated—and continue to participate, as he emphasizes—in the composition of Europe even to the extent of assuming the leading role, due to the power of their *Geist*, their unique spiritual force.

Because the will to survival of Europeanism sought to prevent it, preferring instead the fusion of the races, Nietzsche does not yet contemplate the possible political renaissance of the Jewish people, its return to the status of a nation of warriors and peasants, to the surprise of the world. We may presume, though, both because of his sharp recoiling from the "new god"—the state—and because of his real interest in having the Jews become absorbed into Europe, that Nietzsche would not be counted among the supporters of the renewal of the Old Testament of the Jewish people again in its land, although, if he would be true to his character rather than to his philosophy, who knows, who knows . . . ?

A Literary Judgment

We would not be dealing fully with this topic of Nietzsche and the Old Testament if we did not speak of the strong impact, deep and lasting, that this "Book of Books," as he refers to it, had on his entire work. Of course, while quite important for Nietzsche personally, it is outstanding in its influence on European culture beyond its religious aspects of monotheism, morality, and prophecy. One of the most important biographers of Nietzsche, Bernoulli, provides this fact with a literary-biographical expression in referring to Nietzsche's religiosity: "In the last year of his creativity (1888) . . . , religious signs became recognizable: an enthusiasm for 'the future and hope,' his Zarathustran consciousness bordering on messianism, his Yahwist jealousy against 'foreign gods' even to the point of a fanatical desire to destroy them altogether—these combined with the inner joy of the visionary, the complete piety and prayerful devotion of a psalmist."[32]

With regard to *Zarathustra* everything is quite clear and to the point. Despite the utilization of the figure of a Persian prophet, the founder of the Aryan religion, the volume is entirely "biblical," almost without any reflection of the original Zarathustra. Overbeck wrote to Rohde, who was not excited about the book's biblical style: "Beyond this I do not like the tone and I cannot find any good taste outside his primary homeland which is, of course, the Old Testament prophecy. This caused me added personal worry regarding Nietzsche."[33]

The prophetic stance of a railer at the gates (as well as in the forest or on the hills) is conscious, directed, and even emphasized. Walter Kaufmann claims, if critically, that the main difference between the status of the prophets and that of Nietzsche is the latter's lack of humility: the prophets did not speak in the first person. But in this case Kaufmann should have remembered that *Thus Spoke Zarathustra* is a copy not only of the Old Testament but of the New as well. In the New Testament the stress is on the "I say unto you," as opposed to the "thus says the Lord," "God does speak," and "thus speaks the Lord of Hosts" where the prophet is but a mouthpiece, a messenger to convey what has been told him. In this case, Nietzsche-Zarathustra is closer to the New Testament, with its personal pretentiousness of the single hero of the plot and his prophecy, than to the Old Testament with its many prophets, heroes, and saviors—but not one Messiah.

However, the main link between them is internal: the *will* of Nietzsche to appear as a prophet, as the giver of a new law. This is the root of the idealistic centrality of "On Old and New Tablets." Whereas in the law of Moses the second tablets are exact copies of the first, Nietzsche shatters the old, which symbolize a complete world of values borne by mankind for more than three thousand years, so as to write a completely new set—not in the script of God or from His mouth, but specifically and knowingly by man as creator and lawgiver.

Even though in the New Testament's Sermon on the Mount it is said plainly that the purpose is not to make new, and whereas most of Jesus' parables still remain within the bounds of Old Testament

---

32. Carl Albrecht Bernoulli, *Franz Overbeck und Friedrich Nietzsche: Eine Freundschaft*, 2 vols. (Jena: Eugen Diederichs, 1908), II, 177.

33. Ibid., p. 384.

morality and are only slightly heightened and brought to an extreme, here, in this case, Nietzsche straightforwardly states that the intent is to bring down a temple so as to establish a new one, and to overturn all the old values. This is the basis for the command: "thou shall not pity thy neighbor." It is from here too that he derives the injunction: "surely thou shalt shatter the old tablets" because "there are gods but not one God."[34] This then is the way: contradicting the primary commandment of the Old Testament, even "surely you shall destroy the *righteous and upright* for me."[35]

This conscious awareness—and it is unimportant if this is only pretension—of Nietzsche's, as if he were speaking from a new Mount Sinai or Tabor, is what gives the book its subjective strength. Nietzsche was convinced that this was the best, most important, and most decisive of his works, and not only of his alone. Thus, in this framework I will not draw any specific parallels, since the whole book, in content and style, is in fact a parallel version.[36]

The biblical "philosophy" (if it is possible and permissible to refer to the "philosophy" of a Bible that is anti- or unphilosophical in the strict meaning of the term) extends from "In the beginning" as a central and determinable expression for the entire world of the Bible: there is a creator who directs, knows, wills, and fashions—a reason for everything, a beginning. Therefore there is purpose, at least until the "vanity of vanities" of Ecclesiastes (Koheleth), "the *wisest* of men" but not necessarily the most loyal (one thousand wives) nor he with the most faith ("who knows?"—surely a Socratic agnosticism—is the refrain of the book), which must be viewed as an expression of the paradoxical nihilism of the ultraoptimistic Bible.

Nietzsche, following Schopenhauer, mocks the godly self-satisfaction of "and it was very good." Every nihilist certainly finds something on which to fasten in the book of Ecclesiastes. Many presume to find Greek sources for the book, even though it is clear today, after a comparative study of the various cultures before and after Greece, that every culture reaches, in the end, a stage of self-satiation, denial, and vanity such as this. The "eternal return" of Nietzsche is not bound up with this book and its recurring, seasonal theories because of differences in psychological points of departure: Ecclesiastes is a book of open pessimism and weakness even to the

---

34. Z, III, "On Old and New Tablets," secs. 10, 11.
35. Ibid., sec. 27.
36. See Hans Vollmer, *Nietzsches Zarathustra und die Bibel* (Hamburg: Deutsches Bibelarchiv, 1936), where literally hundreds of verses are shown to have been drawn from the Bible.

point of cynicism, whereas the revelation of Nietzsche's "eternal return" is apparently optimistic, even joyful, and is expressed in an abundance of positive statements. The conclusion of Ecclesiastes—if also the product of an intervening editor: ". . . the conclusion of the whole matter: fear God and keep his commandments for this is the whole duty of man"—is quite anti-Nietzschean. It is a wonder that Nietzsche did not pounce on this hypocritical Pharisaic Philistine, who assumed the guise of a rabbi or pope to cover his naked, laughing, yet unhappy bones, and contrast him with *Zarathustra*, proclaiming the joy of the sun, happy in its might without the laughter of man-beast-monkey ("man in God's image is a monkey," says Nietzsche, not that God is a monkey but rather man, who wishes to copy God). But the undercurrent of opposition I pointed out above, between "in the beginning" and "vanity of vanities," is to be found in Nietzsche in satirical form: "The history of the world is concentrated *in nuce*:—the most serious parody I have ever heard: In the beginning there was vanity of vanities, and vanity of vanities, by God, there was! And God was that vanity of vanities."[37]

Paradoxical usages of biblical verses of this type are frequent and not necessarily a parody, as with the twisting about of the description of man's failure from Adam and Cain, on through to the generation of the flood, until God "grieved at his heart" and repented of his work. Nietzsche's conclusion is: "What? Is man merely a mistake of God's? Or God merely a mistake of man's?"[38] And in the same connection, regarding the creation of woman: "Man has created woman—out of what? Out of a rib of his god—his 'ideal.'"[39] Since we have seen previously how this idealistic act of man "succeeded," it is obvious to us what this rib is.

Nietzsche maintains a special affection for these Genesis tales of the Old Testament, for he views them as brilliant acts, the little containing much, and he also appreciates their sense of humor *vis-à-vis* the New Testament's lack of humor. And yet, man's fate over the centuries has been fixed in these texts of the Creation, the Fall, and the eating of the fruit of the tree of knowledge. The deep connection between knowledge and death has penetrated into man's consciousness ever since ancient times and in many cultures, as seen, for example, in the actions of Oedipus and of the Sphinx, and is reflected in modern times in the Spenglerian tension between *Dasein* and

---

37. MA, II/I, sec. 22.
38. G, "Maxims and Arrows," sec. 7; *The Portable Nietzsche*, p. 467.
39. Ibid., sec. 13; ibid., p. 468.

Wachsen. It is included in the folk-philosophical tale, humorous as it is, of the banishment from the garden of Eden; using as his basis the text there ("and he placed at the east of the garden of Eden Cherubim and a flaming sword which turned every way to keep the way to the tree of life" [Gen. 3:24]), Nietzsche formulates: " 'Paradise lies in the shadow of swords'—also a symbol and motto by which souls of noble and warlike origin betray themselves and divine each other."[40]

Whether intentional or not, there is a contradictory parallel between two passages: one announces the victory of the one God and the other His death, with a satirical whiplash joining the two. The first is Elijah on Mount Carmel in the decisive Israelite struggle against the multiplicity of idols, against Ashtoreth and Baal, the gods of the Zidonites and Canaanites, the lords of nature—a struggle that was a victory for the one and only God of Israel. In this dramatic-satiric scene, Elijah mocks the prophets of Baal, as it is recorded: "and he said, cry aloud for he is a god, he is talking or pursuing or he is journeying, perhaps he sleeps and must be awakened" (1 Kings 18:27), so that he may conclude on a triumphant note announcing "the Lord, he is the God; the Lord, he is the God" (1 Kings 18:39). The definite article is stressed to refer emphatically to the one and only God.

The second happening is at once tragic and satiric, brought about by one of the most famous and stinging of Nietzsche's creations, "the madman": he is a sort of antithesis of Elijah, announcing in the marketplace the death of the God whose victory Elijah announced on the mountaintop of Carmel. Marketplace versus mountain, death versus victory, Nietzsche versus Elijah: " 'I seek God! I seek God!' As many of those who do not believe in God were standing around just then, he provoked much laughter. Why, did he get lost? . . . Did he lose his way like a child? . . . Or is he hiding? . . . Has he gone on a voyage? or emigrated?"[41]

This is a satirical parallel and the fulfillment of tragedy. There and then on Mount Carmel Elijah slaughters the prophets of Baal as an idol-breaker does those who failed the test. Here and now, "the madman" shouts out: "Whither is God? . . . we have killed him—you and I."[42] And from the announcement of God's death—and the pain of this "heretic" because of God's death needs no proof—Nietzsche

---

40. Ibid.
41. FW, sec. 125; *The Portable Nietzsche*, p. 95.
42. Ibid.

moves to the grief of the prophet on the threshold of his end. It is told regarding the death of Moses: "And Moses went up from the plains of Moab to the mountain of Nebo, to the very top . . . and the Lord showed him all the land" (Deut. 34:1). And in Nietzsche: "The *place* where I am today—on the height, where I will no longer speak with words but lightning bolts—ha, how far from this was I then! But *the land I did see* . . . this is the great tranquility of the promise, this the joyful promise even unto the distances of the future that will not remain as only a destiny!"[43] Certainly it cannot be assumed that in writing these words Nietzsche felt his own end—that is, the end of his conscious and willful life—approaching, felt himself on the edge of the breakdown that occurred in a matter of days thereafter. However, his identification at that time with the prophet, one legislating for mankind, was not inconsequential in dictating to him this style of Moses' dying days: "Ich sah das Land," "I *saw* the land" (the emphasis is Nietzsche's; what is the "land" doing here?)—and immediately afterwards "Verheißung," the "promise."

Surely one of the elements that attracted Nietzsche to the Old Testament—one that is missing from the New—is the contest between man the believer and his God. Nietzsche turns around the verse "he whom the Lord loveth He correcteth" (Prov. 3:12) and writes instead: "I love him who chastens his God because he loves his God."[44] (And in the same connection, in *The Dawn of Day*, sec. 15, Nietzsche attributes the verse in Proverbs to Christianity without mentioning the source.)

Most certainly it did not escape Nietzsche that God's correctors and chastisers were his biblical admirers, such as Abraham, Jeremiah, and Job. After all, it is because of this aspect that he calls them heroic. In one of his Dionysian dithyrambs, Nietzsche, the great and loving investigator of the Greek myths and thought, makes use of two biblical images (!) to describe his struggling, truth-seeking soul:

Oh Zarathustra
Cruel Nimrod!
Who, until recently, a hunter before God
you were
And now you yourself have become the game.

.   .   .   .

---

43. *Ecce Homo*, "The Untimely Ones," sec. 3.
44. Z, Prologue, sec. 4; *The Portable Nietzsche*, p. 128.

> Why should you slip away
> to the garden of Eden
> of the ancient snake?
>
> . . . .
>
> You are the man of knowledge
> Zarathustra the wise.[45]

This is a Nietzschean confluence: Nimrod and Zarathustra, Dionysus and Adam, who repeatedly returns—despite the expected punishment—to the tree of knowledge in the garden of Eden.

In conclusion, there is an aphoristic expression that is the epitome of Nietzsche's conciseness on the one hand and the essence of the divine outlook of the Old Testament on the other. Preceding the final formulation were such phrases as *werde der du bist* (become what thou art) or *ich bin der ich sein muß* (I am what I must be), but in the motto of *Ecce Homo* we have: *wie man wird, was man ist*—how one becomes what one is. Is not this phrase, the essence of all the existentialist philosophy of which Nietzsche, together with Kierkegaard, is considered one of the founders, similar to the forced or willing fusion between what must be and the divine image of man that permits him—and obliges him—to choose his fate: the Nietzschean *amor fati*?

One last question arises for which there is no answer, for it pertains to a riddle for every Old Testament commentator that surely is not accidentally phrased. I am referring to God's answer to the query regarding His own very essence (this being the meaning of the biblical concept of "name"): "I am what I am" (Exod. 3:14). Is this not a basis for a divine existentialism? Did Nietzsche knowingly or unknowingly crown the *magnum opus* of his spiritual life in a truly moving similitude between the definition of the essence of the God of Israel, who reveals Himself to Moses out of a bush, and the definition of the essence of Dionysus-Nietzsche-Zarathustra, or man in God's image?

A question for prolonged, unceasing study.

---

45. WKG, VI, 390–91.

IV. Morality and Deity in Nietzsche's Concept of Biblical Religion

Charles Lewis

I

Nietzsche's attempt to reveal the inner character of biblical religion is founded upon his confidence in the modern view, culminating in Hegel, that moral and religious concepts are no more, or less, than creations of the human spirit and its history. He also joins company with the modern view that essential to the biblical concept of God is the concept of moral perfection, of supreme righteousness and justice. Nietzsche's own contribution to this understanding of Western religion is found in his treatment of the idea that the biblical concept of deity owes its most distinctive features to the quality and character of biblical morality.

With Feuerbach, Nietzsche traces the origin of religious belief to the psychology of self-objectification. In this naive form of self-awareness, a people's most impressive powers and feelings appear to them as objective, even alien, realities.[1] When confronted with his own strongest impulses and feelings of power, the religious man attributes their presence to awesome powers that impinge upon him from beyond the limits of his deficient existence. His basic disposition is one of self-denial, the denial of his own value and power; he diminishes and denatures himself through his regard for the otherness of his own highest possibilities. It is because of this pathology of consciousness that Nietzsche finds the religious man alienated from himself, even terrified and humiliated by his Other: "in so far as everything great and strong in man has been conceived as superhuman and external, man has belittled himself—he has separated the two sides of himself, one very paltry and weak, one very strong and

---

1. See WM, introduction to "Critique of Religion" (p. 85 in *The Will to Power*, trans. Walter Kaufmann and R. J. Hollingdale, ed. Walter Kaufmann [New York: Random House, 1967]), and secs. 135, 185, 204, 245; A, sec. 16; G, "Maxims," 13; G, "Skirmishes," sec. 19; GM, Preface, sec. 5; GM, II, secs. 22, 23; GT, sec. 3; Z, I, "Goals"; FW, sec. 139.

astonishing, into two spheres, and called the former 'man,' the latter 'God.'"[2]

In his *Genealogy of Morals* (II, secs. 19ff.), Nietzsche distinguishes three periods of religious consciousness: a prehistoric age of indebtedness to and fear of ancestor-gods; an intermediate age of self-glorification through the ennoblement of deity; and a now dying age, dominated by Christianity, of the consciousness of guilt before an all-seeing, holy Judge. The religion of the ancient Greeks and the earliest period of biblical religion would belong to the intermediate age. In such noble religions, whose gods are destructive as well as creative, evil as well as good, Nietzsche finds the unmistakable beginnings of man's authentic self-revelation, the original form of his discovery and affirmation of his will to power. Thus Israel's preexilic Yahweh "was the expression of a consciousness of power, of joy in oneself, of hope for oneself: through him victory and welfare were expected . . ." (A, sec. 25). Even the justice of Israel's old God was, in fact, inseparable from the ultimate interests of his chosen people.

In spite of its noble origin, biblical religion suffered a fateful decline with the catastrophic defeat and exile of the Hebrews. From the once noble religion of a God beyond good and evil, it was transformed into its opposite by a people now dominated by a priestly caste who nourished an intense resentment and hatred of the natural expressions of power in noble men. The form of their revenge against their conquerors (and, indeed, against all noble types) was supremely spiritual: with their most seductive and effective form of sublimated aggression, with their weapon of *psychological* warfare, they originated a moral-religious inversion of the values of their mas-

---

2. WM, sec. 136. Cf. WM, introduction to "Critique of Religion." All quotations from this source follow the Kaufmann-Hollingdale translation in *The Will to Power*. Subsequent quotations from other sources (except where indicated otherwise) will follow the Kaufmann translations in *The Portable Nietzsche*, ed. and trans. Walter Kaufmann (New York: Viking, 1954); *Basic Writings of Nietzsche*, ed. and trans. Walter Kaufmann (New York: Modern Library, 1968); *The Gay Science*, ed. Walter Kaufmann (New York: Random House, 1974).

Presumably, the religion of sufficiently noble men (as the ancient Greeks, e.g.) is immune to the pathological aspect of the psychology of self-objectification. See, e.g., GM, II, sec. 23. It should be evident from the account provided below in parts II and III that this anomaly in Nietzsche's psychology of religion is exemplified in biblical faith to an extent he does not discern or acknowledge. The existence of this anomaly provokes, in itself, questions about the relation between Nietzsche's concept of deity and his concepts of the *Übermensch* and eternal recurrence. For Karl Jaspers's thought on this point, see his *Nietzsche: An Introduction to the Understanding of His Philosophical Activity*, trans. Charles F. Wallraff and Frederick J. Schmitz (South Bend: Regnery/Gateway, 1979), pp. 429–49.

ters, even of those ultimate values enshrined in the faith of their fathers.

The final consequence, the eventual result, of this "sublime vengefulness" was "that ghastly paradox of a 'God on the cross,' that mystery of an unimaginable ultimate cruelty and self-crucifixion of God *for the salvation of man*" (GM, I, sec. 8). Though the old God had been sacrificed already upon the altar of Israel's humiliation, this crucified God is the New Testament's own judgment upon all that is noble in the concept of deity. Already a pallid reminder of too much bloodletting, the shadow God of the Jews has been supplanted by his Son. A God of perfect, of righteous, love is now the ground and meaning of all true values. Now the justice of the old God, which was coextensive with the interests of his special people, has been universalized in the interest of the general welfare. Now the love of the old God, which was bestowed upon a noble people, has been transformed by its bestowal upon the neighbor, the suffering, the poor, the unfortunate, the powerless. For this, the religion of an oppressed class, the highest values are those of egalitarian justice and a love that secures the least of men from final harm, a love for which the blessed *are* these very childlike souls.

In its fateful dominion over the life of Western man, this ultimate expression of the religion of "sublime vengefulness" has become the ultimate expression of man's capacity to diminish and denature himself. Having been seduced by Christian values, even gifted people, who, in different circumstances, would have naturally thought and acted in other ways, have been led to despise every noble impulse and instinct. In company with ordinary men, they have been taught to oppose and suppress their natural instincts and every desire to assert themselves. Moreover, the archaic feeling of indebtedness to ancestor-gods has become the most severe bad conscience of irremediable guilt before God. The believer thus lacerates himself inwardly for every natural, animal, powerful instinct and for his unremittable debt to the ground and source of his existence. For such guilt even the genius of redemption by divine self-sacrifice can afford only temporary relief. For such a soul even his animal instincts are a form of hostility toward, and thus guilt before, God. And so he "ejects from himself all his denial of himself, of his nature, naturalness, and actuality, in the form of an affirmation, as something existent, corporeal, real, as God, as the holiness of God, as God the Judge, as God the Hangman, as the beyond, as eternity, as torment without end, as hell, as the immeasurability of punishment and guilt" (GM, II, sec. 22).

In such passages Nietzsche makes clear his conviction that a leitmotiv runs through the sundry authors, dramatis personae, and long history of biblical literature. For him the dominant and fundamental character of this religion, in both its Jewish and Christian forms, consists in its attitude of moral guilt before a supreme Lawgiver and Judge. It is true that Nietzsche has called the New Testament the "book of grace" (J, sec. 52), but his point has less to do with qualifying the above characterization than with stressing the sublimity of the (presumably preexilic) drama of divine justice. More significantly, he tends to identify what can be found concerning the spirit of grace and mercy in biblical literature with the life of Jesus, the deeper meaning of which was not grasped by the authors of the New Testament, his own disciples and apostles.[3] Paul was a "genius in hatred," an apostle of vengeance and judgment (A, secs. 42, 45), and the gospels, though saying "'judge not' . . . consign to hell everything that stands in their way" (A, sec. 44). These gospels, he thinks, are steeped to their marrow in the spirit of moral condemnation; in glorifying the divine Judge, the evangels glorify themselves and their own judgments.

In addition to the materials from which Nietzsche constructs his speculative psychology of the Redeemer, there are, however, other biblical sources concerning the grace and mercy of God. It would appear that, in keeping with his conception of the leitmotiv of biblical religion, Nietzsche is content to view them in terms of his understanding of divine love. For the love of God that Nietzsche finds here is an invention of biblical religion, indeed, a new love born of Jewish resentment and raised by Christianity to its highest extent in the form of egalitarianism, pity, and love of the selfless, the weak, and the lowly (GM, I, sec. 8; WM, sec. 246; A, sec. 2). This is not the love that "loves beyond reward and retribution": "Did this god not want to be a judge too?" (Z, IV, "Retired"; FW, sec. 140).

If Nietzsche has, in fact, plumbed the depths of biblical religion with his conception of its guilt and judgment, his understanding of the love of God turns even this otherwise ill-fitting theme into a fundamental part of what can now be seen as an essentially coherent

---

3. See, e.g., FW, sec. 137; A, secs. 32, 37, 39–47; cf. J, sec. 164; GM, II, sec. 10. For a discussion of Nietzsche's ambivalence toward Jesus, see Karl Jaspers's *Nietzsche and Christianity*, trans. E. B. Ashton (Chicago: Henry Regnery, 1961), pp. 88–93. See also Walter Kaufmann, *Nietzsche: Philosopher, Psychologist, Antichrist*, 4th ed. (Princeton: Princeton University Press, 1974), pp. 337–50.

theology of the Old and New Testaments.[4] As indicated, the preexilic Hebrews and Jesus are excluded from this characterization.

II

From the foregoing it is evident that Nietzsche has approached the theology of biblical religion by way of an examination of its morality. This approach is a consequence of his view that it is not gods, but belief in gods, that determines the content of any theology. And, in the case of biblical theology, that which determines the nature and content of theological belief is precisely the morality of *ressentiment* and judgment. It is this morality that is reflected in the concept of deity, this morality that shapes the character and speaks through the voice of God. This God thus assumes the character and voice of moral perfection, the most complete and unconditional realization of the values and imperatives of biblical morality.

A consequence of fundamental significance for this understanding is the conception of the attitude of worship to which it is unavoidably linked.[5] For a basic feature of this posture of belief must be the moral reverence that would be inspired by an exemplar and voice of moral perfection. It is in view of this essentially moral character of the attitude of worship that one should ask whether Nietzsche has, in fact, understood the very heart and soul of biblical religion —whether he has, in fact, discovered there a virtually unequivocal

---

4. I use the expression "biblical religion" to refer exclusively to the religion of biblical sources. As I shall argue in part III, Nietzsche's portrayal of Christianity and Judaism actually has its basis in the theology of postbiblical writers, through whom the transforming power of Greek philosophy occasioned the rise of a new religion.

5. "As was the ancient custom of slaves," Nietzsche says in *The Dawn*, "we are still prostrating ourselves before power"; this power he then assesses with respect to the "worthiness of being venerated" (M, 348; my translation). This aphorism thus contains the germ of Nietzsche's later thought concerning what I have called the attitude of worship. Since Nietzsche does not provide a characterization of this attitude as such, I have constructed a formulation of the sort of account that would conform to his view of the psychology of belief in God. *Phenomenologically* considered, the question is whether the attitude of worship can be understood properly within the moral terms of a Nietzschean account. Considered in this way, the existence or nonexistence of God (or gods) is not the issue; rather, the question is whether the phenomenon of worship in biblical religion can be described adequately by means of what are, essentially, moral categories. The assumption, whether of atheism or otherwise, that such is the only possible or proper description simply begs the question at issue here.

leitmotiv of the guilty conscience before an absolute Lawgiver and Judge. The consideration of this matter will then be seen to raise a further question about the Nietzschean conception of divine justice and love.

In keeping with Nietzsche's moral characterization of the biblical God, the attitude of the worshiper would be understood in terms of both the depth of his guilt before the divine Judge and the height of his regard for the ideal of moral perfection. It is in this guilt and regard that the attitude of Nietzsche's believer may be said principally to consist. From the attention given to the believer's guilt, it appears that Nietzsche would take this to be the more fundamental aspect of the attitude of worship. Originating in the prehistoric feeling of indebtedness to ancestor-gods, whose great sacrifices and accomplishments account for the very existence of the tribe, this debt-guilt (*Schuld*) was intensified in proportion to the perception of the greatness of God. The result was its supreme moralization as the bad conscience and the concept of an irredeemable debt fixed in the idea of a corrupted nature, of original sin (GM, II, secs. 19–22).

This account of the character of the biblical attitude of worship is thus cast in the frame of a consciousness of failed reciprocity—that is, in terms of relations among men. The human relations in this case, however, would not be those that obtain among equals; rather, the worshiper's status would be marked by the distance that separates inferior souls from the superior power and achievements of noble men (cf. J, sec. 257; GM, I, sec. 2). And, as noble men are those who honor, who revere, all that is like themselves—who have deep reverence for age, tradition, ancestors—Nietzsche's worshipers also revere, though here in the form of transcendence, what are, in reality, their own highest ideals (cf. A, sec. 47; G, "Maxims," 13; G, "Reason," 4). In this light the relations that are of the greatest importance for Nietzsche's account are seen to have the dual facets of natural disparity and failed reciprocity.

Yet even when the relations are understood in this manner, it remains the case that they are human relations, relations within the purview of what is essentially natural, known or knowable. And it is just because of this reliance upon such relations that a Nietzschean characterization of the biblical attitude of worship must be called into question.[6] For whatever the merits of Nietzsche's psychological ap-

---

6. The charge that Nietzsche misunderstood Christianity has been made many times in ecclesiastical circles: in tracts, sermons, religious periodicals, etc. For a brief

proach to this matter, the indispensable datum here is the religious self-understanding that can be discerned within the deepest levels of biblical faith. With this in view, it is evident that Nietzsche's worshiper would not, nor could he, possess the same self-perception as one who has experienced the full range and depth of existing *coram Deo* in the context of biblical religion. It is difficult to avoid the impression that what one finds is an irreducibly *religious* phenomenon. No moral relations among types of men, no matter how disparate, can account for the radical condition of this worshiper in relation to his God; no natural relation, however concealed by its guises, can explain his sense of creatureliness or the greatness of the Power before which he is but dust and ashes (e.g., Gen. 18:27; Job 42:6; Ps. 103:14).

The original and fundamental condition in which the creature finds himself in the presence of God is that of sin. "In sin did my mother conceive me," says the psalmist, "the sacrifice acceptable to God is a broken spirit. . . ."[7] But the sin of which the psalmist speaks is not a condition of failed reciprocity, regardless of the intensity with which such failure may become internalized as the bad conscience. In opposition to the moralizing interpretations, whether theological or otherwise, that have been imposed upon this condition of the creature before God, the most extensive and penetrating studies of religion have found something here that defies analysis by means of categories that would otherwise account for moral phenomena and states of consciousness.[8] This uniquely religious form of dread is grounded in the believer's creatureliness; it is not the result of moral failure, however oppressive. It is not what he has done or failed to do, but what he is, that defines the essential character of his creatureliness. His condition, as van der Leeuw has described it, is that of enmity to God: "sin therefore is hostile contact with God . . . subsisting in the deepest essential being of man, it brings him close

---

survey of this area of research, which "up to the present has been completely neglected," see Peter Köster, "Nietzsche Kritik und Nietzsche-Rezeption in der Theologie des 20. Jahrhunderts," *Nietzsche Studien*, 10/11 (1981–82), 626–28.

7. Ps. 51:5, 17. All biblical quotations are from the RSV.

8. See, e.g., G. van der Leeuw, *Religion in Essence and Manifestation*, trans. J. E. Turner (London: George Allen and Unwin, 1938), chap. 78; Rudolf Otto, *The Idea of the Holy*, trans. John W. Harvey (London: Oxford University Press, 1950), chap. 8; Walter Eichrodt, *Theology of the Old Testament*, vol. 2, trans. J. A. Baker (Philadelphia: Westminster Press, 1967), pp. 394ff., 406f.; Paul Ricoeur, *The Symbolism of Evil*, trans. Emerson Buchanan (Boston: Beacon Press, 1969), chaps. 1, 2, and pp. 311, 343.

before God, where will opposes Will, and Power, power."[9] It is this strange conjunction of presence and alienation, of being and nothingness, that stands in the way of every attempt to explain this phenomenon by means of the moral categories obtaining in natural, human relations.

Such relations are likewise the source of the veneration that, with guilt, would characterize a Nietzschean account of the religious attitude. The believer's regard—respect, admiration, veneration—for the divine exemplar and voice of moral perfection would have its natural parallel in the honor and reverence that noble men have for their own superior attributes, for age, for tradition, and for ancestors. With the biblical attitude of worship, however, it is sin and salvation that are the most fundamental aspects of the believer's self-understanding. His encounter with the dreadful presence of the sacred is also characterized by gratitude for the Power that saves him from affliction and annihilation, that brings even beatitude. Thus the psalmist who is struck by his sinful nature asks God to "cast me not away from thy presence. . . . restore to me the joy of thy salvation" (Ps. 51:11–12). The salvation enjoyed by the sinner is received as a gift and not a reward; indeed, for such a one as this there is no capacity by means of which he could establish any worthiness before God.

Situated at the intersection of this original condition of sinfulness and the gratuitousness of salvation is the divine mystery of election. According to Nietzsche's account of the matter, the believer's "humility" in being chosen by God must be a disguise for his pride (WM, sec. 175). The Jews, he says, "feel that they are the chosen people among all the nations because they are the moral genius among the nations" (FW, sec. 136). But the merit of this as a conception of the biblical mystery of election consists only in its faithfulness to the natural, moral relations from which the whole of Nietzsche's account of biblical religion derives. From the perspective of the specifically religious self-understanding of the biblical sources, the election of God's people is a mystery that cannot be turned into a quite palpable reward for virtue or service rendered. The preeminent manifestation of the character of this God is not the moral disposition of his will but the greatness of his power to create and to destroy, to annihilate and to save (e.g., Isa. 45:7; Deut. 32:39). Before such a God there is no worthiness that the creature could turn to his advantage, nor does such a God have any need to justify his actions before men. Hence

---

9. Van der Leeuw, *Religion*, chap. 78, sec. 2.

the Deuteronomist ascribes the privileged status of his people to God's love: "the Lord set his heart in love upon your fathers and chose their descendants after them, you above all peoples. . . ."[10] What else but the unfathomable mystery of gratuitous love could account for the election of a people who must be reproached continually for their rebellious nature and hardness of heart?

In the same vein, the Apostle Paul asks why God entered into a special relationship with Abraham and his descendants (Rom. 4:13; 9:9–11), why he hardened the hearts of these very people against his saving grace in Christ (Rom. 10:7–8; 11:25), and why he extended this grace to disobedient Gentiles (Rom. 11:30). The Apostle's answer is found in his analogy with the choice of Jacob to receive his father's blessing (cf. Deut. 32:8–10): when his mother conceived Jacob and his twin, "though they were not yet born and had done nothing either good or bad, in order that God's purpose of election might continue, not because of works but because of his call, she was told, 'The elder will serve the younger'" (Rom. 9:11–12). With the Deuteronomist Paul ascribes the choice to God's love: "as it is written [Mal. 1:2–3], 'Jacob I loved, but Esau I hated'" (Rom. 9:13). Paul then responds to the question of whether this would be unjust, but, rather than offering morally sufficient reasons for these most fateful expressions of God's will, he juxtaposes the greatness of God's power and mercy with man's "will or exertion" (Rom. 9:16). Declaring that God "has mercy upon whomever he wills, and . . . hardens the heart of whomever he wills" (Rom. 9:18), Paul then asks: "Will what

---

10. Deut. 10:15; cf. 4:37; 7:7–8; 9:6–7; 23:5; 32:8–10. See Walter Eichrodt, *Theology of the Old Testament*, vol. 1, trans. J. A. Baker (Philadelphia: Westminster Press, 1961), pp. 237–39, 286; Gerhard von Rad, *Old Testament Theology*, vol. 1, trans. D. M. G. Stalker (New York: Harper and Row, 1962), p. 223; Gerhard von Rad, *Deuteronomy*, trans. Dorothea Barton (Philadelphia: Westminster Press, 1966), esp. p. 68; G. Ernest Wright, "The Faith of Israel," in *The Interpreter's Bible*, vol. 1, ed. George Arthur Buttrick (New York: Abingdon-Cokesbury, 1952), pp. 352f., 369.

The Deuteronomists gave expression to what must be considered the standing biblical conception, found centuries later in the Pauline epistles, of divine election. Though the central part of their text (4:44–30:20) is thought to have been composed before the major deportations of the Exile, the remaining portions probably extend from the time of the book of Joshua to the end of 2 Kings. According to G. von Rad, "incalculable influences have proceeded from it; we can indeed follow the broad stream of Deuteronomic tradition in the exilic and postexilic age much more clearly than that which issues ostensibly from the Priestly Document. Deuteronomy is the beginning of a completely new epoch in Israel. In every respect, therefore, Deuteronomy is to be designated as the middle point of the Old Testament" (*Studies in Deuteronomy*, trans. D. M. G. Stalker [London: SCM Press, 1953], p. 37). It is also one of the four books of the Old Testament that are most often cited in the New Testament.

is molded say to its molder, 'Why have you made me thus?'" (Rom. 9:20; cf. Isa. 29:16; 45:9).

Such pronouncements from the most sophisticated theological sources in the Greek and Hebrew texts exist alongside and beneath moralizing interpretations of God's choices and actions. Even Paul provides interpretations of this sort, but the die is cast decisively by his portrayal of the most fateful expressions of the divine will. Here the Apostle is led to proclaim: "How unsearchable are his judgments and how inscrutable his ways!" (Rom. 11:33; cf. Ps. 36:6). And whatever may be said in the Hebrew texts about the divine judgment upon disobedience, the fact remains that there is no accounting for God's choice of Israel to be the turning point and center of the destiny of the world (e.g., Isa. 2:60). The divine will becomes essentially perspicuous in the light of interpretations rooted in the sphere of natural, moral relations. But in regard to such choices and deeds, it is not even a matter of the essentially knowable which has not yet come to light: "for my thoughts are not your thoughts, neither are your ways my ways, says the Lord. For as the heavens are higher than the earth, so are my ways higher than your ways and my thoughts than your thoughts" (Isa. 55:8–9).

The mysterious and gratuitous love that can be found in the deepest levels of the biblical texts is not to be found in Nietzsche's understanding of the concept: he sees lying beneath this love, in its various expressions, the vengeance and judgment of a type of humanity. Morality is thus the basis and determinant of this "new love," which reveals and conceals its bitter core of *ressentiment*. In opposition to the high and mighty it affirms the lowly and powerless. In opposition to the natural order of rank and rights, it posits the equality of all men before God (e.g., Z, II, "Tarantulas"; A, sec. 43). But the egalitarianism of this "universal love of men" is not what it appears to be; it is, in fact, "the *preference* for the suffering, underprivileged, degenerate" (WM, sec. 246). With its complete inversion of the natural order of justice, the egalitarianism of this new, biblical type of love is the substance of Nietzsche's understanding of divine justice. What was seen to be a mysterious and gratuitous love is here a form of egalitarian justice that nevertheless favors a type of humanity whose special worthiness deserves a special reward. In the end, this love, Nietzsche says, "wants to be *paid* well" (A, sec. 45).

Such love, in the Nietzschean account, may be predicated indifferently of God and the creature, for both of these expressions of charity are theological interpretations of an underlying morality of inverted justice. This morality is the creation of priestly *ressentiment*, which took the form of a "moral world-order" whose purview extends even into the assumptions and constructions of modern philosophy. In essence, this world-order is the morality of a type of humanity, behind which stands the authority of its God. The commands of this God set forth for all time an absolute opposition of good and evil. The power of this God assures that reward and punishment will be meted out in accordance with the degree of obedience to his will. Thus armed and authorized, the priests interpret all happiness as a reward for obedience and all unhappiness as punishment. In their book, we have "chance done out of its innocence; misfortune besmirched with the concept of 'sin' " (A, sec. 25; cf. G, "Great Errors," sec. 7).

There is no denying that Nietzsche can appeal to an abundance of biblical literature in support of his view of divine justice. Of central importance for his account of the religion of the Jews is their interpretation of the Exile as punishment for disobedience, for their disregard of the hieratic morality enshrined in "holy scripture" (A, sec. 26). But standing squarely in the way of such views is the theology of Job, which can be seen as an anguished affirmation of the mysterious God noted above in relation to the theologies of Deuteronomy and Isaiah, the God whose will and ways are beyond the creature's moral assessment and understanding. The moral interpretation of suffering is represented by Job's friends, whose God is conceived on the scale of Nietzsche's own portrayal of deity in biblical religion. A morally perspicuous God who can be counted upon to reward obedience and punish disobedience is impressed upon a man whose faithfulness is nevertheless insistently asserted. "I will defend my ways to his face," Job proclaims, for "a godless man shall not come before him" (Job 13:15–16).

Why, then, does Job suffer? In posing this question, the writer shakes to its foundations the conception of a God who conforms to the expectations of the creature, no matter how well-disposed by his morality.[11] The very question about Job is seen as a human confrontation with the divine, as enmity to God, and is thus met, not with an answer from the domain of natural, moral relations, but with an impressive reminder of sacred power. In the end, Job submits to this power which can do all things, admits to encroaching upon things beyond his ken, and repents in dust and ashes (42:2–6).

11. For a notable assessment of the significance of Job in biblical religion, see Ricoeur, *Symbolism*, pp. 314ff.; cf. pp. 32, 85, 106ff. See also his "Religion, Atheism, and Faith" in Alasdair MacIntyre and Paul Ricoeur, *The Religious Significance of Atheism* (New York: Columbia University Press, 1969), pp. 82, 89f., 93ff.

It would be shortsighted to dismiss this conception of deity as alien to the spirit of biblical religion, for the theology of Job is both a recollection of the deepest levels of Hebrew thought and an anticipation of their reemergence—most decisively in the Pauline conception of the mystery of divine election. As shown by the Apostle's analogy with the election of Jacob, all considerations bearing upon creaturely disobedience, upon "good or bad," are finally overcome by the power of God's prevenient will. The desire to see this as the election of every person to receive the gift of salvation is motivated, as Nietzsche would argue, by the morality of egalitarianism, of pity, of fairness to those who may otherwise be excluded by a divine predilection shrouded in mystery. But insofar as Paul's theology requires the unconditioned freedom of God to dispose of his power as he wills, this interpretation is an imposition upon the apostolic texts.

And it is the same with attempts to avoid the implications of gospel references to the elect, to the few who will be saved, and to the outer darkness that awaits the rest.[12] Here again, considerations based upon the virtue that one might claim in behalf of his election do not go unchallenged, as when the owner of a vineyard asks of the laborers who thought they had earned more than those who had worked less: "Am I not allowed to do what I choose with what belongs to me?" (Matt. 20:15). It is the sovereignty of divine choice, not the morality of contractual justice, that emerges as the deeper point of this parable. The moral expectations of the elder son in the parable of the Prodigal (Luke 15:11ff.) are likewise dashed by his discovery that the blessings of his father are not based upon the extent of service to him. As with the workers who had labored longer, the elder son could not understand the blessing bestowed upon his profligate brother. The evangel might have recalled the story of Jacob and Esau, as Paul had done.

Both Paul and the evangels are undeniably subject to the lure of the "moral world-order" of law and judgment, punishment and reward, but the fact nevertheless remains that they, with the ancient tradition of faith from which they originated, have also given expression to an elemental aspect of the attitude of worship that cannot be assimilated by the moral point of view. This powerful undercurrent of biblical faith arises from the primordial basis of the uniquely *religious*, the attitude of worship, wherein an original condition of sinfulness is conjoined with gratitude for a mysterious and salvific love. Neither the expectation of reward nor the fear of punishment can

---

12. E.g., Matt. 22:13f.; 24:22–24, 31; Mark 13:20–22, 27; Luke 13:23ff.; 18:7.

account for this enmity and this gratitude for deliverance from alienation and annihilation.

Apart from this original and fundamental aspect of the attitude of worship, the biblical concepts of law and judgment cannot be understood. For in spite of the insistent urging of the moral point of view, the most sophisticated theological sources attempt to draw the vectors of law and judgment within the orbit of divine love. The divine law is then seen as itself a gift rather than a burden borne in return for favor. It is because of his standpoint within this perspective that the psalmist can exclaim "Oh, how I love thy law. . . . thy word is a lamp to my feet and a light to my path" (Ps. 119:97, 105; cf. Deut. 4:8). Even Paul, who saw the law as an end in itself for the Jews, could view it in relation to divine love: the law, he says, "was our custodian until Christ came, that we might be justified by faith" (Gal. 4:24). For the Apostle, this faith is itself a gift of God's love (Eph. 2:8-9).

III

In light of this account of the origin and ground of the biblical concept of deity, it is apparent that Nietzsche's conception has failed to situate the morality of law and judgment within the deeper significance of a love that is beyond moral limits upon its power to bestow and to withhold the gift of salvation. Beneath and within the layers of commandments and judgments in biblical religion there exists the concept of a God who is thus not without attributes dear to Nietzsche's own heart. Yet more notable is the fact that the original and fundamental attributes of this God—creative and destructive power, gratuitous love—are the highest values in the Nietzschean pantheon. Where such values are deified, religion is a "form of thankfulness," whose god "must be able to help and to harm, to be friend and enemy—he is admired whether good or destructive" (A, sec. 16). The deity of a decadent people, on the other hand, is "gelded in his most virile virtues and instincts," a god of the weak, of the "physiologically retrograde" (A, sec. 17). For those who are secure in their power, "a gift-giving virtue is the highest virtue," which Zarathustra calls "love," and "whole," and "holy" (Z, I, "Gift-giving," sec. 1). With such power there is the authentic love that "always occurs beyond good and evil" (J, sec. 153; cf. GM, II, sec. 10).

At this point, a question that can be avoided no longer: If the biblical concept of deity is a reflection of biblical morality, how can the one be centered upon values not found in the other? How can Nietzsche's portrayal of a biblical morality of weakness and judgment be reconciled with the God of power and love in biblical religion? If a people's conception of deity is the reflection of its highest values, then the highest values of biblical morality should include the morally unconditioned power and unlimited will that are basic attributes of its God.

Nietzsche would not be compelled to grant this conclusion as it stands if he were to acknowledge an important distinction that can be found in the context of the attitude of worship. Misled in his understanding of biblical religion by his reliance upon the natural relation of reciprocity and the distance that separates noble men from the weak, Nietzsche was not disposed to see what, for the believer, is an important implication of the disparity between the sacred and the profane: for such a distance as this, attributes that characterize the sacred belong to a realm beyond that which is definitive for creaturely life. Taking the latter as "moral" limits, the creature's attempt to exercise his profane power without regard for morality is to presume for himself the freedom and sovereignty that are God's alone. In worship he is confronted with the absolute limits of his creaturely power. His will to power beyond these limits is the root and branch of his enmity to God. In gratitude for the life that has been given to him, the worshiper seeks forgiveness for his sin, acknowledges his limits, and thus regards the imperatives of morality as ordained for his weakness and well-being as a creature.

From the standpoint of biblical faith, however, the believer's gratitude for life, even creaturely life and its limits, is surpassed by his gratitude for gifts greater than life itself. For beyond the distance between the sacred and the profane is the gift of God's own participation in the life of his chosen people. For his people, creaturely life is thus raised to a higher plane of existence wherein the believer lives under the command, which is a permission, to partake of God's own loyalty to covenants and to share in his own power to love unmotivated by desire. This love, which arises from abundance of power rather than need, Nietzsche attributes to the noble man, of whom it is said that his power "seeks to overflow, the happiness of high tension, the consciousness of wealth that would give and bestow . . . [which] helps the unfortunate, but not, or almost not, from pity, but prompted more by an urge begotten by excess of power" (J, sec. 260; cf. A, sec. 57). The believer, however, unlike Nietzsche, sees this gratuitous love, not as a value-creating power by which man rises to his own highest possibilities, but as a gift bestowed by a value-creating Power that flows from beyond the sphere of human possibilities.

There remains, on the other hand, the biblical portrayal of this God as Lawgiver and Judge, the righteous God who rewards justice and punishes injustice. The God who for Nietzsche occupies the foreground, if not the whole, of the biblical horizon is not to be denied his place within this framework. Yet when viewed from the perspective of the morally unconditioned power and mysterious love of the God portrayed in the foregoing account, the biblical concepts of divine justice and judgment must occupy a far more limited place than that assigned to them by a religion in which the divine power to bestow or withhold salvation must exist within an overarching moral world-order. For such a religion, the moral world-order provides the setting within which the divine power is exercised. Accordingly, those not blessed with the gift of salvation must suffer because of their disobedience. Or, in another version, a morally perfect God excludes no one; his purpose is to see that all men will eventually become morally fit for his heavenly kingdom. Thus John Hick, in his monumental theodicy, postulates existence "beyond the grave in which the moral structure of reality is borne in upon the individual. . . . an idea . . . not far from the traditional Roman Catholic notion of purgatorial experiences occurring (for those who die in a state of grace) between death and entry into the final heavenly Kingdom. . . ."[13]

It is clear enough that Hick has banished the God of unconditioned power and love to the darkness of an unenlightened morality. And, though the theologies of Roman Catholicism and classical Protestantism have retained the old God's power to exclude whomever he wills from salvation, they have, at the same time, tried to reconcile his mysterious ways with a moral world-order. Linked in a common destiny with the genius of Greek philosophy, the concepts of divine law and justice have been lifted from their former position within the scheme of biblical faith and provided with a new, more profound significance. A fateful shifting of the center of gravity in biblical religion has thus begun. Drawn within the orbit of the ethical and metaphysical concepts of Greek philosophy, the prevailing post-biblical traditions of faith have embraced a God who is *worthy* of worship.[14]

13. John Hick, *Evil and the God of Love* (London: Macmillan, 1968), pp. 382f.
14. For an account of Jewish thought on this point, see Louis Jacobs's essay in *Religion and Morality*, ed. Gene H. Outka and John P. Reeder, Jr. (New York: Anchor, 1973), pp. 155–72. For an examination of the meaning of divine goodness in biblical religion and of the meaning it has come to have in the Western world, see my "Divine Goodness and Worship Worthiness," *International Journal for Philosophy of Religion*, 14 (1983), 143–158.

The persistent rationalism of the philosophers has made ever more appealing the idea of a metaphysical Being, at once the timeless ground and source of a universal, rational world-order, the basis of all things, the God of all mankind, the highest Good. With the enlightened Plato, or the Plato of their Platonism, the postbiblical traditions could identify this as the only true God; with his Socrates they could deliver the verdict that evil, arbitrary, provincial gods are not worthy of the best city.[15] It is in view of this development and its significance for the religion of the West that Nietzsche's description of Christianity as "Platonism for 'the people'" (J, Preface) is most revealing.[16] For by way of the synthesis effected in the prevailing theological traditions, the highest Being, the God of perfect goodness, is also the God of religious faith.

But such a coincidence would not have been possible without the prominence that was given to the elements of divine law and justice within biblical religion. Through the synthesis of these elements with concepts arising from the central concerns of the philosophers, a new, *essentially* moral religion came into existence. However higher than all worldly things, the highest Being, above all else, is the highest Good. The dread inspired by a God whose thoughts and ways are beyond human ken has been supplanted by moral reverence. However supreme, the highest Good is not beyond human ken. It can inspire moral reverence because of its relation to human good, to the more or less familiar categories of virtue and lawfulness. Where God is, above all else, the highest Good, worship is, above all else, moral reverence, veneration, adoration.

The God whose mysterious love was related, originally and fundamentally, to his unconditioned power of election has become a God whose love is related, preeminently, to his justice. Wherever the dominant tendency of this new religion is not fully realized, the divine goodness poses an enigma for the believer—as when Saint Anselm cannot understand why "among men who are equally evil, thou dost save some and not others, through thy supreme goodness,

---

15. See Plato *Republic* 379C–E; cf. 364B–C, 391D–E; *Timaeus* 29A, 30A; *Laws* 716A–717B; *Epinomis* 977A. Cf. also Aristotle *Metaphysics* A. 982b, 32ff.

16. On the other hand, it conceals the fact that Plato himself does not share the egalitarian conception of justice that Nietzsche finds at the heart of Christian faith. Furthermore, Max Scheler argues that this faith, in itself, is not egalitarian; see his *Ressentiment*, trans. William W. Holdheim (New York: The Free Press, 1961), chap. 4, esp. pp. 119, 128ff.; also pp. 143f. For a different view of Platonism and Christianity on this point, see Harry Neumann, "Superman or Last Man? Nietzsche's Interpretation of Athens and Jerusalem," *Nietzsche Studien*, 5 (1976), 1–28, esp. pp. 2–3.

and dost condemn the latter, and not the former, through thy supreme justice."[17] It is evident that the moral impulse at work in this counterpoint of motives cannot find rest in such an unhappy alliance of divine love and justice. There is thus no reason for surprise when one finds that the God of an enlightened faith must be a God whose love can exclude no one. From the Nietzschean perspective, this God's love shows itself to be the morality of pity, of identification with the unfortunate, of egalitarian justice. It is here, in relation to this development within the history of postbiblical religion, that Nietzsche's account of morality and deity becomes a genuine confrontation with that faith to which the prevailing morality owes its soul and substance.

Where God is, above all else, the greatest Good, Nietzsche thinks that a "hiding place" for truth has been the attempt to prove God's existence. But that which truly matters, which is truly a revelation, is the *concept* of God (WM, sec. 251). And on this point he is joined by those who, believing themselves to be the true heirs of biblical faith, have nevertheless abandoned the existent God in their veneration of an authentically Jewish or Christian morality. In Nietzsche's prognosis, however, such heirs are also symptoms of failing health and decline.

17. Saint Anselm, *Proslogion* XI. Translation by Eugene R. Fairweather in *A Scholastic Miscellany: Anselm to Ockham*, ed. Eugene R. Fairweather (New York: Macmillan, 1970), p. 81.

V. The Critical Imitator of Jesus: A Contribution to the Interpretation of Nietzsche on the Basis of a Comparison

Eugen Biser
(Translated by Timothy F. Sellner)

I. The Impulse to a Comparison of the Two Figures

In the recently discovered Gospel of Thomas, which came to light as the result of a grave find in Upper Egypt, Jesus addresses Himself to His disciples with the challenge: "Compare me, and tell me whom I am like" (Logion 13[1]). Seen in the context of the 114 statements of Jesus summarized in this gnostic gospel writing, these words are uttered not out of a feeling of uncertainty and the need for identity—such as might be inferred from the biographical context of the parallel canonical text, the scene at Caesarea Philippi (Matt. 16:13–20)—but rather out of the consciousness of an ultimate incomparability, and they are spoken with the unequivocal intention of bringing this incomparability to light.[2]

Over against this we have Nietzsche's appeal to his interpreters: "Above all, do not mistake me for someone else!"[3] He would have considered it an excess of such a "mistaken identity" if he were someday—as he fears in *Ecce Homo* (and quite rightly so, to judge by a number of rampant growths in the history of the interpretation of that work)—to be pronounced holy.[4] To this extent his challenge, in contrast to the intention implied by the words of Jesus, is upheld by

---

1. Cf. Willem Cornelis van Unnik, *Evangelien aus dem Nilsand* (original title: *Openbaringen uit egyptisch zand*) (Frankfurt am Main: Scheffler, 1960).
2. Martin Buber, in his book *Zwei Glaubensweisen* (Zurich: Manesse, 1950), pp. 28ff., interprets this passage in the sense of a fundamental uncertainty; on this point, cf. the exposition in my book *Der Helfer: Eine Vergegenwärtigung Jesu* (Munich: Kösel, 1973), pp. 89ff.
3. *Ecce Homo*, Preface, sec. 1. All translations from the German are by Timothy F. Sellner.
4. Ibid., "Why I Am a Destiny," sec. 1.

the consciousness of a special affinity with the figures being compared with him—and thus of an overarching comparability between himself and the other figures. The extent to which this consciousness took possession of Nietzsche toward the end of his creative life is shown by the note from his *Nachlaß* stating that he had always lived "in that which had moved Zarathustra, Moses, Mohammed, Jesus, Plato, Brutus, Spinoza, [and] Mirabeau,"[5] but it is shown above all by the phrase in the great letter to Jakob Burckhardt from the days of Nietzsche's collapse, in which he states that it is unpleasant for him and offends his modesty "that in the final analysis every name in history" is his own[6] (a statement that finds its negation, however, in the admission stemming from the period of *Zarathustra*: "I longed for people, I sought after people—I found only myself").[7]

In this context it is perhaps relevant to note that there arises from Nietzsche, as from hardly any other figure in modern intellectual history, a permanent impulse to ever new comparisons; the course of his influence consists, in significant measure, in the conclusions derived from an analysis of Nietzsche's relationship with these other figures.[8] The arc formed by the figures brought into comparison with Nietzsche extends surprisingly far, not least by virtue of the affinities made apparent by the glaring light of his love-hate relationship with them: it extends from Hölderlin, whose similarity in type to Nietzsche had already occurred to his contemporaries, back to Pascal (Vaglia), Dante (Biser), Socrates (Sandvoss), Kierkegaard (Jaspers), and Heine (Spencer), as well as forward to Dostoevsky (Shestov), Kafka (Sokel), and to Thomas Mann (Pütz), who wove together significant elements from Nietzsche's biography into the figure of his Doctor Faustus, conceived as the symbolic representation of the decadence of the German *Geist*.[9]

The most extreme position of anyone utilizing this approach was taken by Franz Brentano, in an essay from his *Nachlaß*, when he juxtaposed the author of *The Antichrist* and the founder of Christianity.[10] Conversely, shortly before Nietzsche's death the Russian phi-

---

5. *Nachlaß* (Die Unschuld des Werdens, II), sec. 1117.
6. Nietzsche to Jakob Burckhardt, 6 January 1889.
7. *Nachlaß* (Die Unschuld des Werdens, II), sec. 1167.
8. Cf. the introductory remarks to my article "Nietzsche und Dante. Ein werkbiographischer Strukturvergleich," in *Nietzsche Studien*, 5 (1976), 146f.
9. Cf. further Peter Pütz, "Thomas Mann und Nietzsche," in *Nietzsche: Werk und Wirkungen*, ed. Hans Steffen (Göttingen: Vandenhoeck & Ruprecht, 1974), pp. 91–114.
10. Franz Brentano, "Nietzsche als Nachahmer Jesu," in Franz Brentano, *Die Lehre Jesu und ihre bleibende Bedeutung*, ed. Alfred Kastil (Leipzig: Meiner, 1922), pp. 129–32.

losopher of religion Vladimir Soloviev, in his "Short Story of the Antichrist," had stylized Nietzsche into the precursor of the adversary of God who will appear in the last days.[11] In spite of the distortion caused by Nietzsche's most extreme denial of God, he appears even here to possess a "subliminal" kinship to Jesus, so that the comparison undertaken by Brentano can be considered merely as the consistent elaboration of a thought-model that is already to be found in Soloviev. It is no less consistent that Brentano concentrates his investigation on those specific statements in which the self-interpretation of both figures under comparison can be documented.[12] Just as Jesus understood Himself as the light shining in the darkness, so Nietzsche, according to Brentano, also perceived himself "as a superabundance of light"; just as it is reported of Jesus that He spoke with authority, so Nietzsche, he states, also took to giving orders rather than offering arguments; just as Jesus preaches conversion, Nietzsche also demands "the revaluation of all values"; and just as Jesus lived in the consciousness that "in Him the fullness of time had come," Nietzsche also viewed himself, in Brentano's version, as an event of epochal significance that was determining the course of human history. Yet no matter to what extent Nietzsche took Jesus "as his model," his attempt not only to equal Him, but to surpass Him, becomes for Brentano a mere caricature, especially since his "teaching concerning the pitilessness of the overman" was refuted by his own life history in the sense that he saw himself dependent on pity and compassion as almost no other.

Whoever still wished to speak of similarity in the face of such contradictions would expose himself to not only the ridicule, but also the indignant protest of Nietzsche himself, if the latter had not already challenged him to make comparisons by virtue of his own demand not to be taken for someone else. This is reason enough, it seems, to examine the problem—alluded to by Brentano but not elaborated upon—once again from the distant perspective of the half century or more that has elapsed since his work.

11. Cf. the analysis in my study *"Gott ist tot": Nietzsches Destruktion des christlichen Bewußtseins* (Munich: Kösel, 1962), pp. 267f., where Nietzsche is also compared structurally with Soloviev; cf. also my article "Das Desiderat einer Nietzsche-Hermeneutik," in *Nietzsche Studien*, 9 (1980), 19f.

12. In spite of its sketchy nature, Brentano's article could actually be described as a comparative analysis of christological declarations of nobility; for further information on this topic, see the investigation by Ferdinand Hahn, *Christologische Hoheitstitel. Ihre Geschichte im frühen Christentum* (Göttingen: Vandenhoeck & Ruprecht, 1966).

II. Jesus within the Scope of Nietzsche's Critique of Christianity

In Nietzsche's view, the figure of Jesus does not receive its complete profile until it has been brought into connection with his critique of Christianity.[13] As is made clear in the vehement conclusion to *The Antichrist*—a passage that calls Christianity "the one great curse, the single great innermost corruption for which no means is poisonous, clandestine, subversive, petty enough," and finally "the single immortal blemish of humanity"—this critique has for its goal radical negation and destruction.[14] In the aggressiveness of this statement is reflected the crisis in the development of Nietzsche's work in which *The Antichrist* stood at that time. Originally conceived as the "first book" of the "revaluation of all values" and proclaimed in its subtitle as an "Attempt at a Critique of Christianity," the work was then plucked by Nietzsche from its planned context in the hectic rush of his last creative days—so evident in its concluding passages—and, having been provided with the new subtitle "Curse on Christianity," was brought into action as "heavy artillery" against the embodiment of all life-denying powers, the Christian religion.[15]

The question with which the "madman" concludes his proclamation of the death of God sounds hardly less radical: "What are these churches now if they are not the tombs and sepulchres of God?"[16] The context of these two utterances is rendered apparent through the idea developed by Jaspers that for Nietzsche God dies "through the consequences of Christianity."[17] Nevertheless, this context must be made broader by means of the opposing viewpoint that Christianity as "a system, as a thoroughly conceived and total view of things," is being destroyed by the concept of God on which it is based, a concept that Nietzsche understands as a syndrome of destructive

---

13. Karl Jaspers's essay *Nietzsche und das Christentum* (written 1938) must still be considered the best statement of the problem (1946; 2nd ed., Munich: Piper, 1952).

14. A, sec. 62.

15. The fact that Nietzsche increasingly fell into this attitude of the artillerist can be seen from the letter to Georg Brandes (20 November 1888) in which, alluding to *Ecce Homo*, he declares: "I am after all the foremost psychologist of Christianity and can, old artillerist that I am, bring up heavy artillery. . . ."

16. FW, III, sec. 125.

17. Jaspers, *Nietzsche und das Christentum*, p. 18.

and life-denying tendencies.[18] For, as an institutional manifestation of the frustrating fiction that in the form of the concept of God gained power over man and robbed him of his best qualities, Christianity itself is an intellectual symbol of domination that draws its entire repressive power from the narcotic effect of the illusions unified within it. As such, it is simultaneously the "most disastrous kind of arrogance" ever known, as well as a "monstrous sickness of the will, which undermines, in addition to everything that promotes and favors life, the will to life itself." With its life-denying tendency it was the first really to conjure up the devil of negativism in the world, to raise ignorance to a virtue, to declare doubt a sin, to give Eros poison to drink and thereby to commit a singular crime against life.

In the nature of this fiction, however, lies also the chance for overcoming it. For it is merely necessary to break a single concept away from this fictional system or, better yet, to put a single reality in its place, "and the whole of Christianity hurtles down into nothingness."[19] In the meantime it is not only important for Nietzsche that those "spirits which have become free" should be seen through the "fabric of nineteen centuries of lies"; even more important is the notion that in Nietzsche's view Christianity, of its own accord, presently finds itself in a state of self-destruction that is being brought to light by the process of historical erosion. For like "all great things," Christianity is also condemned to perish of its own creations—first "as dogma," then "as morality," and thereby finally "through an act of self-overcoming": "After Christian truthfulness has drawn one conclusion after another, it must in the end draw its most striking conclusion, the conclusion against itself; this will happen, however, when it poses the question 'what is the meaning of all will to truth?'"[20] Nietzsche sees himself as an observer of this scene, standing at the "deathbed of Christianity," dazed and overcome by this great drama "in a hundred acts, reserved for the next two centuries in Europe," this "most terrible, most questionable, and perhaps also most hopeful of all dramas."[21]

Nevertheless, Nietzsche keeps in readiness not only his criticism of the system of Christianity, but also a "genealogical" explanation of the Christian religion. The first essay of his *Genealogy of Morals*, he assures us in *Ecce Homo*, offers "the psychology of Christianity,"

---

18. Cf. the explanation in my book *Theologie und Atheismus: Anstöße zu einer theologischen Aporetik* (Munich: Kösel, 1972), pp. 27ff.; 55f.
19. A, sec. 39.
20. GM, III, sec. 27.
21. M, I, sec. 52; GM, III, sec. 27.

for it describes, as he states in an allusion to his famous early work, "the birth of Christianity out of the spirit of *ressentiment*."[22] What he has in mind concerning this "birth" he then develops in the notion that Christianity proceeded from a—truly world-altering—act of interpretation, and that for this reason it is to be understood in terms of its development as a unique "history of interpretation." At its beginning stood the fact of the death of Jesus, this "most horrible of paradoxes," which confronted the disciples, who were far from "forgiving this death," with the real riddle: "Who was this? What was this?"[23]

This fact remained to be interpreted. In the course of the history of interpretation that ensued, four interpretations came into play which have thereby "ruled over Christianity": "Judaism (Paul); Platonism (Augustine); the mystery cults (doctrine of redemption, emblem of the 'cross'); asceticism (—enmity toward 'nature,' 'reason,' 'the senses'—the Orient)."[24] The initiator of this process was Paul, who set to work with the logical cynicism of a rabbi and saw to it that the worst of all possible tidings followed on the heels of the glad tidings of Jesus by placing life's center of gravity "in the beyond" with his lie of the "resurrected" Jesus, and who thus for the first time really nailed the Redeemer to the cross—"to his own cross." While the "bearer of glad tidings" died as He lived and taught, and while He attempted with His death if necessary "to give the strongest demonstration, the proof of his teachings," Paul brought to the fore that feeling most alien to the gospel, revenge, by stylizing Jesus' death on the cross into a "sacrifice"; brought the question of the existence of the individual after death into a "causal connection with that sacrifice"; placed "the concepts of guilt and sin into the foreground"; falsified the "assassination attempt on priests and theologians" carried out by Jesus into a "new priesthood and theology"; and thus built up again in the grand style precisely "that which Christ had annulled by means of his life." Consequently, "in the concept 'Church' precisely that was canonized . . . which the 'bearer of glad tidings' felt was beneath him, behind him."

The result of this unfortunate history of interpretation set in mo-

---

22. *Ecce Homo*, "Why I Write Such Good Books": Genealogie der Moral.
23. A, sec. 40. The following quotations are taken from a collage of aphorisms 28–51 of A, along with sections 158–216 of the notes from the *Nachlaß* published under the title *The Will to Power*. The latter, too little acknowledged by scholars, must be considered as that collection of materials from which Nietzsche put together his last broadside against Christianity.
24. *Nachlaß* (WM), sec. 214.

tion by Paul is quite obvious: "'Christianity' has become something quite different from that which its founder did and what he wished"; and "The Church has become precisely that which Jesus preached against—and taught his disciples to fight." Strictly speaking, there is really no room for Jesus in this view of the question. As Jaspers quite appropriately sums it up, He has "actually nothing to do with the history of Christianity."[25] In the final analysis there was for Nietzsche "only *one* Christian, and he died on the cross."[26]

III. Jesus within the Context of Nietzsche's Conflict of Values

By means of this hermeneutic "trick" Nietzsche obtains a view of Jesus that is only slightly encumbered by his anti-Christian polemic. We must emphasize the word "view" (*Blick*) here, for to judge by one of the poems of his youth, which still finds its echo—although not without polemic distortion—in his "Ariadne's Lament" from the "Dionysus-Dithyrambs," Nietzsche's religious development began with the experience of being struck "in the heart" by the gaze (*Blick*) of the Lord, calling him to Himself:

> Thou hast called:
> Lord, I hurry,
> And tarry
> At the steps of Thy throne.
> Burning with love
> Thy gaze so heartily,
> Painfully
> Shines into my heart:
> Lord, I come.

> I was forlorn,
> Enraptured,
> Captured,
> To Hell and suffering born.
> Thou stoodst from afar:
> Thy gaze ineffable
> Impelling

---

25. Jaspers, *Nietzsche und das Christentum*, p. 19.
26. A, sec. 39.

Struck me so oft:
Now I come gladly. . . .[27]

From all indications, with this point of departure the end of Nietzsche's positive relationship to Jesus had already been reached, for only a year later in his satirical poem "Before the Crucifix" Nietzsche challenges the Crucified One half-mockingly, half-pityingly to climb down from His "martyr's-stake" in order together with him to come "down to earth."[28] Long before Zarathustra will entreat his brothers to "remain true to the earth" and not to "believe those who speak to you of otherworldly hopes!"[29] the basic motif of such an appeal is already struck here. From this point on, Nietzsche's relationship to Jesus enters further and further into that state of disunity which arises from his lingering dependence on Jesus and his continually more pronounced movement toward the values of this life and world. This lingering dependence is responsible for the fact that Nietzsche articulates his growing alienation and the criticism that it provokes in somewhat muffled tones—certainly less harshly than he does in comparable instances.

It is significant in this regard that Thomas Mann, in agreeing with the judgment of August Messer (a Nietzsche interpreter from the twenties), comes to the conclusion that Nietzsche had left "the person Jesus of Nazareth" untouched "by his hatred for historical Christianity," although his explanation for this circumstance sounds rather daring: "for the sake of the end, of the cross, which he loved from the depths of his soul."[30] For it was not the convergence that he

27. "Du hast gerufen: / Herr, ich eile, / Und weile / An deines Thrones Stufen. / Von Lieb entglommen / Strahlt mir so herzlich, / Schmerzlich / Dein Blick ins Herz ein: / Herr, ich komme. /
Ich war verloren, / Taumeltrunken, / Versunken, / Zur Höll' und Qual erkoren. / Du standst von Ferne: / Dein Blick unsäglich / Beweglich / Traf mich so oft: / Nun komm' ich gerne . . ." (*Jugendschriften*; HKG [*Werke*], II, 80). In terms of the history of religious expression Nietzsche is here uniting himself with that mystical tradition which finds its most penetrating documentation in Nicholas of Cusa's treatise *De visione Dei* (1454). Cf. further the introduction to the latter work edited by Elisabeth Bohnenstädt (Leipzig: Meiner, 1944), pp. 1–52.
28. *Jugendschriften*; HKG (*Werke*), II, 188.
29. Z, Preface, sec. 3.
30. Thomas Mann, "Nietzsches Philosophie im Lichte unserer Erfahrung," in *Neue Studien* (Berlin: Suhrkamp, 1948), pp. 133f.; according to August Messer (*Erläuterungen zu Nietzsches Zarathustra* [Stuttgart: Strecker und Schröder, 1922], p. 20), Nietzsche always maintained for Jesus "a tender reverence in spite of his hostility to Christianity."

anticipated in his end—it is well known that Nietzsche in his insanity spoke of being crucified by his doctors in "a complicated way," after he had been signing his messages of madness alternately "Dionysus" and "the Crucified One"—but rather his sense of having been affected by the figure of the living Jesus that colored all his criticism and that caused Jesus for Nietzsche to become the basis for repeated attempts at interpretation in spite of all his resistance and rejection.

It sounds very much like an attempt to understand Jesus from the standpoint of his own sociocultural presuppositions when Nietzsche concludes in *The Gay Science* that a Jesus Christ was possible only in a landscape "over which the melancholy and sublime thunderclouds of the angry Jehovah continually hung," so that "the rare and sudden breakthrough of a single ray of sunlight through the gruesome, all-encompassing, and perpetual day-night could be experienced as if it were a miracle of 'love.' "[31] To be sure, Christ, as Nietzsche concludes in *Human, All-Too-Human*, fostered the stupefaction of mankind by placing Himself "on the side of the intellectually weak"; yet one must think of Him "as the warmest of hearts."[32] Thus Nietzsche asks himself how much has to be overlooked in the total evaluation of a people "to which the world owes the most noble man (Christ), the most truly wise man (Spinoza), the most powerful book, and the most effective moral law in the world."[33] In line with this positive "prejudice" he would have us ponder the question he poses in *Beyond Good and Evil* of whether "underneath the holy fable and disguise of Jesus' life" there does not lie "hidden one of the most painful cases of the martyrdom of knowledge about love."[34] Even in *The Antichrist* he is still of the opinion that one could, "without stretching the meaning of the expression too much, call Jesus a 'free spirit,' " for "he does not care for anything solid."[35]

Thus it is that in *Zarathustra*, in which Nietzsche takes his final position opposing the message of Jesus, he creates an image of the latter that leaves open for Him the possibility of a "conversion" to Zarathustra's doctrine of belief in this world:

> Truly, too early died that Hebrew whom the preachers of slow death honor: and that he died too early has ever since spelled doom for many. . . .

31. FW, III, sec. 137.
32. MA, I, sec. 235.
33. Ibid., sec. 475.
34. J, IV, sec. 269.
35. A, sec. 32.

Had he but stayed in the wilderness and far from the good and the just! Perhaps he would have learned to live and to love the earth—and to laugh as well!

Believe me, my brothers! He died too early; he himself would have recanted his teaching if he had lived to my age! He was noble enough to recant![36]

Eventually, however, the criticism inflicted upon Christianity penetrates through to its founder. Now Jesus appears in Nietzsche's view as the "holy anarchist," who, by summoning "the lowest classes, the outcasts and the 'sinners,' the chandalas within Judaism to opposition against the dominant order," became a "political criminal" and brought upon Himself the punishment of the cross.[37] In the final analysis, according to Nietzsche, it was Jesus Himself who was responsible for the fact that Christianity developed into a "form of mortal enmity against reality" that has never been surpassed.[38] Thus nothing would be more preposterous than to make a hero out of Jesus and to raise Him to the level of a "genius": "Speaking with the severity of a physiologist, an entirely different word would be more nearly fitting here: the word *idiot*."[39]

All the more surprising, then, is the sympathetic picture that Nietzsche draws in contrast to the "crude fable of the miracle-worker and redeemer" developed by Christian dogma regarding Jesus and His gospel. For Nietzsche the gospel is that "True life, eternal life has been found—it is not promised, it is here, it is in you: as a living in love, in love without removal or exclusion, without regard for station."[40] Accordingly, the "kingdom of heaven" proclaimed by Jesus is a "state of the heart—not something that is to come 'above the earth' or 'after death,'" nothing that we expect; "it has no yesterday and no day after tomorrow, it will not come in 'a thousand years'—it is an experience of the heart; it is everywhere, it is nowhere. . . ."[41]

This approach toward Jesus—which nevertheless keeps its distance—reaches its highest point when Nietzsche sums up "the en-

---

36. Z, I, "On Free Death."
37. A, sec. 27.
38. Ibid.
39. A, sec. 29. As is well known, this expression was suppressed by Nietzsche's sister in the early editions of A, and was finally brought to light through the investigations of Josef Hofmiller in his article "Nietzsche," in *Süddeutsche Monatshefte*, 29 (1931), 74–131.
40. A, sec. 29.
41. Ibid., sec. 34; cf. also *Nachlaß* (WM), sec. 161.

tire gospel" in the words of the Crucified One to His fellow sufferer on the cross: " 'This was truly a godly man, a child of God!' says the malefactor. 'If you feel this'—answers the redeemer—'then you are in paradise, then you, too, are a child of God.' "[42] In fact, Nietzsche had already formulated this paraphrase of the crucifixion scene in Luke (23:39–43) perhaps even more cogently in the preliminary study to this text: "The malefactor on the cross: when even the criminal himself, suffering a painful death, judges: 'As this Jesus is dying, without rebellion, without enmity, benevolently and submissively—this alone is the right way,' then he has affirmed the gospel, and with that he is in paradise. . . ."[43]

IV. Jesus within the Field of Tension of Nietzsche's Own Self-Descriptions

Just as Nietzsche's youthful impression that he has been struck by the gaze of Christ finds its echo in "Ariadne's Lament" and, even earlier, in the accusations of the "ugliest man" (revealed by Zarathustra to be the murderer of God),[44] so we can also notice in the utterances of the Jesus-critic an existential disquietude brought about by the figure of Jesus, regardless of whether these utterances are intended to perform a critical or an analytical function. If we pursue this further, we come in the end to those role-figures through which Nietzsche plays in the—ultimately vain—hope of finding his own identity in them.

Beginning with the most strident formulation, the figure of the "Antichrist," we find that Nietzsche had already (in his "Attempt at a Self-Criticism" at the beginning of the new edition of *The Birth of Tragedy* of 1886) asked in the form of a barely concealed reference to himself: "who could claim to know the rightful name of the Antichrist?" And because during the writing of *Ecce Homo* the right time seems to have come to let the last of his masks fall, he also assures us very openly here: "I am, in Greek and not only in Greek, the Anti-

---

42. Ibid., sec. 35. In his Nietzsche article (above, n. 39) Hofmiller points out (pp. 94f.) that this passage as well was suppressed by the editors of the early editions of A (ostensibly because it was exegetically indefensible).

43. *Nachlaß* (WM), sec. 162; the extent to which this interpretation coincides with my own understanding of the scene is made clear in my article "Der Leidensgefährte," in *Geist und Leben*, 48 (1975), 40–50.

44. Just as the lamenting Ariadne feels herself wounded by the gaze of the god who is pursuing her, the gaze of the allseeing God also becomes the central motif for the murder of God by the "ugliest man" (Z, IV, "The Ugliest Man").

christ. . . ."⁴⁵ In spite of this, and although in the brief concluding aphorism of his hyperbolic autobiography he plays off "his" god Dionysus against the Crucified One, he does not hesitate to imitate the air of Jesus when he assures us: "And in all seriousness, nobody before me knew the right way, the way upward; it is only beginning with me that there are hopes once again, tasks, ways that can be prescribed for culture—I am the bearer of these glad tidings.—And for this reason I am also a destiny."⁴⁶

He subsequently even gives the reason for this sudden turning from critique to affinity. It is his will to drive a contradiction to such an extreme that it is transformed into a new affirmation: "I contradict as no one has contradicted before, and am nonetheless the antithesis of a No-saying spirit. I am a bearer of glad tidings like no one before me, I know tasks of such magnitude that up to now the very idea of them has been lacking; it is only beginning with me that there are hopes once again."⁴⁷

In the same context Nietzsche gives us the motivation for the publication of his biography by stating that he has a "terrible fear" of someday being canonized—he does not wish "to be a saint, but would prefer to be a buffoon."⁴⁸ This preference for the role of the fool is not merely a manifestation of the hectic rush of a will to expression driven to its limits, for it is but a small step from the "buffoon" to the role-figure of the "madman," through whom Nietzsche first proclaimed the convincingly formulated message of the death of God.⁴⁹ In the proclamation of this "bearer of glad tidings" as well, a contradiction has been extended to the point where it becomes an affinity.

Not only does the "madman" expect consequences from the death of God that immediately remind us of Jesus' proclamation of the kingdom of God ushered in by Him, it is even more significant that he relates the story in such a way that it can function as a perfect reformulation of the type of parable that Jesus preferred to use in his proclamation of this kingdom of God.⁵⁰ Thus the possibility arises for

---

45. *Ecce Homo,* "Why I Write Such Good Books," sec. 2.
46. Ibid., Twilight of the Idols, sec. 2.
47. *Ecce Homo,* "Why I Am a Destiny," sec. 1.
48. Ibid. See also what has been said above (Part I of this article).
49. The aphorism "Die Gefangenen" from MA (II/II, sec. 84) must be considered more as a "provisional" formulation in this regard; cf. my study "Nietzsches Kritik des christlichen Gottesbegriffs und ihre theologischen Konsequenzen," *Philosophisches Jahrbuch,* 78 (1971), 34–65, 295–305.
50. This is further discussed in the work cited above (n. 49).

a text-immanent solution to the problem, which then presents itself in the form of the shocking designation of Jesus as an "idiot." But before we begin to consider, along with Jaspers, Nietzsche's dependence on Dostoevsky's novel of the same name and to speculate whether Nietzsche was aware at least of the title of the work, which at the time of the writing of *The Antichrist* was not yet available in German translation, we should first take hold of this key offered by Nietzsche himself.[51] For when it is said of Jesus in *The Antichrist* that He not only "denied any breach between God and man," but that He "lived" precisely this proclaimed unity between God and man as His glad tidings,[52] it is basically that very thing being imputed to Him which is intended by the proclamation of the "madman," namely, the reclaiming of the attributes "wasted" on God for mankind itself.[53]

All this leads us to the conclusion that Nietzsche's criticism of Jesus, measured against the vehemence of his criticism of Christianity, is a great deal more restrained, because in his critical encounter with Jesus Nietzsche was confronted by the remains of a bond he had never quite given up. Zarathustra's relationship to the priests is also characterized by the same "disassociated affinity":

> Here are priests: and even if they are my enemies, pass by them quietly and with a sleeping sword!
> There are heroes even among them; many of them have suffered too much: thus they want to make others suffer....
> But my blood is related to theirs; and I want to see my blood honored even in theirs.[54]

It is this feeling of a "blood relationship" withstanding all estrangement that determines Nietzsche's relationship to Jesus and makes it possible for us to hear in his No a repressed assent and in his accusations a suppressed homage. However far Nietzsche moves away from Jesus, it is still in the sense of the consciousness described in the aphorism "Star Friendship," of being inescapably associated with Him, the One he passed by and left behind.[55] This residual

---

51. Jaspers, *Nietzsche und das Christentum*, pp. 22f.
52. A, sec. 41.
53. The aphorism "Excelsior" (FW, III, sec. 285) deals expressly with this anthropological objective of the denial of God.
54. Z, II, "On Priests."
55. FW, IV, sec. 279. The aphorism must be considered as Nietzsche's most subtle self-revelation concerning his relationship to Richard Wagner.

feeling of a bond between them may have moved Nietzsche to superscribe that exorbitant self-portrait he placed before mankind—in the last outbreak of his desire to communicate with it—with the "most Christian title of all," *Ecce Homo*.[56]

56. Mann, "Nietzsches Philosophie im Lichte unserer Erfahrung," p. 123.

VI. Dionysus versus the Crucified One: Nietzsche's Understanding of the Apostle Paul

Jörg Salaquarda
(Translated by Timothy F. Sellner)

I

Nietzsche's explicit statements concerning Paul are predominantly negative.*[1] He describes the Apostle as a "typical *décadent*" and calls him—borrowing a term from the Manu Lawbook[2]—a "chandala-type." In his sharp polemic in *The Antichrist* he designates it as "the greatest, most evil assault on *refined* humanity" that in the New Testament every Peter and Paul is granted "immortality," thereby furthering decisively "the revolt of everything crawling on the earth against that which has nobility."[3] In a few places he singles out Paul in particular from the ranks of others he considers *décadents* in order to polemicize against him with special vehemence. In such passages Paul appears as the exponent of that Judaism which in Christianity

---

*This chapter is a slightly modified English version of Jörg Salaquarda, "Dionysos gegen den Gekreuzigten: Nietzsches Verständnis des Apostels Paulus," *Zeitschrift für Religion und Geistesgeschichte*, 26 (1974), 97–124; the German version was again published in *Nietzsche*, ed. Jörg Salaquarda, Wege der Forschung, no. 521 (Darmstadt: Wissenschaftliche Buchgesellschaft, 1980), pp. 288–322.

1. Nietzsche's works and literary remains (*Nachlaß*) are cited from the *Kritische Gesamtausgabe* edited by Giorgio Colli and Mazzino Montinari (WKG); material that has not yet appeared in this edition is quoted from the *Großoktavausgabe* (GOA) or the *Kleinoktavausgabe* (KOA). Quotations from letters are drawn mainly from the *Gesammelte Briefe*, abbreviated as GB. Translations from the German are by Timothy F. Sellner.

2. Cf. G, "The 'Improvers' of Mankind," secs. 3 and 4; WKG, VI-3, 94f. In the philological commentary to G (KSA, XIV, 420) Montinari points out that Nietzsche drew his information from the following book, which can still be found in his library: Louis Jacolliot, *Les législateurs religieux. Manou—Moïse—Mahomet* (Paris: Lacroix, 1876). Cf. Nietzsche's letter to Gast of 31 May 1888; GB, IV, 381f.

3. A, sec. 43; WKG, VI-3, 216.

had asserted itself victoriously;[4] in others he figures as the example *par excellence* of the "ascetic priest," a type that Nietzsche had already developed in the *Genealogy of Morals*.[5] In *The Antichrist* Nietzsche writes, referring expressly to his earlier psychology of the "ascetic priest": "Paul was the greatest of all the apostles of revenge. . . ."[6] Already in his earlier writings we find characterizations that unmistakably express aversion and condemnation, as for example: "Such natures as that of the Apostle Paul have an 'evil eye' for the passions; they come to know of them only what is dirty, deformed, and heartbreaking. . . ."[7]

A number of the authoritative interpreters of Nietzsche's criticism of religion and Christianity have apparently derived his understanding of Paul from this and other similar passages. Thus Karl Jaspers, for example, names Paul as the foremost of those figures who "are always rejected by him [sc. Nietzsche]."[8] Ernst Benz expresses himself in more detail, but in the same vein: "To no other Christian does Nietzsche betray such animosity, such an explosive and measureless hate as he does to Paul. In no other case do the most negative designations, the sharpest accusations pile up as in that of Paul; moreover, no one is the object in the same way of Nietzsche's personal mockery, abhorrence, disgust, and repugnance as this particular apostle."[9] Walter Kaufmann finds Nietzsche's "attack on Luther's *sola fide* and on Luther's great example Paul, . . . even more impassioned than his diatribes against the Church."[10] And even Overbeck noted with consternation the vehement polemical form in which his friend had expressed his understanding of Paul, though with regard to the contents he preferred it to other interpretations.[11]

Other writers have viewed as questionable any one-sided attempt

---

4. Cf., for example, *Nachlaß*, November 1887 to March 1888, 11 [364]; WKG, VIII-2, 403 (WM, sec. 214).
5. GM, III; WKG, VI-2, 355ff.
6. A, sec. 45; WKG, VI-3, 221.
7. FW, sec. 139; WKG, V-2, 166f.
8. Karl Jaspers, *Nietzsche. Einführung in das Verständnis seines Philosophierens*, 3rd ed. (Berlin: de Gruyter, 1950), p. 27.
9. Ernst Benz, *Nietzsches Ideen zur Geschichte des Christentums und der Kirche* (Leiden: Brill, 1956), p. 36.
10. Walter Kaufmann, *Nietzsche: Philosopher, Psychologist, Antichrist*, 3rd ed. (Princeton: Princeton University Press, 1968), p. 343.
11. "An evaluation [sc. of Paul] by Nietzsche diametrically opposed to that of Wellhausen. I prefer it, as repugnant as its invective character is to me" (Franz Overbeck, *Christentum und Kultur*, 2nd ed. [1919; reprint, Darmstadt: Wissenschaftliche Buchgesellschaft, 1962], p. 55).

to impute certain opinions to Nietzsche on the basis of any of his extreme statements. According to this approach, if we were to judge by the rules of formal logic, then Nietzsche frequently "contradicted" himself. But we are not simply to follow the customary (pre)judgments of "common sense"; rather, we ought to understand that Nietzsche always brought different perspectives to bear on a subject and that he made full use of the "magic of an opposite way of thinking."[12] Is it not possible that this basic tendency in his thought could provide insight into his understanding of Paul as well? Could not the vehemence of the polemic correspond to the closeness of the kinship?

The thesis stated here in question form has been advocated most decisively by Ernst Bertram. For Bertram, accordingly, Nietzsche is

> also Paul, the vanquisher of the Law, of the "old tablets," the proclaimer, servant, and interpreter of a new Lord of our souls. Not the Paul, of course, whom the "Antichrist" out of vengeful self-hate and using all the techniques of a malicious and fanatical psychoanalytical approach intentionally misconstrues as a *décadence*-type. Not Paul the "dysangelist," the theatrical "genius of hate," the "chandala-type." . . . Rather, the affirming half of his existence is "rather" akin to the Paul of Albrecht Dürer, who, with book *and* sword, composed, half imbued with Attic wisdom, half with Northern melancholy, looks out at us from the panel of the "Four Apostles" in the Alte Pinakothek in Munich. . . .[13]

Yet even when we divest this thesis of its inspirational phraseology it fails to be convincing. Bertram proceeds from the correct observation that Nietzsche taught and practiced a mode of perspectival cognition, and he concludes correctly that a polemic never signifies for Nietzsche mere rejection or repudiation. But when he wishes to show the other side, that is, the "kinship" of Nietzsche with Paul, then he makes use of images and turns of phrase that he cannot prove have their origin with Nietzsche himself. The fact that no image of Paul as imbued partly with "Attic wisdom," partly with "Northern melancholy" is to be found in Nietzsche's writings does not, of course, vitiate Bertram's thesis, since he assumes from the very beginning that Nietzsche did not wish to acknowledge such a

---

12. *Nachlaß*, autumn 1885 to autumn 1886, 2 [155]; WKG, VIII-1, 140 (WM, sec. 470).
13. Ernst Bertram, *Nietzsche: Versuch einer Mythologie*, 7th ed. (Berlin: Bondi, 1929), p. 54; cf. the context and pp. 61, 129, 133, and 314. Cf. also Fritz Wenzel, "Das Paulusbild bei Lagarde, Nietzsche und Rosenberg" (Diss., Breslau, 1937), pp. 29f. Wenzel is heavily dependent on Bertram for his concept of Nietzsche's image of Paul.

kinship. Nevertheless, the thesis fails to hold even if it can be shown that Nietzsche's intentions were nothing of the kind—which, in fact, is precisely the case.

Carl Bernoulli also added his opinion to this complex of views, agreeing to a certain extent with the thesis of Bertram, but arguing more cautiously for a positive interpretation. While discussing Nietzsche's relationship to Calvin he appends an interesting remark: we can "be certain," he says, "whenever [Nietzsche] takes someone especially severely to task that a secret kinship is always behind it."[14] To support this he includes two references, which he fails, however, to think through to their conclusion. In the one case he draws a connection between Nietzsche's "vision" of Sils-Maria and the Damascus experience of Paul;[15] in the other he considers the question of whether kinship and opposition need to be judged from two separate sides. But when in addition he establishes "love" as the common and deciding factor,[16] he loses the firm footing provided by that which can be substantiated from the text.

II

If we examine all the passages in which Nietzsche does not merely mention Paul in passing but deals with him with some degree of thoroughness, then it becomes clear that while he treats Paul in polemic fashion most of the time, this is not always the case. A crude division, left undifferentiated until a later time, may serve to point the way to further examination of the problem: Paul is interesting to Nietzsche as a "Christian" and as a "great man." These two aspects doubtless merge continuously into each other, yet their division

---

14. Carl A. Bernoulli, *Franz Overbeck und Friedrich Nietzsche: Eine Freundschaft*, 2 vols. (Jena: Eugen Diederichs, 1908); here, II, 4.

15. "Nietzsche had experienced . . . in that first summer at Sils his day of Damascus; it was as if the scales were falling from his eyes; he completed the progression from No to Yes; Saul became Paul; the pessimist became the optimist" (ibid., I, 316). The comparison between "Sils-Maria" and "Damascus" is more significant than Bernoulli was aware; it is also correct that Nietzsche advanced by means of his insight at Sils from No to Yes. But one can maintain that Nietzsche became an "optimist" only when one uses this term in a quite different sense from that in which Nietzsche himself used it.

16. "The cause of his [sc. Nietzsche's] hatred of the Apostle Paul could have been that the latter had debased his immortal song to the glorification of love as the basic force through which man first becomes man because of his teleological allusion to the goal and fulfillment of man as lying in the world beyond" (ibid., II, 267).

helps us to recognize more clearly certain characteristics of Nietzsche's understanding of Paul. Nietzsche did not (as, for the most part, the interpretation of Jaspers one-sidedly maintains he did)[17] from the very beginning see in the "Christian" Paul the antipode of Jesus. In many of his notes Nietzsche leaves the question open as to whether he considers Jesus or Paul to be the authoritative "founder" of Christianity. In a passage typical of this attitude he states that "Jesus (or Paul)" had possessed that decisive psychological insight to which Christianity owed its triumphant progress.[18] At another point Nietzsche even names other possible "founders": "Half the earth now bends its knee" before "*three Jews*, as we know, and *one Jewess*" who succeeded in overcoming "Rome"—namely "Jesus of Nazareth, the fisherman Peter, the tentmaker Paul, and . . . Mary."[19] Even in a late note from the *Nachlaß* that he accompanied with the caption "against Jesus of Nazareth as a seducer," Nietzsche leaves unanswered the question concerning the decisive impetus for Christianity: he did "not like it at all about that Jesus of Nazareth or his Apostle Paul that they *put such big ideas into the heads of the little people*. . . ."[20]

It is not until *The Antichrist* that Nietzsche achieves an unequivocal differentiation of the roles of Jesus and Paul in the origin of Christianity, and at the same time arrives at an unrestrained opposition to the Apostle. The following formulation is typical of the trend in his late work: "In Paul is embodied the antithesis-type to the 'joyful herald' [sc. to Jesus], the genius of hatred, in the vision of hatred, in the unbending logic of hatred."[21] To be sure, this differentiation had been proposed much earlier. Among the fragments and notes of the *Nachlaß* from 1880–81 are to be found a few notes that anticipate the antithesis of *The Antichrist* but in a milder form. In the middle of the deliberations stands Paul; Jesus is brought under consideration only insofar as Paul is said to have "used" him. "Paul believed in Jesus," reads one of these notes, "because he had need of an object that would concentrate, and thereby satisfy him."[22] These and other notes reflect Nietzsche's musings following his reading of Hermann

---

17. Cf. especially Karl Jaspers, *Nietzsche und das Christentum*, 2nd ed. (Munich: Piper, 1952), pp. 25ff.

18. FW (Book Five), 353; WKG, V-2, 271.

19. GM, I, sec. 16; WKG, VI-2, 301.

20. *Nachlaß*, beginning of 1888, 12 [1]; WKG, VIII-2, 448; and *Nachlaß*, autumn 1887, 10 [86]; WKG, VIII-2, 172 (WM, sec. 205, offers an abbreviated version).

21. A, sec. 42; WKG, VI-3, 213f.

22. *Nachlaß*, summer 1880, 4 [261]; WKG, V-1, 495.

Lüdemann's description of Pauline anthropology.[23] The thrust of his excerpts[24] and the accompanying musings show clearly what it was in Lüdemann's study—today little regarded by New Testament scholars[25]—that attracted and interested him: the thesis that in Pauline theology the Law was denied any power of salvation. Nietzsche drew from this a more far-reaching conclusion: he understood the positive statements concerning the Law in Romans as a temporary accommodation on the part of the Apostle to the "Jewish-Christian congregation in Rome, which was as yet unknown to him."[26] With

23. Hermann Lüdemann, *Die Anthropologie des Apostels Paulus und ihre Stellung innerhalb seiner Heilslehre. Nach den vier Hauptbriefen dargestellt* (Kiel: Toeche, 1872). Nietzsche had probably heard about this study from Overbeck; in any case he borrowed it from his friend in July 1880 (cf. Nietzsche's letters to Overbeck from 22 June and 7 July 1880 and Overbeck's letter of 10 July 1880). In a letter dated 19 July 1880 Nietzsche thanked Overbeck for the forwarding of several books and indicated that he had at least read this particular study: "Lüdemann's work," he writes, is "a masterpiece in a very difficult field," but the author is "unfortunately . . . no writer."

24. The information that the notes cited below deal with excerpts from Lüdemann's *Anthropologie des Apostels Paulus* was obtained from Mazzino Montinari. The excerpts—partly word-for-word quotations, partly paraphrases—are to be found in the *Nachlaß*, summer 1880 (WKG, V-1), in the following fragments (the corresponding pages of Lüdemann's book are included in parentheses): 4 [217] (13); 4 [218] (16–19); 4 [219] (this major excerpt refers to pp. 8–206, although omitting or only briefly touching upon a great deal of material). Nietzsche's musings in connection with his reading are most likely contained in the following fragments: 4 [220]; 4 [231]; 4 [253–55]; 4 [258]. For a complete listing of Nietzsche's excerpts from Lüdemann, see *Nietzsche*, ed. Jörg Salaquarda, Wege der Forschung, no. 521 (Darmstadt: Wissenschaftliche Buchgesellschaft, 1980), pp. 321–22, and Montinari's commentary in KSA, XIV, 361ff.

25. In this regard cf. above all Rudolf Bultmann, *Theologie des Neuen Testaments*, 2nd ed. (Tübingen: Mohr, 1959), pt. 2, I, A. 1. ("Die anthropologischen Begriffe," within the section "Die Theologie des Paulus").

26. This is clearly expressed in the major excerpt 4 [219] (WKG, V-1, 484–86), which is chiefly concerned with the equation of "flesh" and "Law." The note concludes with the observation: "pp. 204–5 contain the gist of the matter." Lüdemann writes in this passage: "First of all, there can be no doubt that the impossibility of fulfilling the Mosaic Law was an axiom for Paul which he at no time in any of his letters lost sight of. . . . How does he come now to speak, as he apparently does in Romans 2:7, 10, 13, and 4:2, in such a way that he maintains the objective validity of the Law and treats as an open question the capability of man, which might perhaps aid him in attaining justification through its fulfillment?" (204). According to Lüdemann, Paul cannot have meant that to be taken seriously, for the idea of a *"self-correction of God,"* namely the replacement of one means to salvation (Law) by another (Jesus), would have been impossible for Paul's "theological-deterministic way of thinking." Paul thus comes to the conclusion: "if the Law has never been fulfilled, then fulfillment must have been impossible because of its very nature; consequently, the Law was never meant to be fulfilled in the first place" (205).

this thesis he deviates from Lüdemann, who reports on the theory and considers it, but who ultimately rejects it.[27]

In conjunction with his work of 1887 and 1888—first for his planned book *The Will to Power*, then for the four-part *Revaluation of All Values*—Nietzsche read other works that were directly or indirectly relevant to the theme "Jesus and Paul." The most important of these is "My Religion" by Tolstoy, followed by Dostoevsky's *The Possessed* and works by Wellhausen and Renan.[28] Tolstoy's understanding of the message of Jesus may perhaps have provided the final impetus for Nietzsche's fundamental differentiation between Jesus and Paul; in addition, Nietzsche was indebted to this author for hints and suggestions for the "Psychology of the Redeemer" presented in *The Antichrist*. "No God died for our sins; no redemption through faith; no resurrection after death"—these were the tendencies of the "joyful message" of Jesus that Nietzsche noted to himself while reading Tolstoy. "These are all forgeries of true Christianity, for which we must hold that pernicious crank [sc. Paul] responsible."[29] Among the musings that Nietzsche wrote down in connection with this subject we find turns of phrase that he transferred almost word-for-word into *The Antichrist*, as for example: "*That is the humor of the matter*, a tragic humor: Paul built up again in the grand style precisely that which Christ had annulled by means of his life."[30] "We see what had become of the death on the cross. *Paul* appears as the daemon of the dysangelium. . . ."[31]

I maintain that Nietzsche initially regarded Paul as *one* of the decisive figures in the origin of Christianity, and finally as *the* decisive figure alone. With that we have obtained the prerequisite for Nietzsche to observe and analyze Paul under the aspect of the "great man."

At this point we can identify formally the first characteristic of the alleged "kinship" behind Nietzsche's polemic against Paul: it is a kinship with regard to "greatness" in the sense of one's being ele-

---

27. To be sure, Lüdemann's rejection is not convincing. It is based on a solution that is remarkably pallid in comparison to the problem worked out earlier with such clarity. Paul, he maintains, neither attributed a direct power for salvation to the Law, nor did he—even in his Epistle to the Romans—ever effect a mere accommodation; rather, he understood the Law as an "eternal moral idea." Accordingly, in Romans "that idea comes into play which is constantly in the thought of Paul . . . , that the moral idea basic to Mosaic Law has eternal value and enduring significance" (ibid., p. 214).

28. In this regard cf. the "Vorbemerkung der Herausgeber" in WKG, VIII-2, vff.

29. *Nachlaß*, November 1887 to March 1888, 11 [275]; WKG, VIII-2, 345.

30. Ibid., 11 [281]; ibid., 350.

31. Ibid., 11 [282]; ibid., 351.

vated from the masses. To be sure, the "greatness" that Nietzsche grants the Apostle he views as destructive; but the more vehemently he opposes it, the more he obviously feels compelled to regard it as definitive. A closer examination of Nietzsche's differentiation between Paul and Jesus will show this even more clearly. Nietzsche rejects the thesis of Renan that the terms "hero" and "genius" had anything to contribute to the understanding of Jesus. He writes: "Speaking with the strictness of the physiologist, a quite different word would sooner be appropriate here: the word idiot."[32] Nietzsche understands "idiot" essentially in terms of its Greek meaning, that is, as the designation for an "apolitical man," a private citizen refraining from participating in the business of the state.[33] Jesus is an "idiot" for him, because the way of life he practiced and taught is only possible as the *most private* form of existence," which presupposes "a narrow, solitary, and completely unpolitical society." Nietzsche states that such a way of life belongs "in the conventicle"; it is "still possible at any time," providing similar conditions are present.[34] Nietzsche thought he recognized *one* such unpolitical society in the Russian peasants, who were repressed and yet accommodated themselves to their repression. He praised Dostoevsky, who as a consequence of his knowledge of the Russian people had understood the "psychological type" Jesus. "I only know of one psychologist who has lived in that world where Christianity [sc. in Jesus' sense] is possible, where a Christ can arise at any moment . . . that is Dostoevsky. He *fathomed* Christ." A few lines later he states, in the middle of his critical encounter with Renan: ". . . can one make a worse error than to make a genius out of Christ, who was an idiot?"[35] In another passage—representing, as does the one quoted above, preliminary work to section 29 of *The Antichrist*—Nietzsche utilizes the

---

32. A, sec. 29; WKG, VI-3, 198.
33. Nietzsche uses the word "idiot" several times with this meaning, and herein agrees with Dostoevsky. On this point, cf. Martin Dibelius, "Der 'psychologische Typ des Erlösers' bei Friedrich Nietzsche," *Deutsche Vierteljahresschrift für Literaturwissenschaft und Geistesgeschichte*, 22 (1944), 61ff. Remarkably, no notice has been taken of this study, the best and most detailed one by those authors who later concerned themselves with Nietzsche's use of the word "idiot" (cf. Erich Podach, *Nietzsches Werke des Zusammenbruchs* [Heidelberg: Rothe, 1961], pp. 61ff.; Walter Kaufmann, *Nietzsche*, pp. 340f., n. 2; and Karl Jaspers, *Nietzsche und das Christentum*, p. 21 and n.—although one can at least excuse Jaspers for the reason that he agreed in 1952 to the *unaltered* reprinting of his study of 1938).
34. *Nachlaß*, autumn 1887, 10 [135]; WKG, VIII-2, 198 (WM, sec. 211); and *Nachlaß*, November 1887 to March 1888, 11 [365]; WKG, VIII-2, 404 (WM, sec. 212).
35. *Nachlaß*, spring 1888, 15 [9]; WKG, VIII-3, 203.

word "idiot" expressly in *differentiating* between Jesus and Paul. He begins with the proposition: "Jesus is the *antithesis of a genius*: he is an idiot," and supports it with the same argument that he puts forth in *The Antichrist*. At the conclusion of the characterization Nietzsche finally turns to its further development: "One must keep this in mind: he is an *idiot* in the midst of a very clever people. . . . Yet his disciples were not that at all—Paul was definitely no idiot!—the history of Christianity depends on this fact."[36]

In a note written somewhat earlier Nietzsche had formulated in a general and problematic way what he later coined primarily with reference to Jesus and Paul and put forth as a definite thesis: "The founder of a religion *can* be insignificant,—a match, nothing more!"[37] Another note reads: "The concept 'originator' is so ambiguous that it can even signify the mere cause of a favorable opportunity for a movement. . . ." The concrete example for this idea is once again furnished by the relationship between Paul and Jesus: "Consider the *freedom* with which Paul treats the problem concerning the person of Jesus, coming near to juggling the facts—Someone who has died, whom people have seen after his death, someone who was delivered to death by the Jews. . . . A mere 'motif'; he then creates the music for it. . . . A cipher at the beginning. . . ."[38]

We see that to the extent that Nietzsche divests Jesus of the "responsibility" for the origin and rise of Christianity, Jesus also decreases for him in "greatness" in the sense of his effectiveness in determining the events of history. The fact that the name "Jesus Christ" has attained world-historical significance is due to its propagation and promotion by Paul, whereby he neither carried out nor developed the intentions of Jesus, but twisted them completely around. As we have seen, Paul was not an "idiot" in Nietzsche's eyes, but a man of genius.[39] Nietzsche accords him "greatness" and, in his later writings, even towering "greatness"; in his writings of 1888 Paul—next to Socrates[40]—is the most decisive promoter of *décadence* morality.

36. Ibid., 14 [38]; ibid., 29.
37. *Nachlaß*, spring 1884, 25 [419]; WKG, VII-2, 118 (WM, sec. 178).
38. *Nachlaß*, spring 1888, 15 [108]; WKG, VIII-3, 263. This fragment was previously known as No. 177 of the WM, where of course the pointed final phrase was omitted.
39. Cf., for example, A, sec. 58; WKG, VI-3, 244f. Also *Nachlaß*, autumn 1887, 10 [181]; WKG, VIII-2, 230 (WM, sec. 175). Note the comparison between "genius" and "idiot" in the fragment cited in n. 32.
40. On the later Nietzsche's understanding of Socrates, cf. especially G, "The Problem of Socrates"; WKG, VI-3, 61ff. For an interpretation, see Hermann Josef Schmidt, *Nietzsche und Socrates. Philosophische Untersuchungen zu Nietzsches Socratesbild*, Monographien zur philosophischen Forschung, no. 59 (Meisenheim am Glan: Hain, 1969).

In the writings and notes of the years before 1888 are to be found a few passages in which Nietzsche in other contexts treats directly or indirectly the question of the "greatness" of the Apostle. Of interest in this regard is the thesis that the founder of a system of morality must stand above this system, and may not be "moral" in precisely the sense of the system that he sets out to establish.[41] Since for Nietzsche religion is essentially morality (that is, a complex of values), then Paul, too, as the founder of a religion, is—according to this thesis—elevated above the mass of merely religious or merely moral men. In a note in the *Nachlaß* he writes in this context: "*Paul—who is one of those great immoralities in which the Bible is richer than we think.*"[42] Nietzsche also considers Paul's case when he occupies himself with the problematic question of the "ascetic priest."[43] The ambiguity of this type—in that on the one hand it is guided by the instincts of *décadence*, and on the other is nevertheless "strong" enough to channel the "will to nothingness" of the *décadents* for a time into another direction—Nietzsche apparently sees personified especially in Paul. In a fragment put on paper relatively early, Nietzsche sought to comprehend genealogically the raptures of the ascetic martyr, and in this connection Paul came to mind. "It is not entirely impossible that even the souls of Paul, Dante, Calvin, and others of their kind have penetrated at one time into the terrible secrets of such ecstasies of power."[44] In another note, this one rather isolated from its context, Nietzsche singled out because of their psychological insights three of the "Christians" he used to oppose most vehemently: "All deeper men are in agreement—Luther, Augustine, Paul come to mind—that our morality and its attendant actions do not coincide with our *conscious will*. . . ."[45]

In summarizing the results of this section of the investigation it can be said that Nietzsche's estimation of Paul generally is the same as that of all "great men" whose "greatness" he views as the promotion of a *décadence* movement. He dealt in similar fashion with Socrates, with the great theologians of antiquity and the Middle Ages, with the reformers, with the exponents of "modern ideas," and with

---

41. Cf. G, "Morality as Anti-Nature," sec. 5; WKG, VI-3, 96: "It may be established as a primary tenet that to *make* morality one must have the definite will to do the opposite. . . . To put this in terms of a formula, one might say: *all* means whereby humanity was previously to have been made moral were from the very outset *immoral*."
42. *Nachlaß*, July–August 1879, 42 [57]; WKG, IV-3, 463.
43. Cf., as the most important text, the third essay of GM; WKG, VI-2, 357ff.
44. M, sec. 113; WKG, V-1, 102.
45. *Nachlaß*, autumn 1885 to autumn 1886, 1 [55]; WKG, VIII-1, 20.

others.[46] In a number of aphorisms and notes Paul figures as only one of many. In *The Antichrist*, however, Nietzsche emphatically singles him out from the large number of promoters of the values of *décadence*. By polemicizing against him with previously unequaled severity, he simultaneously elevates him by means of stylization to *the* promoter of the decline.

III

In the course of the year 1888 Nietzsche's impression intensified that on the basis of his insights he was depicting a decisive crisis in the history of humanity. Excluding *Ecce Homo*, he speaks of his world-historical significance in the introductory passages to his last writings,[47] in his correspondence,[48] and in a number of fragments in his *Nachlaß*.[49] He maintains that only "from him on" was there "great politics" (i.e., that which calls "life" in its total development to account);[50] that he is breaking world history into two pieces;[51] that he must undertake an enormous task[52]—these and similar utterances are characteristic of his later work. The process that brought about this extravagant presentation of himself Nietzsche designates as the "revaluation of all values."[53] As the negative side of the "revaluation" he understands the opposition to, and vanquishing of, the values of *décadence*; as the positive side, the erection and reinforcement of new values stemming from those who have turned out well (*die Wohlgeratenen*).[54] For the designation of the positive side Nietzsche made use

---

46. In this regard, cf. A, sec. 4; WKG, VI-3, 169.
47. Cf. the Preface to G; WKG, VI-3, 51f.; and above all, section 1 of the Preface to *Ecce Homo*; WKG, VI-3, 255.
48. Cf., for example, his letters to Brandes of 20 October 1888, to Strindberg of 7 December 1888, and to Overbeck of 24 December 1888, among others.
49. From among a profusion of notes, cf., for example, the two fragments from the *Nachlaß*, December 1888 to the beginning of January 1889, 25 [6 and 7]; WKG, VIII-3, 453f.
50. Cf. ibid., 25 [1]; WKG, VIII-3, 451f.
51. Cf. his letter to Strindberg of 7 December 1888.
52. Cf. G, Preface; WKG, VI-3, 51.
53. Cf. in this regard my article "Der Antichrist," in *Nietzsche Studien*, 2 (1973), 91ff.; here, 93f., especially nn. 10–12.
54. Cf. the plan in the *Nachlaß*, September 1888, 19 [8]; WKG, VIII-3, 347. The first three books were to establish the tendencies of *décadence* and proclaim their defeat. Nietzsche wanted to oppose Christianity as the *Antichrist*, philosophy up to his time as a *free spirit*, and *décadence* morality in general as an *immoralist*. Under the superscription *Dionysus* the fourth book was to establish the new and positive valuation—a "philosophy of the eternal recurrence."

of the symbols "Dionysus" and "Zarathustra" as well as formal titles such as "philosophy of the future."[55]

In order to render credible the necessity and inevitability of his "revaluation," Nietzsche placed his morality of *décadence* before the eyes of his readers in a continuous onrush of ideas: he speculated about their origin, exposed their inner contradictoriness, described in strident fashion their negative consequences, and attempted at the same time to root out their fundamental indefensibility. This tendency found its clearest expression in *The Antichrist*, from which Nietzsche expected a powerful effect.[56] At the end of *Ecce Homo* Nietzsche finally coined what is probably the most easily remembered formula for the direction of his "revaluation": *"Dionysus versus the Crucified One."*[57] Whoever propagates the new values, the "disciples of the philosopher Dionysus,"[58] must oppose the values designated by the symbol of "the Crucified One." The accurate decoding of these two symbols and their formal comparison is thus the most appropriate path to Nietzsche's later philosophy. When Nietzsche says "the Crucified One," "God on the Cross," or "Christ on the Cross," he does not have the "historical Jesus" in mind, and consequently we cannot connect these symbols in any relevant way with his "psychology of the redeemer."[59] Rather, these symbols sum up the basic inclination of later Christianity, whose true founder Nietzsche identified as Paul. Nietzsche reminds us of "the inestimable words of Paul: 'The *weak* things of the world . . . hath God chosen': *that* was the formula, *décadence* was victorious *in Hoc signo.*—God on the Cross—do we still not understand the terrible ulterior motivation behind this symbol? Everything that suffers, everything that hangs

---

55. On "Dionysus," cf. n. 54 above and the text below; "Zarathustra" needs no further reference; on "philosophy" and "philosophers" "of the future," cf., for example, J, secs. 42 and 210; WKG, VI-2, 55 and 146ff. The subtitle of J is "Prelude to a Philosophy of the Future."

56. Cf. in this regard my article "Der Antichrist" (above, n. 53), p. 93 and n. 8.

57. *Ecce Homo*, "Why I Am a Destiny," sec. 9; WKG, VI-3, 372.

58. *Ecce Homo*, Preface, sec. 2; WKG, VI-3, 256. Cf. the study by Rose Pfeffer, *Nietzsche: Disciple of Dionysus* (Lewisburg, Pa.: Bucknell University Press, 1972), and my review in *Nietzsche Studien*, 2 (1973), 315ff.

59. It is thus incorrect and can lead to untenable conclusions when a critic such as Jaspers takes "the Crucified One" as Nietzsche's symbol for (the historical) Jesus: "For Nietzsche, the great adversary of Jesus was Dionysus. Almost all statements of Nietzsche are expressed in terms that are against Jesus and for Dionysus. Jesus' *death on the cross* was for him the expression of declining life and an indictment of life . . ." (*Nietzsche und das Christentum*, p. 73). This criticism can also be made of Paul Wolff—cf. his "Dionysus oder der Gekreuzigte. Zur Lebensidee Nietzsches," in Wolff, *Denken und Glauben. Reden und Aufsätze* (Trier: Paulinus Verlag, 1963), pp. 85ff.

on the cross, is divine. . . . We all hang on the cross, consequently we are divine . . . we alone are divine. Christianity was a victory, a *more noble* sentiment perished because of it,—Christianity has been mankind's greatest misfortune so far. . . ."[60]

If it is in Christianity that the life-hostile morality of *décadence* receives especially clear expression, and if it has shown itself in this form to have been a factor in history such as no other, then it is understandable that the "revaluator" Nietzsche viewed Paul, the "inventor" of Christianity, as one of his great adversaries, and finally as *the* great adversary. In his reflections on the symbol of "the Crucified One" Nietzsche expresses both his decisive rejection of this symbol and his respect for the overwhelming significance of it and its "creator." Nietzsche states emphatically that "God on the Cross" was and is far superior to all earlier and later symbols of *décadence* in terms of its power and range. An indication of this is his thesis that all countermovements to Christianity that have been produced up to now were in fact merely propagating secularized variations of the Christian ideas of morality. Nietzsche notes, for example, "irony against those who believe Christianity has been overcome by the modern natural sciences. The Christian value-judgments are absolutely not overcome by means of these. 'Christ on the Cross' is the most sublime symbol—still. . . ."[61] Acknowledgment of the greatness and decisive rejection of the tendency complement each other. Thus while Nietzsche speaks of the "*grandiose* paradox" expressed in the formula "God on the Cross," he adds, however, that with that "all *good taste* in Europe for millennia" has been destroyed.[62]

In a note from within the compass of *The Antichrist* Nietzsche expressly places in juxtaposition "The two types: *Dionysus* and the *Crucified One*." In his opinion, the two types differ "not . . . with regard to their martyrdom; it is merely that in each case this has a different significance," namely, in the one the negation of life and the denunciation of its essential impulses as "evil," in the other the "*promise into life*"—it "will be eternally reborn and return from the destruction."[63] In order for a disengagement from Paul's symbol and the consequences of its propagation by him to take place, fortunate circumstances are needed, in Nietzsche's view. Even those who have turned out well and the brave, who are capable of taking steps in

---

60. A, sec. 51; WKG, VI-3, 230.
61. *Nachlaß*, autumn 1885 to autumn 1886, 2 [96]; WKG, VIII-1, 106.
62. *Nachlaß*, spring 1884, 25 [292]; WKG, VII-2, 82. Cf. ibid., 25 [344], 98f.
63. *Nachlaß*, spring 1888, 14 [89]; WKG, VIII-3, 57ff.

this direction, will not remain without "attack," as the following note reveals: "What kind of character traits a person must have to dispense with God,—what kind, to dispense with the 'religion of the cross'? Courage, sternness of mind, pride, independence and hardness, decisiveness, no melancholy, etc. Christianity is victorious again and again by means of a *retrogression.*—Certain circumstances must be favorable."⁶⁴

It is well known that Nietzsche already uses the term "the Dionysian" as well as the symbol "Dionysus" in his early work *The Birth of Tragedy*. While he still uses them equivocally in this work—on the one hand as the designation for one of the poles in the contrasting pair Apollo-Dionysus, and on the other, however, as the overriding unity of both—they later become more and more Nietzsche's symbol for the *one* reality.⁶⁵ This is revealed above all in Nietzsche's self-interpretations.⁶⁶ In the Preface of 1886 he writes in retrospect: "It was *against* morality that my instinct . . . turned at that time; it was an instinct that aligned itself with life and that discovered for itself a fundamentally opposite valuation of life . . . [I] baptized . . . it . . . in the name of a Greek god; I called it *Dionysian.*"⁶⁷ At the end of *The Twilight of the Idols* Nietzsche likewise comes to speak of his early work and stresses: "*The Birth of Tragedy* was my first revaluation of all values." He emphasizes that he still cherishes the symbol "Dionysus," for he himself is "the last disciple of the philosopher Dionysus," and as such "the teacher of the eternal recurrence."⁶⁸ At another point Nietzsche states with emphasis what is negated by means of the symbol "Dionysus" and how fundamental is this negation: "Whoever does not merely comprehend the word 'Dionysian,' but comprehends *himself* in the word 'Dionysian,' has no need of a

---

64. *Nachlaß*, spring 1884, 25 [404]; WKG, VII-2, 113.
65. Cf. the beginning of GT: "We will have gained much for the science of aesthetics when we . . . perceive with absolute certainty that the further development of art is bound up with the *Apollonian* and *Dionysian* duality . . ." (GT, sec. 1; WKG, III-1, 21), and in contrast to this the identification of the Dionysian with the *single* world-will in sec. 18 of the same work (WKG, III-1, 111ff.). On the interpretation of the "Dionysian," cf. the studies of Peter Köster, esp. *Der sterbliche Gott. Nietzsches Entwurf übermenschlicher Größe*, Monographien zur philosophischen Forschung, no. 103 (Meisenheim am Glan: Hain, 1972), and "Die Renaissance des Tragischen," in *Nietzsche Studien*, 1 (1972), 185ff.
66. "Attempt at a Self-Criticism," that is, the later Preface (first pub. 1886) to GT; WKG, III-1, 5ff. Cf. further *Ecce Homo*, "Why I Write Such Good Books": The Birth of Tragedy; WKG, VI-3, 307ff.; and FW (Book Five), 370; WKG, V-2, 301ff.
67. GT, "Attempt at a Self-Criticism," sec. 5; WKG, III-1, 13.
68. G, "What I Owe to the Ancients," sec. 5; WKG, VI-3, 154.

refutation of Plato, or of Christianity, or of Schopenhauer—he *smells the decay*. . . ."⁶⁹

The thrust of the above-cited statements reveals that with the symbol of "the Crucified One" Nietzsche does not have in mind merely Christianity in the stricter sense, but rather its chief characteristic, which also receives expression in other *décadence* teachings. With the formula "Dionysus versus the Crucified One" he is, accordingly, concerned with the question of revaluation in general, with the struggle of the values of ascending life (= of those who have turned out well) against the values of declining life (= of the *décadents*). With the invention or "creation"⁷⁰ of God, which is expressed in the symbol "God on the Cross," Paul, according to Nietzsche's analysis, brought about a "revaluation" whose boldness even his most resolute opponents can only stand back and admire. To be sure, an "untimeliness," an elevation of one's self above the standards of the time, is necessary in order to be able to see and evaluate this. Only whoever is a "revaluator" himself can judge the greatness of the deed of an earlier "revaluator" in proper fashion. "Modern men, dulled to all Christian nomenclature, no longer sense the awful superlative for a classical taste that lay in the formula 'God on the Cross.' Never yet and nowhere else has there been such boldness in reversing course, never anything as horrible, questioning, and questionable as this formula; it promised a revaluation of all the values of antiquity."⁷¹

Nietzsche expressed in *Ecce Homo* in coded form the manner in which the "Dionysian revaluator," who intends with his "revaluation" to bring about a *dialectical*⁷² return to the original valuation of those who have turned out well,⁷³ must confront and at the same

---

69. *Ecce Homo*, "Why I Write Such Good Books": The Birth of Tragedy, sec. 2; WKG, VI-3, 310.

70. A, sec. 47; WKG, VI-3, 223. Cf. Eberhard Jüngel, "Deus qualem Paulus creavit, dei negatio. Zur Denkbarkeit Gottes bei Ludwig Feuerbach und Friedrich Nietzsche. Eine Beobachtung," in *Nietzsche Studien*, 1 (1972), 286ff., esp. 296.

71. J, sec. 46; WKG, VI-2, 65.

72. If I am advocating the thesis that certain of Nietzsche's lines of thought must be interpreted, in the words of Rose Pfeffer, as most nearly "analogous to the Hegelian dialectical movement" (*Nietzsche: Disciple of Dionysus*, pp. 39ff.), then it should be carefully noted that it is a matter here of analogy and not of identity. The reader will find a more detailed explanation at the beginning of Section V.

73. Although Nietzsche saw in the Greeks before Socrates an enduring prototype for all those who had turned out well and their system of values (cf., for example, *Nachlaß*, June–July 1885, 37 [7]; WKG, VII-3, 306–308), he did not wish simply to return to them with his "Dionysian philosophy." He wanted certainly to be "the Anti-

time be a match for the one who brought about the "revaluation" in favor of the values of *décadence*.

People have never asked me, although they ought to have, what precisely in my mouth, in the mouth of the first immoralist, the name Zarathustra means, for that which constitutes the enormous historical uniqueness of this Persian in history is exactly the opposite of this. Zarathustra was the first to observe in the fight of good and evil the very wheel in the machinery; the transposition of morality into the metaphysical realm . . . is *his* work. But this question would in fact be its own answer. Zarathustra created this disastrous error, morality; consequently he must be the first to *recognize* it. Not only because he has had more experience in this matter, and for a longer time, than any other thinker—the whole of history is after all the refutation by experiment of the principle of the so-called "world order"—but what is more important, Zarathustra is more truthful than any other thinker. His teaching and his teaching alone regards truthfulness as the highest virtue—this means the opposite of the *cowardice* of the "idealist," who flees from reality; Zarathustra has more intestinal fortitude than all other thinkers put together.[74]

Nietzsche is saying in this passage concerning the relationship between "his Zarathustra" and the "historical Zarathustra" that the former is inimical to the latter in that it draws *conclusions* from the latter's teachings. This corresponds to what he says in other passages concerning the "self-overcoming" of Christianity. The "truthfulness" he speaks of in the above quotation Nietzsche designates at other points as the Christian virtue par excellence,[75] and he places value on the conclusion that it is precisely this consequence of Christianity of which it will ultimately perish.[76] When Nietzsche in his late phase confronts the "revaluator" Paul as a "Dionysian revaluator" with the

---

christ . . . in Greek," but by no means "only in Greek" (*Ecce Homo*, "Why I Write Such Good Books," sec. 2; WKG, VI-3, 300).

74. *Ecce Homo*, "Why I Am a Destiny," sec. 3; WKG, VI-3, 365.
75. Cf., above all, FW (Book Five), 344; WKG, V-2, 256ff.
76. Cf. *Nachlaß*, autumn 1885 to autumn 1886, 2 [127]; WKG, VIII-1, 123–25 (WM, sec. 1): "the sense of truthfulness, developed highly by Christianity, is *nauseated* by the falseness and mendacity of all Christian interpreters of the world and of history." Cf. FW (Book Five), 357; WKG, V-2, 282: "We see *what* was actually victorious over the Christian God: Christian morality itself, the ever more rigorously understood concept of truthfulness. . . ."

formula "Dionysus versus the Crucified One," then this signifies that he conceives of his relationship to the Apostle essentially in terms of neither a mere conflict nor a secret kinship, but rather in terms of a *dialectical overcoming*.[77]

IV

If Nietzsche comes to speak of the *great* representatives and promulgators of the values of *décadence*, then he chiefly names Socrates and the "founder of Christianity" (i.e., Jesus or Paul; ultimately, Paul alone). In the end Paul apparently became more important for Nietzsche than Socrates—*this*, at least, seems unmistakable to me. Nietzsche's polemic against the Apostle is much more vehement;[78] he favors the title "Antichrist" over that of the "free spirit"; and most importantly, he sums up in *Ecce Homo* his entire struggle precisely with the formula "Dionysus versus the Crucified One." *Why* Nietzsche finally came to view Paul as the decisive "revaluator" in favor of the values of *décadence* can perhaps be explained by the following more detailed examination of his understanding of Paul. For the time being it can be said that in general he conceives of Christianity as the most comprehensive movement in which the values of Western philosophy have been preserved, so to speak.[79] Moreover, the fact that Socrates' design for a system of values exists merely in isolated fragments[80] that do not give us as clear a picture as in the case of Paul may also have played a role here.

As we have mentioned, Nietzsche twice dealt with Paul more thoroughly: on the occasion of his work on *The Dawn*, and in his last creative year. If we want an overview of his understanding of the person and work of the Apostle, then it is best to proceed from the more objective, less polemic notes and reflections from the years

77. This is the true gist of Bernoulli's thesis regarding kinship in opposition (cf. nn. 14–16 above).
78. Compare A, secs. 37ff., with G, "The Problem of Socrates."
79. Thus "in the final analysis" Nietzsche sees in Kant only an "*underhanded* Christian" (G, " 'Reason' in Philosophy," sec. 6; WKG, VI-3, 73), and "German philosophy" in particular is for him "basically . . . an *underhanded theology*" (A, sec. 10; WKG, VI-3, 174).
80. Regarding the best-known and most influential image of Socrates, that of Plato, Nietzsche cannot free himself from the suspicion that behind this image lies a drama similar to Pascal's: Plato, originally one of those who had turned out well, was weakened and "moralized to death" by Socrates (cf. on this point the Preface to J; WKG, VI-2, 4f.; and *Nachlaß*, spring 1888, 14 [94]; WKG, VIII-3, 64).

1880–81. The most detailed passage of this period, the sixty-eighth aphorism of *The Dawn*,[81] is basic to the characterization that follows. Its heading—"The First Christian"—betrays that in it Nietzsche for the first time presents to the public that thesis to which he did not always hold at first, but which in his late phase became decisive for him: namely, that Paul and not Jesus is to be regarded as the "founder" of Christianity. Nietzsche introduces this thesis in the following way: without the "remarkable history" of Paul, "without the confusion and turmoil of such a mind, such a soul, there would be no Christianity; we would scarcely have heard of a small Jewish sect whose master died on the cross." The fact that this insight had not long been known and acknowledged was due, in Nietzsche's view, to our reluctance—which had become a matter of habit—to read and interpret the New Testament just as any other book. Since people either believe "in the authorship of the 'Holy Spirit' " or stand in some way "under the influence of this belief," they pay as a rule little attention to *who* is writing here and *with what intent*. For a millennium and a half, he states, nobody had read the New Testament writings from a new standpoint, and later on only "a few scholars" at the most.[82] But if we were to begin to read the New Testament "not as the revelation of the 'Holy Spirit,' but rather with an open and honest mind of our own, and also without thinking thereby of our own personal need"—if we were to begin to read the New Testament in a philological sense,[83] we would then discover in the writings of Paul the true origin of Christianity, and its effectiveness would soon be at an end.

Further passages have it as their goal to investigate what lies behind the writings of Paul and the reports concerning him, and by means of a "psychology" of the Apostle Paul[84] to understand the genesis of Christianity. Paul is exposed in Nietzsche's analysis as nature in conflict with itself, and thus as a *décadent*. He was "hot-

---

81. WKG, V-1, 60ff. If not otherwise noted, the citations that follow are taken from this aphorism.
82. This remark is probably an allusion to Lüdemann (cf. n. 23 above).
83. Cf. A, sec. 36; WKG, VI-3, 206: "For the first time we, we who have become *free spirits*, have the presuppositions for understanding something that nineteen centuries have misunderstood. . . ."
84. "On the Psychology of *Paul*," reads the heading to a note in the *Nachlaß*, spring 1888, 14 [57]; WKG, VIII-3, 36 (WM, sec. 171). In A Nietzsche only briefly repeated his earlier "Psychology of Paul" published in M, essentially taking it for granted. On the other hand, his *"Psychology of the Redeemer,"* namely Jesus, nowhere received such clear contours before (cf. A, sec. 28; WKG, VI-3, 196).

headed, sensual, melancholy, malicious in his hatred"; his extant utterances are suggestive of all that lay on his conscience, namely, "hostility, murder, idol worship, filthiness, drunkenness, and a desire for dissolute revelry." The concept *sarx*, with which Paul himself summed up all such tendencies as these, is rendered by Nietzsche as "carnality."[85] In opposition to this "carnality," Paul had always passionately striven to fulfill the Jewish Law and its demands. Just like Luther later on, Paul must have had moments in which he gave vent to the contradictoriness of his inclinations with the lament: "It is all in vain! The torment of the unfulfilled Law cannot be overcome."[86]

The fanatical zeal with which Paul persecuted the Christian sect is taken by Nietzsche as a double indication: on the one hand, of Paul's difficulty in fulfilling the Law, which he wished to overcome by means of such activities; on the other, of the fact that the Apostle suspected that a way out, that a possible solution to his problem might lie with this sect. His thoughts at this time must have revolved more and more around the problem of why he "*could* not fulfill the Law itself; in fact, and this is what seemed strangest to him, that his wanton lust for power was continually stimulated to overstep it, and that he had to give in to this thorn." One step further and he would not have been able to rid himself of the suspicion that it was not "carnality" that was causing him to transgress the Law, but "the Law itself, which *must* continually prove to be unfulfillable and tempts us with irresistible fascination to transgression."[87] Nietzsche here breaks off briefly and remarks that Paul "at that time" had "not yet [seen] this alternative" clearly. A special event was necessary to convey these reflections all at once fully into his conscious mind—the vision before the gates of Damascus.[88] As Nietzsche depicts it, this key experience had the function of making Paul immediately aware of his problem and its solution; further, it allowed him to understand these insights as having been revealed from God or the resurrected

---

85. Among Nietzsche's fragments from Lüdemann's book cf. fragments 4 [231] and 4 [251]; WKG, V-1, 488 and 492.

86. In this regard a clear parallel can be found in Nietzsche's image of Socrates. In Nietzsche's opinion, Socrates also had "every evil vice and desire" within him, but overcame them nevertheless through the erection of a "tyranny of reason" (cf. G, "The Problem of Socrates," esp. secs. 3, 9, and 10; WKG, VI-3, 63 and 65f. Nietzsche's source was Cicero, Tusc. IV, 37, 80, where the "physiognomist" is identified as Zopyrus. Cf. also Georg Christoph Lichtenberg, an author whom Nietzsche admired and whose works he possessed ("Über Physiognomik" in *Vermischte Schriften*, 8 vols. [Göttingen: Dieterichsche Buchhandlung, 1867], IV, 31).

87. Here Lüdemann's interpretation comes into play (cf. above, nn. 26 and 27).

88. Cf. Acts 9:1–9; 1 Cor. 9:1 and 15:8.

Christ. "And finally the saving thought occurred to him simultaneously with a vision—as it could not otherwise have been the case with this epileptic: to him, the fanatical zealot of the Law who was inwardly sick unto death of it, to him appeared on a lonely road that same Christ with the glory of God on his countenance, and Paul heard the words: 'Why persecutest thou *me*?' "

What is of interest here in terms of Nietzsche's psychological analysis could be described as a process within the *"mind"* of the Apostle. His mind became clear—Paul understood all at once the cross and the resurrection of Christ as the convincing answer to his problem. According to Nietzsche, Paul later declared that Jesus Christ had fulfilled the Law on the cross and with his resurrection had overcome it. He is the "destroyer of the Law." As a consequence of this experience Saul, the zealot of the Law, becomes Paul, the "teacher of the *destruction of the Law*." What gives the "conversion" of Paul the rank of a "world-historical event" in the eyes of Nietzsche and elevates it above a merely private experience is its illustrative character; here the "genius" of Paul becomes manifest, for he found a solution that many who came after him could understand and accept as a solution to their own problems. In an earlier work Nietzsche had described "genius" in the following way: "To desire a lofty goal *and* the means to attain it."[89] As mentioned above,[90] he later conceived of this "desire also for the means" in terms of involvement in political activity, and contrasted the "man of genius" with the unpolitical "idiot." In our aphorism Nietzsche describes Paul in such a way that we must understand him as such a "man of genius." "The enormous consequences of this idea, of this solution to his problem, whirl before his eyes; suddenly he becomes the happiest of men— the fate of the Jews, no, of all people seems to be bound up with this idea, with the very instant of his sudden inspiration; he has the thought of thoughts,[91] the key of keys, the light of lights; from henceforth history will revolve around him!"[92]

As an addendum to this climax of his exposition Nietzsche paraphrases or quotes a few more statements of Paul, placing his main emphasis on the idea that for the Apostle "carnality" and the Law work together in tempting man to sin. With the conclusion to the aphorism Nietzsche finally returns to its title.

89. Cf. MA II/I, sec. 378; WKG, IV-3, 162.
90. Cf. WKG, IV-3, 5f.
91. It is important to note the use of this phrase, which Nietzsche otherwise only applies to his idea of recurrence.
92. Cf. also *Nachlaß*, autumn 1887, 10 [181]; WKG, VIII-2, 230f. (WM, sec. 175).

Just a short time longer amid this decay!—that is the lot of the Christian before he, having become one with Christ, rises again with Christ, takes part in the divine majesty along with Christ, and, like Christ, becomes the "son of God."—With that Paul's ecstasy is at its peak, and likewise the obtrusiveness of his soul—with the thought of becoming one with Christ every bit of shame, subordination, every barrier is removed from his soul, and the intractable will of the desire for power manifests itself as an anticipatory reveling in *divine* majesty.—This is the *first Christian*, the inventor of Christianity! Up to then there had only been Jewish sectarians.

V

The "kinship" to Paul that has been correctly assumed to lie behind Nietzsche's vehement polemics against the Apostle has been characterized above as a "dialectical resemblance." A sketch from Nietzsche's attempt to draft a "history of morals" will help to shed light on this thesis.[93]

According to Nietzsche's view of history, originally (that is, in the long periods of prehistory) only those who had turned out well were value-creating and value-determining.[94] The establishment and promulgation of values was accomplished in spontaneous, instinctive acts of life; it was not supported by theories and was thus, so to speak, pretheoretical. The victorious ones at any given time, the superior caste, the tribe that had subjugated another—these succeeded in making their value-judgments valid within the sphere of their domination. Whenever the rulers lost their dominant position, then their values as well had to make way for those of the new victors. Thus only very little remains of these early forms of "master morality";[95] what we have left are mere traces that extend forward into the historical period in the form of codices and the like. For example, Nietzsche regarded the Greeks up to the fifth century before Christ

---

93. An important section of Nietzsche's work in this regard is the fifth book of J ("Natural History of Morals"; WKG, VI-2, 105ff.). Cf. on this point Wolfgang Müller-Lauter, *Nietzsche. Seine Philosophie der Gegensätze und die Gegensätze seiner Philosophie* (Berlin/New York: de Gruyter, 1971), pp. 34ff.

94. Cf., for example, J, sec. 260; WKG, VI-2, 218: "The noble type of man feels *himself* to be value-determining . . . he knows himself as that which first gives honor to things, he is *value-creating*."

95. J, sec. 260; WKG, VI-2, 218 and 221f. Cf. *The Case of Wagner*, Epilogue; WKG, VI-3, 44.

as a well-turned-out, value-setting people whose system of values in outline was basic to the thought of the great "tragic philosophers" before Socrates. As regards the pre-Socratics themselves, Nietzsche's position is not consistent: he first viewed them as strong types in whom the antithetical tendency to Socratic *décadence* was expressed;[96] but soon his judgment began to vacillate.[97] In his late phase his interest in these philosophers diminished; when he reproaches the philosophers as a group for lacking a sense of history and distrusting the witness of the senses, then he excepts only Heraclitus to a certain extent.[98]

If one interprets the "history of morals" that can be ascertained from Nietzsche's numerous statements as a dialectic movement, then this first epoch stands as the *thesis*. The establishment, promulgation, and supersession of values is carried out during this epoch in close harmony with life and its vicissitudes, and lacks all theoretical foundation. When value-systems in rough outline of the type of the "master morality" become codified, fixed in constitutions, or are even written down or expounded philosophically at the beginning of the historical period, then, in Nietzsche's view, an ambiguous situation arises: the danger exists thereby that a certain complex of values may become cut off from its supporters and from the conditions under which it is meaningful and promotes life, and that this complex of values may then become entrenched.

The way for the second phase in the history of morals was prepared, according to Nietzsche, in various areas and cultural realms by means of this sort of severing and entrenchment. Nietzsche speaks in terms of *décadence* movements and he attempts in greater or lesser detail to describe them. His most frequent and intensive critical encounters have been with the Jews, who "brought into being that marvelous achievement of the inversion of values" by holding fast to their God and the values he represented even after they (the Jews) had lost their dominance. Nietzsche claims that he can also read with particular clarity in the further development of the Jews and their religion the difficulty that was caused by this "inversion." In Nietzsche's view, the inner consequence of their attempt forced the Jews more and more to reinterpret and falsify their history—to write as if their past greatness were the cause of their pres-

---

96. Cf. *Die Philosophie im tragischen Zeitalter der Griechen* (1873); WKG, III-2, 293ff.

97. Nietzsche writes accordingly in one of his notes in the *Nachlaß* (summer 1875, 6 [35]; WKG, IV-1, 188) that the disunity of the Greeks and the Persian Wars were to blame that the beginnings of a higher and further development did not last.

98. Cf. on this point G, " 'Reason' in Philosophy," secs. 1 and 2; WKG, VI-3, 68f.

ent decline. Nietzsche is even able to say at one point that it was with the Jews that "the *slave rebellion in morals*" began—namely, the establishment and promulgation of values that have arisen from the perspective of powerlessness.[99] Nietzsche believed he could perceive in Buddhism, especially Chinese Buddhism, a less aggressive attempt to hold to traditional values in spite of a decline.[100] From his late period we should also mention his reading of the Manu lawbook, in whose caste system he saw delineated a relatively acceptable classification of the values of *décadence*.[101]

An even more interesting *décadence* movement for Nietzsche, and one which by virtue of its effect is of greater importance in the long run, is that of Greek philosophy after Socrates. In contrast to the Sophists, the post-Socratic philosophers were, from Nietzsche's standpoint, typical reactionaries who were striving to get back to "the *old virtues*." The philosopher "desired the *ideal polis*, after the concept 'polis' had become obsolete (much the way the Jews held on to the idea of themselves as a 'people' after they had fallen into bondage)." Here, too, reinterpretation and falsification were immediately put into practice. "Gradually everything *genuinely Hellenic*"— thus, precisely that which was to be protected and preserved—"was made responsible for the decline (and Plato was just as ungrateful to Homer, tragedy, rhetoric, and Pericles as the prophets to David and Saul)—*the decline of Greece* is understood *as an objection to the foundation of Hellenistic culture: fundamental error of the philosophers. . . .*"[102]

If we follow Nietzsche's reasoning, then these transitional forms remained for a long period merely local movements, or those restricted to certain portions of society (namely, the "lower" levels). Nietzsche begins by saying that similar tendencies will always exist—in fact, must always exist. For, as he writes in a note from the *Nachlaß*, "*décadence* . . . belongs to all epochs of humanity; there exists everywhere discarded and decayed material; it is a process of life itself, the elimination of decaying and degenerate creatures."[103] Nietzsche questions in passing whether his own time, which he considers "in a certain sense *ripe* (namely, *décadent*)," does not need a

---

99. J, sec. 195; WKG, VI-2, 118f. Cf. also GM, I, sec. 10; WKG VI-2, 284ff.; and A, sec. 25; WKG VI-3, 191f.

100. Nietzsche took "chinoiserie" (*Chineserei*) as his symbol for the "deepest leveling" (FW [Book Five], sec. 377; WKG, V-2, 311); Kant was designated disapprovingly as the "great Chinaman from Königsberg" (J, sec. 210; WKG, VI-2, 148).

101. Cf. G, "Morality as Anti-Nature"; WKG, VI-3, 76ff.

102. *Nachlaß*, November 1887 to March 1888, 11 [375]; WKG, VIII-2, 410.

103. Ibid., 11 [226]; ibid., 329.

new "Buddhism," which could supersede "aggressive Christianity" and its secularized daughters; "a European Buddhism might perhaps be indispensable."[104] Along with the "*décadence* movements, according to Nietzsche's analysis, there also existed in this transitional period value-systems in outline form of those who have turned out well, and these have been the determinant and dominant ones. Nietzsche names the Romans as the chief bearers of the master morality during this period. The growing threat of the values of *décadence* was compensated for by the overwhelming strength of the ruling Romans, and the victory procession of the "decline" was delayed. The Romans were "the strong and noble, and none stronger and nobler has ever existed on earth or has ever been dreamed of; every remnant of them, every inscription delights us, provided that we divine *what* was writing there."[105]

According to this thesis of Nietzsche's late philosophy, the situation did not change until the rise of Christianity. *This* particular *décadence* movement succeeded in seizing power and holding it for an extended period of time. That it was able to do this was due chiefly to the work of Paul. To a certain extent we have already shown how and with what arguments Nietzsche presents this thesis; the following comments will serve to round out his argumentation.

Among Nietzsche's statements concerning the origin of Christianity two above all are of interest in regard to the theme of the present investigation. The first has to do with his thoughts on the "triumphant progress" of Christianity. He establishes as decisive the fact that Christianity was successful in taking up and binding to itself the main tendencies of all the important *décadence* movements of antiquity: it took its "basic foundation" from Judaism, from which it arose and which, as Nietzsche maintains, it simply carried on in freer form; from Greek philosophy it drew the structures of its method of reasoning and verification; the idea of redemption and its practical applications it took over from the Near Eastern mystery religions; contemplation and asceticism from the older Asiatic *décadence* movements; and so on. Secondly, in Nietzsche's opinion it has been decisive for Christianity that it directed itself from the beginning to the lowest segment of society, to those who were never integrated, to the "chandala," without thereby disregarding the other groups—the oppressed, the weary, the mediocre, and finally even those who had turned out well. Christianity, he says, was conceived from its

---

104. Ibid., 11 [366]; ibid., 404; and *Nachlaß*, autumn 1887, 9 [35]; WKG, VIII-2, 14–16.
105. GM, I, sec. 16; WKG, VI-2, 300.

inception as a mass movement and was successful in promoting this idea. As we have seen, in Nietzsche's analyses the "slave revolt in morality" *begins* "when *ressentiment* . . . becomes creative and gives birth to values," which occurs chiefly in the Jewish *décadence* movement. It should be added here that Nietzsche views the "symbol of the holy cross" as the true sign of victory for this "revolt": "At least it can be said for certain that *sub hoc signo* Israel with its revenge and revaluation of all values has triumphed again and again up to now over all other ideals, over all *more noble* ideals."[106]

It should now be clear that according to Nietzsche's ultimate thesis the aggregation of the basic characteristics of all the *décadence* movements in Christianity, their concentration in the symbol "God on the Cross," and their orientation primarily toward the lower classes were the work of Paul. Thus the latter becomes for him the true "revaluator" in favor of the values of *décadence*—he becomes that "world-historical personality" who definitively ends the first epoch in the history of morals and ushers in a new one. As the creator of the *victorious décadence* movement, Paul serves as the exponent of *antithesis* in Nietzsche's view of history.

As a consequence of this development brought about by Paul, Nietzsche states, "Judea" (that is, Pauline Christianity) was victorious against "Rome" and "*morality in Europe today is herd animal morality.*"[107] True, there was no lack of countermovements by those who had turned out well, yet as a whole "slave morality" prevailed.[108] In his own conception of the "revaluation" of all values Nietzsche saw now the necessary third step. If we survey the numerous statements in which he characterizes his "revaluation," it becomes apparent that he describes it in a formal sense as a kind of synthesis akin to that of Hegel. Nietzsche's *synthesis* is first of all a return to the thesis: the type of the "master morality" is again to become valid. In a second sense, it is a negation of the antithesis: it opposes the values of *décadence* and seeks to overthrow their (exclusive) legitimacy. Thirdly, it is preservation: Nietzsche does not want a *mere* return to the "master morality," but is interested in a forward movement in which the experiences of humanity on its way to the present are to be overcome and yet preserved. The first two impulses, return to the thesis and negation of the antithesis, are undisputed by Nietzsche scholars and have been examined continuously. Simultaneously problematic

---

106. Ibid., secs. 10 and 8; ibid., 284 and 283.
107. GM, I, sec. 16, and J, sec. 202; WKG, VI-2, 301 and 126.
108. Cf. my article "Der Antichrist," pp. 100–102.

and interesting is the third impulse, however—that of "overcoming preservation."

Nietzsche does not merely intend with his philosophy of a "revaluation of all values" to propose a new *interpretation* of the reality of the world. Neither is it his aim to increase by one the series of world models thought up by Western philosophers from Socrates on. Rather, he wishes to establish a new "emphasis," by means of which the strivings and tendencies of the well-turned-out are furthered, and those of the *décadents* are hindered. Only when we take into account this far-reaching intent do we become aware of the sovereignty with which Nietzsche surveys the future in his last writings and notes—the sovereignty with which, in fact, he believes he can even look back from the future to the present.[109] Nietzsche the "revaluator" is here laying a cornerstone and mortaring it so firmly that it is to last for millennia. All architects to come will be able, in his opinion, to further the structure he has begun and to shape it in different ways—but they must proceed from the cornerstone that has already been laid.

In conformity to the preaching of Paul and yet simultaneously surpassing it, Nietzsche offers his "gospel of the future." His "formula"—*"The Will to Power.* Attempt at a Revaluation of All Values"— stands for "a *countermovement* . . . with respect to principle and task," which finally is to overcome the *décadence* valuation altogether, not merely one of its transitory forms. This all-encompassing countermovement will not come to pass merely in the form of an abstract contesting of this valuation, as can be seen from the fact that in Nietzsche's opinion it "logically and psychologically" presupposes the basic inner characteristic of *décadence* values, namely "nihilism"; it can "in the final analysis only come *after it and from it.*" "For why is the advent of nihilism," that is, the "truth" now becoming evident of all valuations of the *décadents,* "now *necessary*? Because it is our previous values themselves which draw their final conclusion in it; because nihilism is the logic of our great values and ideals thought out to its conclusion—because we must first experience nihilism in order to get behind what was actually the *value* of these 'values.'

---

109. Cf. *Nachlaß*, November 1887 to March 1888, 11 [411]; WKG, VIII-2, 431f., a text that Nietzsche had planned to use as a preface for his book *The Will to Power* and to which the later editors assigned the same function in their compilation of that name: "Conversely, he that speaks here [sc. in opposition to the *décadents* of his time] has so far done nothing but *reflect*; a philosopher and recluse by instinct . . . who has already lost his way once in every labyrinth of the future; a soothsayer-bird spirit who *looks back* when prophesying what will come" (p. 432).

... ."[110] Whoever *has* already experienced that, whoever "as Europe's first complete nihilist . . . [simultaneously] has within himself already lived nihilism to its end, whoever has it behind himself, under himself, beside himself"—Nietzsche is maintaining this all of himself—"is the called 'revaluator.' "[111] Nietzsche describes himself as a man who, as his opposite Paul once did, has already lived out in exemplary fashion that which still lies in the future of other men. In the course of the coming centuries, he believes, more and more people will have to agree with his insight and the consequences that he drew from it.

VI

It is thus of interest to work out that particular understanding of Paul from which Nietzsche directs his harsh attacks in his late work, since it provides an important resource for the proper interpretation of Nietzsche's own philosophy of the "transvaluation of all values."[112] To pursue such an interpretation further, however, no longer lies within the framework of the present investigation. The following more detailed examination of the symbol "God on the Cross" is consequently intended merely to support the above thesis and to indicate its direction.

In Aphorism 68 of *The Dawn* Nietzsche established that Paul understood the "Crucified One" as the "destroyer of the Law." As has already been shown, *the* law plays a role as well in Nietzsche's "history of morals": the *décadents* of the transition phase shore themselves up against the tyranny of the well-turned-out—who are continually seeking to establish *their* own law—by appealing to *the* (universal) law. As a "typical *décadent*," Paul cherished *the* law and defended it against all despotism before his Damascus experience. According to Nietzsche, in that vision it became clear to Paul that this attitude of advanced *décadence*—his own, first, and then that of the many who would come after him—was no longer appropriate. For in the face of increasing disgregation of the drives and desires it becomes less and less possible for the advanced *décadent* to see *the* law as a protection; from a certain stage on, he suffers more from it than from any despotic act of the strong. It seems unavoidable that

110. Ibid.
111. Ibid.
112. Cf. my article "Umwertung aller Werte," *Archiv für Begriffsgeschichte*, XXII/2 (1978), 154–74.

one weakened in such a way will gradually perish. This path of a "Buddhistic peace movement," forbidding itself action of any kind, was introduced and taught by Jesus, according to the thesis put forth by Nietzsche (above all in *The Antichrist*). Here Paul did not follow Jesus: he made possible what was apparently impossible by opening up a new source for the feeling of power, with whose help the advanced *décadents* could once again hold back their destruction. Alongside the effective sources up to that time, namely the values of those who had turned out well and universal law, Paul placed a third source, that is, the concept of a redeemer in the world to come, who chooses the *weak* and removes them from the observation of *the* law. Paul's "solution," as Nietzsche sees it, can consequently be described in the following way: precisely that which the "weary one" (= the *décadent* of the first stage) plays off against the despotism of the strong and which gives him strength and security, namely *the* law, tortures the advanced *décadent* (= the *décadent* of the second stage) most of all; whoever, therefore, overcomes *the* law in a way that can become a new source of the feeling of power for the one suffering from *the* law, "redeems" him. Thus Nietzsche calls the idea of the "destruction of the Law" the "thought of thoughts, the key of keys, the light of lights."[113]

The "revaluator" Nietzsche confronts the "revaluator" Paul. In the symbol "Dionysus" he believes he has found that formula which no longer draws its strength from the formula "God on the Cross," and which therefore is uniquely in a position to drive the former gradually from the field. If we proceed from the idea that Nietzsche understood the "subject" preserved in the Pauline formula as a basic tendency, then we are not far from the conjecture that the situation is the same for the "subject" designated by the term "Dionysus." The "subject" to which the late Nietzsche refers in the symbol "Dionysus" he calls, as we are reminded by several quotations above, the "eternal recurrence of the same."[114]

A few observations show that Nietzsche in fact draws a parallel between "destruction of the law" and "eternal recurrence of the same," so that for these two doctrines the same dialectic relationship can be posited that we have already worked out between Nietzsche and Paul. As the first manifestation of this can be cited the fact that Nietzsche owed his recurrence idea to an experience similar to that of Paul before Damascus. Nietzsche's first report of this experi-

113. M, sec. 68; WKG, V-1, 63.
114. See above, n. 54, as well as pp. 112, 113 and nn. 63 and 68.

ence—"*The recurrence of the same.* First draft"—is furnished with the postscript: "The beginning of August, 1881, in Sils-Maria, 6000 feet above the sea and much higher above all human concerns!"[115] The fact that he had a kind of "vision" may not have been all that surprising to Nietzsche, for he had previously engaged in various musings on the subject of "elevated moods," inspirations, and the like. To be sure, this tendency increased with him after the year 1881, as *Thus Spoke Zarathustra* clearly shows. To a few friends and acquaintances Nietzsche gave hints, partly orally, partly in writing, that have to do with his "vision" and its "contents." Because of the exceptional nature that Nietzsche himself attributed to his experience in the Swiss mountains, the report of Lou Andreas-Salomé, which he allegedly was able to relate to her only softly and haltingly,[116] is particularly informative. Nietzsche indicated that his experience took on a plastic and visionary nature by drawing imagery for his description from the visual realm, for example, in the coded reference made to Gast: "Thoughts have arisen on my horizon the likes of which I have not yet seen."[117] Shortly before his experience at Sils, Nietzsche had used a similar image in his description of the vision of Paul: "finally the saving thought struck him."[118] A further parallel is the most obvious of all: Nietzsche calls the two thematic tendencies here—and *only* these tendencies—"thoughts of thoughts."[119] He thus considers them and only them as central thoughts, which bind together and give structure to all other thoughts. A final important common factor becomes apparent when we look at the consequences that Nietzsche drew for himself with respect to the two experiences: as Paul became the "teacher of the *destruction of the Law*," Nietzsche himself became the "teacher of the eternal recurrence."[120]

115. *Nachlaß*, spring–autumn 1881, 11 [141]; WKG, V-2, 392. Cf. also Nietzsche's own quotation of this note in *Ecce Homo*, "Why I Write Such Good Books": Thus Spoke Zarathustra, sec. 1; WKG, VI-3, 333. Ryogi Okochi, "Nietzsches Amor fati im Lichte von Karma des Buddhismus," in *Nietzsche Studien*, 1 (1972), 36ff. (here: 49ff.) gives an overview of the most important texts pertaining to this theme.

116. Lou Andreas-Salomé, *Friedrich Nietzsche in seinen Werken* (Vienna: Konegen, 1894), p. 224.

117. Letter to Gast of 14 August 1881; GB, IV, 70. Cf. the reference to the striking phrase "to see a thought" in Okochi, "Nietzsches Amor fati," p. 46.

118. M, sec. 68; WKG, V-1, 62.

119. Concerning Paul, cf. M, sec. 68; WKG, V-1, 63; concerning Nietzsche's idea of eternal recurrence, cf. *Nachlaß*, spring–summer 1881, 11 [143]; WKG, V-2, 394; and *Nachlaß*, summer 1888, 20 [133]; WKG, VIII-3, 375.

120. M, sec. 68; WKG, V-1, 63; and G, "What I Owe to the Ancients," sec. 5; WKG, VI-3, 154.

In the idea of the eternal recurrence of all things Nietzsche felt he had found that "emphasis" with which he could successfully combat the tendency "destruction of the law" (and also, naturally, the "establishment of the law," which proceeds from it). To be sure, the supersession of the old values, which he takes to be unavoidable, can, in his opinion, be completed only by means of a long, drawn-out process. "Let us be on our guard against teaching such a doctrine like a sudden religion! It must soak in slowly, whole races must contribute to it and become fruitful—so that it may become a great tree overshadowing all humanity yet to come. What are the couple of millennia during which Christianity has existed! For the greatest idea many millennia are necessary—it must be small and powerless for a *long, long* time!"[121]

121. *Nachlaß*, spring–autumn 1881, 11 [158]; WKG, V-2, 401. For a detailed discussion of the doctrine of eternal recurrence see the excellent study by Bernd Magnus, *Nietzsche's Existential Imperative* (Bloomington and London: Indiana University Press, 1978) and my review in *Nietzsche Studien*, 9 (1980), 432–40.

VII. *Amor dei* and *Amor fati*: Spinoza and Nietzsche

Joan Stambaugh

The aim of this paper is to try to make some sort of comparison between Spinoza's *amor dei*, love of God, and Nietzsche's *amor fati*, love of fate. I do not wish primarily to deal with what Nietzsche thought of Spinoza (although that would be a valid and interesting topic), but rather to throw some light on the extraordinary phenomenon that both thinkers, independently of each other, *experienced*: the love of God or fate. I shall begin by centering on two questions: (1) What is it that is loved, and (2) What kind of "love" is involved here? A discussion of (1) will point up some fundamental similarities, perhaps identities, between Spinoza and Nietzsche.

Spinoza's God and Nietzsche's fate have at least the following qualities in common: neither is a personal creator-God, neither has anything to do with teleological purposes (and thus the world utterly lacks these), and both are strictly necessary and could not be otherwise in any way. Both thinkers stress the "immanence" of God or fate, and both could be called "pantheistic" in a qualified sense.

Of course, Spinoza's concept of God is more developed than is Nietzsche's concept of fate because God is the very core and foundation of Spinoza's thought. Novalis had called him a "man drunk with God" ("ein gottbetrunkener Mensch"). In contrast, what Nietzsche means by fate is intertwined with his basic ideas and is scarcely coherent or meaningful without them. In other words, God is the all-encompassing reality for Spinoza, whereas what Nietzsche says about fate is by itself not sufficient to delineate the originality of what he had in mind.

1. What it is that is loved—Spinoza

Having briefly stated what the two thinkers have in common—which will be the substance of this paper—let us examine some of the unique features of Spinoza's God. Spinoza begins his *Ethics* by defining *causa sui*, the cause of itself whose essence involves existence,

God; but this does not tell us what is unique about Spinoza's conception because it is the traditional definition going back to medieval times, with its ultimate roots in Greece. How to think a cause of itself concretely is problematic anyhow. It seems to be primarily a way of asserting the absolute independence of God; no one else caused Him.

Negatively speaking, God is not a person, and He does not create the world. The world follows from God with an immediate necessity which Spinoza describes in geometrical terms. Because we are concerned with the *naturans* and not the *naturata* right now, with God and not with the world, we shall focus on what it means to say that God is not a person. For Spinoza, man is not created in the image of God, rather it is man who in his ignorance tries to "create" God in the image of man. Intellect and will in God are entirely different from human intellect and will in both essence and existence, so much so that all they have in common is the mere name.[1] Most importantly, God's intellect is spontaneous, not receptive, to use Kantian terms. What He thinks, He thereby creates. In God, intellect, will, and power are one and the same thing, and God's very essence is power.[2] If we can conceive of God as power and spontaneous intellect together, we approach the nonanthropomorphic and non*anthropological* dimension of Spinoza's God. He is absolutely necessary and cannot possibly be other than He is. Necessity and freedom coincide; to be free is to be self-determined from the necessity of one's being. This is what is distinctive about Spinoza's conception. The rest of what he says coincides more or less with traditional ideas.

2. What kind of love

What kind of relation does man bring to this God whose intellect and will are so different from his that they have nothing in common but the name? Spinoza defines love as joy accompanied by the idea of an external cause.[3] Joy he defines as a man's passage from a lesser to a greater perfection,[4] stressing that joy is not perfection itself since that would not involve emotion. Joy is, so to speak, on the way to perfection. Emotions always move in a certain direction; they take us somewhere.

1. Baruch Spinoza, *Ethics*, I, prop. XVII.
2. Ibid., prop. XXXIV.
3. Ibid., III, prop. XIII.
4. Ibid., def. 11.

But what does Spinoza mean by perfection? He states that the most common way of speaking about perfection and imperfection is analogous to the way men talk about good and evil. They have an ideal standard in mind, say of a house, and according to how something does or does not measure up to this standard it is judged perfect or imperfect, good or evil. These are merely human ways of thinking and feeling; essentially they say nothing about the actual nature of what is being judged. Furthermore, such judgments make sense for Spinoza only in relation to man-made objects, objects of *techne*; they are totally inapplicable and inappropriate to things of nature, which just are as they are and cannot be otherwise.

Spinoza's own use of the word "perfection" (*perficere*) is closer to the nonjudgmental quality of being accomplished, completed, in this sense per-fected.[5] In keeping with his constant and vigorous rejection of final causes, Spinoza states that things are not put in the world by God in order to attain some end that they (and He) lack, but rather they endeavor to persist in and increase their being, coming as close to perfectedness as possible. But perfection and reality are the same things.[6] Reality, however, is God or nature or substance. Thus, man's relation to God is that of love, of increasing his being and thus becoming like nature: more free, more independent, more powerful because the very essence of God is his power.[7]

This love is intellectual. What does Spinoza mean by this? What kind of love can man have for God, particularly for Spinoza's God? The common image of the love of the child for the father seems totally out of place here. The Greeks had three words for love: *eros*, the love of the lower for the higher, closest to "erotic" love; *philia*, the love between equals, closest to friendship; and *agape*, the love of the higher for the lower, closest to selfless love, or even compassion. None of these seems to help us understand what Spinoza is talking about.

Let us try to throw some light on what Spinoza meant by *intellectual* love. Intellectual love arises from the third and highest kind of knowledge, which is intuition or immediate insight: "From the third kind of knowledge necessarily springs the intellectual love of God. For from this kind of knowledge arises joy attended with the idea of God as its cause, that is to say, the love of God, not insofar as we

---

5. The last line of Sophocles' *Oedipus at Colonos*, usually rendered "For all this is determined," could also be read "For all this is perfected."
6. *Ethics*, II, def. 6; IV, preface.
7. Ibid., I, prop. XXXIV.

imagine him as present, but insofar as we understand that he is eternal; and that is what I call the intellectual love of God."[8]

This love of God is identical with understanding his true nature; it does not represent him as some present thing, but understands him, has a direct insight into him, in his eternity which has nothing to do with duration, time, or space. Understanding God in his eternity becomes love for God when man grasps his identity with substance and realizes that he is one of its modes. "The intellectual love of the mind toward God is the very love with which he loves himself."[9]

Let this rather schematic presentation suffice for now, and let us turn to Nietzsche.

3. What it is that is loved—Nietzsche

Nietzsche repeatedly speaks of *amor fati* as his innermost nature.[10] To begin with, it might be helpful to look at his distinction between "Turkish" and "Russian" fatalism. We should note that he makes no consistent demarcation between the terms "fate" and "fatalism" (and, in one passage, even "determinism"); they are interchangeable in his usage.

> Turkish fatalism. Turkish fatalism contains the fundamental error of placing man and fate opposite each other like two separate things: Man, it says, can strive against fate, can try to defeat it, but in the end it always remains the winner, for which reason the smartest thing to do is to give up or live just any way at all. The truth is that every man himself is a piece of fate; when he thinks he is striving against fate in the way described, fate is being realized here, too; the struggle is imaginary, but so is resignation to fate; all these imaginary ideas are included in fate. The fear that most people have of the doctrine of determinism of the will is precisely the fear of this Turkish fatalism. They think man will give up weakly and stand before the future with folded hands because he cannot change anything about it; or else he will give free rein to his total caprice because even this cannot make what is once determined still worse. The follies of man are just as much a part of

---

8. Ibid., V, prop. XXXII, corollary (trans. William Hale White, rev. Amelia Hutchinson Sterling, 4th ed., rev. and corr. [London: H. Frouder, 1910]).
9. Ibid., prop. XXXVI.
10. See *Nietzsche contra Wagner*, Epilogue; *Ecce Homo*, "Why I Write Such Good Books": The Case of Wagner, sec. 4.

fate as his cleverness: this fear of the belief in fate is also fate. You yourself, poor frightened man, are the invincible Moira reigning far above the gods; for everything that comes, you are blessing or curse and in any case the bonds in which the strongest man lies. In you the whole future of the human world is predetermined; it will not help you if you are terrified of yourself.[11]

That "Russian fatalism" of which I spoke manifested itself to me in such a way that for years I clung tenaciously to almost unbearable conditions, places, habitations, and companions, once chance had placed them in my way—it was better than changing them, than *feeling* that they could be changed, than revolting against them. . . . He who disturbed this fatalism, who tried by force to awaken me, seemed to me then a mortal enemy—in fact, there was danger of death each time this was done. To take one's self as a destiny, not to wish one's self "different"—this, in such circumstances, is the very highest wisdom.[12]

Turkish fatalism conceives of man and fate as separate. Fate is something to which man is subjugated and against which he is powerless. This form of fatalism Nietzsche connects with traditional religion, with the demand for obedience to a power external to oneself.

To consider: to what extent the fateful belief in divine providence—the most paralyzing belief for hand and reason there has ever been—still exists; to what extent Christian presuppositions and interpretations still live on under the formulas "nature," "progress," "perfectibility," "Darwinism." . . . Even fatalism, the form philosophical sensibility assumes with us today, is a consequence of this long belief in divine dispensation, an unconscious consequence; as if what happens were no responsibility of ours.[13]

Thus, the brand of fatalism that Nietzsche calls Turkish fatalism is basically an instance of man robbed of his autonomy and his freedom by a religion imposing a moral order on him from without. Let us now make the linguistic distinction that Nietzsche did not make, and call this Turkish fatalism "fatalism" as opposed to what he describes under the term Russian fatalism, which we shall henceforth call "fate." Fate is his own positive concept; fatalism is his polemical target. He loved fate, not fatalism.

11. S, sec. 61 (author's translation).
12. *Ecce Homo*, "Why I Am So Wise," sec. 6 (trans. Fadiman).
13. WM, sec. 243 (trans. Kaufmann).

To sum up, by fatalism we understand the traditional popular view of determinism, that man is completely determined by outside forces or, more importantly for Nietzsche, by an outside Force, God, and His moral decrees of good and evil. In the face of this, man can do either of two things: he can give up and cease to will or do anything, or he can devote himself to total caprice and arbitrariness, just aimlessly doing anything at all for the sake of doing something. Both of these options are fundamentally nihilistic. In contrast to this, Nietzsche's own conception of fate, expressed as Russian fatalism, lies in understanding oneself as fate.

What does it mean to understand oneself as fate? Apart from some abstract consideration of fate as a decree of God, as some sort of predestination, or as a kind of world order (*moira*), what Nietzsche really emphasizes most about fate is that things cannot be in any other way than they are. It is in this that he and Spinoza are in complete and astonishing agreement. But in keeping with his more personal and poetic style, Nietzsche stresses the relation of the individual to fate. Because fate is not bound up with the Judaeo-Christian idea of God, the question arises as to the "source" of fate, of who or what planned it—if indeed that is the case—and whether the individual is then free or determined. This latter question had become absolutely central in the nineteenth century, especially with Schelling. If you understand human freedom and its role in the scheme of things, you also understand the Absolute, nature, and essentially everything else. The question of freedom or determinism of the individual brings us to the second aspect of our inquiry, to the question of what kind of love is at stake here. But first we need to say something more about the source of fate and about what exactly fate is. The two questions actually blend into each other in Nietzsche's case: our two initial aspects, what it is that is loved and what kind of love, collapse into one.

As we have said, one of the main traditional sources of fate would be a decree of God. This is obviously ruled out for Nietzsche. The alternatives would seem to be some theory of heredity or environment or, most likely, some inscrutable combination of both; or else some dimension of the individual that escapes sociopsychological analysis. The trouble with sociopsychological analyses is that they inevitably lack precision and reliability; there are too many "exceptions." For example, identical twins can grow up in the same environment and turn out to be quite different from each other. Heredity and environment are indisputably influences on everyone, but "influence" is too vague and inconclusive to deserve the name of fate.

So we are left with the question of a nonsociopsychological dimension of the individual. If fate is not to be understood as an external decree or power, then it must be grasped philosophically, not just genetically or environmentally, as something within the individual that molds him. "The highest state a philosopher can attain: to stand in a Dionysian relationship to existence—my formula for this is *amor fati*."[14]

The philosopher strives for a Dionysian relation to existence as his highest state. What is a Dionysian relation? It is a way of being or living, perhaps best to be conceived in the Kierkegaardian fashion where what matters is not the "what" but the "how." Kierkegaard says something to the effect that it is better to be an authentic pagan than an inauthentic Christian. Dionysus, the wine-god, the god of intoxication, is the god of destruction and creation, of death and birth, of rebirth. To live in a Dionysian relation to existence means to live the creation and destruction that lie at the very heart and core of existence. The opposite of the Dionysian relation would be the Platonic quest for unchanging being that Nietzsche so vehemently rejects. Plato sought the eternal *eidos* or Form that has nothing to do with change and is inaccessible to the senses; Nietzsche absolutely denies the possibility of any static persistence and seeks "eternity" in becoming itself, in change, in creation and destruction, in eternal recurrence.

To live in a Dionysian relation to existence means to affirm the elements of creation and destruction as inherent in eternal recurrence. Nietzsche, as perhaps no one before him, discovered and expressed the paradox that one can create nothing new unless one affirms what is already there. And this "already-there-ness," this givenness, is what he means by fate.

The passage in *Zarathustra* entitled "On Redemption" contains the pithiest presentation of Nietzsche's thoughts on the will's attitude of revenge. We do not want to go too deeply into that here, but only to state that revenge is one of several of man's extremely negative and crippling attitudes or feelings. Pity, envy, *ressentiment*, and hate would be other examples. Revenge is the will's antiwill against time and the "it was" or the past. Time is irreversible. What once happened I cannot undo or change; what once was, I cannot get back or regain. The past slips away from me off into some inaccessible "region" where I can neither get at it in order to change it nor possess

---

14. Ibid., sec. 1041 (trans. Kaufmann).

it again. And from this "region" it intractably exerts its influence on my present situation; it affects me, but I am powerless to affect or change or regain it. It is out of my reach, forever; and yet it affects me.

Zarathustra states that the will must learn reconciliation with time, and something higher than reconciliation. The "it was" is a fragment, an enigma, and dreadful chance until the creative will says to it: "I willed it thus!" Having said that, the will can then say: "I will it thus! I shall will it thus!" Only when the will can affirm the past *as it is* is the will capable of willing creatively, not reactively, in the present moment and capable of freely willing the future: "Has the will yet become his own redeemer and joy-bringer? Has he unlearned the spirit of revenge and all gnashing of teeth? And who taught him reconciliation with time and something higher than any reconciliation? For that will which is the will to power must will something higher than any reconciliation; but how shall this be brought about? Who could teach him also to will backwards?"[15]

After these words Zarathustra falls fiercely silent, badly shaken. He is thinking thoughts that he apparently decides not to utter. Reconciliation with time occurs as willing back. This could mean either of two things: (1) to will backwards in time, so to speak, turning time around, reversing it, or (2) to will things and events back, to will them to come again, to return. Both of these ideas are unusual, to say the least, and might strike us as impossible. No one that we know of has ever succeeded in reversing the direction of time in the sense of literally willing *backwards*. This first alternative is so obscure that we are not even certain what it would *mean*, to will backwards. But it is fairly certain that the general import is to change what has already occurred, to reverse time.

The second alternative at least makes more sense, even if it seems implausible. To will back things and events of my life means to will them *again*. This is Nietzsche's repeated question: Can I will that everything come again, can I will to live my life again and again exactly *as it is*? If I can say yes to this question, then I have a Dionysian relation to life. Strictly speaking, this does not reverse time, which continues to occur in a "forward" direction; however, nothing gets lost, it all comes back again. "My formula for greatness in man is *amor fati*: that one wants nothing different, neither forwards nor backwards nor for all eternity. Not just to bear what is necessary, still

---

15. Z, II, "On Redemption" (trans. Kaufmann).

less conceal it—all idealism is falsehood in the face of necessity—but *love* it."[16]

4. What kind of love

The above passage may serve to introduce the last section of our study, the question of what kind of love is at stake here. As we remarked earlier, the kind of love has really ceased to be a separate issue since the question of what it is that is loved now completely defines the kind of love involved. One has a certain kind of love for a child, for a parent, for a man or woman, for an animal, for a piece of music, for a painting, for a landscape. They are all different feelings, which get lumped together under the well-worn blanket term, "love." But in each case the type of love is attuned to its "object," to what is loved. Thus, if the soul loves fate, the kind of love must be appropriate to fate, must be fate-ful—in other words, the soul itself becomes fate. This is a bold statement which we must consider very carefully. Let us look at a passage from *Zarathustra* entitled "On the Great Longing":

> O my soul, I taught you to persuade so well that you persuade the very ground—like the sun who persuades even the sea to his own height.
>
> O my soul, I took from you all obeying, knee-bending, and "Lord"-saying; I myself gave you the name "cessation of need" and "destiny."
>
> O my soul, I gave you new names and colorful toys; I called you "destiny" and "circumference of circumferences" and "umbilical cord of time" and "azure bell."[17]

This passage dramatically expresses why we are no longer dealing with two separate questions: fate is a name for the soul. The soul is placed in a cosmic dimension in that it is compared to the sun, just as Zarathustra often speaks with the sun and, like it, periodically goes under. This means that the soul is not to be understood in a personal or psychological way, but as part of the cosmos, indeed as a very important part. Playing on the word for necessity, *Not-wendigkeit*, Nietzsche gives it the very concrete meaning of "turning the

---

16. *Ecce Homo*, "Why I Am So Clever," sec. 10 (author's translation).
17. Z, III, "On the Great Longing" (trans. Kaufmann).

need" and couples it with fate. The soul is fate and necessity, fate and turning the need. Of the other, more poetic, names for the soul, the phrase "azure bell" occurs earlier in the section "Before Sunrise," when Zarathustra speaks cosmically, this time with the heavens. He begins,

> Together we have learned everything; together we have learned to ascend over ourselves to ourselves and to smile cloudlessly—to smile down cloudlessly from bright eyes and from a vast distance when constraint and contrivance and guilt steam beneath us like rain.
>
> And when I wandered alone, for *whom* did my soul hunger at night, on false paths? And when I climbed mountains, *whom* did I always seek on the mountains, if not you? And all my wandering and mountain climbing were sheer necessity and a help in my helplessness; what I want with all my will is to *fly*, to fly up into you . . .[18]

and continues with the azure bell functioning almost as a leitmotiv,

> But I am one who can bless and say Yes, if only you are about me, pure and light, you abyss of light; then I carry the blessings of my Yes into all abysses. I have become one who blesses and says Yes; and I fought long for that and was a fighter that I might one day get my hands free to bless. But this is my blessing: to stand over every single thing as its own heaven, as its round roof, its azure bell, and eternal security; and blessed is he who blesses thus. For all things have been baptized in the well of eternity and are beyond good and evil. . . .
>
> This freedom and heavenly cheer I have placed over all things like an azure bell when I taught that over them and through them no "eternal will" wills.[19]

Here, Zarathustra speaks of himself as of a heaven, a rounded, rooflike, azure bell that eternally protects and shelters everything in a joyful, eternal blessing. This poetic "imagery" for the soul is about as far removed from the Cartesian *res cogitans* as possible; the soul is not a separate substantial thinking thing, but rather a sheltering protection that grants eternal and blissful safety to all things. The sheltering heaven is not oppressive and opaque, but free and luminous,

---

18. Ibid., "Before Sunrise" (trans. Kaufmann).
19. Ibid. (trans. Kaufmann).

transparent light. The pure, deep heaven is an abyss of light. As so often in *Zarathustra*, the imagery here is paradoxical. The heaven above is an abyss; to throw himself into its height is Zarathustra's depth; it speaks mutely to him. In another passage he says: Listen! for I want to hear you. The ordinary ways of thinking about things collapse here, and we are forced to experience them in a new way.

Finally, we need to look at the section in *Zarathustra* entitled "At Noon," where Zarathustra falls into a unique kind of sleep while his soul remains awake. He speaks of and speaks to his strange, wonder-full soul, comparing it to a ship that has finally come into a still harbor. It is midday, and all is still; the world is perfect. Zarathustra muses about happiness, about how little is needed for happiness, and then corrects himself: more radically, precisely the very least makes up the best kind of happiness.

> Precisely the least, the softest, lightest, a lizard's rustling, a breath, a breeze, a moment's glance—it is *little* that makes the *best* happiness. Still!
>
> What happened to me? Listen! Did time perhaps fly away? Do I not fall? Did I not fall—listen!—into the well of eternity? What is happening to me? Still! I have been stung, alas—in the heart? In the heart! Oh break, break, heart after such happiness, after such a sting. How? Did not the world become perfect just now? Round and ripe? Oh, the golden round ring—where may it fly? Shall I run after it? Quick! Still![20]

The best happiness is experienced in a moment (*Augenblick*) that is so much the very least that it has nothing to do with time or duration at all. Zarathustra asks, What happened to me? What is happening to me? Am I not falling, did I not fall into the well of eternity? There is no distinction between past and present. This whole experience of noon is timeless, for when it was all over the sun stood in exactly the same place as when it started. It is clear that Zarathustra had some sort of experience of eternity. We cannot and need not go into the meaning of eternity here; what concerns us is the effect of that experience on his soul:

> "Who are you? O my soul!" (At this point he was startled, for a sunbeam fell from the sky onto his face.) "O heaven over me!" he said, sighing, and sat up. "You are looking on? You are listening for my strange soul? When will you drink this drop of dew which

---

20. Z, IV, "At Noon" (trans. Kaufmann).

has fallen upon all earthly things? When will you drink this strange soul? When, well of eternity? Cheerful, dreadful abyss of noon! When will you drink my soul back into yourself?"[21]

Suddenly, Zarathustra becomes aware that his soul is strange; what we all take for granted as being the most familiar thing in the world, our souls, our selves, suddenly becomes totally unfamiliar, unknown. Who are you? Zarathustra asks his soul, and then asks the heaven, the well of eternity, when it will drink his soul back into itself.

To sum up the question of what kind of love is involved here: strictly speaking, it is less a matter of love than it is of a kind of identity. The soul not only loves fate; the soul *is* fate. Here the "is" is used in a transitive sense to mean the soul is, exists fate in much the same way that Sartre said, "I exist my body." Thus, to say the soul is fate is not tantamount to saying flatly soul equals fate, soul is the same thing as fate; but soul lives out fate, soul is the living occurrence of fate. This identity also characterized what Spinoza was talking about when he said that "The intellectual love of the mind toward God is the very love with which He loves Himself."[22]

By way of conclusion, we shall attempt once more to clarify what Nietzsche meant by fate. First of all, he did not mean what most people mean by that word: he did not mean some kind of predestination. In this sense he is closer to the Greek idea of fate (*moira*), to the Greeks for whom the gods themselves were subject to fate, rather than to the Judaeo-Christian idea. We shall gain a last insight if we take a look at the world-view that both Nietzsche and Spinoza rejected, at teleology. God and fate are, so to speak, the opposite or the negation of teleology, to use the *via negativa*.

If I have a purpose or goal or *telos*, it is something that I lack now and must strive after. This was Spinoza's objection to the purposeful "will of God," that His goals should be lacking to Him. Rather, Spinoza says, everything is already there and cannot possibly be otherwise. It must be just as it is. Nietzsche reached this insight when he realized that not only can we affirm the world process if we remove the idea of purpose from it; removing the idea of purpose first enables us to affirm the world process *as it is*, not as it ought to be. To consider the world process as it ought to be lands us back in the realm of good and evil, of Platonic backworlds, a world behind this

21. Ibid. (trans. Kaufmann).
22. *Ethics*, V, prop. XXXVI.

world judging our world to be imperfect and without value. Nietzsche strives for the innocence of becoming, becoming affirmed as it is with no reference to anything outside it. The innocence of becoming names the "world" aspect of fate, just as the soul names the "self" aspect.

> Question: does morality make impossible this pantheistic affirmation of all things, too? At bottom, it is only the moral god that has been overcome. Does it make sense to conceive a god "beyond good and evil"? Would a pantheism in this sense be possible? Can we remove the idea of a goal from the process and then affirm the process in spite of this—This would be the case if something were attained at every moment within this process—and always the same. Spinoza reached such an affirmative position insofar as every moment has a logical necessity, and with his basic instinct, which was logical, he felt a sense of triumph that the world should be constituted that way.[23]

If something is attained in every moment of the world process, no moment ever exists for the sake of another; each moment has its own necessity. In conclusion, we can say that both Spinoza and Nietzsche experienced fate as inner necessity, not as predestination or some kind of compulsion from without. To find and follow your inner necessity is to find freedom. The freedom of a painter is to find the inner necessity of his painting, to get it just right, neither too much nor too little, to get it the way it has to be. One could say the same thing for many activities in the arts, in acting, in writing, even in sports. Spinoza defined that thing as free which exists from the necessity of its own nature alone. And Nietzsche echoed this thought when he wrote, "The unconditioned necessity of all occurrence has no compulsion about it; he stands high in knowledge who has thoroughly realized and felt this,"[24] and "*Fatum* is an elevating thought for him who comprehends that he belongs to it."[25]

23. WM, sec. 55 (trans. Kaufmann).
24. GOA, XIII, 63.
25. GOA, XIV, 99.

VIII. Nietzsche and Luther: A Testimony to Germanophilia

Max L. Baeumer

A few years ago, students at the University of Wisconsin in Madison were allowed to inscribe their criticism and concern on a temporary wooden fence surrounding a building-site on the campus.* One of the graffiti read: "Nitsche says: God is dead." The spelling of the name was wrong, but the quotation was right and apparently still prevails among our young people.

What gives the statement "God is dead" its pungent quality is the fact that it is the message of a descendant of a line of Lutheran clergymen and theologians reaching back into the seventeenth century. Friedrich Nietzsche, who, in his relentless critique of Western civilization, rejects and attacks Christianity and teaches superman as the highest type of humanity without God and religion, was the son of a Lutheran pastor, a devout Lutheran who started his academic career as a student of Lutheran theology at the university in Bonn in 1864. Fourteen years later, he became the archenemy of religion, Christianity, and Lutheranism, to use his own words, "in thunders and lightnings against everything that is Christian or infected with Christianity."[1]

Everything that is Christian, whether good or bad, is personified for Nietzsche in Martin Luther. In *The Birth of Tragedy* (1872), Nietzsche praises Luther as the "deep, courageous, and spiritual" reformer, one "of our sublime protagonists," "of our great artists and poets" (sec. 23).[2] In Luther's Reformation, he sees the youthful "im-

---

*This is the text of a lecture given at Wake Forest University in April 1981. Therefore, its style is that of an oral discourse, and introductory remarks may seem elementary to the Nietzsche scholar. But on the advice of the editors, I have decided to print it in the form in which it was delivered.

1. Georg Brandes, *Friedrich Nietzsche*, trans. A. G. Chater (London: Macmillan, 1909), p. 94.

2. W, I, 128. Except where further specification is necessary, I shall refer, for the sake of convenience, to sections that are preserved in all of the various editions of Nietzsche's works. For English versions of Nietzsche's texts I am indebted to the translations by Walter Kaufmann, published by Random House, New York, and to the less

pulse of the free spirit" (in 1878: MA, I, sec. 26). But nine years later, Nietzsche proclaims: "Luther's Reformation [is the] coarsest form of moral mendaciousness under the guise of 'evangelical freedom' in which the slandered instincts try to create a right for themselves" (WM, III, sec. 786). Luther, whom Nietzsche in 1872 praises as the healthy-minded son of an ore miner (W, I, 261), is fifteen years later only a pathological fanatic, "the reverse type of the strong spirit that has become free" (A, sec. 54), a "monk, with all the vindictive instincts of an abortive priest in his body" (sec. 61).

Nietzsche's brilliant language can be harsh to the ear, crude in expression and provocative and aggressive in style, especially when he attacks bourgeois morals and Christianity. He arouses not only the young and discontented, but also the scholar and academic. The theme "Nietzsche and Christianity" has been treated in more than 140 publications since Nietzsche's death in 1900. More has been written on this subject than on "Nietzsche and Superman" or "Nietzsche and Richard Wagner." The topic "Nietzsche and Luther" has been discussed from various viewpoints in more than twenty scholarly investigations.[3] The greater number of these publications deal with our topic less critically, either from a German nationalist point of view[4] or under the catchy headline "Luther-Nietzsche-Hitler."[5] Theological discussions mainly emphasize partial aspects of the religious controversy "Luther-Nietzsche."[6] The most important literary

---

reliable translations of the edition of *The Complete Works of Friedrich Nietzsche*, ed. Oscar Levy (1909–13; reprint, New York: Russell and Russell, 1964). However, I have felt free to modify existing translations deviating too much from the original German.

3. Cf. *International Nietzsche Bibliography*, revised and expanded, comp. and ed. Herbert W. Reichert and Karl Schlechta, University of North Carolina Studies in Comparative Literature, no. 45 (Chapel Hill: University of North Carolina Press, 1968), and *Nietzsche Studien* (Berlin/New York: de Gruyter, 1972–).

4. For instance Jules Paquier, *Le protestantisme allemand, Luther-Kant-Nietzsche*, 10th ed. (Paris: Bloud et Gay, 1915); Jean-Edouard Spenlé, *La pensée allemande de Luther à Nietzsche* (Paris: A. Colin, 1924, 1935, 5th ed. 1955; German ed.: *Der deutsche Geist von Luther bis Nietzsche* [Meisenheim: A. Hain, 1949]); Bernhard Schulz, "Die Sprache als Kampfmittel. Zur Sprachform von Kampfschriften Luthers, Lessings und Nietzsches," *Deutsche Vierteljahresschrift für Literaturwissenschaft und Geistesgeschichte*, 18 (1940), 431–66.

5. Gerhard Hultsch, *Friedrich Nietzsche und Luther*, Diss. Breslau 1940, Schriftenreihe der Luthergesellschaft, Heft 13, (Gütersloh: C. Bertelsmann, 1940). William M. McGovern, *From Luther to Hitler: The History of Fascist-Nazi Political Philosophy* (1st ed. by M. Sait, Cambridge, Mass.: Harvard University Press, 1941; reprint, Boston: Houghton, Mifflin, and New York: AMS Press, 1973). J. de Courberive, *Génies dévoyés, Luther-Nietzsche-Hitler* (Avignon: E. Aubanel, 1953).

6. Arvid Runestam, "Nietzsches Übermensch und Luthers freier Christenmensch," *Zeitschrift für systematische Theologie*, 1 (1924), 520–32. Fritz Buri, *Kreuz und Ring. Die*

and historical investigations of Nietzsche's ideas and views of Martin Luther are Emanuel Hirsch's study "Nietzsche und Luther" of 1921; a series of four articles on Nietzsche, Luther, and the Reformation, by Heinz Bluhm, in *The Publications of the Modern Language Association of America* between 1943 and 1956; and the book by Ernst Benz, *Nietzsches Ideen zur Geschichte des Christentums und der Kirche* (Nietzsche's Ideas on the History of Christianity and the Church) of 1956.[7]

These scholars concentrated on two main questions: How can Nietzsche's radical change from an ardent admirer to a deadly enemy of Martin Luther be explained? Secondly, what ideas and which writers influenced Nietzsche to launch the most violent attack on Christianity and Luther in modern times? Emanuel Hirsch (p. 67) believes that Nietzsche's turn to hatred and contempt toward Luther was "nothing but the echo from the infamous *History of the German People* written by the Catholic priest Johannes Janssen" in 1879, of which Nietzsche remarked in a letter of 5 October 1879 to his friend Peter Gast that after having read this book, he was no longer capable of saying honestly anything good about Luther. But Heinz Bluhm ([2], pp. 1053–68) proved in 1950 on the basis of newly available records that the sharp turn in Nietzsche's attitude toward Luther and the Reformation occurred well before the appearance of Janssen's book and differs greatly from Janssen's, Heinrich Denifle's, and Hartmann Grisar's Roman Catholic criticism of Luther.

According to Bluhm's thorough investigation, Nietzsche changed his view on Luther radically between 1876 and 1878 with the appearance of *Human, All-Too-Human*. His praise of Martin Luther expresses nothing but the general and superficial opinion held by most Protestants of the time, while in his attack, Nietzsche evaluates Luther increasingly against the background of his own *Weltanschauung*.[8] Ernst Benz (pp. 10–13) infers that Nietzsche basically blames Luther

---

Kreuzestheologie des jungen Luther und die Lehre von der ewigen Wiederkunft in Nietzsches "Zarathustra" (Bern: P. Haupt, 1941).

7. Emanuel Hirsch, "Nietzsche und Luther," *Jahrbuch der Luther-Gesellschaft*, 2/3 (Leipzig, 1921/22), 61–106 (also in: Emanuel Hirsch, *Lutherstudien II* [Gütersloh: C. Bertelsmann, 1954], pp. 168–206). Heinz Bluhm, "Das Lutherbild des jungen Nietzsche," *PMLA*, 58 (1943), 264–88 (hereafter cited as Bluhm [1]); "Nietzsche's Idea of Luther in *Menschliches, Allzumenschliches*," *PMLA*, 65 (1950), 1053–68 (hereafter cited as Bluhm [2]); "Nietzsche's View of Luther and the Reformation in *Morgenröte* and *Fröhliche Wissenschaft*, *PMLA*, 68 (1953), 111–27 (Bluhm [3]); "Nietzsche's Final View of Luther and the Reformation," *PMLA*, 71 (1956), 75–83 (Bluhm [4]). Ernst Benz, *Nietzsches Ideen zur Geschichte des Christentums und der Kirche*, Beihefte der Zeitschrift für Religions- und Geistesgeschichte, 3 (Leiden: Brill, 1956). In the following text these three commentators are quoted by page numbers.

8. Bluhm (4), p. 83.

for preventing, through his Reformation, the victory of the strong, healthy, and pagan Renaissance over the weak and backward Christianity in Germany and all of Europe. These are the general conclusions of previous research on Nietzsche and Luther.

However, we want to base our investigation on Nietzsche's own statements about Luther and consider his assertions in their historical context, a task that hitherto has been neglected. The first of a few meager autobiographical remarks of the fifteen-year-old Gymnasium student, on the occasion of a visit to places associated with Luther in Jena and Eisleben, is already typical of Nietzsche's attitude toward Luther: "It gave me much pleasure to visit the greatest leaders of our nation: Luther, Goethe, Schiller, Klopstock, Winckelmann, and many others" (W, III, 41–42). Fourteen years later, in his preliminary notes to the second part of his *Untimely Meditations*, Nietzsche writes in the same vein: "When we speak of the German spirit ["vom deutschen Geiste"], we mean Luther, Goethe, Schiller, and some others" (GOA [2], X, 278). In spite of being destined by his pious family and by himself to become a Lutheran pastor, young Nietzsche prefers to see the founder of his Church only in connection with the greatest and rather worldly and un-Christian German writers. Secondly, he values Luther not as the reformer but as a leader of the German nation.

From his earliest years, Nietzsche saw the Prussian State (or later the German Empire) and the Lutheran Church as the two institutions that determined the national life and glory of Germany. He was proud to share his birthday, the fifteenth of October, with the reigning king of his Prussian fatherland and he found it "appropriate," as he says, to have received "in holy baptism" the king's name "Friedrich Wilhelm" (W, III, 13, 90, 93). During the victorious war against Austria in 1866, he called himself an "enraged Prussian" (ibid., p. 1360). Just as he was taken by the festive "German music" of Richard Wagner, he enjoyed the *Nationalfest* of Schiller's One Hundreth Anniversary in 1859 as "a significant omen for the reawakened German national consciousness" (ibid., pp. 75–77).

In 1864, as a student in Bonn, he complained bitterly that "our Reformation festival is ignored by the university" (HKG, *Briefe*, I, 313). Three years later, in 1867/68 when Nietzsche joined the Prussian army, the combined 350th anniversary of the Reformation and dedication of the Luther Monument in Worms marked the climax of the many national festivals of that time. All the Lutheran princes of Germany were present when the colossal monument by Ernst Rietschel, the creator of the magnificent Goethe and Schiller statues in

Weimar, was unveiled with the words: "German folk, the highest crown bestowed by you rightfully belongs to this glorious miner's son."[9] As far as I know, Nietzsche did not mention this Luther festival, but thenceforth he adopted the famous epithet "the miner's son" for his own association of Luther with German nationalism. In the fifth of his lectures "On the Future of Our Educational Institutions" (1872), Nietzsche characterizes the patriotic spirit of the Deutsche Burschenschaft (the nationalist German Student Association, founded in 1813 during the Wars of Liberation from the yoke of Napoleon) with the words: "That earnest, manly, stern, and daring German spirit; that spirit of the miner's son, Luther, which has come down to us, healthy and unbroken from the time of the Reformation" (W, III, 261).

Nietzsche's nationalistic view of Luther becomes even clearer when we consider my abbreviated introductory quotation from his earliest work—*The Birth of Tragedy*—in its wider context. Here in section 23, Luther is called "our sublime protagonist" as the model and leader for "a restoration of all things German." Talking about the desperately hopeless situation "von unserem deutschen Wesen," of "our German substance and character," in modern civilization, Nietzsche implores his German readers:

> All our hopes stretch out longingly towards the perception that beneath this restlessly palpitating civilized life and educational convulsion there is concealed a glorious, intrinsically healthy, primeval power, which, to be sure, stirs vigorously only at intervals in stupendous moments, and then continues to dream of future awakening. It is from this abyss that the German Reformation came forth: in the choral-hymn of which the future melody of German music first resounded . . . , this chorale of Luther . . . , the first Dionysian luring call breaking forth from dense thickets at the approach of spring. To it responded with emulative echo the solemnly wanton procession of Dionysian revelers, to whom we are indebted for German music—and to whom we shall be indebted for the *rebirth of the German myth*.

What Nietzsche proclaims here in 1871 is a national rebirth of Germany out of a unification of Dionysian blissful ecstasy, as revealed in the music and choruses of Richard Wagner, with the youthful and glorious Reformation, as it burst forth from Luther's chorale. Nietz-

---

9. Cf. Max L. Baeumer, "Lutherfeiern und ihre politische Manipulation," *Deutsche Feiern*, ed. Reinhold Grimm and Jost Hermand (Wiesbaden: Athenaion, 1977), p. 53.

sche continues: To reach this goal we must, first of all, "hold fast to our shining leaders, the Greeks," from whom we "borrowed the two divine forms" of aesthetic knowledge, the Dionysian and the Apollonian. Then, to eliminate the foreign Romanic element from "the pure and vigorous kernel of the German character," "the German spirit . . . must begin its struggle" and be encouraged by "the victorious bravery and bloody glory of the late war." This is the Franco-German War of 1870/71, which ended with the proclamation of a German Kaiser and in which Nietzsche participated as a volunteer medical orderly for three weeks until he became sick with infectious diarrhea. In this struggle, Nietzsche says, the German spirit must "be eternally worthy of our sublime protagonists on this path, of Luther as well as of our great artists and poets. . . . And if the German should be looking around timidly for a 'Führer,' a leader, to guide him back to his long-lost homeland . . . , let him but listen to the ecstatic luring call of the Dionysian bird, which hovers above him and will show him the way." Again, Luther is supposed to be the leader and luring idol for a second, a Dionysian reformation "of all things German." That, in those years from 1871 to 1873, was Nietzsche's strange German-Dionysian perception of Martin Luther. Nietzsche was, in his nationalistic attitude—and as some scholars argue[10]— little influenced by Richard Wagner, who also glorified the "German spirit" of the Reformation and "Luther's magnificent chorale."[11]

If we give due consideration to the close connection and politically motivated affiliation of Lutheranism and German nationalism during the nineteenth and twentieth centuries, if we bear in mind how the state, the Lutheran and Reformed Landeskirchen, cities and towns, schools and universities taught, solemnly declared, and glorified Luther as a national hero, if we can imagine the high national feelings of the Bismarck era, the successful Prussian wars, and the splendid foundation of the so-called Second Reich and new German Empire, then we realize to what a great extent Nietzsche, Wagner, and other contemporaries appear as part of this general national movement and how they are totally immersed in this new national environment of religion and patriotism, of Luther and "all things German." Wagner's Teutonic operas and Nietzsche's *Birth of Tragedy out of the Spirit of Music* (that is, out of the spirit of Wagner's German music) were determined in many respects by the national condition and by nationalistic attitudes of the time, as much as the vehement attacks by

---

10. Cf. Ernst Bertram, *Nietzsche. Versuch einer Mythologie* (1918; 7th ed., Berlin: G. Bondi, 1929), passim. Hirsch, p. 64. Bluhm (1), pp. 276–80.

11. Richard Wagner, *Gesammelte Schriften und Dichtungen* (Berlin: Bong, n.d.), IX, 116 and 95.

Arthur Schopenhauer, Ludwig Feuerbach, David Friedrich Strauß, Bruno Bauer, Paul de Lagarde, Karl Marx, and Nietzsche, a few years later, were directed *against* the same German nationalism, its hero Martin Luther, and the Church that he personifies. Nietzsche himself was fully aware of the dialectic process of his own change from the affirmative view of a Luther of the "German spirit" to a totally negative judgment of a backward Luther of "German barbarians" (FW, III, sec. 149). Referring to his passage about the Dionysian luring call (quoted above), he says in the book "We Fearless Ones," added to his *Joyful Wisdom* in 1887: "I interpreted for myself German music as the expression of a Dionysian power in the German soul: I thought I heard in it the earthquake by means of which a primeval force ['the German Reformation'], that had been imprisoned for ages, was finally finding vent. . . . It is obvious that I then misunderstood what constitutes the veritable character both of philosophical pessimism and of German music—namely, their Romanticism" (sec. 370), which he calls in his Preface an "imprudent spiritual diet and pampering" in opposition to "the frolicking of returning energy, of newly awakened belief in a tomorrow and after-tomorrow."

Nietzsche never repeated his daring, if not incomprehensible, conception of Luther as the Dionysian lurer and leader for a new Reformation of "the German spirit"—"der deutsche Geist." But he does restate in his lectures of 1872, mentioned before, that the healthy spirit of Martin Luther, the miner's son, is a sublime example of the tough and courageous German character and that "the rebirth of real culture must emerge from the true German spirit . . . , which speaks to us so marvelously from the innermost core of the German Reformation, German music, and German philosophy . . . , from which we can expect a victory over that voguish pseudo-culture of the present day."[12]

In Nietzsche's *Untimely Meditations* of 1873 and 1874, it is "Luther's Reformation" and "the German Reformation" to which religion, art, and culture in Germany are indebted for the continuation of their existence and for their liberation from the shackles of governmental power (W, I, 254, 332). In his "Thoughts: Reflections on Philosophy in Distress," written at the same time, Nietzsche sees Luther even as a sociopolitical revolutionary: "If a Luther were to arise today, he would revolt against the loathsome disposition of the capitalist classes, against their stupidity and thoughtlessness."[13] Although this is only a one-time assertion—Luther as a liberator from capitalism—it

---

12. GOA (2), IX, 416, 370, and 350. See also Bluhm (1), pp. 274–75.
13. GOA (2), X, 302. See also Bluhm (1), p. 282.

clearly shows Nietzsche's predominantly political conception of Luther and the Reformation. A few years later, Nietzsche again was to call Luther a revolutionary, but this time in a directly opposite meaning: Luther as the backward leader of the Reformation as a mob rebellion in Germany and Northern Europe. Yet in 1875, Nietzsche still enjoyed the "good and pure air of Protestantism" when he wrote to his friend Erwin Rohde on February 28: "Never before have I felt more strongly my innermost dependency on the spirit of Luther than now." Nietzsche's last positive utterance about Luther, in his fourth *Untimely Meditation*—"Wagner in Bayreuth" (1876)—is in connection with his praise of Wagner's *Meistersinger von Nürnberg, Tristan,* and the *Nibelungen Ring*: these operas demonstrate "the life and substance of all truly great Germans," based on "that exclusively German serenity (*Heiterkeit*) of Luther, Beethoven, and Wagner, which other nations can never comprehend and which the present-day Germans seem to have lost" (W, I, 408–9). The concept of *Heiterkeit*, serenity, has been identical, since Winckelmann's day, with the spirit of classical art and the Greeks. Nietzsche's presumptuous and nationalistic glorification of Luther, Beethoven, and Wagner has its climax in bestowing on them the shining and august quality of serenity, by which German writers have always characterized the greatness of classical Greece.

But why did Nietzsche's view of Luther now change to the negative? It has been widely assumed among scholars and biographers that Nietzsche's break with Wagner resulted also in an adverse position to Luther.[14] This is not the case, as Nietzsche's own "Thoughts of January 1874 about Richard Wagner" demonstrates. Here, he expresses a negative opinion about Wagner for the first time, specifically by comparing him negatively with Luther, whom he still estimates very positively. Wagner is too arrogant, Nietzsche writes, to be a true German or a Martin Luther. He does not possess the straightforwardness and unselfishness that Luther had, and he has the particular ambition to relate himself to the greatest men—Schiller, Goethe, Beethoven, Luther, the Greek tragedians, Shakespeare, and Bismarck.[15] Of course, Nietzsche does the same thing of which he accuses Wagner, comparing Luther and Wagner (and also himself) with the greatest ones of mankind, and above all, with the great Germans. Here Luther even appears in line with Bismarck.

---

14. See Hirsch, p. 64; Bertram, passim; Benz, p. 14. Against this position: Bluhm (1), p. 283.

15. GOA (2), X, 441, 433, and 446. See also Bluhm (1), p. 283.

Nietzsche's turn against Luther four years later can therefore hardly be explained as a consequence of his break with Wagner. He never again mentions Luther and Wagner together. But since Nietzsche so obviously and consistently relates his estimation of Luther not to theology and religion, but to the greatest German personalities, the German scene, and to a rebirth of Germany, I would like to suggest that we continue to direct our attention to Nietzsche's judgment of Germany at the time when he changed his view of Luther so drastically and unexpectedly.

In regard to "the German scene," Nietzsche was not only a spectator from the outside, but since 1873 he had been fleeing Germany and the Swiss-German border town of Basel as often as possible. He felt estranged in the German environment, took sick leaves from the University of Basel after 1876, and lived mostly in Italy and in the south, which he considered his "promised land" (W, III, 1365–70). His nationalistic "Exhortation to the Germans," the *Mahnruf an die Deutschen*, supporting the foundation of the Bayreuth Wagner-Festspielhaus, had been publicly rejected in Germany and one of his closest Lutheran friends, Heinrich Romundt, had turned Catholic. Nietzsche's letters show him to be increasingly disgusted with the educational, cultural, and political conditions of imperial Germany—plagued by Bismarck's *Kulturkampf*, by his struggle with the Catholic Church, by two attempted murders of the Kaiser, by rising socialism, and by the effects of a rapidly growing economy and life of luxury. At the same time, Nietzsche sharply criticizes, in his four *Untimely Meditations*, the religion, history, philosophy, and culture of contemporary Germany as lifeless, philistine, and un-German. His changing view of Luther corresponds exactly to his new and negative attitude toward Germany and to his criticism of German culture. His new estimate of Luther and the Reformation found its first literary expression in the aphorisms of *Human, All-Too-Human* (1878–80).

Nietzsche himself confirms this break and change of direction in autobiographical notes (*Ecce Homo*, "Human, All-Too-Human," sec. 1) and in the introduction to this book when he says: "*Human, All-Too-Human* is the monument of a crisis. It is entitled: A book for *free* spirits . . . meaning a spirit that has become free." In his previous writings and in his comments on Luther, he was concerned about the "German" spirit. Now it is in the name of the "free spirit" and "the liberation of the spirit" that Nietzsche attacks Luther; first in a section (26) on "Reaction as Progress," where he calls him one "of the rugged, powerful, impetuous, but nevertheless backward-lagging spirits which conjure up once more a past phase of mankind" and adds that Luther's Reformation stopped "all the movements of freedom of the spirit, [that is] of the whole Renaissance." In another section (237), entitled "Renaissance and Reformation," Nietzsche explains his stand more precisely:

> The Italian Renaissance contained within itself all the positive forces to which we owe modern culture: The liberation of thought, disregard of authorities, the triumph of education over the darkness of tradition, enthusiasm for science, and . . . the unchaining of the individual. . . . On the other hand, the German Reformation stands out as an energetic protest of backward spirits, who were by no means tired of the medieval views of life. . . . With their northern strength and stiff-neckedness they threw mankind back again. [So] the great task of the Renaissance could not be completed; it was prevented by the resistance of the contemporary backward German spirit. But if Luther at that time had been burnt like Huss,—the morning sun of enlightenment would probably have risen earlier and with a splendor more beautiful than we can now imagine.

Two things have become clear from this and the previous quotations. First of all, Nietzsche totally reverses his positive view of Luther. But positively as well as negatively, he sees Luther first as the representative of the so-called rebirth, then as the reactionary spirit of German backwardness and resistance in Europe.

Secondly, it is evident that Nietzsche's estimate of Luther, whether affirmative or negative, always portrays Nietzsche's image of the German national character. Whether praised as an ideal of hopeful renovation or condemned as a force of retrogression and decadence, Luther personifies for Nietzsche *the* German spirit, and the Reformation and Lutheranism equal everything German. "Essentially, we are still the same people as those Reformation men," Nietzsche tells the Germans. Only the fact that we no longer burn our adversaries or resort to the methods of the Inquisition distinguishes us from the age of the Reformation and proves that we belong to a so-called higher culture (MA, I, sec. 633).

The Reformation itself, Nietzsche says, is "the disaster of modern German history" and hindered "the unity of the German nation," because "Luther's thick head full of suspicious and strange misgivings struggled against it" (MA, II, sec. 226). In *The Dawn of Day* (1881), Luther is "the great pessimist," who impressed the German soul with that typically "German logic": *credo quia absurdum est*, which for every true Latin is a sin against the intellect (M, Preface, sec. 3). Nietzsche continues: While the Catholic Church has somehow preserved the fine spirit and a sense of beauty for European humanity, Luther is responsible for the "brutalization of the clergy" (I, sec. 60) and is possessed by a deadly hatred against the whole priesthood (sec. 68). In the eyes of Nietzsche, Luther remained "that uncompromising miner's son, who was always suspicious of the *vita contemplativa* and the saints" and edified the Germans—to their liking—that the saints were no better than the rest of us (sec. 88).

In a paragraph on "The Attitude of Germans to Morality," Nietzsche states that since a German is capable of great things but is unlikely to accomplish them because he obeys whenever he can, submission and obedience—whether public or private—are the German virtues. Luther taught the Germans that they must obey a being in whom they can trust implicitly. This is indeed the worship of the German, the more so, as there is now less worship left in his religion (MA, III, sec. 207). Exploiting the semantics of the word "Reich," meaning "empire" as well as "the Kingdom of God," Nietzsche suggests that Luther in his processional hymn "A Mighty Fortress Is Our God" has expressed, better than he himself could have done, "the demon of power" that satisfies man more than all his possessions and enjoyments. Then he quotes Luther's fourth stanza: "And though they take our life, / Goods, honor, children, wife, / Yet is their profit small, / These things shall vanish all, / The Kingdom [*das Reich*] it remaineth." Nietzsche adds (V, sec. 262), "Ja! Ja! Das 'Reich'!"—"Yea, Yea, the German Empire!"

When these words were written, Bismarck had just strengthened the *Kaiserreich* by an alliance with Austria and Russia. A year before, the thirty-eight-year reconstruction of the Gothic Cathedral of Cologne had been completed, to which Luther's wedding ring had been presented with great fanfare and then recognized as an embarrassing forgery. So the Catholic Cologne Cathedral, still a famous showpiece for travelers, was dedicated in a splendid celebration by the Protestant Kaiser Wilhelm I as a magnificent national symbol for the reestablishment of the old German Empire.[16]

It is exactly this boisterous celebration and mutual dependence of German nationalism and Protestantism that was personified for Nietzsche and his contemporaries in Martin Luther and that Nietzsche attacked now in Luther more and more violently. We can show

---

16. Quoted after Erwin Mühlhaupt, *Der Kölner Dom im Zwielicht der Kirchen- und Geistesgeschichte* (Düsseldorf: Presseverband der Evangelischen Kirche im Rheinland, 1965), p. 21.

this development only in a few typical examples from a multitude of available quotations. In *The Joyful Wisdom* of 1882, which Nietzsche calls "the Saturnalia of a spirit of hope" and a "seriously frivolous book" (Preface to the second edition), he makes Luther responsible for putting an end to a blooming Christian culture in Germany (FW, sec. 148) and argues that the success of Luther's Reformation in the north was possible only because "the north had remained backward in comparison with the south of Europe" (sec. 149).

Above all, he explains the Reformation under the heading "The Peasant Revolt of the Spirit" (FW, sec. 358). Here he says that Luther, as a man from the lower people, lacked all the hereditary qualities of a ruling caste, and all the instincts for power, so that his work, his intention to restore, merely became the commencement of a work of destruction. He unraveled, he tore asunder with honest rage, where the old spider (the Church) had woven longest and most carefully. He gave the sacred books into the hands of everyone. He demolished the conception of "the Church." He gave back to the priest sexual intercourse and thereby destroyed the respect and belief of the simple people, especially the women, in something superhuman in an exceptional man. "Every man his own priest"—behind such formulae and their boorish slyness, there was concealed in Luther the profoundest hatred of the "higher man" and of the rule of "higher men." As a matter of fact, he, the impossible monk, repudiated the rule of the "homines religiosi." He consequently brought about precisely the same thing within the ecclesiastical social order that he combated so rigorously in the bourgeois civic order, namely a "peasant revolt." His Reformation is also responsible for the degeneration of the modern scholar, with his lack of reverence, of shame, and of profundity. In short, it is responsible for the "plebeianism" of the spirit that is peculiar to the last two centuries. Lastly, the "modern ideas" of the state belong to this peasant revolution of the north against the cooler, more ambiguous, more suspicious spirit of the south (sec. 358).

It has not hitherto been recognized that Nietzsche's conception of Luther's Reformation as a "peasant revolution" puts him right into the Marxist camp of his time, which he regarded as "decadent," and "rabble."[17] And Voltaire, whom Nietzsche praised as "a grand seigneur of the spirit: exactly that which I am," had already considered the Reformation a great—the first—"révolution d'esprit," but still a "barbaric pollution" of that splendid sixteenth century of arts and

---

17. G, sec. 37; A, sec. 57.

enlightenment.[18] Nietzsche calls Luther the "German barbarian" (J, sec. 46) and attacks him and the Reformation for resisting "the liberation of the spirit" during the splendid era of the Renaissance, as we have seen.

In 1850 Friedrich Engels, the clarion of Karl Marx, proclaimed (with the same words used by Nietzsche thirty-two years later) Luther's Reformation as a peasant revolution.[19] In 1884, when Nietzsche was expounding the same thesis, but under different premises, Engels stated: "The Reformation—the Lutheran as much as the Calvinist—is the first bourgeois revolution in which the Peasants' War constituted the critical episode." Marx asserts that this revolution was "the most radical fact of German history, an undertaking that was wrecked by theology."[20]

But here the basic difference between Marx and Nietzsche becomes evident. Marx sees the Reformation solely as an appendix to the Peasants' War. He defines and thereby canonizes Luther's Reformation for Marxism as "the first bourgeois revolution in religious disguise."[21] Nietzsche, however, considers the Reformation negatively as a religious and ecclesiastical revolt, led by that one peasant, Martin Luther. Therefore, Nietzsche calls Luther's Reformation "the peasant revolt of the spirit," while Marx insists on a nonreligious "bourgeois revolution" of the exploited German peasantry. We do not know whether Nietzsche was influenced by Marx and Engels in formulating his own and opposite conception of the Reformation. However, as we have seen, he holds Luther's Reformation responsible for the "plebeianism" of modern political ideas about "this peasant revolution of the north." Nietzsche's remark could easily be read as an indication that he was well aware of the affinity *and* the difference between his own and Marx's stands on the Reformation and that he intentionally used the punning expression "peasant revolt" for satirizing Luther's Reformation and poking fun at the socialism of this time, of which he says that it also "appeals to the Christian instincts" (W, III, 821).

In *Beyond Good and Evil* (1886) Nietzsche continues the theme of Luther, the "Germanic barbarian," and his "belligerent slave-faith" (J, sec. 46). Luther's "passion for God" is "boorish, naive, and trou-

---

18. François Marie Voltaire, *Essai sur les moeurs et l'esprit des nations*, chap. 128.
19. Friedrich Engels, "Der deutsche Bauernkrieg" (1850), Karl Marx, Friedrich Engels, *Werke*, 5th ed. (Berlin: Dietz, 1973), VII, 327–413.
20. Karl Marx, Friedrich Engels, *Werke*, ed. Institut für Marxismus-Leninismus beim ZK der SED, 39 vols. (Berlin: Dietz, 1956–68); here, XXI, 402–3, and I, 386.
21. Ibid., XXXVII, 274.

blesome" (sec. 50). The book *On the Genealogy of Morals* (1887) portrays the Reformation as "that radically plebeian, German and English movement of revenge" against "the brilliant revival of the classical ideal in the Renaissance" (GM, I, sec. 16). When Nietzsche explains his "ascetic ideal," he points to Luther as a negative example: "This most eloquent and insolent peasant whom Germany has had, that typical Lutheran tone, in which he felt quite the most in his element during his tête-à-têtes with God." "Luther's opposition," Nietzsche says, "was at bottom the opposition of a boor, who was offended at the 'good etiquette' of the Church. . . . But for Luther the peasant that was simply not German enough. He wanted to talk directly, to talk personally, to talk 'straight from the shoulder' with his God. Well, he has done it" (III, sec. 22).

Some scholars, however, would like to take note of two positive statements about Luther in Nietzsche's writings on morals and "good and evil." In the one case Nietzsche remarks, in connection with Richard Wagner's alleged intention to compose a play about "Luther's Wedding" for his German audience, that it would be a good idea to write "a bold and pleasing Luther comedy" for the many libelers of sensuality among the Germans and that "perhaps Luther's greatest merit lies just in the fact of his having had the courage to live up to his 'sensuality,' which was called at that time and delicately enough, 'evangelical freedom'" (GM, III, sec. 2). However, there seems to be sufficient reason to doubt the positive character of this assertion.

In the other case, Nietzsche argues that in Germany there has been only one kind of public and approximately artistic discourse—that delivered from the pulpit. "The masterpiece of German prose is therefore with good reason the masterpiece of its greatest preacher [Luther]: The Bible has hitherto been the best German book. Compared with Luther's Bible, almost everything else is merely 'literature'—something which has not grown in Germany, and therefore has not taken . . . root in German hearts, as the Bible has done" (J, sec. 247). In order to value and understand these remarks about Luther, the greatest preacher and master of German prose, more fully, we have to consider a statement in Nietzsche's letter of 22 February 1884, written two years earlier to his friend Erwin Rohde after he had finished the three main parts of *Thus Spoke Zarathustra*: "To you, as a 'homo litteratus,' I shall make a confession—I pride myself on having brought the German language to its perfection with this *Zarathustra*. After Luther and Goethe, one more step had to be taken. . . . I excel Goethe in a more vigorous and bolder line of expression, yet without falling among the boors, like Luther" (W, III, 1215).

Nietzsche was very much aware of the excellence and brilliance of his own language. He acknowledged how much his *Zarathustra* owes to the language of Luther and Goethe. But he was not willing to deviate from his negative estimation of Luther as the rebellious peasant in German history.

Nietzsche's last two works, written the year before he collapsed, insane, on a piazza in Turin, bear the religious titles *Ecce Homo* and *The Antichrist* (the subtitle "A Curse upon Christianity" is usually translated "An Attempted Criticism of Christianity"). Here Nietzsche once more summarizes his stand on Luther and Germany. The *Ecce Homo* section of scathing criticism, "Nothing shall prevent me from being rude, and telling the Germans some unpleasant truths,"[22] is repeated, with a few minor changes, in section 61 of *The Antichrist*. Referring to Friedrich Theodor Vischer's *Aesthetics or Theory of the Beautiful* (1846–57), Nietzsche repeats (in the above section of *Ecce Homo*) Vischer's so-called "truth, which made the rounds of German newspapers: The Renaissance and the Reformation . . . constitute a whole—the aesthetic rebirth and the moral rebirth." Nietzsche continues:

> Such sentences exhaust my patience, and I feel . . . it my duty, to tell the Germans . . . : Every great crime against culture committed during the last four hundred years lies on their conscience! . . . The Germans deprived Europe of the fruits, the whole meaning of her last period of greatness—the Renaissance. . . . Luther, that fatal monk, not only restored the Church, but what was a thousand times worse, restored Christianity the very moment that it lay prostrate. . . . Catholics would have good reason to celebrate Luther festivals, produce Luther plays—Luther and the "moral rebirth"! To the devil with all psychology!

It is interesting to note that Nietzsche, who, it will be recalled, had written about the "Lutherfest" in Bonn and the need for a Luther comedy on sensuality, refers here again to Luther festivals and plays. Shortly before, in 1883, the 400th birthday of Martin Luther had been celebrated in festivals, plays, historical processions, and military parades all over Germany and with all the pomp and display of German nationalism. Full of resentment against the chauvinism of the Bismarck era, Nietzsche satirized the vogue and cult of these nationalistic Luther festivals. Here in *Ecce Homo*, he continues his scolding of the Germans: "With this [that is, Luther's Reformation] they incurred the responsibility for everything that resulted, every-

---

22. *Ecce Homo*, "Why I Write Such Good Books": The Case of Wagner, sec. 2.

thing that exists—the sickliness and stupidity that opposes culture, the neurosis called nationalism, from which Europe suffers" ("The Case of Wagner," sec. 2). The same section on Luther and Germany closes in *The Antichrist* with an even stronger rebuke: "They [the Germans] also have the most unclean, the most incurable, and the most irrefutable kind of Christianity—Protestantism—on their conscience. If we shall never be able to get rid of Christianity, the Germans will be to blame" (A, sec. 61).

Nietzsche's last two statements only confirm our findings that, in his eyes, Luther is just the embodiment of everything German. For Nietzsche, Luther's Reformation is the cause of all the cultural ills and national evils of Germany, including socialism. After praising Luther during his first thirty years as an incarnation of the "daring German spirit" and as "leader" to another German reformation, Nietzsche then made him the scapegoat for the sins of modern Germany. In Nietzsche's writings, Luther is nothing but a cleverly chosen symbol for the author's own and radically changing attitudes toward his German and Protestant inheritance, a symbol for "everything German." Nietzsche is, therefore, not interested in Luther the writer, the theologian and religious reformer, unless he can use these aspects of his work for his own purpose of praising or condemning German nationalism.

More than ninety percent of Nietzsche's statements about Luther refer to German culture, history, and nationalism. Why has this fact been overlooked? Why have Nietzsche's assertions about Luther never been critically investigated and judiciously evaluated? A few less thorough and mostly sensational publications deal with German nationalism from Luther to Nietzsche, or to Hitler, in general—but they do not examine Nietzsche's political views of Luther in any detail.[23] Theological investigations can hardly shed any light on Nietzsche's nationalistic interpretations of the reformer, and have failed to do so (Benz, pp. 2-7). Let us therefore turn once more to earlier scholars of literature and history who have dealt with Nietzsche and Luther.

Emanuel Hirsch judges the pro-German attitude of the earlier Nietzsche toward Luther as "so genuinely German" (p. 63) and is "ashamed" that Nietzsche obtained his negative view of Luther allegedly from that un-German Catholic priest Janssen (p. 67). Ernst Benz emphasizes Nietzsche's "German way of thinking," his "German conception" (p. 13) and "German consciousness of history"

---

23. See the publications by Spenlé, Schulz, and McGovern listed above, nn. 4 and 5.

(p. 79). Heinz Bluhm considers Luther's Reformation not only "German," but "Germanic." He states that Nietzsche, in *The Birth of Tragedy*, "summons the true and deep German character . . . in his creed, written with blood, [and] opposed to a shallow, essentially un-German presence." He considers Nietzsche's joining the Lutheran Gustav-Adolfsverein in Bonn an "ebullition of his Protestant blood inheritance," and his confession of a "heartfelt dependence on the spirit of Luther" in his letter of 28 February 1875, mentioned above, "the instinctive voice of the Protestant blood in Nietzsche."[24] It must be added that this strange "blood and soil" estimate of Nietzsche and Luther appeared in March 1943, when the United States and the free world were fighting the horrible excesses and dangers of that same "blood and soil" ideology on the battlefields.

Benz and Bluhm refer to Ernst Bertram's book on Nietzsche, in which we are assured that "Martin Luther is the oldest name in Nietzsche's line of intellectual ancestors" and that "Nietzsche's unrestrained and odious Luther-enmity is only a symbol of fraternal strife in his own heart: Faustian and super-German." It is out of his "nordic Christianity" that Nietzsche "attacks that Asiatic, decadent-Hellenistic Christianity, the slave-religion of Paulus."[25] While Benz rejects Bertram's "super-German" interpretation as racist and folk romantic (p. 14), Bluhm fully acknowledges this "intellectual-spiritual kinship of Nietzsche to Luther," expressed not only by Bertram, but also by Kurt Hildebrandt,[26] as "far more grandiose" than his own rather modest investigation (Bluhm [1], p. 265).

The result of this brief retrospect into the prevailing scholarship on our topic is astounding as well as pretty obvious: so far, all the investigators of the Nietzsche-Luther relationship follow only the tracks of Nietzsche himself. Either they have accepted, uncritically and unconditionally, Nietzsche's philosophy and his nationalistic view of Martin Luther, or their own attitude toward Luther, Protestantism, and Germany is exactly the same as the one that Nietzsche characterizes so perfectly as bourgeois German. Others, especially Karl Jaspers and Ernst Benz,[27] want us to believe that Nietzsche's unrelenting fight against Christianity, the Reformation, and Luther has, in

---

24. Bluhm (1), pp. 272–73, 284–85.
25. Bertram (see above, n. 10), passim.
26. Kurt Hildebrandt, *Wagner und Nietzsche. Ihr Kampf gegen das neunzehnte Jahrhundert* (Breslau: F. Hirst, 1924).
27. Karl Jaspers, *Nietzsche und das Christentum*, 2nd ed. (Munich: R. Piper, 1952), especially p. 25 (1st ed., Hameln: F. Seifert, 1946; English ed., *Nietzsche and Christianity*, trans. E. B. Ashton [Chicago: H. Regnery Co., 1961]). Benz, p. 178.

the last analysis, the positive meaning and purpose of a criticism that opens up "a wide range of new possibilities" for a reform of modern Christianity. While this is certainly a good way for a Christian to value Nietzsche's assault, the latter himself has never given any indication that he meant anything but the destruction of Christianity.

For an admirer of Nietzsche, there is also the distressing if not painful conclusion of our investigation that Nietzsche's estimate of Martin Luther is basically superficial and conceived exclusively under the notion of German nationalism. Nevertheless, Nietzsche was very right when he caricatured the national-heroic Luther image of his time, an image that still prevails in our day. Forty-five years after Nietzsche's *Antichrist*, the "Deutsche Christen" movement within the Protestant Church of Germany greeted Hitler's seizure of power as "*a German revolution in the spirit of Martin Luther*,"[28] while many other Lutheran pastors and Christians resisted the Nazi onslaught and suffered imprisonment, concentration camp, and death. In 1967, Luther was celebrated in East Germany as "the most courageous organizer of the most important revolution in German history before 1945."[29] A few years ago, the official newspaper of the German Democratic Republic, *Neues Deutschland* (14/15 June 1980), announced the formation of a planning committee under the chairmanship of the state and party chief Erich Honecker to prepare a grand celebration to mark the 500th anniversary of Luther's birth in 1983. Honecker stated in his opening speech: "Martin Luther is one of the greatest sons of the German people . . . , whose precious heritage the German Democratic Republic has accepted as her own."

There seems to be no end to "Luther the great German." Therefore, Nietzsche's antiproclamation of "Luther the impossible German" still has its justification in the domain of politics and nationalism.

28. Cf. Baeumer, "Lutherfeiern," p. 58.
29. Ibid., p. 60.

IX. "The Only Logical Christian": Nietzsche's Critique of Pascal

Brendan Donnellan

In a letter written shortly before the eclipse of his creative life by madness, Nietzsche compared his ambivalence toward Dostoevsky with his relationship to Pascal, "whom I almost love, since he has enlightened me infinitely: the only logical Christian."[1] It was the challenge presented by the most formidable apologist of Christianity that increasingly fascinated and exasperated Nietzsche to the point of obsession, especially in the later works. This mixed attitude is perhaps summed up most revealingly in his confession in *Ecce Homo*: "I do not read but *love* Pascal, as the most instructive victim of Christianity, murdered slowly, first physically then psychologically—the whole logic of this most gruesome form of inhuman cruelty" (WKG, VI-3, 283). Yet, alongside horror at Pascal the Christian, and admiration for Pascal the thinker and psychologist, there is identification with Pascal the man far exceeding Nietzsche's relationship to most previous philosophers. In the famous "Journey to Hades" aphorism from *Human, All-Too-Human* (VM, sec. 408), Pascal belongs to the select company of great minds whom Nietzsche has sought out in the Underworld and whose "eternal liveliness" he commends. An unpublished sketch from the time of the composition of *The Gay Science* even asserts that when Nietzsche speaks of Plato, Pascal, Spinoza, and Goethe, "then I know that their blood rolls in mine—I am proud when I speak the truth of them—the family is good enough not to need invention or concealment" (WKG, V-2, 483).

It is a consistent feature of Nietzsche's dialogue with past thinkers that vehement disagreement is by no means a sign of personal disparagement: "attack is in my case a sign of good will, sometimes even of gratitude. I honor, I distinguish by associating my name with

---

1. Nietzsche to Brandes, 20 November 1888 (*Gesammelte Briefe*, vol. 3 [Berlin/Leipzig: Schuster & Loeffler, 1905], p. 322). Translations from the German are by the author. Pascal translations are taken from Blaise Pascal, *Pensées*, trans. A. J. Krailsheimer (Harmondsworth, Middlesex: Penguin, 1966). References are given in the text, specifying the *Pensée* number according to Louis Lafuma's classification, which Krailsheimer follows.

that of a cause or person: pro or con—that makes no difference to me at this point" (WKG, VI-3, 273). This profound respect for intellectual opponents is specifically related to Pascal in another sketch from Nietzsche's middle period: "I have the contempt of Pascal and the curse of Schopenhauer on me! And can anyone be more affectionately inclined toward them than myself! But admittedly with that affection which remains frank in order to remain a friend and not become a lover and fool" (WKG, V-1, 686).

Nietzsche's encounter with Pascal's thought represented the clash of the most aggressive modern spokesmen of two militant and mutually inimical *Weltanschauungen*: Christianity and atheism. Pascal presented an irresistible challenge to the German through the riddle of a strong and brilliant personality rejecting anthropocentric values for the absolute claims of an increasingly moribund religion. The spectacle of a proud and powerful mind falling prey to the "illusions" of Christian transcendence never failed to fascinate and horrify Nietzsche, not least because of the obvious sense of kinship that he felt toward an incisive and original thinker who in many ways anticipated his philosophical views. Nietzsche's attempts to reconstruct the emotional—and physiological—motivation of his rival reach their pitch in the later works, but the story of his relationship to the Jansenist can be traced back to the earliest stages of his philosophical development. In general, one can say that Nietzsche's preoccupation with the *content* of Pascal's thought is at the forefront in his early and middle works, while in the later works it is the *pathology* of his spiritual opponent that whips him up to a fever pitch of personal involvement.

In his early and middle works, dominated as they were successively by the ideals of the "genius" and the "free spirit" who stand above their time, Nietzsche felt a particular affinity to Pascal as an embodiment of the contemplative life. In the first *Untimely Meditation* he supports his criticism of the unreflecting industriousness of modern man with a summary of the urge to diversion (*divertissement*) that is born of restlessness and boredom: "Now, Pascal suggests that men only endeavor to work hard at their businesses and sciences with the view of escaping those questions of greatest import which every moment of loneliness or leisure presses upon them—the questions relating to the *wherefore*, the *whence*, and the *whither* of life" (U, I, sec. 8; cf. *Pensées* 132–39). Throughout his life, with similar intensity, Nietzsche himself was to put Pascal's question as to the purpose of life, although, unlike the Frenchman, he could not allow himself a supernatural solution. Several years later, when he laments in *Human*,

All-Too-Human the modern mis-estimation of the *vita contemplativa*, which has been replaced by the "disease" of industriousness, he cites Pascal as one of the former great moralists who are now unjustly neglected (MA, I, sec. 282).

Both Nietzsche and Pascal offer an ideal beyond man's constant alternation between an ultimately purposeless flight from the self in diversion and the barren misery of loneliness and boredom. At one point in *Human, All-Too-Human* Nietzsche defines boredom as a state of being accustomed to work, and envisages a stage beyond work (a task performed out of need) and play (work undertaken with no other purpose than to satisfy the desire for work): the blissful, tranquil vision of happiness of the artist and the philosopher (MA, I, sec. 611)—which corresponds, in essence, to the picture of the free spirit's serene detachment from life given at the end of the first section of *Human, All-Too-Human* (MA, sec. 34). For Pascal the misery associated with the realization of one's condition is a result of original sin. Besides the instinct for external diversion we have a higher instinct for the true source of peace and happiness: "God alone is man's true good, and since man abandoned Him it is a strange fact that nothing in nature has been found to take His place" (148; cf. 136). Both Nietzsche's solution to man's dilemma—a superior personal culture—and Pascal's promise of spiritual union with God thus equally depend on the abandonment of meaningless activity for a life dedicated to contemplation.

It was not until his apparent conversion to rationalism and science in *Human, All-Too-Human* that Nietzsche concerned himself with the Christian apologist as a phenomenon in his own right who was to be taken seriously and overcome on the moral and religious levels. The subsequent tenor of his polemic against Pascal is struck in a short but crucial aphorism that marks the beginning of his intellectual battle with the Frenchman by proclaiming the rights of the self against Christian attempts to discredit and abuse it: "*Contrasts.*—The most senile thought ever conceived about men lies in the famous saying, 'The self is always hateful,' the most childish, in the still more famous saying, 'Love thy neighbor as thyself.'—With the one, knowledge of men has ceased; with the other, it has not begun" (VM, sec. 385).

Thus Pascal, with his conviction that "le moi est haïssable" (597), stands at the end of the religious tradition of denial of the self through love of one's neighbor inspired by the "childish" words of Christ. The "senility" of Pascal is symptomatic of his role as the last serious apologist of a dying religion, whose precepts now emphasize, instead of the immature but outgoing idealism of the founder, a negativistic criticism and contempt of the human self. This principle of self-abasement constituted the major stumbling-block for his German reader, whose moralism consisted of a vindication of the rights of the higher self and a sense of the undesirability, not to mention the impossibility, of purely altruistic behavior. Despite its other changes of course, Nietzsche's philosophy remained consistent in its emphasis on the self as both the starting-point and the goal for development in the postsupernatural understanding of man's role in life.

Pascal's supposedly perverse degradation of the self is a main theme of *The Dawn*, where the Frenchman comes to the forefront as a moral rival and opponent of Nietzsche. The latter begins to interpret Pascal's religiosity, like Rousseau's, in terms of self-hatred. This leads him to ironic conclusions concerning the doctrine of loving one's neighbor as oneself: if one also follows the Christian concept of the self as hateful, most dramatically expressed in recent times by Pascal, the natural consequence is bound to be the latter's misanthropy (M, sec. 63). Nietzsche again plays on the paradoxical notion of self-hatred when he objects: "If our self, according to Pascal and Christianity, is always hateful, how could we even permit and accept others loving it—whether God or man!" (M, sec. 79).

Pascal had eloquently summed up his doctrine of hatred of the self while at the same time positing a presence of the divine within each person that Nietzsche would certainly have interpreted as a disguised love of part of the natural self:

> The true and only virtue is therefore to hate ourselves, for our concupiscence makes us hateful, and to seek for a being really worthy of our love in order to love him. But as we cannot love what is outside us, we must love a being who is within us but is not our own self. And this is true for every single person. Now only the universal being is of this kind: the kingdom of God is within us, universal good is within us, and is both ourselves and not ourselves. (564)

For Pascal the human ego is criminal both in its self-absorption and in its instinctive injustice: "In a word the self has two characteristics. It is unjust in itself for making itself center of everything: it is a nuisance to others in that it tries to subjugate them, for each self is the enemy of all the others and would like to tyrannize them" (597). Love of self implies hatred of truth: self-love is the source of all injustice and disorder (617, 978). Love of God implies hatred of the self, and hatred of the self implies love of God (618). It was this awareness of the exclusive claims of the Christian deity that led Nietzsche to rejoice in the nonexistence of God, since otherwise man could not bear being unable to become a god himself (WKG, VI-1, 106), an attitude that Pascal had already known and condemned: "Anyone who does not hate the self-love within him and the instinct which leads him to make himself into a God must be really blind" (617).

Nietzsche's fundamental argument with Pascal was precisely on this issue of the *moi haïssable*. On the one hand, he felt this to be typical of the Christian denial of the legitimate rights of a self free from the tyranny of external sanctions. On the other hand, he saw Pascal's *Apology* as appealing, ironically enough, to the most selfish instincts: man consoles himself for his weakness and anxiety by inventing belief in a supernatural life—in Nietzsche's eyes one of the lowest forms of self-seeking. He accuses Pascal of sacrificing the life-enhancing passions for the sake of a sterile private preoccupation, of stressing the self-absorbed individual at the expense of the phenomenon of Becoming (WKG, V-1, 700). For him, Pascal, like all saints, is a self-centered egoist (WKG, V-1, 654, 669–70). To religious egoism he opposes the philosophical ideal by which the individual paradoxically renounces himself to proclaim and further the maximum intensification of the life force, an all-consuming task making him indifferent to his personal fate: "'What do I matter!' is the expression of true passion, the utmost stage of *seeing something outside of oneself*" (WKG, V-1, 656).[2] One might observe, however, that Nietzsche did not fully realize that it is only man's concupiscence that Pascal finds hateful, that he allows a legitimate self-love (cf. 119, 450), and that the apparently negative element of self-hatred is balanced by the positive vision of charity in his system of values.

In *The Dawn* Nietzsche demonstrates his detailed knowledge of the *Pensées* when he attacks other specific aspects of that work, including the confidently argued defense of the "hidden God," which he sees as masking Pascal's inner uncertainty (M, sec. 91), perhaps subscribing to the notion current in the nineteenth century of Pascal as a secret skeptic, desperately suppressing his own doubts. In a note from this time he also criticizes Pascal's theory of the "automaton," which recommends that man at first go through the motions of reli-

---

2. Elsewhere, examining the "psychology of the psychologist," Nietzsche contrasts his own approach with the morbid introspection of the Frenchman even more explicitly: "We are no Pascals, we are not especially interested in the 'salvation of the soul,' in our own happiness, in our own virtue.—We have neither the time nor the curiosity to rotate about ourselves in that way" (WM, sec. 426).

gious observance mechanically in order to acquire the habit of belief (418, 821): for Nietzsche this is simply "making one's dishonesty pay" (WKG, V-1, 719). Particularly, he condemns the tactic adopted in the *Pensées* that aims to bring home to the reader the misery of human life in order to create utter dissatisfaction with his condition, describing Pascal's works as typical of the ignoble attempt by Christianity to exploit the capacity for despair of a certain kind of men, stalking them like a hunter his prey. Pascal, he reflects, attempted to determine "whether with the help of the most cutting knowledge everyone could be brought to despair;—the attempt failed, to his second despair" (M, sec. 64).

The Christian calumniation of life as a means of ruining men's pleasure in existence—in order to bring them in despair to the Church—was a practice that Nietzsche censured at first comparatively mildly, in *Human, All-Too-Human* (e.g., MA, I, secs. 119, 555), but then with ever-growing rigor, ending in a crescendo of hatred and disgust in his final diatribe against Western religion, *The Antichrist*, in which he accuses the Christian Church of "living on states of distress, *creating* states of distress in order to eternalize *itself*" (A, sec. 62). That Pascal personifies for Nietzsche this kind of Christian nihilism becomes increasingly clear in the course of his works. On the one hand, he considers Pascal to have exaggerated the ills of human life (cf. WKG, V-1, 683); on the other he calls into question the validity of the Christian alternative so movingly evoked in the *Pensées*. Nietzsche does not deny that Christianity may bring happiness and peace of mind (cf. GM, III, sec. 24), but he objects that this effect is no argument for its truthfulness.

Pascal had presented the positive advantages of Christian faith as justifying the gamble that it entailed: "No one is so happy as a true Christian, or so reasonable, virtuous, and lovable" (357). Nietzsche, however, is impressed neither by the "proof of pleasure" (MA, I, sec. 120), nor by the logic that a need necessitates the means to the relief of this need, which he considers the ultimate in impertinence (cf. M, sec. 90), and still less by the faculty of intuition so extolled by Pascal: "Hunger does not prove that a food exists to satisfy it, but it desires the food. 'Divining' something does not mean perceiving the existence of a thing in any way, but considering it possible, to the extent that one wishes or fears it; 'divination' does not take us a single step further into the land of certainty" (MA, I, sec. 131).[3]

3. Cf. Nietzsche's later refutation of Christian "proofs by potency" (A, sec. 32), and specifically of Pascal's proof by necessity: "Pascal's main error: he thinks he can prove

In *The Dawn*, repudiation of Pascal's doctrines is balanced by an ineradicable respect for Pascal the man, and by acknowledgment of his passionate Christian conviction. The aphorism in which this is expressed is entitled, appropriately, "Wishing Perfect Opponents for Oneself." Nietzsche's adversaries in this case are the great religious spokesmen produced by the French nation, which he describes as "the most Christian people in the world: not in the sense that the piety of the masses is greater in them than elsewhere, but because the most difficult Christian ideals have transformed themselves among them into men, and not just ideas or attempts. Take Pascal, in the union of passion, spirit, and honesty the leading Christian,—and consider what had to unite here!" (M, sec. 192). Despite Nietzsche's violent criticism of Pascal's methods and conclusions, he recognizes the sincerity and genius that animate his vision. His respect for the impossible task of reconciling reason and faith that Pascal almost carried out is further attested by his comment that the perfect examples of Christianity found among the seventeenth-century French produced perfect counterparts in the later *libertins*: "The French freethinker always combated great men and not merely dogmas and sublime abortions, like the freethinkers of other nations!" (ibid.). Here, as always, it is the incorporation of a belief in a great and original personality that impresses Nietzsche despite all disagreement.

After *Zarathustra* it is above all the simultaneous intellectual and physical destruction of Pascal by Christianity that fascinates and appalls Nietzsche. He had already suggested that Pascal's addiction to Christianity had been responsible for the breakdown of his health.[4] The later analyses are variations on this theme of the bodily and spiritual ruin of the Frenchman by religion, which in Nietzsche's opinion led to his early death. Pascal's faith is described as "a pro-

---

that Christianity is true because it is necessary—this presupposes a good and true providence, which makes everything necessary true as well: but there could be necessary mistakes! And finally! The necessity might only seem that way because one has become so used to error that it dominates like a second nature" (WKG, V-1, 696).

4. Cf. Ida Overbeck: "The problem of the relationship between the body and thought in Pascal preoccupied him very much. Already in 1878 or 1879 he was claiming that Pascal's dependence on Christianity could well have wrecked him" (Carl Albrecht Bernoulli, *Franz Overbeck und Friedrich Nietzsche: Eine Freundschaft*, 2 vols. [Jena: Diederichs, 1908], I, 133); and Nietzsche's sister: "He loved Pascal as a kindred spirit; he was as moved by his end as if it had been that of a beloved friend, indeed, as if he himself were threatened by it" (Elisabeth Förster-Nietzsche, *Das Leben Friedrich Nietzsches*, 2 vols. in 3 [Leipzig: Naumann, 1895–1904], II, 883–84).

tracted suicide of the intellect" (J, sec. 46) and a sacrifice of the intellect (J, sec. 229), illustrating the loss of all freedom and pride that Christian self-abasement brings. The struggle to reconcile religion with knowledge that *homines religiosi* had to undergo could only be understood fully, Nietzsche comments, by one whose intellectual conscience was "as profound, as wounded, as monstrous as Pascal's" (J, sec. 45). At the end of the section on the religious nature in *Beyond Good and Evil*, Pascal is cited as the most notorious example of the destructive power of Christianity and its waste of precious human potential, provoking the angry concluding indictment: "He who . . . with some divine hammer in his hand, approached this almost deliberate degeneration and stunting of man such as constitutes the European Christian (Pascal for instance), would he not cry out in rage, in pity, in horror: 'O you fools, you presumptuous, pitying fools, what have you done!' " (J, sec. 62).

Subsequent (mostly unpublished) references continue to emphasize the masochistic, self-torturing nature of Pascal's attempt to accommodate reason to religion. He is presented, for example, as a brooding hypochondriac (WKG, VI-3, 88), or as the most deplorable case of Christian depravation of even the intellectually strongest natures to the point where they find their very intellectuality misleading and sinful (A, sec. 5).

Pascal is claimed by Nietzsche to have praised sickness as a state superior to health (WM, secs. 227, 246), although there is no evidence that he actually did so, and Pascalism is even reduced to "a pathological condition of the *nervus sympathicus*" (WM, sec. 312). Nietzsche's central explanation of the origin of religious feelings as a misinterpretation of physiological states of discomfort or pleasure (G, "The Four Great Errors," sec. 6) had been anticipated by an earlier analysis tracing Pascal's sense of man's sinfulness back to a misunderstanding of unknown bodily states as moral and religious phenomena (M, sec. 86).

Pascal and Schopenhauer are cited as prime examples of the gloomy capacity of the strong to believe in the implications of herd values more earnestly than do the mediocre themselves, and thus to calumniate precisely the superior features that set them off from the mass (WM, sec. 276). Nietzsche's tragic pity over the annihilation of Pascal's *noblesse* is summed up when he polemicizes: "Christianity should never be forgiven for destroying such men as Pascal. One should never cease to combat exactly this in Christianity: That it has the will to break above all the strongest and noblest souls" (WM, sec. 252).

We have seen how Pascal the Christian apologist intensely interested and provoked Nietzsche throughout his philosophical career. At this stage we may take a closer look at the areas in which the concerns of Pascal and Nietzsche overlap, and in particular at Nietzsche's increasingly vehement critique of the aims and tactics of the *Apology*.

One of the most crucial differences between Pascal and Nietzsche is in their respective assessments of the compatibility of reason and belief. Although a mathematician and physicist of genius, Pascal was convinced that the conclusions of science and logic are valid only on one plane, while questions that belong to another dimension can only be solved by correspondingly different faculties. He distinguished a hierarchy of three separate but complementary modes: the order of the body, or senses; of the mind, or reason; and of the heart, or intuition. Of these the order of the heart is the highest faculty, since it alone can sense the basic premises from which the reason develops its systems: "Principles are felt, propositions proved" (110). Instinct and logic belong to different orders that can never meet on the same plane, a postulate most tellingly expressed in the famous pun "The heart has its reasons of which the reason knows nothing" (423), while the last step of the rational intellect lies in recognizing that there are an infinite number of things beyond it (188). Feeling is thus portrayed as a pre- and supra-rational knowledge of the truth beyond the superficial and unreliable constructs of deductive thought, a certainty that no process of logical reasoning will be able to challenge or replace.

The fact that religion cannot be completely proved by the reason is of no relevance, since religious truth can only be apprehended by the heart. Since they are such separate faculties, there is no question of a conflict between reason and religious intuition, although in his system of converging proofs Pascal also uses the findings of the mind (rational argument) and of the senses (biblical proofs and miracles) to support the insights of the supreme faculty of the heart. Even though he himself recognized that "there is something astonishing about Christianity" (817), he found it an eminently *reasonable* religion: he does not try to destroy the limited authority of reason, but to show how Christianity conforms to it and confirms it, to the extent that it can do so without ceasing to be a religion. Nietzsche was to object vehemently that "Christianity is incompatible with science, religion, truth" (A, sec. 47), while Pascal used precisely these realms of experience, in an intricately intermeshed system of emotional, logical, and factual argumentation, to prove how they all are meaningless *without* Christianity.

For Nietzsche the issue was clear-cut, despite his own radical skepticism as to the power of reason: Christianity is incompatible with the present state of knowledge; it is indecent for modern man to be a Christian (A, sec. 35). Religion and knowledge are natural enemies: "The priest knows only *one* great danger: that is science" (A, sec. 49). Hence the fascination of the case of Pascal for him: he was particularly intrigued by the tension of soul that arises when a strong and noble soul submits to Christian ideals. Pascal was for Nietzsche the noble exponent of a faith that mainly catered to the low, the vulgar, and the unintelligent. At the same time, Nietzsche remained aware of the paradox that the modern scientist's and philosopher's devotion to truth was also a form of the religious instinct. He described his own thought as having grown *out of* Christianity, as a severer form of piety, now *forbidding* him to be a Christian (WKG, VII-1, 163). Another unpublished note reveals that his profound interest in truth is indebted to Christianity—and specifically to Pascal (WKG, VII-2, 235).

The dialectics of Nietzsche's relationship to Pascal are sustained above all by Pascal's position at a great historical watershed between the age of religion and the age of science. Pascal, in Nietzsche's eyes, came at the *end* of the truly Christian era, just as Paul, "the Jewish Pascal," had actually begun it (Nietzsche's dissociation of the harmless idealist Christ from the sect that sprang up after him is amply documented [cf. A, secs. 27–40; WM, secs. 158–72]). The Christian word was already perverted in the pages of Paul's Epistles, which, read honestly, would have done for Christianity by exposing its origins, "just as the pages of the French Pascal expose its future and what will destroy it" (M, sec. 68). At first sight, the comparison of Paul, considered by Nietzsche to be a crude, fanatical, and superstitious bully, with the exquisite genius of Pascal is startling—until one realizes that it is exactly Nietzsche's intention to show how Christianity, as a movement, started as an expression of the lowest classes of the Jewish nation by feeding on resentment and vengefulness (cf. GM, I, secs. 8–10; A, sec. 27); became more refined in time; and, with the independent cultivation of the ideal of truthfulness that evolved from it in the form of modern rationalistic science, collapsed, despite the attempts of increasingly subtle intellects to rescue it from the tide of skepticism sweeping it away at the end of its natural course.

Nietzsche found Pascal's depiction of the fallen state of man and his immersion in sin all the more ironic since Jesus Himself had abolished the concept of "guilt" and denied the existence of any chasm between man and God (A, sec. 39). Paul is consistently presented in Nietzsche's work as the actual founder of the *institution* of Christianity, and it is apparent that Pascal would not have been exempted either, despite—or rather, because of—the consistency of his doctrine, from the philosopher's scathing judgment that "in reality there has been only one Christian, and he died on the Cross" (ibid.).

Pascal represented for Nietzsche not only the last, and most intellectual, expression of the Christian tradition, but also the prophet of the new age of nihilism. Pascal's remark that without God man is "a monster and a chaos" (131) is applied to the development that was brought by the erosion of Christian faith in the nineteenth century, and that was diagnosed by the modern Pascal, Schopenhauer, in his life-negating writings (WM, sec. 83; WKG, VIII-2, 109). Both these thinkers intensified Nietzsche's awareness of the challenge presented by the modern rise of nihilism and disorientation, which he sought to overcome with a purely anthropocentric philosophy.

Perhaps the most revealing tribute to Pascal as a kindred strong, skeptical mind of genius, whose fatal infection by Christianity was only the result of historical circumstance, is paid in an analysis of the profundity possessed by apparently unlikely figures. Among these Nietzsche counts Pascal, "who died only thirty years too early to laugh at and scorn Christianity from the depths of his furious and magnificent soul, just as he did earlier, when younger, with the Jesuits" (WKG, VII-3, 190). One senses that Nietzsche felt Pascal to possess all the qualities that go to make up the ideal free spirit—incisive intelligence, uncompromising honesty, and the personal strength to bear the acutest pessimism—only to be led by some chance influence or impulse into the spiral of self-destruction through religion.

Pascal's *Provincial Letters* indicting the Jesuits rival the best of Nietzsche's polemical writings in masterly use of cutting irony, rigorous logic, and devastating rhetoric. It is perhaps also due to this powerful and aggressive skepticism that Nietzsche recognizes himself in the Frenchman. The historical irony of Pascal's life lies in his double role not only as the most formidable postmedieval representative of the Christianity of Paul and Augustine, but also as an innovative thinker standing on the threshold of an age of science, reason, and skepticism—values that would have been epitomized in his both analytical *and* intuitive genius if he had not felt compelled to use weapons from this very arsenal to defend an increasingly vulnerable religion. Pascal's tragedy, in Nietzsche's eyes, consisted in the mortal conflict between religious and freethinking tendencies, in the course of which the latter, and with them the vast potential of his proud and creative character, were slowly and cruelly annihilated, when it would have taken little to tip the balance the other way to a unique flowering of the human mind and personality.

It has already been suggested that much of Nietzsche's increasing hostility toward Pascal is attributable to unconscious identification with traits in the other's character that he rejected in himself. This may be especially relevant in his attitude toward the austere asceticism of Pascal. In Nietzsche's later works Pascal is presented more and more as the supreme example of the Christian self-chastiser who abuses both mind and body. The German's distaste at the spectacle of Christian self-abnegation cannot, however, mask the fact that his own way of life was strictly ascetic in character, requiring the renunciation of comfort for a hermitlike existence, and the most rigorous self-discipline in his habits, to overcome ill health and dedicate himself to his writing. There are also decidedly ascetic strains in his philosophy itself, which demands unsparing pursuit of the often cruel truth before one enters into the joy of free knowledge, and on the moral level denial and overcoming of the lower self to achieve sublimation of the passions. There is thus a certain similarity between the high aims and uncompromising demands of his philosophy and the self-denying severity of the Christian saintly life, a fact that he partly recognizes in *The Genealogy of Morals* when he describes religious asceticism as a major, if misguided, form of the will to power (GM, III, secs. 1, 28).

Despite this suppressed sense of kinship, Nietzsche's overall attitude in a highly complex relationship, tempered as it is by a certain amount of sympathy and identification, seems to be acute revulsion at the profound and often unimaginative denial of the worth of life that religious asceticism, in his view, involves. Anticipating later psychological theories of drive frustration, Nietzsche defines asceticism as a "defiance of the self," the turning of a need for violence and tyranny in on oneself in the absence of other objects (MA, I, sec. 137). The ascetic makes it easy for himself, he claims, by subjecting himself to an external will, and thus escaping boredom without the painful excitement of his own will and passions (MA, I, sec. 139). Nietzsche undoubtedly saw Pascal's resolution of the oppressive problem of the restless will as a similar avoidance of the issue. Pascal might certainly be seen as incorporating the dialectic between pride and self-contempt discerned by Nietzsche in the saint and the ascetic (M, sec. 69). Equally applicable to Nietzsche's picture of Pascal are other passages where the ascetic and the martyr are seen as the ultimate expressions of paradoxical Christian pride and domineeringness (cf. MA, I, secs. 137, 142).[5]

---

5. Cf. *The Genealogy of Morals*: "For an ascetic life is a self-contradiction: here rules a *ressentiment* without equal, that of an insatiable instinct and power-will that wants to

Nevertheless, as Nietzsche himself admits, his analyses of the ascetic in *Human, All-Too-Human* are based on the lowest common denominator of the species (MA, I, sec. 144), and inevitably there are more appealing examples. Nietzsche's attitude toward Pascal is constantly marked by great respect, if also by increasingly violent disagreement, and it is apparent that he places him on a higher level of asceticism than that of the crude and unintelligent men of religion of former times to whom he usually seems to refer with this term. Nietzsche's assessment of the ascetic ideal was far more differentiated than his criticism of the psychology of the Christian version might suggest. His work abounds in prescriptions of a "personal régime" in the conduct of life demanding restraint, sobriety, and self-denial (cf. M, sec. 553). Later he was to suggest that the scientific spirit—which had dominated him on one level at least during his middle period, and which had then been presupposed and, at last, transcended in his later nihilistic skepticism—is itself a manifestation of the ascetic spirit (GM, III, sec. 23). In his notes for the projected *Will to Power* he even proclaims his wish to renaturalize asceticism, with the emphasis on strengthening instead of denying the will: asceticism represents a positive principle that was unfortunately ruined by the Church (WM, sec. 916). Pascal probably offered Nietzsche the best example of this misplaced capacity for self-discipline.

Indeed, Pascal's opposition to the pleasure principle and his stress on mastery of the self show obvious correspondences with Nietzsche's doctrine that the most urgent task is to "give style to one's character" (FW, sec. 290). The criticism of human weakness that comes to the forefront particularly in *Zarathustra* and the later works is anticipated by Pascal's dismay at man's giving way to his animal nature and wasting his potential. Although he does not envisage the superman in Nietzsche's sense, Pascal, too, wishes man to fulfill the dignity demanded by his unique status in nature and to become again "the most excellent of creatures" (430) by realizing his inherent greatness. Both the atheist and the Christian aspire to transcend a merely biological existence of pleasure-seeking by rejecting crude materialism for an ideal of perfection. The following *Pensée* on self-mastery, for example, is in a way a harbinger of Nietzsche's heroic moral philosophy: "There is no shame in man giving in to pain, but it is shameful for him to give in to pleasure. . . . In pleasure it is man who gives in to pleasure. Now, glory comes only from mastery and control, shame only from subjection" (795). These are essentially the

---

become master not over something in life but over life itself, over its most profound, powerful, and basic conditions" (GM, III, sec. 11).

same ideas that are expounded, in more polemical form, in the Prologue to *Zarathustra*.

Although Nietzsche accused Christianity of destroying the vital passions, at more than one point Pascal expresses opinions resembling the German's central doctrine of the harnessing and sublimation of the instincts: ". . . the righteous man takes nothing from the world or its applause for himself, but only for his passions, which he uses like a master, saying to one 'Go' and [to another] 'Come.' *Thou shalt rule over thy desire.*[6] Thus mastered his passions become virtues; avarice, jealousy, anger, even God ascribes these to Himself. And they are just as much virtues as mercy, pity, constancy, which are also passions" (603).

Pascal, too, takes a fresh look at the conventional moral concepts of good and evil, the topic later treated in such exhaustive detail by Nietzsche, when he comments, for instance, that "A certain sort of evil is as hard to find as what is called good, and this particular evil is often on that account passed off as good. Indeed it takes as much extraordinary greatness of soul to attain such evil, as to attain good" (526; cf. 783, 813, 905 for further analyses of the inextricable nature of good and evil), an observation that incidentally shows that Nietzsche's justification of the great man's evil was by no means an unprecedented notion. Pascal has a similar awareness to Nietzsche's of the realities of the master mentality and the struggle for power (cf. 97, 597, 828), although, proceeding from the standpoint of Christian humility, he makes no attempt to idealize these phenomena, as Nietzsche does. Perhaps most revolutionary of all, in the orthodox tradition, is a passage where Pascal, imbued with the true spirit of Christian faith and charity, transcends the narrow, Pharisaic legalism often associated with Catholicism and hints at his own revaluation of values: ". . . morality has no time for morality. In other words the morality of judgment has no time for the random judgment of mind. For judgment is what goes with instinct, just as knowledge goes with mind" (513). These explorations were, however, all directed toward a reanimation of Christian values, and not their abolition.

It is on the level of their intentions that the Christian moralist and the atheist approach each other most intimately. Both are intensely earnest philosophers dissatisfied with the empty, materialistic life led by the majority of mankind, and with apostolic zeal both propose higher ideals either to fulfill or to restore man's greatness. Nietzsche himself recognized this shared sense of dedication: "Com-

---

6. Matt. 8:9.

parison with Pascal: Does not my strength also lie in self-overcoming, as his does? His in the service of God, mine in the service of honesty?" (WKG, V-1, 702). The very intensity and tension of their thought may have been what eventually led to their breakdowns, collapsing as they did at the prime of their productive lives and leaving behind crucial works in tantalizingly incomplete form. Nietzsche's horror at Pascal's fate has in retrospect a strangely prophetic tone of identification, just as his boast that he had more endurance than Pascal and would not burn out like a candle[7] was invested with the deepest tragic irony. It could be argued that both were the victims of their obsessive convictions.

Their belief in the potential grandeur of man, encouraged by a spiritual dialogue with a few chosen higher minds, is in dialectical antithesis to their misanthropic disgust with the animality and purposelessness of the mass of mankind.[8] They were equally aware of the special status of man in nature: animals do not suffer spiritually from their condition, but man, with his consciousness of his predicament, experiences dissatisfaction and wretchedness. Each might have accused the other of resorting to mythological solutions in his effort to provide human fate with dignity. There is even a similarity in the structures of these "mythologies." Beyond the palpable limitations of human life, an awe-inspiring perspective opened up for each of them: the possibility of eternal damnation or salvation for one, or of the Eternal Recurrence of the Same for the other. Ironically, the Antichrist Nietzsche invented his own religion, with the prophet Zarathustra and the god Dionysus to announce the good news of this Eternal Recurrence.[9]

Their solutions to the problem of the human predicament were as opposed as their basic presuppositions: for Nietzsche the superior man's good was to be created from his own resources, while Pascal could rescue human nature from contradiction and despair only by

---

7. "We are less embittered than Pascal, and also less vengeful toward the world; we have less strength at any one time: on the other hand we do not burn out too quickly like candles, but have the strength of endurance" (WKG, V-1, 702).

8. Frequent comments in the works of both stress this aspect of human nature, e.g., "Man is properly speaking *wholly animal*" (664); "Man as a species does not represent any progress compared with any other animal" (WM, sec. 684); "Man's nature is entirely natural, *wholly animal*" (630); "Man is both beast and superanimal; the higher man is both monster and superman: that is the way things go together" (WKG, VIII-2, 90).

9. Nietzsche's warning against misinterpretation, "There is nothing in me of a founder of a religion—religions are affairs of the rabble" (WKG, VI-3, 363), is to be understood in a more literal context.

postulating a supreme being both immanent and transcendent. Pascal envisages the rehabilitation of man through Christ's intervention with divine grace, while Nietzsche preached the miracle of man's becoming his own god. The urgent necessity of overcoming and perfecting human nature was, however, the central concern of both. The spiritual destinies of Pascal and Nietzsche converged when they found themselves unable to accept worldly compromises, and felt impelled to signpost the way to a nobler life for man regardless of sacrifice or risk.

X. Lessing and Nietzsche: Views on Christianity

Diana Behler

Although separated by a century in time and considerable differences in intellectual milieu, moral outlook, and temperament, Lessing and Nietzsche shared the kind of keen intellectual acumen, critical audacity, and stylistic élan that have drawn attention to their roles as "modern" critics of their own heritages of Christianity.[1] Lessing's avowed perspective as an "admiring amateur" rather than a professional theologian and Nietzsche's unfettered stance of a "free spirit" whose intellectual curiosity recognized no inviolable "truths" placed them in the position of outsiders whose perspectivistic outlooks and existential loneliness, deemed by Nietzsche a prerequisite for critical thinking, drove them to raise issues that threatened orthodox positions and seemed to betray their own Protestant educations.

Their intimacy with Christian theology, coupled with its cardinal virtue of "truthfulness" honed to its ultimate refinement and aided by intellectual courage and stylistic virtuosity, made them subjects of indignant outrage—Lessing among his contemporaries, and Nietzsche posthumously.[2] Lessing, motivated by concern for the moral education of humanity as a whole, remained well within the circum-

---

1. Nietzsche is quoted from the KSA. Most translations are my own, although various works by Nietzsche contained in the following translations have been consulted: Walter Kaufmann, *Thus Spoke Zarathustra* (New York: Viking, 1954), *The Birth of Tragedy and the Case of Wagner* (New York: Vantage, 1967), *The Portable Nietzsche* (New York: Viking, 1968), and *Basic Writings of Nietzsche* (New York: Random House, 1966); with R. J. Hollingdale, *The Will to Power* (New York: Random House, 1967); R. J. Hollingdale, *Nietzsche: Thus Spoke Zarathustra* (Baltimore: Penguin, 1961); Francis Golffing, *The Birth of Tragedy and The Genealogy of Morals* (New York: Doubleday, 1956).

2. In his book *Lessings Christentum* (Göttingen: Vandenhoeck & Ruprecht, 1980) Arno Schilson points to the lack of unified opinion among scholars and notes that hardly another modern thinker has experienced such contradictory interpretations as Lessing in his attitude toward Christianity (p. 7). Critics along the lines of O. Mann and H. Thielecke conclude that in the final analysis, Lessing wished to serve orthodox Christianity, whereas J. Schneider, B. Bothe, M. Bollacher, and E. Heftrich claim that he broke decisively with Christianity in an unparalleled radicality. Mediating between

ference of rational enlightenment, however, whereas Nietzsche, with a shriller voice and in sharp defense of individual potential, burst the confines of nineteenth-century convention.

Nietzsche valued Lessing's clean intellectual tenacity and polemical drive, seeing in him a "universality of spirit" that strained at the boundaries of his narrow bourgeois German existence (KSA, I, 183). In *Beyond Good and Evil* he praised Lessing's "free thinking," his "galloping tempo," "cheerful mood," and paradoxical style that challenged long and dangerous thoughts with stylistic grace and speed befitting a Machiavelli. Indeed, he sensed the "dry, fine air of Florence" in Lessing's "mischievous artistic feeling" and admired him as a philological and theological polemicist, while glossing over his other role as dramatist and aesthetician. Lessing, as the "most honest theoretical person," had even dared to annoy his contemporaries by announcing that he was "more interested in the search for truth than truth itself" (I, 99). Such an "excess of honesty" (first manifested in the figure of Socrates) may suffer from the illusion, however, that thinking itself can not only comprehend, but also correct existence—a function Nietzsche reserves to art. Theoretical thinking must necessarily turn over into art when it has reached its limitations, Nietzsche claims here, an insight Lessing certainly displayed when he brought his message of religious tolerance and plurality, his moral perspectivism cloaked in parable and dialogue, onto the stage with *Nathan the Wise*.

A recognition of the primacy of art over theory reveals an underlying sense of kinship in cognitive perception and stylistic expression, traits that are actually constitutive elements in Lessing's and Nietzsche's critiques of Christianity. Both question the objectification of knowledge that takes place in the historical process and then solidi-

---

these two extremes are critics such as G. Fittbogen, G. Pons, G. Rohrmoser, and L. Wessell, who interpret Lessing's criticism of Christianity as one of "Doppelbödigkeit" based on his high regard for the "Vernunftgehalt" of Christian "Glaubenswahrheiten" and ethics. Wessell stresses that Lessing's actual philosophical speculations about God, which occupy only a few pages, utilize Lutheran phraseology in the "letter" of his discourse, irrespective of what he may have meant esoterically, and claims that Lessing took "Christian supernaturalism very seriously in his attempt to integrate history and rationality" ("G. F. Meier and the Genesis of Philosophical Theodicies of History in 18th-Century Germany," *Lessing Yearbook*, 11 [1979], 64, and *G. E. Lessing's Theology: A Reinterpretation* [The Hague: Mouton, 1977]). Schilson provides a bibliography organized according to various facets of theological problems in Lessing scholarship. See also my article "Nietzsche and Lessing: Kindred Thoughts," *Nietzsche Studien*, 8 (1979), 157–81, for additional aspects of intellectual links between these two thinkers.

fies into orthodox belief, for such objectification of a singular experience into a general belief fundamentally denies the spirit of free inquiry that both sought to further. Lessing and Nietzsche polemicized against established, orthodox Christianity in its coercive forms for the sake of achieving greater authenticity and maintaining the process of speculative discourse rather than coming to a specific conclusion to the argument, for any such "result" would contradict the goal of widening the field of debate. It is not my intent to formulate any evolution of religious thought here or to discuss the manifold differences between these two thinkers, but to highlight some analogous features of their critiques of Christianity and their modes of communicating them. Lessing and Nietzsche engaged in "hermeneutic readings" of the Gospels to arrive at a possibly original view of Jesus through the optics of necessarily flawed and distorted historical transmission of experience: Lessing through his dealings with the Reimarus fragments, and Nietzsche chiefly in *The Antichrist*. Inherent in this distinction between the "original" and the "copy," the "spirit" and the "letter" of religion is the Kierkegaardian skepticism about whether historical accidental "truth" with all its proofs and the force of longevity has any relationship whatsoever to the qualitatively altogether different realm of what he termed eternally real, unadulterated authenticity.[3] In other words, their main quarrel with Christianity was with its claim to exclusivity in truth and the resulting implication of authority to determine individual conscience based on "belief."[4] For Lessing the consequence of a relativization of church

---

3. Søren Kierkegaard, *Concluding Unscientific Postscript*, trans. David F. Swenson and Walter Lowrie (Princeton: Princeton University Press, 1974). In his "Introductory Remarks concerning the Objective Problem" of the *Unscientific Postscript* Kierkegaard states that the "truth of Christianity must be determined through a critical examination of the various sources" when viewed as historical (p. 23), but in the first chapter dealing with the "Historical Point of View" he states that since "anything historical is merely an approximation . . . essentially incommensurable with an infinite personal interest in eternal happiness" (pp. 24–25), scholarly critical theology and philology are inadequate tools to evaluate Christianity (p. 27). Religion is an "infinite personal passionate interest" which precludes historical objectivity (p. 28). Faith and not proof is the determining factor for Christianity, which in Kierkegaard's terms is essentially spirit, inwardness, and subjectivity (p. 33). In a chapter devoted to Lessing, he denies objective truth, which he considers to be "personal appropriation" (p. 71), and sees double reflection as the appropriate mode for communicating the "secrets" not conveyed by ordinary communication ("Attributable to Lessing," p. 73).

4. While varying in their specific assessments of the degree of distortion and misconstruction inherent in the temporal process of history, Lessing and Nietzsche utilize the same driving force of intellectual probing and ironic shift of perspective in an attempt to grasp the reality from which history separates us. It is an essential aspect of

authority was to establish a more rational basis for human moral action, whereas for Nietzsche it was to attack the foundations of one of the pillars of the sociopolitical structure of European civilization, to destroy it in the expectation of a moral anarchy that he hoped would generate a new kind of individual. With Lessing human autonomy would stem from an inculcation of moral values beyond the necessity for external coercion or religious codes; for Nietzsche, autonomy would come from a self-affirmative power and concentration on individual potential irrespective of societal consequences or external ethical imperatives.

Nietzsche's *Antichrist* is a compact and strident depiction of what the "discipline for truth . . . a triumph achieved finally and with great difficulty by the European conscience," sublimated and transformed from Christian into intellectual conscience (III, 600), has reaped in its effort to strip away layers of historical reception of what Jesus really was and how he lived. The heretical title appears at first to be the product of an irreverent, even atheistic will to truth, "where the intellect is strong, mighty, and at work without counterfeit today" (V, 409), divested of any guiding ideal. Nietzsche, however, recognized this as the last consequence of Christian morality stripped of all extrinsic factors, the Christian virtue of truthfulness turned against itself to arrive at the authentic reality of the "redeemer type," upon whose supposed teachings a world-historical religion was founded.[5] His antithesis is seen emerging not prior to

---

their critique of Christianity because it reflects what both perceive to be the paradoxical condition of man, in Friedrich Schlegel's terms "a finite being conceived in terms of the infinite," or in Kierkegaard's formulation for Plato's Eros of the *Symposium*, "the child born of the finite and the infinite" (*Kritische Friedrich-Schlegel Ausgabe*, ed. Ernst Behler, Jean-Jacques Anstett, and Hans Eichner [Munich: Schöningh, 1958–], II, "Ideen" No. 98, p. 266; Kierkegaard, *Unscientific Postscript*, p. 85).

5. In his *Positives Antichristentum: Nietzsches Christusbild im Brennpunkt nachchristlicher Anthropologie* (The Hague: Nijhoff, 1962) Hermann Wein emphasizes the anthropological significance of Nietzsche's assessment of God's death and its positive meaning for immanence, concluding: "Nietzsche nimmt Christus als Zeichen, als Gelegenheit zum Gleichnis vom nicht verleumdenden, vom Ja-tuenden Menschen, der nicht Richter sein will" (p. 114), whereby the rule of priestly teachings as the standard of morality has been broken. Dieter Henke's *Gott und Grammatik: Nietzsches Kritik der Religion* (Pfullingen: Neske, 1981) analyzes reason, morality, and decadence in religion as well as what remains after Nietzsche's criticism of religion with regard to mankind, and provides a fine bibliography of the relevant scholarly literature. In a chapter on "Nietzsche und das Christentum" (pp. 137–60), in his book *Zeitliches und Ewiges in der Philosophie Nietzsches und Schopenhauers* (Frankfurt am Main: Klostermann, 1977), Otto Most highlights not only the distinction Nietzsche makes between Jesus and Christianity, but also his evaluation of Jesus as a figure of decadence (p. 138), and maintains that

the final judgment, but in the first historical rendering of his significance, the entire Christian "truth" that Nietzsche terms "idle falsehood" and "deception," the opposite of what inspired the Christian movement in the beginning. Precisely that which is Christian in the ecclesiastical sense is anti-Christian in essence, Nietzsche claims: "things and people instead of symbols; history instead of eternal facts; forms, rites, dogmas instead of a way of life" (XIII, 162). Christ denied "everything that is today called Christian" (XIII, 517), and for this reason a true Christianity, not bound to dogma, might still be possible as a practice, as a "means to being happy," but not as an article of faith. One should take heed not to confuse Christianity as a historical reality with the source called to mind by its name, for such decadent manifestations as "Christian church," "Christian faith," and "Christian life" are seen as "an unparalleled misuse of words." The Jesus of *The Antichrist* is shown as depicting how one should live to feel "divine," "blessed," "in heaven," and does not point to transcendence, but to life as a "condition of the heart" (VI, 205–6; XIII, 154). As the great symbolist and master of sign language, semiotics, and metaphors, Jesus carried the "glad tidings" within himself and made them manifest in his actions, abrogating all concepts of sin, guilt, reward, and punishment—and all other connotations for the distance separating man and God (VI, 205). Jesus' essence, which defied formulation, was to signify that there were no longer any opposites, and he constituted a "new way of living, not a belief."

---

the history of Nietzsche's mind, his works, and his illness can be found in his attempts to find a replacement for his "verlorenen Gott in den verschiedenen Formen der Selbstvergottung" (p. 144). In his article on "Nietzsche's Mitigated Skepticism," *Nietzsche Studien*, 8 (1980), 260–67, Bernd Magnus discusses the basic problem of "knowledge" as that of reconstructing a text in much the same way as I view Nietzsche's attempts to reconstruct his image of Jesus. See also Jochen Kirchhoff, "Zum Problem der Erkenntnis bei Nietzsche," *Nietzsche Studien*, 6 (1977), 16–44; and Konrad Hilpert, "Die Überwindung der objektiven Gültigkeit," *Nietzsche Studien*, 9 (1980), 91–121, for a discussion of truth as process ("etwas, das zu schaffen ist und das den Namen für einen Prozeß abgibt" [p. 105]), rather than a static reality. Peter Köster, in his study "Nietzsche Kritik und Nietzsche-Rezeption in der Theologie des 20. Jahrhunderts," *Nietzsche Studien*, 10/11 (1981–82), 615–85, discusses the problems inherent in viewing Nietzsche's theological polemics as a hidden affinity to and support for Christianity in the vein of Karl Jaspers; he concludes that the theological reception of Nietzsche has its center in a "Krisis des Christlichen, die in ihren Ursachen kaum zureichend erfaßt werden kann" (p. 619). See also Bernd Magnus, *Nietzsche's Existential Imperative* (Bloomington and London: Indiana University Press, 1978), pp. 13–21, for a discussion of Nietzsche's views on morality and Christianity; and John T. Wilcox, *Truth and Value in Nietzsche* (Washington, D.C.: University Press of America, 1982), pp. 67–97, where the critique of Christianity is utilized as a test case for Nietzsche as a cognitivist.

Nietzsche sees him as eschewing the word, for "the word kills, everything fixed kills" (VI, 204), and as neither denying nor seeking to prove by exhortation, Scripture, or the sword, but constituting his own proof, his "kingdom of God" (VI, 203). Thus for Nietzsche the "Son of God" refers not to an historical person, but to an "eternal" reality in every moment, a state to which any individual, but never an entire society, can aspire at any time, in every epoch.

God is seen as nothing other than this immanent practice, whereby the "life," "truth," or "light" of which Jesus spoke are not to be taken literally, but as expressions of the "innermost," defying the limiting, fatal concretization of the word. All else—nature, reality, language itself—is merely symbolic, signs of inner feelings of joy and self-affirmation independent of any religion, cult, history, politics, psychology, books, or art. Nietzsche interprets Jesus as a living denial of the entire theological apparatus that has held mankind hostage to the promise of future happiness through the coercion of morality (VI, 204–6). His death signified that there was no transition to something else: "The 'Kingdom of God' is nothing to be anticipated: it has no yesterday and no tomorrow, it does not come 'in a thousand years'—it is an experience within a heart; it is everywhere; it is nowhere . . ." (VI, 206, 207). By holding out false promises beyond this, Nietzsche writes in the posthumous fragments, Christianity inevitably promotes nihilism in European civilization, for disappointed expectations lead to despair and defeat (XIII, 296).

Jesus—whether naive, sovereign, or "idiot," as he is variously presented by Nietzsche—represented undialectical instinct without denial, resistance, or resentment, whose death was the natural consequence of his "being," and Nietzsche views the disciples, especially Saint Paul, as having altered this death into a banner of martyrdom for their own political ends. Their inability to accept the tragic aspect of existence made Jesus' death a great puzzle for them, but they used this symbol to set in motion an entire system of sin and redemption, reward and punishment, eternal happiness or damnation —these "forms of systematic cruelty"—out of a sense of revenge and resentment against the ruling class of Judaism who had killed their "Messias." Thus instead of truth, error became the motivating principle, and conviction a powerful means of oppression and enslavement to their will (VI, 210). The newly powerful Christian priests misunderstood Jesus' essential message, his superiority over any feeling of resentment, and embraced the unevangelical feeling of revenge, transforming their "redeemer" into a theologian (VI, 240) to promote the coercive "thou shalts" to the masses (VI, 216).

For Nietzsche the subtle fragility of such types as Jesus is always destroyed in every age by rationalist philologists of the letter and not the spirit, "dysangelists" with political goals and tyrannical intentions who distort the elegant simplicity of the symbol to a flat and lifeless abstraction for purposes of propaganda and self-aggrandizement (XI, 201, 202). Such a manipulative priestly psychology seeks to prevent individual understanding and tame inquisitive man by means of the moral world-order, the instrument for man's torture, he claims: "Man shall not look beyond himself, he shall look down within himself, he shall not look prudently and cautiously into things in order to learn, he shall not see at all: he shall suffer" (VI, 228). Sin, the greatest "self-violation" of man, was invented to render every knowledge, every culture, every nobility of man impossible (VI, 228–29), and the shift of emphasis from this world to the hereafter deprives actual existence of its intrinsic value. Instead of earthly fulfillment, this priestly psychology promises heaven, and instead of knowledge, belief. The story of creation in Genesis was promulgated to drive home the moral that man should not think, and original sin, Eve's arrogance in attempting to share in that godly quality of knowledge, is punished by the loss of Paradise and the correlative hardships, all "nothing but expedient means in the battle against knowledge! Misery does not permit man to think" (VI, 227), Nietzsche concludes. In other words, the immanent possession of blessedness symbolized in the figure of Jesus is seen as having been perverted through historical religion to its opposite—suffering and resentment, loss and alienation. Love, the quality Nietzsche deems Christianity's "finest artistic device" and source of its lyrical and universal appeal, becomes an absurdity when contrasted with Paul's depiction of Jesus as sending to hell everyone who didn't believe in him. Paul appears as a contradictory psychological type whose "goodness," the "feeling of making judgments against everything beautiful, rich, powerful," his hatred against the laughing ones, made him rather the "wickedest of all people."[6] This paradox had assumed an ironically comic side in *Human, All-Too-Human*, when

---

6. K, pp. 83, 343. In "Dionysus versus the Crucified One" (see Chapter VI above) Jörg Salaquarda discusses Nietzsche's recognition of Paul's historical "greatness" as the essential promoter of the decadence movement heralded by Christianity. While perceiving God on the cross as the ultimate symbol of decadence and decline, Nietzsche attributes this cultivation of the value-laden name "Jesus Christ" entirely to Paul. In this sense, Paul was for him no "idiot," but rather a man of genius (p. 294). See also Salaquarda, "Der Antichrist," *Nietzsche Studien*, 2 (1973), 91–136, for a discussion of the meaning of the term "Antichrist" and its ramifications.

Nietzsche portrayed Paul as "God's persecutor" (II, 591). Just as absurd as the "hellish fear" that panicked God into driving out Adam and Eve from Paradise in his fear of rivals to his omniscience, as portrayed in Nietzsche's *Antichrist* (VI, 226), is the thought that God would establish the moral world-order of heaven and hell in order to satisfy his own vanity. This thought gains a more serious note when Nietzsche insinuates in a Feuerbachian anthropomorphic vein that the very cruelty projected into the Godhead must actually have been the incitement to the concept: "What a cruel and insatiable vanity must have flickered in the soul of whoever thought up such a thing, by himself or with another! Paul remained Saul—God's persecutor."

Nietzsche goes so far as to make Christianity responsible for the death of God and the demise of true morality, claiming in his unpublished manuscripts that "God suffocated from theology; and morals from morality."[7] Christianity represents in *The Antichrist* the revolt of the disappointed and embittered who, in their absolute misunderstanding of the type and dissatisfaction with immanent reality, sought "justice" by a revaluation of the very values Jesus embodied, producing the herd mentality, the modern antithesis to what he had actually symbolized.[8] They turned a great ahistorical symbol into an historical vain and petulant God, a living reality into a false literary abstraction, an individual God into a tyrannical generalization: "Decay of a God. God became the thing in itself" (VI, 184).[9] The historical success of Christianity, its tenacity and longevity, do not prove anything about the greatness of its founder, "but would rather testify

---

7. K, p. 337.

8. This is the central argument of *The Genealogy of Morals* (KSA, VI, 247ff.), of course, especially Book I, in which Nietzsche presents the revaluation of values or the slave revolt in morals (p. 268) brought about by those resentful of the autonomy of the ruling class. Jesus certainly represents another kind of autonomy, which expresses itself neither in ruling nor in reactive power in Nietzsche's portrayal, but in the freedom of existence that seeks no confirmation or denial. For this reason, Nietzsche can call him, "with some tolerance," a "free spirit," whose "symbolics par excellence" remains external to any religion, any specific experience or knowledge (VI, 204). Nietzsche's understanding of the type seems to rest on his comprehension of this symbolic representation, a perception or intuition beyond philosophical proof.

9. Throughout *The Antichrist* Nietzsche expresses his disdain for anything that remains fixed, any attempts to display validations or proofs because of an alleged philosophical or historical permanence rather than remaining subject to the constant test of reason (pp. 234–36). Thus Kant's imperatives appear as sacrifices to abstraction, a relinquishing of one's personal choice in morals to a concept of duty itself, a "recipe for decadence" (pp. 177–78). All easy generalizations fall into this fatal category for Nietzsche, but especially those having moral implications for human behavior of a regulative nature.

against him" (I, 320, 321).[10] In a "world-historical irony" (VI, 208) Jesus, the "bold anarchist," became a tool for the propagation of oppressive dogma (VI, 198), and modern man, in his insistence on the security of the word, the letter, has succumbed to the easy tyranny of "belief": "The formula of our happiness: A Yes, a No, a straight line, a goal . . ." (VI, 169).

Thus Christianity has become for Nietzsche, from his perspective of "the heights," a religion visible only in its negative components, in those detrimental to life—a mere "spectacle for the gods" serving to enslave mankind and paralyze action, a vivid incorporation of life-denying decadence (VI, 211–12).[11] Nietzsche's portrayal of the figure of Jesus, however, is that of a life in which opposites were reconciled and death accepted with equanimity, a symbolization of the merging of dissonances within life rather than a promise of future happiness. The semiotics and imagery of Jesus were artistic rather than theological, representational rather than regulative, accepting rather than denying of earthly life, Nietzsche insists, but his unreflective possession of godliness was thwarted to a codified repressive system of moral imperatives alienating mankind from itself and corrupting his natural state.

During the period of *The Birth of Tragedy*, Nietzsche considered the crucial metaphysical activity of man as art and not morality, postulating that only the "metaphysics of the artist" could decipher and embrace the chaos of being, a spirit that fundamentally denied the "moral interpretation and significance of existence" (I, 17). Although

---

10. Such success may be attributable in part to the martyrdom of Jesus and his followers, but Nietzsche denies that this has any relation to truth, that the cross is any argument (KSA, VI, 234–35). His basic view of historical Christianity is that it takes a stand against reason and intellectual independence, emphasizing intellectual pride as the greatest sin, whereas the ancients believed in the divine origin of reason and independence of mind as the highest virtue. See KSA, X, 26. Its worldly success may also be a result of the transformation of its God into a cosmopolitan deity "for everyone," an "anchor for all those drowning in sin and sickness," a reflection of man's own decadent state (VI, 183–84).

11. Here Nietzsche seems to continue a tradition of thinking in German literature in which the poet or philosopher assumes an elevated perspective and gives his assessment of the historical significance of an event or phenomenon by virtue of the "height" of his perception, his "distance" from the event or position as a late-comer within an era; e.g., Lessing's stance in *The Education of the Human Race*, "from a hill from which he believes he surveys more than the prescribed path of his present day," and Novalis's "Die Christenheit oder Europa," where the poet is "high enough to be able to smile back upon those above-mentioned earlier times." Cf. my article on "Lessing's Legacy to the Romantic Concept of the Poet-Priest," *Lessing Yearbook*, 4 (1972), 72.

Nietzsche's early purely aesthetic justification of existence was soon to be surpassed by a more comprehensive and profound acceptance of being in all its contradictoriness and admixture of pain and joy in his tragic vision of life, his posthumous writings during the period of *The Antichrist* evidence his repeated recourse to aesthetic terminology to depict the state of man faced with the dilemma of modernity, when past "philosophical" and "moral" truths have unmasked themselves as impotent, even retarding, forces. These explanations of the world appear as hurdles to be overcome rather than as guideposts to be respected. Philosophical decadence, which signaled the decay of Greek instincts, was followed by moral decadence, which promulgated Christian "virtue" while lacking any methodical means to test these "truths," and Nietzsche heralds a third stage of an "aesthetic" grasp of life overcoming the nihilistic decadence of its predecessors (XIII, 296). Indeed, the aesthetic condition is the source of language and communication; it represents the "power of suggestion" involving psychological and physiological dimensions, whereby the modern artist may even exhibit a form of "neurosis" in his heightened sense of perception and suggestibility (a condition, however, attributable to the inhospitable environment of "modernity" rather than to the type itself) (XIII, 298). "Pleasure is a feeling of power," Nietzsche claims here, noting that "reason" and "intoxication" are opposites that are nevertheless inextricably necessary to each other (XIII, 311). Here too Nietzsche's tragic perception is cloaked in aesthetic terms when he wistfully points to the fleeting duration of any kind of beauty, a transitoriness that should not serve to negate life in the Schopenhauerian vein, but rather should impel us toward exultation and embrace (XIII, 317).

Christianity with its moral world-view is consistently regarded as the nihilistic antithesis of the artistic world-view, but Jesus, who used sign language, semiotics, and images, "was no theologian" (VI, 203), Nietzsche asserts in *The Antichrist*. Nietzsche's image of the redeemer type is rather that of an effortless reconciliation of life's dissonances, with death accepted as a kind of seal on the transitory and fragile nature of life (VI, 203). This is not to say that he was lacking his usual ambiguity in his evaluation of the type he recognized in the historical figure of Jesus; as with all types he distilled from historical reality, Nietzsche was chiefly interested in utilizing Jesus as an illustration of something contrary, as a foil for exemplifying a basic flaw he perceived in a cultural tradition or value. The more positive aura that Jesus assumes in *The Antichrist* says less about what Nietzsche really thought of him than about what he thought of institutionalized religion, and what better way to hurl invectives against the edifice of Christianity than to demonstrate the absolute otherness of its cornerstone? By denying the authenticity of the founder's image, Nietzsche drew his sharpest weapon, and although he also terms Jesus a decadent lacking any will to power in his passivity, the great "indifferent" whose psychological reality should have been plumbed by a Dostoevsky (XIII, 180, 409; also VI, 202), one should be careful not to heap all those termed "decadent" into one barrel. As with most of his designations, the term "decadent" gains various shades of meaning and tone depending on the point the label is used to make. In both *The Antichrist* and the posthumous writings Nietzsche is careful to reject the heroic interpretation of Jesus according to Renan, and mocks any attempt to make him into a more complex or ironic figure (VI, 199–202). Faced with the poverty and "pinched existence" of the Jewish culture into which he was thrown by the accident of birth, Jesus chose to call his reality "good" instead of "bad" by choosing an "inner reality" that contrasted with his external historical frame (XIII, 296). His lack of concern for tomorrow or yesterday, his quiescent static existence, which Nietzsche variously associates with Buddhistic attitudes and Saint Francis of Assisi (XIII, 162, 160), belied any notion of progress and certainly failed to fulfill the role assigned to him as savior or political leader.

There is no element of destiny in Nietzsche's portrayal of Jesus in the posthumous fragments, and in one instance he terms him the "opposite to a genius," an "idiot" because of his inability to comprehend reality, who remains within the confines of his "world," his "truth," a stranger to the rest (XIII, 237). Kant too had been termed an idiot by Nietzsche, as one who did not face up to the reality of his times, an antirealist—and thus the term itself is subject to interpretation. Nietzsche probes rather sharply into the possible psychological causes for such a type as Jesus, attributing his childlike behavior to perhaps an arrested adolescence, a failure to mature, resulting in an inability to understand anything intellectual, "an idiot in the midst of a very clever people," the cleverest of whom was Paul (XIII, 237). This projection of characteristics is secondary, however, to Nietzsche's main thrust of anti-Christianity, for which the type serves him well. One should remember too that in *Ecce Homo* Nietzsche referred to himself as both a decadent and its opposite (VI, 266), and that while penning sharp and strident critiques of late nineteenth-century Christian culture, the "reality" of his own environment, he was slipping ever more into the unreality of isolation and madness, a poignancy that has not escaped notice by critics—among them Giorgio Colli, in his postscript to the volume containing *The Antichrist* (VI, 452ff.).

It is important to note here that despite his castigation of Christianity in *The Antichrist* and the fragments relating to it, Nietzsche credits this religion with two significant contributions to modernity: the legacy of antiquity, and the refinement of thought to a high level of self-reflection. Both are elements of much of his later thinking concerning the emergence of a new type of individual combining the insights of antiquity with contemporary refinement, the qualities of "nobility" with the power of the mind. He saw Christianity as contradicting not only Jesus' life, but also the entire heritage of antiquity. In heathendom he found the "type of spirit that absorbs and redeems internally the contradictions and questionable aspects of existence" (XIII, 266), whereas he regarded Christianity as a negative interlude and a retarding force. Despite spoiling the glorious spontaneity of heathen Greek culture, however, Christianity simultaneously preserved and transmitted it to us in an imperfect and distorted image, which must be carefully reconstructed to its original state by the discerning mind. Not a return to antiquity is envisioned, but rather a surpassing of Christian civilization, "to overcome everything Christian by something super-Christian and not just cast it aside" (XI, 682), a dialectical process reminiscent of Novalis's vision (in his *Christenheit oder Europa*) of a new age reflecting the past as "a mirror image of its father" and encompassing all stages leading to its flowering.[12]

One is to discover the south again, Nietzsche says, and "spread out a bright, glittering southern sky above oneself to reconquer the southern health and hidden power of the soul." Step by step this recapturing of the amoral spirit of antiquity is to unfold and surpass the confines of ancient Greece to become "more supranational, European, supra-European, more Oriental, and finally more Greek—for the Greek was the first great union and synthesis of everything Oriental and with that the beginning of the European soul, the discovery of our 'new world'—" (XI, 682). This will perhaps bring about a new day and may even produce an individual surpassing the "perfected Christian" and the "perfected artist of the Romantic ideal," the noblest types Nietzsche had encountered previously, both elements of his own past. Thus Christianity assumes the contours of a transitional stage with a specifically educational value, and even Nietzsche

---

12. Novalis (Friedrich von Hardenberg), *Schriften*, ed. Paul Kluckhohn, Richard Samuel, et al. (Stuttgart: Kohlhammer, 1960–), III, 519.

is proud of his Christian heritage with its rhetorical subtleties, considering it an honor to derive from a family stock that in every sense of the word took its Christianity seriously (X, 382).

It was of course the "semblance of Greek serenity" that had raised the hackles of the "profound and formidable natures of the first four centuries of Christianity." The life of the immediate present rather than a preoccupation with the past and future—"the moment, wit, and levity" of the Greeks—was envied by the slave mentality of Christianity, but this too, ironically, was a false image of Greek antiquity, "that pale red color of serenity" steadfastly maintained by the tenacity of Christian conviction and canonized by Winckelmann and German Classicism. As they had "misread" Christ, so too did they misconstrue antiquity and selectively omit the Greece of the sixth century B.C., with its birth of tragedy, mysteries, art, Pythagoras, and Heraclitus (I, 78). Modern man, however, now lives suspended between the values of two realms of his historical heritage—ancient Greece and Christian Europe, both in need of authentic reconstruction—between an intimidating Christianized morality and a similarly dispirited dilettantish emulation of antiquity by scholars. Christianity had placed its ideals on such a high and unattainable level that the virtues of antiquity and the naturalness they radiated were outdone, even to the degree that this spontaneity appeared repugnant and dull. "Later on, however, after one had indeed recognized that which was better and higher, but could no longer aspire to it, one could no longer return to the good and noble, to that virtue of antiquity, as much as one may have wished to" (I, 345), Nietzsche continues in *The Birth of Tragedy*.

Compounding the perplexity of man's modern soul is the fact that both of the images—that of ancient Greece and that of Jesus—transmitted through history and impacting him, are distortions. Jesus was not transcendent, nor was Greek culture superficially happy; both were complex entities cloaking inner realities by means of artistic representation. "Christ and Christianity—Dionysus and Winckelmann's Greece: these are the two comparable world-historical antitheses that have confounded modern man and led him to a low moral ebb, unfruitful and unhappy," Nietzsche claims, a state from which man must recover (I, 345–46).[13] The ancients became susceptible to

---

13. While it might seem inimical to link the figure of Christ with that of Dionysus and see in his traits of passive acceptance any similarity to the dynamic and ascendant Dionysian life-forces, Nietzsche does present them here analogically as misrepresented entities, whose distorted images have brought about decline. Furthermore, in their significance as Nietzschean types both demand symbolic, rather than literal,

the charms of Christianity only after they themselves had become soft and decadent, when it was a "blessing to meet those creatures who were more souls than bodies, . . . timid, flitting, chirping, well-disposed characters with a prospect of the 'better life' and because of that so modest, so proudly patient!"; but for the barbaric peoples, it was poison to their heroic, childlike souls. Here again, however, we see Nietzsche's shifting perspective, his capacity for seeing more than one side of a phenomenon, even one so roundly chastised as Christianity, when he turns the coin over and asks: "To be sure: without this weakening what would we still have of Greek culture? what of the entire cultural heritage of humanity? for the barbarians, untouched by Christianity, knew how to make a clean sweep of old cultures." If the lens of history causes distortion, then it is still to be preferred to complete obliteration of the past, and with the demise of Christianity diagnosed by Nietzsche from his modern historical standpoint, a good portion of antiquity has also become unintelligible, especially the entire religious basis for life (II, 478–79). For this reason too, it would be a false tendency to attempt an imitation of antiquity, to turn back the historical time clock and traverse the path of history into the past (II, 586). Christianity may have spoiled the glorious spontaneity of heathen Greek culture, but it simultaneously

---

comprehension. In *The Birth of Tragedy*, Dionysian music incites man to "strain his symbolic faculties to the utmost" and "express the very essence of nature symbolically," to tear asunder the Mayan veil of illusion in order to effect a "total emancipation of all the symbolic powers" of musical dynamics and recognize the unity of nature, an activity requiring that one reach the same level of self-expression manifested by these powers themselves (I, 33–34). Just as the Apollonian Greek with his unsymbolic logical orientation must have gazed upon the Dionysian entity with "awed surprise" (I, 34), so too did the disciples "misread" the symbol of Jesus, for they and their aims were qualitatively different from what he actually constituted. Symbolic understanding indeed becomes the key to perceiving figures such as Jesus and Dionysus in their essential reality beyond time and space, and for the discerning, although historically distant, reader, they contain within their own typologies that very demand for hermeneutic deciphering which their historical transmissions would obliterate. Symbols such as Jesus, Dionysus, and Zarathustra have a universal, eternal dimension, which in Nietzsche's grasp of the totality of existence emerge within an historical age and shimmer through the distortions of temporality, accessible only to those who comprehend symbolic representations, neither demanding nor permitting philosophical proofs of existence. Paul Ricoeur recognizes the creative aspect of modern man's "deciphering of illusions of religious consciousness," for in this process of demythologization, the "semantic charge" is virtually inexhaustible: "With symbolic language, we are in turn faced with a language which says more than what it says, which says something other than what it says and which, consequently, grasps me because it has in its meaning created a new meaning" (*The Philosophy of Paul Ricoeur*, ed. Charles E. Reagan and David Stewart [Boston: Beacon Press, 1978]).

preserved it and transmitted it to us, just as Nietzsche's attempts to "overcome" Christianity serve to underscore its significance for modern man.

Christianity also contributed the very quality Nietzsche so splendidly employs in his own analysis of the past in *The Gay Science*, namely, moral skepticism (III, 478), which certainly deprived man of his self-understood "virtues" and security, but permitted "free thinkers" to exist to show us the errors in history! Thus one cannot know "if God should be more grateful to the Devil or the Devil to God that everything has occurred as it has" (II, 479–80). Even Saint Paul is credited by Nietzsche for having given Christianity the linguistic depth and finesse without which it would have died of intellectual poverty (II, 322). Had Christianity lacked the "complexities and storms of such a mind, such a soul," we would hardly have heard of this small Jewish sect whose master died on the cross (III, 65), and had Paul not been such a tortured personality suffering from the fixed idea of the fulfillment of the Judaic code, Christianity might not have fared so badly in its historical transmission. There seems to be in Nietzsche's analysis, however, a certain necessity about the course of history with its biases and errors, with all the fallibility of its recorders, and in this sense, it serves a function similar to historically revealed religions in Lessing's *Education of the Human Race*. There is, in other words, an intimate connection between "truth" and "error," an implicit interrelationship denoting the impossibility of conveying any "truth" directly (or, as Michel Foucault notes in his essay on Nietzsche and genealogy, referring to Nietzsche's speculations in *The Gay Science*, perhaps truth is merely the "history of error," "the sort of error that cannot be refuted because it was hardened into an unalterable form in the long baking process of history").[14] The underlying "truth" remains inaccessible and inexpressible in the realm of historicity except through the indirect means of parable and symbol—and with Lessing, precisely through error.

There is furthermore the tendency in both Lessing and Nietzsche to view history in terms of successive stages in triads, whereby one stage is seen as necessary to the flowering of the next, which then in turn both negates and carries forward the essential quality of its predecessor until a third, critical level is reached—either a utopian view of human potential or, as is often the case with Nietzsche, a crucial

---

14. Michel Foucault, *Language, Counter-Memory, Practice*, Selected Essays and Interviews, trans. Donald F. Bouchard and Sherry Simon (Ithaca: Cornell University Press, 1977), p. 144. See also p. 146 for Foucault's definition of genealogy and Nietzsche's method.

stage of cultural degeneration demanding reversal. With Nietzsche, however, such schematized speculations are quite tentative and illustrative rather than attempts to depict any linear development; they are shortcuts to lengthier explanations. In Aphorism 25 of *The Antichrist*, for instance, Nietzsche reveals this tendency toward triadic thinking in his compressed analysis of the degeneration of the concept of God, where the thundering god of revenge, Jahweh, is supplanted by the milder version for sinners, and then reduced to a complete moral abstraction (VI, 193–94). In the posthumous writings nihilism is seen as residing in a vain promise for more than one can actually deliver, a discrepancy resulting in disappointment. Thus Jesus is not nihilistic, but Christianity is. Nietzsche delineates this cultural movement as an initial stage of philosophical supremacy and degeneration with the decay of Greek instincts; a second reign of morality with Christian virtues as the dominant force, until its bankruptcy in the hypocritical reaction to the disappointment of unfulfilled expectations in contemporary European civilization (XIII, 296); and a third stage of aesthetic freedom is envisioned, promoting individual autonomy along with enhanced communicative ability, an aesthetic condition he terms "will to power," since art always "wants more." This "will to power" generally expresses a will to change in the posthumous fragments, even a will to "lie," meaning here a recognition of the need for dissimulation, gesture, symbol—in short, a will to art in order to promote life, which is dependent on artifice or the veil of illusion for sustenance and growth. Above all, such a will requires antitheses, opposition (XIII, 260). Thus the task of the modern intellect is that of good reading of the text of history, which with an achievement of greater veracity could establish a basis for promoting a new internalized form of freedom, an emancipated individual not unlike that of Lessing's prophetic ideal in his *Education of the Human Race*.[15]

Lessing's analyses of Christianity are certainly more ambiguous and tentative than Nietzsche's, and commentators still disagree as to whether he was a firm believer in its main tenets such as transcendence. Certainly the hide-and-seek game he had to play with the

---

15. Secs. 25, 26, 31, 38, and 42 of *The Antichrist* are examples of Nietzsche's thesis that our perception of Jesus is distorted by falsifications and a denaturalized reading of his essence. In sec. 42 (KSA, VI, 218) he cautions that one cannot read the Gospels enough because of the difficulties residing behind every word, the artistry utilized in words and gestures communicated to falsify, for which reason they can be read as "just literature." The art of reading consists in reading things without falsifying them through interpretation, however (sec. 52; p. 233).

censors, the sensitivity of his immediate public to such massive criticism of prevailing religious beliefs, the controversy surrounding the publication of the "anonymous" Reimarus fragments, and the fierce battle with Pastor Goeze, along with the ensuing withdrawal of the freedom from censorship and the simultaneous publication ban, provide obstacles to a clear picture.[16] Just such considerations impelled him to be circumspect in his pronouncements, to mask his true intent and radical views with an esoteric language of semiorthodoxy (as Henry Chadwick claims of the *Education of the Human Race*), even ostensibly to choose sides with his orthodox opponents rather than ally himself with newer, more liberal groups. The mask of orthodoxy was also useful as a smoke screen for being on closer guard against his secret enemies: "I get along with my public enemies in order to be on even better guard against my secret ones," he wrote to his brother Karl in March of 1777.

Lessing's intellectual honesty is coupled with his renowned stated preference for the pursuit of truth above its possession in his *Rejoinder*, not merely because of his humility before the uniquely godly prerogative of omniscience and the practical considerations of threatened censorship, but, as Hannah Arendt has pointed out, precisely because he wished to continue the discourse and maintain the possibility for further debate in the world.[17] Thus Lessing states:

> The worth of a man does not consist in the truth he possesses, or thinks he possesses, but in the pains he has taken to attain that truth. For his powers are extended not through possession but through the search for truth. In this alone his ever-growing perfection consists. Possession makes him lazy, indolent, and proud. If God held all truth in his right hand and in his left the everlasting striving after truth, so that I should always and everlastingly be mistaken, and said to me, "Choose," with humility I would pick the left hand and say, "Father, grant me that. Absolute truth is for thee alone."[18]

---

16. See Schilson, pp. 18–20; and *Lessing's Theological Writings: Selections in Translation*, trans. Henry Chadwick (Stanford: Stanford University Press, 1967), in his introduction, pp. 105f.
17. *Gotthold Ephraim Lessings sämtliche Schriften*, ed. Karl Lachmann and Franz Muncker, 3rd ed. (Stuttgart/Leipzig: 1886–1924), XVIII, no. 546, pp. 226–27 (hereafter cited as LM); Hannah Arendt, *Men in Dark Times* (New York: Harcourt, Brace & World, 1968), p. 27.
18. LM, XIII, 23–24. For Nietzsche the search for truth was preferable to its possession because a certain amount of illusion is necessary for the maintenance of life.

The optics of perspectivism inherent in the famous parable of the three rings that is central to Lessing's drama *Nathan the Wise* conveys not only the message of human tolerance, but also that of the impossibility of human perception of one single truth valid for all at any time. It is a difficult task for the critic to make any definitive assessment of Lessing's personal beliefs in terms of Christianity precisely because of what Søren Kierkegaard called Lessing's evasiveness, his ability to "carry himself circumspectly . . . while achieving the still more difficult task of keeping silent through speaking." It was Lessing's merit that he prevented direct admiration, says the ironic Kierkegaard, and that he did not become "world-historical and systematic," so that he isolated himself within his own subjectivity focused solely on the religious and God and not men, and his religious sensibility had no result at all! Thus he had seized upon the Archimedean point of the religious life and was an "essential individual . . . of decisive subjectivity" who maintained his dialectical insights within himself to prevent their diversion into the hands of some merely external possessor.[19] Kierkegaard emulates and illustrates Lessing's bilevel hermeneutic style by ironically stating that he lacked "seriousness and dependability," and by chiding him for not having stated outright: "I defend Christ." He was one of those religious subjects with the "remarkable trait that it [religion] comes into being for the individual and closes behind him," Kierkegaard claims, although one could argue that Lessing left this door sufficiently ajar to allow us to ponder just what he actually thought. He was such a remarkable teacher for Kierkegaard because he defied any objectification and evaded the "stupid attempts of fanatics to enroll him in the service of positive social ends" as well as their "presumptuous attempts to exclude him." Not slogans or systems, but artfulness marks the style that complements the sensibility, whereby jest and earnestness confound each other and the emphasis "is often placed upon the indifferent, so that the initiated may precisely in this manner best grasp the dialectically decisive point, while the heretics get nothing to run with."[20]

Lessing's prose functions on two levels, confiding to the reader "sub rosa" that he keeps up with the thought and managing to convey to others a truth, whose chief feature it is that it is intensely personal and cannot really be transmitted, "that one must be alone about it." This paradoxical communication—indirect, ironic, Socratic,

---

19. Kierkegaard, *Unscientific Postscript*, p. 71.
20. Ibid., pp. 61–65.

and elusive—requires creative activity on the part of the reader in his historically advanced position, a kind of contemporaneity despite historical distance, which "excludes every historical illusion . . . every perverse objective falsification." Lessing as a teacher never made appeals, never coerced, never pronounced doctrine, for that would have contradicted the very essence of his intellectual position. Thus he does not attack or defend Christianity, but always changes the letter of his discourse to maintain the spirit. He solved the problem Kierkegaard saw as germane to the modern religious sensibility by living the paradox and communicating the incommunicable, by refusing the objectification of a profoundly subjective experience. He was free and wished to make all others free in relation to himself, was secure without binding others to his security, and engaged in the kind of double reflection that emancipates the recipient by communicating with him artistically and eschewing the need for majority approval or the certainty of witnesses, these "town criers of inwardness," these disciples who invert the message of their teacher.[21]

Kierkegaard's reception of Lessing is significant in this context, not especially for its uniqueness in presenting this product of the Enlightenment in bourgeois German society as a model existentialist religious thinker, but because what he says about Lessing and his mode of thought and communication is so applicable to the hermeneutic problem at the core of Nietzsche's critique of Christianity: the distinction between Christ and the religious structure he unwittingly generated. It parallels the underlying insight that the best religion, the most effective teacher, forgoes convictions, proofs, doctrines, claims to historical objectivity, paralyzing ritual, and promises for the future.

Nietzsche's complex will to truth (III, 575–77) is tempered by the recognition that our perceptions are constantly subject to a variety of shifting perspectives and the filter of subjective values, that there are no absolute truths that enjoy universal validity (a view compatible with Lessing's). He thinks that man will never exhaust the possibilities for interpreting existence, and he can therefore state that "nothing is true and everything permitted" (V, 398–401; XI, 88, 155; IV, 340). Nothing should be exempt from the process of continual testing and experimentation (III, 415–16). The only form of "truth" Nietzsche admits is that of symbolic or metaphoric expression, subject to interpretation—but these too, however, may easily become "illusions about which one has forgotten that they are illusions," and

---

21. Ibid., pp. 67–71.

"a sum of poetized and rhetorically exalted human relations" may experience such embellishment and long tradition that they eventually appear as canonical beliefs (I, 880–81). The will to truth is not only experimentation, but also manifests itself as a temptation to seek security, to ascertain and force transitoriness into the framework of permanence. Truth is only a label for a process, a "processus in infinitum," an ever-active determination rather than a consciousness of something stable and definitive (XII, 384–85), and language may be ultimately an inadequate expression of reality (I, 878).

Thus the imperative of "belief" so central to the Christian religion is for Nietzsche a weakness, an illness, the condition of unwillingness to maintain the unending pursuit of truth. The doctrine of personal immortality is nothing more than a comforting human preference for the illusion of a beautiful lie (VI, 225, 232–34, 229–30), and belief is still only belief, the enemy of knowledge. Intellectual honesty demands strength, sacrifice, and a noble soul. The conviction that God is interested in our personal welfare may be heartening, but it is an abuse of godly dexterity to interpret the "finger of God" as a power that will cure a cold or hold off the rain until we have safely entered the coach! Indeed, any god so constructed would be an absurdity, an errand-boy or postman, a negative factor of belief, and that is what Christian philology has produced! (VI, 232–33). It is indeed human, all-too-human, to cling to such convictions, to experience "miracles and being born again," to "hear the voices of angels!" (III, 551).[22]

When we hear church bells on a Sunday morning, Nietzsche says, this is a reminiscence of the crucifixion of one who long ago claimed to be the Son of God, but "the proof for such a contention is completely lacking" (II, 116–17). Martyrdom is ineffective as a proof, and Nietzsche questions whether anything is changed about a matter simply because someone sacrificed a life for it. Truth is not something one person has and another does not, and martyrdom has perhaps better served the cause of error. "Today one needs only the crudest persecution of an ordinary sect to give it an honorable name" (VI, 234–35). But perhaps the greatest danger in the drive for the certainty of belief is not that of false hope or security, but rather fanaticism. Convictions are but prisons, means for keeping individu-

---

22. See also sections 109, 121, 319, and 347 of *The Gay Science* for examples of Nietzsche's ideas about belief as a desire for something definitive that is, however, mere belief and not truth. "But we, we other ones, thirsty for understanding, want to look our experiences straight in the eye, hour by hour, day by day! We ourselves want to be our own experiments and guinea pigs!" (KSA, III, 551).

als dependent, subject to control, and alienated from themselves (VI, 236–37).[23] The objectification of knowledge that takes place in this historical process and forms the basis for belief in orthodox Christianity fundamentally denies the spirit of free inquiry that links Lessing to Nietzsche's intellectual process.

Kierkegaard had recognized a similar cognitive mode in Lessing's deliberate evasiveness in matters of belief and his desire to forgo being understood by everyone. Stupidity is the prerequisite for such success, whereas subtle religious meaning—or the attempt to "win disciples to the doctrine of not having disciples," as Lessing had done—is another matter entirely and requires infinite patience and an understanding of the "secrets" of artistic communication. Lessing thus reflects the paradox of expressing the conviction "that it is not the truth but the way which is the truth, that is, that the truth exists only in the process of becoming, in the process of appropriation, and hence that there is no result."[24] For Nietzsche, too, this remained the last virtue, the last remnant of Christian morality, and it is central to the similarly elusive style of his prose and the relentlessness of his inquiry.

Upon publication of the Reimarus fragments that postulate a relationship between Jesus and the evangelists surprisingly like that depicted in Nietzsche's *Antichrist*, Lessing foresaw that his motives would be misconstrued. "I take the risk that my intentions will be misunderstood and my suggested goals misinterpreted," he wrote, and he cautioned against identifying Reimarus's theory with his own views.[25] Yet Reimarus's "proof," illustrated by contradictory passages from the Gospels stating that Christianity is a falsification and Jesus of Nazareth was a person different from the Son of God, provided Lessing with a welcome stimulus for debate about the relationship between revealed truth and human understanding. Such proofs have little value other than that of attacking the letter, but not the spirit, of religion, whose claim to "truth" lies outside the realm of the written word of the Bible—which is not necessarily the word of God, as Lessing assures Goeze in his *Axiomata*. Religion existed before evangelists and apostles wrote a single word of the Bible, which in any case can never encompass the entire truth of the Christian reli-

---

23. Fanatics such as Savonarola, Luther, Rousseau, Robespierre, and St.-Simon suffer from a pathological optical restriction according to Nietzsche, but because they are picturesque and humanity would rather see gestures than listen to reason, they are quite effective with the masses (KSA, VI, 236–37).
24. Kierkegaard, *Unscientific Postscript*, p. 71.
25. LM, XIII, *Eine Duplik* I, p. 21.

gion.²⁶ Lessing seeks to maintain the distinction between religion and its history, disdaining the "myopic hermeneuts" with their theological explanations and proofs.²⁷ Furthermore, the subjective realm of religion, which Goeze fears is impaired by exposure to the Reimarus fragments, is for Lessing something insusceptible to any external corruptive influence, for it is "the disposition of the human heart with respect to religion," involving the most internal religious spirit.²⁸

Lessing's posthumous fragments, "The Religion of Christ," delve further into the separation of Christ and Christianity and give convincing testimony to his personal view of Jesus as one who lived and practiced a religion that could be shared by all individuals according to their own assessments of the nobility and worthiness of Jesus as a person, while the Christian religion made Jesus more than a man and the object of adoration. Whereas the religion of Christ is manifested in the Bible, that of Christianity is ambiguous to such a degree that it is "incomprehensible" that both religions could exist simultaneously in this figure.²⁹ Lessing reiterates his assessment that

26. LM, XIII, Axiomata V–VII, pp. 116–21.
27. LM, XIII, Axiomata X, p. 134. Lessing distinguishes between "inner" and "hermeneutic" truth when he chides Goeze for testing inner truth by means of the hermeneutic, concluding: "Als ob die innere Wahrheit eine Probe noch brauchte! Als ob nicht vielmehr die innere Wahrheit die Probe der hermeneutischen sein müßte!" (p. 128). Kierkegaard refers to Lessing's essay "Über den Beweis des Geistes und der Kraft" (LM, XIII, 1–8) to support his own thesis that the "attempt to create a quantitative transition to a qualitative decision" must fail, and cites Lessing's attack on the "direct transition from historical trustworthiness to the determination of an eternal happiness" (Kierkegaard, *Unscientific Postscript*, p. 88). In this essay Lessing makes a clear separation between the power of the "original" acts of prophecy and miracles and that of the accounts of such miracles transmitted by the apostles: the power of the former resided in the immediacy of the witnessing, whereas the subsequent reporting of the events has only the reliability of all historical truths; he concludes: "Wenn keine historische Wahrheit demonstriert werden kann: so kann auch nichts durch historische Wahrheiten demonstriert werden. Das ist: zufällige Geschichtswahrheiten können der Beweis von notwendigen Vernunftwahrheiten nie werden" (LM, XIII, 5). See also Klaus Bohnen, *Geist und Buchstabe. Zum Prinzip des kritischen Verfahrens in Lessings literaturästhetischen und theologischen Schriften* (Köln: Böhlau, 1974), for a discussion of Lessing's distinction between the letter and the spirit of communication as it relates to his *Education of the Human Race*.
28. LM, XIII, "Anti-Goeze III," p. 155. Here Lessing states unequivocally that he would publish the controversial Reimarus fragments again even if Goeze should damn him to the deepest abyss of Hell.
29. LM, XVI, "Die Religion Christi," nos. 1–8. Schilson points out that Lessing strives to maintain the separation of religion from its history and that the rock of Christ is seen as faith and not the written word (Schilson, *Lessings Christentum*, p. 24).

"Christ was simply a teacher inspired by God." The brief posthumous fragments motivate Claus Träger to conclude: "Lessing was a heretic. It was not the Christian religion, but rather the religion of Christ with which he identified. . . . The dominant ideology naturally falls apart when confronted with the impression of a human example that man makes for himself out of the religious founder."[30] If one agrees with Lessing's own description of a heretic as "a person who at least wants to see with his own eyes," a title that has its "very good aspects" and in certain centuries constitutes "the best recommendation that a scholar can bestow upon future generations," then this is a label he wore with ease.[31]

The specific image of Jesus conveyed by Lessing is not as central to our topic as the nature of his dispute with the orthodoxy that maintained the validity of the letter of the evangelists' interpretation, a literal validity doubted by Lessing and vehemently denied by Nietzsche. The question of whether or not Lessing believed the details of Reimarus's "primary assault upon the Christian religion" is irrelevant to the issue of the letter and the spirit of Christianity, that discrepancy existing between the figure of Jesus historically transmitted through the written word and imprinted on mankind by means of theological proofs and historical validation and the type perceived hermeneutically beneath the accretions of the historical church by his spiritual contemporaries. It is precisely this quality of contemporaneity in spirit with the past that so indebted Kierkegaard to Lessing and that Nietzsche in unstated fashion assumed as his own basis for interpretation. It is a subjective quality, a trust in one's individual perceptive capacity, which makes it possible for such critics to rattle the structure of historical edifices for the sake of a better understanding of the great types who originally inspired them. There is perhaps no area sensitive toward its claims to validity as religion, which in Christianity is seen by Lessing and Nietzsche to have objectified the elusive spirit of its unwitting founder and thus turned into his antithesis. Authenticity and ideology are rendered incompatible.

To be sure, Lessing's *Education of the Human Race* has been interpreted as his attempt to reconcile the Christian concept of revelation

---

30. Claus Träger, "Lessing—Kritik und Historizität," *Sitzungsberichte der sächsischen Akademie der Wissenschaften zu Leipzig*: Philologisch-historische Klasse, Band 121, Heft 5 (Berlin, 1981), p. 9.
31. LM, XI, 62–63. Otto Best, in his article "Noch einmal: Vernunft und Offenbarung. Überlegungen zu Lessings 'Berührung' mit der Tradition des mystischen Rationalismus," *Lessing Yearbook*, 12 (1980), 123–56, takes up the question of Lessing as "Ketzer" (pp. 123–24) as a point of departure for his study.

with the Enlightenment ideal of human understanding, the supernatural with the reasonable, the eternal with the temporal. Lessing projects the historical process as a progressive enlightenment of mankind through piecemeal revelation, represented in past religions and leading to a third stage of development when Judaism's system of immediate retribution and Christianity's doctrine of rewards and punishments in the hereafter are abandoned because the moral good has become completely internalized, automatic, and instinctive.[32] Published as a balance to Reimarus's hypothesis, the first fifty-three paragraphs of the *Education* seek to defuse the arguments against the validity of revealed religion, against the error of inconsistency of biblical transmission, by presenting even error as a rational means of education, a tool in the hands of a providential deity of infinite patience with man's still-limited receptive capacities. In such a scheme, where miracles serve as educational devices and the "inner purity of the heart" characterizing Jesus reflects man's own goal, progress is seen as a "large, slow cycle," which by means of "smaller, faster cycles . . . brings the human race closer to its perfection."[33] Absolutes thus become relativized in history, and error justified. The "truth" of revelation is purposeful, and Lessing's skepticism toward revealed religion grows with the strength of its claims to knowledge. Citing the hero of his drama of tolerance, Lessing states that "Nathan's attitude to all positive religions has long been mine."[34] All differences of opinion can be harmonized in the shared recognition that truth is piecemeal, hidden, conditional, and ultimately unknowable to mankind, and Lessing concludes in his fragment entitled "The Christianity of Reason" that man as a moral being has but one choice: "Act according to your individual perfections." Noting that "in the series of beings there cannot possibly be a jump," he speculates that there "must also exist beings who are not sufficiently clearly conscious of their perfections," a thought underscoring both the need for progression in Lessing's basic approach and the individualistic nature of this human development.[35]

Although many passages in *The Antichrist* and in others of Nietzsche's speculations present a skeptical, even negative, view of that idea of progressive human development toward a higher goal which is so germane to Lessing's *Education*, others reveal a fervent expectation of a self-overcoming and emancipated form of human existence

32. LM, XIII, "Die Erziehung des Menschengeschlechts," nos. 1–100, pp. 415–36.
33. LM, XIII, no. 61, p. 428; no. 92, pp. 434–35.
34. LM, XVI, 399–400, 444.
35. LM, XIV, 175–78.

unparalleled in history and surpassing its limitations. While claiming that "future development" is not necessarily progress, heightening and strengthening, and that humanity does not represent development toward a something better (VI, 171), Nietzsche provides another reading of mankind's future in the *Genealogy of Morals* and *Thus Spoke Zarathustra*. It is my contention that beneath the surface of despair about the declined state of human affairs, behind the words of anger at what Christian morality has wrought, there resides within his thought more than a glimmer of hope for individuals willing to see and exchange the "false optic" of belief—the "mental cobwebs" of abstract moral imperatives—for personal choices, and to reject vain hopes of projected heavenly bliss in favor of one's immanent fate (VI, 175, 177–78). Christianity, castigated on the one hand as a decadent will to decline directed against the very instinct for life and growth (VI, 172–75), is recognized as still possible as an "intensely private form of existence"—a paradox only if one does not distinguish the subjective, individual option from that of political Christianity (XII, 532).

In its negation of sensuality and procreation Christianity seems antithetical to life (II, 130), a corruption of everything natural by its impression of sin upon mankind, an inversion of morality in order to create an artificial need for redemption. Its goal for man may not be "that he become increasingly moral, but that he feel as sinful as possible" (II, 134–37). Even the Enlightenment, with its emphasis upon human reason, may have worsened the sorry lot of man by applying stark rationality to human problems and giving them a pessimistic note. "Around 1770 one could notice a decline in joyfulness," Nietzsche claims, and he sees superficial optimism as the culprit, the beautiful belief that glosses over suffering, but cannot eliminate it from man's consciousness: man "alone suffers so deeply, that he had to invent laughter" (XI, 571).

Progress may be mere illusion, and mankind may reach a lower ebb in the future (III, 51, 52). But seen from the perspective of one who views life not as an ascending progression toward a utopian ideal, as Lessing did, but rather as an anarchic and dynamic wellspring for ever-new forms of human potential, these ups and downs (the low point symbolized in Christianity) may be positive and negative stimuli to renewal and change. Out of the enormous ruins of history, "where some things still tower, where much remains decayed and dismal," where the belief in God has become incredible and ascetic ideals are on the wane, there may emerge something more powerful and vital (III, 602). Like Novalis's assessment of his contemporary age, these "beautiful ruins" may constitute the productive anarchy for a new emergence of mankind in which the subtleties and intellectual refinements of Christianity, its self-doubt and questioning will to truth, will be preserved and made fruitful to produce an autonomous and authentic human existence cleansed of bad conscience and external coercions.

To be sure, Nietzsche will not admit even a symbolic guiding hand of Providence through revelation in his reflections, for even as a pedagogical device, such a God appears too ridiculous for belief. A God who sacrifices himself for human sin out of love for his debtor taxes credibility (V, 330–31), and all the means that have been utilized to render man moral, were "basically immoral" (VI, 102). Furthermore, historical experience has taught Nietzsche to be wary of projecting God into the accidents of history: "If human affairs seem wild and disorderly, I certainly don't believe that God had a purpose for this or permits it," he admonishes. "Such thinking robs chance of its innocence!" (VI, 194). A false belief in Providence has enabled man to justify the ways of history, to absolve himself from personal responsibility. The conviction that God "who, although he loves the dark and crooked paths, in the last analysis still leads everything to a 'marvelous end'" is a fable, and one should question "whether the tile that falls from the roof is really thrown off by 'divine love.'" These means are not God's, he suggests, but ours: "And our own nets are torn apart by ourselves just as often and just as clumsily as by the tile. And not everything is a purpose that is labeled as such" (III, 120–22). Providence is a term that makes things easy for us, and accidental events cannot serve as proofs for it. Furthermore, it is highly questionable to assume that this chaos of life, "this whirlpool is reasonable and has a reasonable purpose,"[36] or to interpret nature as a "proof of God's goodness and care" (III, 600). Thus, while Lessing in the *Education of the Human Race* utilizes the letter of orthodox Christianity to convey his hopes for mankind's eventual release from error and growth to autonomy, Nietzsche rejects not only any comforting idea of a providential hand in the process, but even the likeli-

---

36. This posthumous passage is quoted from K, II, "Wir Philologen," no. 158, p. 584. Here Nietzsche muses that the only understanding we possess is the "little bit of understanding of the human being," and it is always to one's own disadvantage to relegate anything to "Providence." He highlights the intuitive, artistic quality of "understanding" (Vernunft) and considers the artist as the individual who possesses this faculty to the highest degree and therefore derives a special happiness from his work. If a work is created through consciousness, there is perhaps an even greater feeling of "understanding and happiness" to be achieved, Nietzsche speculates.

hood of reason or goals in history. Lessing's spiral of development tends to reach progressively higher levels, whereas Nietzsche's projection is one of cyclical emergence and retreat, augmentation and decline, in which entire cycles may rise and fall, but remain dynamic. There is one particular pattern he discerns in a cycle, which he illustrates through Christianity, but everything in the course of history is seen as the result, not of divine guidance or reason, but of man's own actions.[37]

Just as Nietzsche had been able to view Christianity as both the reaction against and the preserver of antiquity, so does he present this religious phenomenon in the *Genealogy of Morals* as the beginning of another cycle moving from man's condition of external moral compulsion to one of a potentially new innocence that emerges by way of an intermediary second stage of human rebellion against moral domination (V, 293–97). As an animal who can make promises, man has had to learn to resist the natural impulse toward forgetfulness by creating memories for himself, "a proper memory of the will," in order to repress immediate desires. He must alter the instinctive urge for momentary gratification to that which is "calculable, regular, and necessary," in order to be able to keep promises for the future (V, 292). Such is the history of human responsibility, the tremendous task of "the morality of mores," which seeks to transform and tame the sovereign individual through the inculcation of bad conscience, guilt, and sin by the cruelest rituals common to religious cults and ideals (V, 294). Brutal punishments of man's sensual and spiritual existence are inflicted by religion to drive him to asceticism and painful self-reflection and thus to impress memory upon him: "Ah, reason, earnestness, mastery over the affects, this entire dismal thing called reflection, all these prerogatives and showpieces

---

37. In his "New Education of the Human Race" (III, 26), Nietzsche disputes the interpretation of "cause and effect" as necessarily that of "cause and punishment," whereby even existence itself has been construed as the punishment. He exhorts all well-meaning individuals to help eradicate the concept of punishment, which has spread like a weed throughout the globe. Clearly referring to the same kind of scheme Lessing drew upon for his *Education of the Human Race*, Nietzsche chides the simplistic Christian theologians who explain the concept of God as developing from the "God of Israel," the "folk" God, to the "Christian God," and ultimately to the quintessence of everything good (VI, 171). He evaluates this alleged "progress" as a reduction of the godly to an anchor for the drowning, to a god for the multitude, a democratic cosmopolitan. Taken literally, Lessing's *Education* would thus have to be rejected as another "false Idea," but as I have tried to show, Lessing's "letter" of discourse often betrays its subversive spirit, and the affirmation of human potential should be understood symbolically within the context of his epoch.

of man: How dearly they have been bought! how much blood and horror lies at the bottom of all 'good things!' " (V, 296–97).

The cruelest form of memory-making, however, is man's own consciousness of being indebted to God: "The feeling of guilt toward the divinity has not stopped growing for thousands of years," Nietzsche claims, and it increases in proportion to the strength of the concept and reverence for God on earth. The emergence of the Christian God as the "maximum-God" has also created the maximum of guilt, an apex for which the inevitable decline, even reversal, is already visible. Along with this decline in the belief in God, one can even anticipate a concurrent waning of human feelings of guilt, and a "complete and definitive atheism might even free mankind from this whole feeling of indebtedness toward its origin, its *causa prima*," for atheism and a kind of second innocence go hand in hand (V, 329–30).

Just as in Zarathustra's tale of the "Three Metamorphoses" the camellike existence of the "herd" man who suffers the humiliation of the imperative "Thou shalt" is followed by the rebellious and powerful lion, only to be supplanted by the third symbol of the child born into a new innocence and characterized by playfulness, so too does Nietzsche envision an emergence of a new human being out of the two previous stages of morality (IV, 29–31). Punishment meted out by an autonomous power for transgressions against it, wherein the spirit and the letter of the retribution are one, is refined through Christian conscience to the internalized agony of guilt, self-doubt, and torment. This self-inflicted punishment for one's perceived sins against a self-defined God reaches a feverish pitch until the propelling force of the Christian moral imperative to truthfulness is driven to its utmost power and turns on its own premises. Dogma becomes subversive to its own authority and is capable of self-annihilation. Christian truthfulness and the internalization brought about by bad conscience have the potential to lead human reflection to the last stage of doubt—atheism, out of which man's new innocence is born and the autonomous individual emerges.

This history of "responsibility" concludes its cycle of development from oppression to freedom, from domination to sovereignty, by means of the same force that initiated it, and when Nietzsche gazes down upon the final stage from his perspective he can place himself "at the end of the tremendous process, to that place where the tree finally bears ripe fruit." Morality and social convention are only the means of a previous stage in the process, whose "ripest fruit on the tree is the sovereign individual who is equal only to himself," having reached complete autonomy as a "supramoral individual." Such a person has surpassed the previous stage of morality, which is mutually exclusive to autonomy, to become his own independent will carrying in every muscle a consciousness of power and freedom, "a feeling of the perfection of mankind as a whole." This individual is envisioned by Nietzsche as superior by virtue of an achieved sovereignty and self-mastery and is the "free individual," the possessor of a long and unbreakable will requiring nothing external to itself and capable of maintaining itself against all misfortune, "even against fate" (V, 293–94). Responsibility has become instinct in the consciousness of freedom.

Thus, in Nietzsche's analysis, the last consequence of Christian morality must be the emergence of the autonomous individual, who has internalized the entire system of inducements to moral behavior to such a degree that what was first impressed from without to curb natural instinct is later refined to self-conscious reflection. Driven to its ultimate peak, reflection returns man to a new freedom, instinct raised to a higher power. This of course does not mark a reversion to either a previous amoral state of barbarism or the natural spontaneity of Greek heathendom, but is the result of a painfully developed refinement of conscience and consciousness—a classical idea reminiscent of Schiller's reconciliation of freedom and necessity and Kleist's return to graceful innocence through the cyclical movement of heightened consciousness.

Viewed from the perspective of utopian idealism, Lessing and Nietzsche both appear as thinkers who absorbed the subtlest ramifications of their religious heritages and made them fruitful for their own speculation, whereby the spirit of Christianity as symbolized in the figure of Jesus surpassed and obliterated its letter. Just as Lessing had called for a third gospel for mankind, and the Romantics for a new Bible, so did Nietzsche exhort free thinkers to make the old scriptural gospel superfluous through new words and deeds: "a new Bible should emerge through you!" (II, 418). Not faith—that "leap" to something qualitatively different which Lessing humorously avoided in his famous excuse of legs too feeble for its accomplishment—will bring mankind to its fulfillment, but a realization of what is within human potential. The "realm of grace" is not to be found elsewhere for Nietzsche: "Is love of fellow man a grace? Is your sympathy a grace? If this is possible, then go one additional step: love yourself out of grace, then you won't need your God any more, and the whole drama of original sin and redemption plays itself out within yourself!" (III, 77–78).

XI. Nietzsche, Heine, and the Otherness of the Jew

Sander L. Gilman

I. The Problem

Nietzsche's works are full of false dichotomies. Of these, the most problematic politically has been his distinction between the Greek and the Jew. Indeed, if this is a polarity, the very labeling of Plato as the quintessential anti-Hellene and Semite must force the reader to ask exactly what Nietzsche understood by the generalized terms "Jew" or "Semite" or "Hebrew."[1]

Nietzsche perceived three moments in the natural history of the Jew: the Jew as the prophet of the Old Testament, serving the angry and holy Jehovah; the Jew as the archetypal wandering Christian (Saul), weak and destructive; and the Jew as contemporary, the antithesis of all decadence, self-sufficient and incorruptible.[2] All three of these images serve as stereotypes incorporating qualities that Nietzsche wishes to present as either positive (as in the first and last cases) or negative. All of these moments are, in the last analysis, negative, in that they reduce the perception of a group of single individuals to the generalities of a class. The search for the source

---

1. All references to Nietzsche's works are to KSA (here, XIII, 114), which is at present the most complete and accurate edition of *all* of Nietzsche's works; translations have been taken from Walter Kaufmann. The question of the false dichotomy between the Hebrew and the Hellene may rest on the reading of Nietzsche's thought in the light of "Max Stirner's" faulty distinction between "Die Alten" and "Die Neuen," which is itself riddled with anti-Semitic references. In general on the question see Werner J. Dannhauser, *Nietzsche's View of Socrates* (Ithaca: Cornell University Press, 1974).

2. KSA, III, 45–46; VI, 246–47; VI, 192–93. The following recent titles are of interest for the present essay: Gerd-Günther Grau, *Christlicher Glaube und intellektuelle Redlichkeit: Eine religionsphilosophische Studie über Nietzsche* (Frankfurt am Main: Schulte-Bulmke, 1958), pp. 201–39; Hermann Wein, *Positives Antichristentum: Nietzsches Christusbild im Brennpunkt nachchristlicher Anthropologie* (The Hague: Nijhoff, 1962), pp. 89–93; Wiebrecht Ries, *Friedrich Nietzsche: Wie die "wahre Welt" endlich zur Fabel wurde* (Hannover: Schlüter, 1977), pp. 62–64; J. P. Stern, *A Study of Nietzsche* (Cambridge: Cambridge University Press, 1979).

and structure of these images of otherness forces the reader to the foundation of Nietzsche's own sense of self, for it is in terms of his sense of otherness that the boundaries of his own self were drawn. The most evident place of departure for an examination of Nietzsche's understanding of the Jew is that oft-quoted passage from *Beyond Good and Evil*—oft-quoted, at least, by a number of Jewish writers and anthologizers of the fin de siècle who wished to see Nietzsche as the ultimate philo-Semite, in contrast to Elisabeth Förster-Nietzsche's propagation of his image as the philosopher of proto-fascist anti-Semitism.[3] In the chapter on "Nations and Fatherlands" ("Völker und Vaterländer") Nietzsche praises the Jews as the purest race in Europe:

> I have not met a German yet who was well disposed toward the Jews; and however unconditionally all the cautious and politically-minded repudiated real anti-Semitism, even this caution and policy are not directed against the species of this feeling itself but only against its dangerous immoderation, especially against the insipid and shameful expression of this immoderate feeling—about this, one should not deceive oneself. That Germany has amply *enough* Jews, that the German stomach, the German blood has trouble (and will still have trouble for a long time) digesting even this quantum of "Jew"—as the Italians, French, and English have done, having a stronger digestive system—that is the clear testimony and language of a general instinct to which one must act. "Admit no more new Jews! And especially close the doors to the east (also to Austria)!" thus commands the instinct of a people whose type is still weak and indefinite, so it could easily be

---

3. Of the early attempts to categorize Nietzsche as a philo-Semite the most interesting works are: Josef Schrattenholz, ed., *Anti-Semiten Hammer* (Düsseldorf: E. Lintz, 1894); Anon., "Friedrich Nietzsche über die Juden," *Allgemeine Israelitische Wochenschrift Teschurim*, 29 March 1895; Anon., "Friedrich Nietzsche über die Juden!" *General-Anzeiger für die gesamten Interessen des Judentums*, 30 October 1902; Achad Ha'am, "Nietzscheanismus und Judentum," *Ost und West*, 2 (1902), 145–52, 242–54; Samuel Jankolowitz, "Friedrich Nietzsche und der Antisemitismus," *Israelitisches Wochenblatt* (Zurich), 13 November 1908; Anon., "Wie klein mancher Große ist . . . ," *Deutsche Sociale Blätter*, 12 December 1908; Josef Stolzing, "Friedrich Nietzsche und Judentum," *Deutsche Tageszeitung* (Berlin), 10 January 1909; Eberhard Kraus, "Wie Friedrich Nietzsche über das Judentum urteilte," *Deutsche Zeitung* (Berlin), 1 January 1909; and Gustav Witkowsky, "Nietzsches Stellung zum Zionismus," *Jüdische Rundschau*, 2 May 1913. On Elisabeth Förster-Nietzsche's anti-Semitism see H. F. Peters, *Zarathustra's Sister: The Case of Elisabeth and Friedrich Nietzsche* (New York: Crown, 1977). See also Alfred D. Low, *Jews in the Eyes of the Germans: From the Enlightenment to Imperial Germany* (Philadelphia: Institute for the Study of Human Issues, 1979).

blurred or extinguished by a stronger race. The Jews, however, are beyond any doubt the strongest, toughest, and purest race now living in Europe: they know how to prevail even under the worst conditions (even better than under favorable conditions), by means of virtues that today one would like to mark as vices—thanks above all to a resolute faith that need not be ashamed before "modern ideas"; they change, *when* they change, always only as the Russian Empire makes its conquests—being an empire that has time and is not of yesterday—namely, according to the principle, "as slowly as possible." (KSA, V, 193)

This passage is clearly linked to Nietzsche's later statement in *The Antichrist[ian]* that the Jews are the antithesis of all decadence:

Psychologically considered, the Jewish people are a people endowed with the toughest vital energy, who, placed in impossible circumstances, voluntarily and out of the most profound prudence of self-preservation, take sides with all the instincts of decadence—*not* as mastered by them, but because they divined a power in these instincts with which one could prevail against "the world." The Jews are the antithesis of all decadents: they have had to *represent* decadents to the point of illusion; with a *non plus ultra* of histrionic genius they have known how to place themselves at the head of all movements of decadence (as the Christianity of *Paul*), in order to create something out of them which is stronger than any *Yes-saying* party of life. (KSA, VI, 192–93)

Nietzsche wrote both of these seemingly positive passages about the Jew at a very special moment in the history of the Eastern European Jew. After the assassination of Tsar Alexander II in 1881, extensive anti-Semitic pogroms drove literally millions of Eastern European Jews toward the West. They spilled through Central Europe on their way to England and the United States. Their presence was viewed as a threat to the false sense of cultural homogeneity felt both by the European nationalists and by those communities of Westernized Jews who had already been assimilated (at least in their self-perception) for a number of generations. Thus the influx of Eastern Jews became the enemy, *in nuce*, threatening to disrupt the fabric of European society as had the Turks centuries before.

The Western European mind needed to create a mental structure through which to cope with the movement of the Eastern Jews. Here was a class of individuals readily recognizable not only through their dress and appearance, but also through their language and rhetoric.

This was the Other par excellence, the reification of the anti-Semitic caricature of the Jew in the West. Indeed, they were living proof of one of the basic tenets of late nineteenth-century popular thought. These Eastern Jews were clearly degenerate: one could sense it in their dirty, smelly, barbaric essence; one could hear it in the decayed mock German and their crude, loud, and boisterous love of argument. For the Western mind this was proof enough of the true nature of the Jew as degenerate; the Westernized Jew, on the other hand, was presented with the fearful specter of that which he feared he had been—the Eastern Jew seemed to be the embodiment of the image of the Jew fossilized in the bedrock of Western myth.

It was not, however, merely within the popular mind that the Jew was categorized as the degenerate Other. Here Nietzsche's comments on the nature of the Jew as the antidecadent can be understood. For the common ground of all Nietzsche's examples of decadence (and decadence is but a subclass of the concept of degeneracy) is the morose, mad figure—Poe, Kleist, Leopardi, Gogol, the madman as degenerate.[4] Late nineteenth-century medicine certainly supported Nietzsche in his linking of exactly such figures with degenerate madness, but it also saw the decadence of the Jew in a very special light: the Jew, more than any other outsider in the West, was perceived as having a special tendency toward madness. The giants of nineteenth-century German psychiatry—Emil Kraepelin, Richard Krafft-Ebbing, and Theodor Kirchhoff—all agreed that the Jew was inherently degenerate.[5] Theodor Kirchhoff's view is representative: "Perhaps the Jews exhibit a comparatively greater predisposition to insanity, but this may be explained by another peculiarity apart from race, viz., the fact that the Jews intermarry very often in close family circles, the crossing is insufficient, and heredity thus gives rise, by in-breeding, to a rapidly increasing predisposition to insanity."[6]

Kirchhoff's etiology for the prevalence of insanity among the Jews is inbreeding. But Nietzsche, as with his understanding of the nature of the physiology of the Black, inverts this accepted wisdom concern-

---

4. KSA, V, 224. See especially Annemarie Wettley, "Zur Problemgeschichte der 'dégénérescence,' " *Sudhoffs Archiv*, 43 (1959), 193–212.

5. A detailed survey of this was undertaken by Alexander Pilcz, "Geistesstörungen bei den Juden," *Wiener klinische Rundschau*, 14 (1901), 888ff. and 908ff. That this was not merely a question of esoteric medical interest can be seen in a popular essay on this topic, "Einfluß der Rasse auf pathologische Erscheinungen," *Proschaska's illustrirte Monatsbände*, 8 (1896), 198–201, which contains much the same information about Jews and insanity.

6. Quoted from the contemporary English translation, Theodor Kirchhoff, *Handbook of Insanity for Practitioners and Students* (New York: William Wood and Co., 1893), p. 23.

ing the Other.[7] For the very condemnation of the Jew as degenerate by the accepted authorities of Western society gave Nietzsche the fulcrum he needed to move the world: he simply turned it on its head. If the anti-Semites need to see the Jew as the essence of decay, Nietzsche, placing himself in the role of the opposition per se, must see in the imposed isolation of the Jew a source of strength. Nietzsche is thus not a philo-Semite but rather an anti-anti-Semite. His sense of the contemporary Jew is colored by his personal opposition to the self-assumed role of the anti-Semite (including his brother-in-law Bernard Förster) as the guardian of the truths of Europe in opposition to the invading Eastern hordes. Nietzsche's antiestablishment view could never accept this; as he became more and more alienated from this view he came to identify himself with the outsider: the Pole in Germany, the Easterner in the West.

II. Jews and Christians

If Nietzsche found that he must defend the contemporary Jew from the attacks of the anti-Semites in the West, he had no such compunctions about the Christian, for the Christians were the powerful majority against which he wished to define himself. However, he saw the softness and weakness of Christianity, its degeneracy, as lying specifically in its Jewish roots. The strength of the Old Testament became the smothering "love" of the New Testament. Nietzsche was writing about texts, about books, about language. This becomes clear when, in *The Antichrist[ian]*, he contrasts the primitive law of Manu with the New Testament:

> Ultimately, it is a matter of the end to which one lies. That "holy" ends are lacking in Christianity is *my* objection to its means. Only *bad* ends: poisoning, slander, negation of life, contempt for the body, the degradation and self-violation of man through the concept of sin—consequently its means too are bad. It is with an opposite feeling that I read the law of Manu, an incomparably spiritual and superior work: even to mention it in the same breath with the Bible would be a sin against the spirit. One

---

7. See my essay "The Image of the Black in the Works of Hegel and Nietzsche," *German Quarterly*, 53 (1980), 141–58. The concept of Otherness, which is rooted in the nature of projection, is discussed in the first chapter of my *Seeing the Insane* (New York: Wiley, 1982) as well as throughout my *Introducing Psychoanalytic Theory* (New York: Brunner/Mazel, forthcoming).

guesses immediately: there is a real philosophy behind it, in it, not merely an ill-smelling Judaine of rabbinism and superstition; it offers even the most spoiled psychologist something to chew on. Not to forget the main point, the basic difference from every kind of Bible: here the *noble* classes, the philosophers and the warriors, stand above the mass; noble values everywhere, a feeling of perfection, an affirmation of life, a triumphant delight in oneself and in life—the *sun* shines on the whole book. All the things on which Christianity vents its unfathomable meanness—procreation, for example, woman, marriage—are here treated seriously, with respect, with love and trust. (KSA, VI, 240)

The laws of Manu are positive, strengthening the nature of man in the world; the New Testament is destructive of life.

Nietzsche's understanding of the nature of the New Testament is important, for he sees it as an "ill-smelling Judaine of rabbinism and superstition" ("Judaine" is Nietzsche's neologism for the evil essence of Jewishness). The entire phrase points not to an image of the Jews of the New Testament, but to the rhetoric of late nineteenth-century anti-Semitism with its stress on the false logic, the rabbinical sophistries, and the superstitions of the Jews linked to their appearance and smell. The latter was associated by anti-Semites such as Theodor Fritsch with "their uncleanliness and use of garlic."[8] The synesthesia of smelling the illogic, of dirty sophistry, reappears in *The Antichrist[ian]* in a much more specific context: "*What follows from this*? That one does well to put on gloves when reading the New Testament. The proximity of so much uncleanliness almost forces one to do this. We would no more choose the 'first Christians' to associate with than Polish Jews—not that one even required any objection to them: they both do not smell good" (KSA, VI, 223). The first Christians were really just Eastern Jews. They contaminated through their very presence. Their presence, however, is felt through the word, through their language, through their rhetoric. It is the mode of discourse of the New Testament that Nietzsche is attacking, as much as its content. The common ground of the New Testament and contemporary rabbinic tradition lies in their shared lying and corrupting rhetoric. But Christianity is the rhetoric of power with which, whether he wishes it or not, he is condemned to be linked. His attempt at exorcising the Christian demons that lurk within his self-perception, his violent parodies of the style of the New Testament in *Thus Spoke Zara-*

8. Fritsch was a contemporary of Förster. Cited here from Theodor Fritsch, *Handbuch der Judenfrage*, 38th ed. (Leipzig: Hammer, 1935), pp. 27–28.

thustra, only heighten his self-awareness of his existence as a representative of the most dominant of all groups, of the most powerful, of the most frightening: the German Christians.[9] Yet even when he attempts to vilify the rhetoric of that which he hates most within himself, he accepts the rhetoric that labels the Eastern Jew as the epitome of Otherness. Nietzsche acknowledges, if but as a reflex, his role as a member of the dominant society in condemning that society. He is, for the moment, the self-conscious Antichrist damning the Christians as merely Eastern Jews.

Thus, Nietzsche invests with the most anger those otherwise inarticulate hatreds that reflect his inner fears. To no little extent these fears are associated with Christianity. We might speculate that his concept of Christianity is loaded with the anger and disappointment felt by the young Nietzsche at the death of his father, who not only represented the Church in his role as a minister but also held the same patriarchal position in the youthful Nietzsche's world as does the Church in the philosopher's mental universe. When Nietzsche addresses the question of Jews qua Jews, he sees a problem that is the direct result of this paternalism and he is able to condemn anti-Semitism as a social evil; when he strives to characterize the inconstant nature of Christianity, he falls back upon that rhetoric which for him (as a German Christian) and his time possessed the greatest negative force, the rhetoric of anti-Semitism. Thus the Jews can be both a positive and a negative image within Nietzsche's system: positive, when seen as the objects of Christian anti-Semitism (a fact that reveals the true nature of Christianity as evil and destructive); negative, when used as the most accessible analogue for that which Nietzsche feared most within himself—the German Christian. The result is a complex form of self-hatred, a self-hatred that draws upon anti-anti-Semitic rhetoric as well as anti-Semitic rhetoric for its articulation. Yet his rhetoric is not unique even in this very specific context: it has an analogue in an earlier writer's sense of self and his use of the image of the Eastern Jew.

III. Analogue and Paradox

Nietzsche's sense of the Otherness of the Jew, typified by his reaction to the Eastern Jew, would be merely an informative corrective

---

9. See Donald F. Nelson, "Nietzsche, Zarathustra and *Jesus redivivus*," *Germanic Review*, 48 (1973), 175–88.

to the false dichotomy of "Greek" and "Jew" if it did not have a striking historical analogue within the works of the emblematic (at least from the standpoint of the Germans) Jewish writer in Germany, Heinrich Heine. Nietzsche's fascination with Heine has been amply documented but little understood.[10] One of the more common observations in modern discussions of the use of "Hebrew" and "Hellene" as aesthetic paradigms in the nineteenth century is that Heine's contrast between "Greek" and "Nazarene," art and spiritualism, is the major forerunner of Nietzsche and Arnold.[11] Heine observed in *Shakespeare's Girls and Women* (1838): "This old, implacable rejection of the theater is but one side of the enmity that has existed for eighteen centuries between two completely heterogeneous manners of perceiving the world, one of which stemmed from the dry earth of Judea, the other from flowering Greece. Yes, this resentment between Jerusalem and Athens, between the Holy Sepulcher and the cradle of art, between the life in spirit and the spirit in life has lasted eighteen centuries."[12] Like Nietzsche's complex understanding of the Jew, Heine's seemingly clear antithesis is illusionary. More than Nietzsche, Heine has a complex, shifting image of the Jew, which reveals his own attempts to define himself through identification with—or in opposition to—the European images of the Jew and those that evolved within German Jewry in the generations following emancipation.[13]

Heine perceived himself as the absolute outsider. Unable to assume a position within the dominant society, he isolated himself from it. Unlike Nietzsche, who achieved more or less everything that the European bourgeoisie could hope for itself—status, position, acceptance, and thus power—Heine achieved none of these. In

---

10. For a summary of the literature on Nietzsche and Heine, see my chapter on these authors in my *Nietzschean Parody: An Introduction to Reading Nietzsche* (Bonn: Bouvier, 1976), pp. 57ff.

11. David J. DeLaura, *Hebrew and Hellene in Victorian England* (Austin: University of Texas Press, 1971).

12. Heine's works are cited to the ed. by Ernst Elster (Leipzig: Bibliographisches Institut, 1887–90); here, V, 384. Where volumes of the new critical editions exist, the texts have been checked against them; except where otherwise noted, the translations are my own.

13. For many years the only major study of Heine's "Jewishness" was Israel Tabak, *Judaic Lore in Heine* (Baltimore: The Johns Hopkins University Press, 1948). In recent years there has been a series of studies that complement Tabak: Hartmut Kircher, *Heinrich Heine und das Judentum* (Bonn: Bouvier, 1973); Ruth L. Jacobi, *Heinrich Heines jüdisches Erbe* (Bonn: Bouvier, 1978); and Ludwig Rosenthal, *Heinrich Heine als Jude* (Frankfurt am Main: Ullstein, 1973).

no little measure this conflict was the cause of his sense of isolation. For German society is dominated by the sense of the Jew as the outsider, as the essential Other; in accepting the language and rhetoric of this society, even ironically, Heine chose to write with a contaminated pen. How German society viewed the sense of the Jew can be seen in Karl Gutzkow's autobiography. In attempting to reconstruct his understanding of the Jew when he was a young man he recalls: " 'Christian-Germanic' anti-Semitism was already present in the fraternity system (*Burschenschaften*). In school I got to know the Jew as a traitor and braggart. What was feared by all was a hunchbacked monster from Poland, as vengeful as Shylock."[14] This image of the Polish Jew, of the Eastern barbarian, dominated the negative image of the Jew in Germany. How easy it was for the emancipated German Jew living in the Free Hanseatic city of Hamburg to accept the view that this image had little to do with himself!—indeed, that it was the very antithesis of himself. Heine was first confronted with the reality of the "Eastern" Jew when, in 1815, he journeyed to Frankfurt and saw the Frankfurt Ghetto.[15] He felt himself transported back to the Middle Ages, back to the horror of the physical isolation of the Jew before emancipation.

Heine traveled to the Prussian province of Poland under the influence of the "Society for the Culture and Science of the Jews," a group that (according to one of its founders, Eduard Gans) wished to destroy the wall separating the Jew from the Christian, the world of the Jew from the European world.[16] His report on this trip, "On Poland" (1822), devoted a much longer segment of the book to the Polish Jews than their presence in the population would have seemed to warrant. Heine's basic tenet seems to be that if the Jews and the peasants were better treated, then the Jews would become peasants toiling on the land. This idyllic image of the Jew as farmer played a role in many nineteenth-century attempts at colonizing the Eastern Jew outside of Europe. But Heine's generally positive image of the Eastern Jew has a number of strikingly negative aspects, at least some of which seem to be independent of his sense of political and economic causes of the Jews' hardships:

14. Karl Gutzkow, "Rückblicke auf mein Leben," in his *Werke*, ed. Peter Müller (Leipzig: Bibliographisches Institut, n.d.), V, 65.
15. Cited by Kircher (above, n. 13), p. 99. See also his references to Yiddish on pp. 97 and 111.
16. The best discussion of this question is to be found in Walter Kanowsky, *Vernunft und Geschichte: Heinrich Heines Studium als Grundlegung seiner Welt- und Kunstanschauung* (Bonn: Bouvier, 1975), pp. 182–89. Kanowsky cites Gans's description of the goals of the "Verein."

A sense of horror overcomes me when I remember how, beyond
Meseritz, I first saw a Polish village inhabited mainly by Jews. The
Wadzeck Weekly Newspaper, cooked into a real porridge, could
not have nauseated me more than these ragbag figures of dirt; and
the high-minded speech of a third-former enthusiastic about gym-
nastics (*Turnplatz*: a reference to the nationalism of *Turnvater* Jahn)
and Fatherland could not have martyred my ears so excruciatingly
as the Polish Jew-Jargon (*Juden-Jargon*). However, this disgust was
soon replaced by pity, after I had observed these individuals at
closer range and saw the pig-sty-like holes in which they lived,
spoke bad German (*mauscheln*), prayed, haggled—and were miserable. Their language was a German sprinkled with Hebrew and
decorated with bits of Polish. . . . But they evidently did not progress with the rest of European culture and their spiritual world
sank into a morass of unedifying superstition, which was forced
into them by a sophistic scholastic in a thousand miraculous
forms. . . . I still prefer the Polish Jew with his dirty fur, with his
lousy beard and his garlic breath and his bad German (*Gemau-
schel*), to many others in their state-paper majesty.[17]

The Polish Jews not only speak a false, degenerate language but also,
like the German-nationalists, have a false rhetoric; they have degenerated from the poetry of the Bible to a primitive, scholastic rhetoric
(which Heine is constrained to find better than that of the assimilated Jews who have become completely Germanized); and lastly,
they smell. Heine set out to write a defense of the Eastern Jew as
possessing the potential for improvement. But his positive image
was still haunted by Gutzkow's image of the deformed Eastern Jew—
the Jew as freak—as the true reality of all Jews, in contrast to the
mask of the assimilated individual Jew.

Later, in *The Baths of Lucca*, Heine repeated this striking contradiction. In attempting to sketch the portrait of the Jew as one with the
world through his religion, Heine stresses the corruption of the language of the Jew as well as the odor of garlic permeating him:

> Thus an old Jew with a long beard and a torn cloak, who cannot
> speak an orthographic word and is a bit mangy, feels himself hap-
> pier than I do with all my education. There lives in Hamburg . . .
> a man called Moses Lump [*Lump* = rascal], also called Moses
> Lümpchen or, in short, Lümpchen. He runs around during the
> entire week through wind and weather with his pack on his back
> in order to earn his couple of marks. When he comes home on Fri-

17. Heine, *Werke*, VII, 194–95.

day evening he lays down his bundle and all his cares, and sits down at table with his misshapen wife and even more misshapen daughter, partakes with them of fish cooked in a tasty garlic sauce, sings the most splendid psalms of King David, rejoices wholeheartedly at the exodus of the Children of Israel from Egypt, rejoices also that all the miscreants who behaved wickedly toward them died in the end, that King Pharaoh, Nebuchadnezzar, Haman, Antiochus, Titus, and all such people are dead, while Lümpchen is still alive and partaking of fish with his wife and child—And I tell you, Herr Doktor, the fish is delicious and the man is happy, he does not have to worry about culture, he sits wrapped contentedly in his religion and green dressing gown like Diogenes in his tub, he gazes cheerfully at his candles. . . .[18]

The Eastern Jew is not defined by his geographic locus, for Moses Lump lives in neither Hamburg nor Poland. Rather, he inhabits the netherworld of myth. For Heine it is a world projected from his own self-perception.

Heine spoke and evidently wrote Yiddish (one anecdote has him translating bits of Homer and Ovid into Yiddish as a joke).[19] He had more than a slight familiarity with the modes of rabbinic discourse, with the pilpul as a mode of the presentation of argument. Yet no matter how deep his knowledge of rabbinics was, and this is not a matter of importance for the present argument, he understood how one presented an argument. He saw himself as one who had moved from the ghetto with a mangled nonlanguage, with a barbaric mode of discourse, *to* the world of a civilized language and an acceptable manner of discussion and analysis. Indeed, one can understand the entire motivation of the "Society for the Culture and Science of the Jews" in this light. The religion of the Other becomes acceptable when cast in acceptable language and rhetoric, at least according to the assimilationists.

When Heine's works depicting Jews are examined, it can be seen that this striving for an acceptable mode of discourse is perceived retrospectively in the myth of the Jew. The Rabbi of Bacharach and his beautiful wife speak a German carved out of the marble of Isaac of York's English. Only when they flee to the Frankfurt Ghetto is the shadow of the future of the language of the Jews cast upon the work by Jäckel the Fool.[20] The world of myth is distanced: it can exist in

---

18. Ibid., III, 328. The translation is adapted from S. S. Prawer, *Heine, The Tragic Satirist* (Cambridge: Cambridge University Press, 1961), p. 192.
19. Kircher, p. 97.
20. Heine, *Werke*, IV, 474.

the Middle Ages, but exists especially in the Golden Age of Spanish Jewry, when the Jews existed as equals to all within the world of myth. One can turn to those problematic three poems, the Byronic "Hebrew Melodies," written by the late Heine—a Heine who had moved from a type of philo-Semitism to a mode of atheism, and then back to some type of reconciliation with the ethics of the Jew (or so the common wisdom would have us believe).

What is most puzzling about these poems is the numerous "mistakes" in them, which everyone has been at pains to point out. They all have to do with Heine's "knowledge" of Judaism and have been used to show his ignorance. But as Leopold Zunz observed, "who learns history from Heine?"[21]—perhaps no one, but what can be learned from him is the creation of the world of myth and its undermining.

"Princess Sabbath," Heine's poetic reworking of the tale of Moses Lump, is the tale of the "little Jew," and yet it begins with the thousand and one nights of Arabia. It recounts the tale of the little Jew who has been condemned to a dog's life except on the Sabbath when he becomes again the Prince of Araby. This magical transformation is heralded by his singing of the Sabbath hymn written by Jehuda ben Halevy, "Lecho daudi lekras kalle"—"Come, my friend, meet the bride." It closes with the Havdallah and the shaking of the ritual spice container, Bessamim, exuding the aroma of the Orient. The ritual lamp is extinguished and the Sabbath is gone.

The error has been noted almost from its first publication: the hymn does not happen to be by Jehuda ben Halevy. Why then mention him after citing the opening line of the hymn in Hebrew? Because Jehuda ben Halevy is one of the very few figures of the mythical age of Spanish Jewry whom even the least knowledgeable reader would have automatically associated with the Golden Age. (The Golden Age, at least within the mythology of the German-Jewish Enlightenment, the *Haskala*, was bounded by Jehuda ben Halevy and Salomon Ibn Gabirol in the eleventh century and Maimonides in the twelfth. It was seen as the age in which Jews were able to live as equals among Christians as well as among Moslems in Spain. This idyll ended with the rise of anti-Semitism in Christian Spain during the late fourteenth century and the final expulsion of the Jews from Spain in 1492.) If Heine had mentioned the actual author, the sixteenth-century Galilean poet Salomon Alkabets, who would have as-

---

21. Leopold Zunz, cited by E. R. Malachi, *Mekubolim in Eretz Israel* (New York: n.p., 1928), p. 83. Zunz is also the source of the myth, repeated in Heine, that all German Jews spoke perfect German until the seventeenth century; see his *Haderashot biYsrael*, ed. H. Albeck (Jerusalem, 1954), pp. 202ff.

sociated his name with any specific world of myth? Heine was in fact working from an actual source, Michael Sachs's 1845 history of the religious poetry of the Jews in Spain,[22] but the introduction of the figure of Jehuda ben Halevy was quite consciously in contradiction to his source: this figure links the world of the synagogue with the greater tradition of Spanish Jewry, with the integrated and meaningful myth of the Golden Age. Here Heine's gustatory comments on the Sabbath cholant and his contrapuntal evocation of the aroma of the Havdallah spices contrast the reality of the daily life of the Jews with the mythic image of the Golden Age.

It is not really surprising that the second of the poems of the "Hebrew Melodies" is devoted to Jehuda ben Halevy, for Heine stressed the function of Hebrew as the pure language that, like the aroma of the spices, evokes the lost world of the mythic past, in contrast to the street stench and the linguistic barbarisms of the ghetto Jews. Thus Jehuda ben Halevy becomes the epitome of the Jew as holy poet. In a mock hagiography Heine tells of the poet's journey to Jerusalem and his death at the hands of an Arab while singing the opening phrase of his hymn "Lecho daudi lekras kalle." The poem to this point has had an ironic undertone. Heine wants to believe in the magical world he has begun to conjure for us in "Princess Sabbath," but it is a world of myth, too pure, too willing to have its great poets accepted and honored in their own time. The language of this world is represented either by exquisite German translations from the Hebrew or by the Hebrew itself, never by Yiddish or Yiddish-accented German. Indeed, when Heine, in passing, used a Yiddishism in the poem, he deleted it in the published version.[23] The contemporary Jew thus intruded into the world of the myth of the Golden Age. The Yiddish-speaking ghetto inhabitant, hidden within the poet, sneaks into this world of myth, contaminating it. The final extant section of the poem turns inward, not into the world of myth, but to the daily realities of Paris and Germany. Heine comments on his wife's reading of the poem, and on the assimilationist tendencies of German Jews such as Julius Eduard Hitzig. His critique of Hitzig leads in a convoluted manner to the one Yiddishism actually contained in the poems, one that suddenly assumes a life of its own: for Heine begins to spin out a mock etymology for the Yiddishism "Schlemiel," seeing its origins in the Old Testament, and the Jewish poet as the true *schlemiel*. This intrusion of the world of daily reality into the world of myth leads then to Jehuda ben Halevy, and the poem, a paean to

---

22. Cited by Rosenthal (above, n. 13), pp. 290ff.
23. Prawer (above, n. 18), p. 193.

the myth of the true poet without the supposed conflicts of the present, ends as a fragment, a metacommentary on the nature of poetic expression.

The reader has thus moved from the world of the little Jew in the opening poem to the seemingly self-contained world of the myth of Spanish Jewry. He has moved from the daily life of the German Jew with his potentially contaminated language and rhetoric (present under his mask of assimilation, according to the anti-Semite), to the Golden Age, to the final world, the world of the "Disputation." This poem concludes not only the mythic world of the "Hebrew Melodies," but also the entire volume of the *Romanzero*; yet despite its vital position in the volume it has been little discussed.[24] It is a problematic poem because it seems to be a break from the earlier works. It is set in Christian rather than Moorish Spain, after the Golden Age, but before the Inquisition was in complete control. A debate is to be held between a Brother José, a Franciscan monk, and a Rabbi Judah of Navarre. It is to be held before Pedro IV, "The Horrible," and his exotic wife Donna Blanca, the former Blanche de Bourbon, to determine which is the true religion. The party lines are drawn, each group awaits its victory. The mendicant preacher begins with a proselytizer's invective against the Jew, one which would echo down the centuries to Heine's own time:

"Juden, Juden, ihr seid Säue,
Paviane, Nashorntiere,
Die man nennt Rhinozerosse,
Krokodile und Vampire,

. . . . . .

"Ihr seid Vipern und Blindschleichen,
Klapperschlangen, gift'ge Kröten,
Ottern, Nattern—Christus wird
Eu'r verfluchtes Haupt zertreten."

["Jews, Jews, you are swine,
Baboons, long-nosed beasts
Which one calls rhinoceroses,
Crocodiles, and vampires,

. . . . . .

24. See Gerhard Sauder, "Blasphemisch-religiöse Körperwelt: Heinrich Heines 'Hebräische Melodien,' " in Wolfgang Kuttenkeuler, ed., *Heinrich Heine: Artistik und Engagement* (Stuttgart: Metzler, 1977), pp. 118–43; and Helmut Koopmann, "Heines 'Romanzero': Thematik und Struktur," *Zeitschrift für deutsche Philologie*, 97 (1978), 51–70. See also Jürgen Brummack, ed., *Heinrich Heine: Epoche—Werk—Wirkung* (Munich: Beck, 1980), pp. 281–85.

"You are vipers and snakes-in-the grass,
Rattlesnakes and poisonous toads,
Adders, serpents—Christ will
Crush your damned heads."]

The answer by Rabbi Judah echoes the gustatory sense of "good taste"[25] that Heine had used from the beginning of *Die Harzreise*. Good taste is the mark of the refined, nondisputatious observer. The rabbi describes how the Leviathan will be prepared on the Day of Judgment:

"In der weißen Knoblauchbrühe
Schwimmen kleine Schäbchen Rettich—
So bereitet, Frater José,
Mundet dir das Fischlein, wett ich!"

["In the white garlic sauce
Swim bits of radish—
Thus prepared, Brother José,
I'm sure you'll enjoy the fish!"]

The contrast between the raging, angry rhetoric of the monk and the tempting, cajoling argument of the rabbi could not be more striking. This ironic contrast continues until the monk is forced to reply:

Aber welche Blasphemie
Mußt er von dem Mönche hören!
Dieser sprach: der Tausves-Jontof
Möge sich zum Teufel scheren.

[But what blasphemy
he had to hear from the monk!
The monk spoke: the "Tausves-Jontof"
Can go to the Devil.]

The Rabbi's reaction to this is at first angry puzzlement, but then he begins to vituperate his opponent:

"Da hört alles auf, o Gott!"
Kreischt der Rabbi jetzt entsetzlich;
Und es reißt ihm die Geduld,
Rappelköpfig wird er plötzlich.

---

25. See especially chap. 2, "A Most Superior Mass of Broth," in Jocelyne Kolb, "Wine, Women, and Song: Sensory References in the Works of Heinrich Heine" (Diss., Yale, 1979), pp. 93ff. Professor Kolb was also kind enough to provide me with her unpublished talk on "Literary Decorum or the Absence of Taste," in which the aesthetics of taste in the nineteenth century is related to broader aesthetic problems.

"Gilt nichts mehr der Tausves-Jontof,
Was soll gelten? Zeter! Zeter!
Räche, Herr, die Missetat,
Strafe, Herr, den Übeltäter!"

["That is the limit, O God!"
The Rabbi shrieked horribly;
And, his patience ended,
Suddenly became enraged.

"If the 'Tausves-Jontof' has no meaning,
What then will have? Help! Help!
Revenge, O Lord, this evil,
Punish, O Lord, the evildoer."]

What has caused this radical turn in the rabbi's rhetoric? What is the "Tausves-Jontof"? As early as the first critical editions of Heine's work, the editors have been at pains to point out that here, too, Heine erred. For the *Tosefot Yom Tov* is an amended edition of the *Mishna*, not really a detailed commentary but a series of footnotes contributed by Yom Tov Lipmann Heller (1579–1654), a rabbi in Vienna, Prague, and Cracow. As each editor of Heine's works is constrained to explain, this work appeared some three or four centuries after the debate depicted in the poem (depending on whether one takes Heine's date or the date of the actual debate upon which it was modeled).[26] No one has asked the obvious question: Why does the mere mention of this tractate alter the rabbi's rhetoric, why does it raise it from its "gustatory" reasonableness to a pitch of anger reminiscent of the monk's diatribe? It is clear that Heine is satirizing the "scholastic" nature of Jewish legalistic argument. Once an authority is attacked, no authority is safe, even if the authority under attack is the most minor one. For Heine the idea of footnotes to a commentary on a fragment of Holy Scripture must have seemed an ironic authority, especially if it stemmed from a pen wielded by an Eastern Jew, rather than by one who came from the world of the Golden Age. The autobiography of Lipmann Heller had appeared in German in 1836. Heine certainly was aware of the provenance of Heller's commentary, even if he had been unaware of its detailed content (which of course is never mentioned and has absolutely no bearing on the poem). Here the reader is returned to the world of Moses Lump and the little Jew in the "Princess Sabbath," but through the back door of the world of myth. It is the Eastern Jew with his barbaric rhetoric

26. Heine, *Werke*, I, 464–77.

who suddenly appears in the "Disputation" in the guise of the Spanish Rabbi of Navarre.

The reaction of the audience caps the poem, for Pedro and his exotically described wife must judge the disputation. Out of Donna Blanca's "ruby, magical lips" is to come the decision:

"Sagt mir, was ist Eure Meinung?
Wer hat recht von diesen beiden?
Wollt Ihr für den Rabbi Euch
Oder für den Mönch entscheiden?"

Donna Blanka schaut ihn an,
Und wie sinnend ihre Hände
Mit verschränkten Fingern drückt sie
An die Stirn und spricht am Ende:

"Welcher recht hat, weiß ich nicht—
Doch es will mich schier bedünken,
Daß der Rabbi und der Mönch,
Daß sie alle beide stinken."

["Tell me, what is your opinion?
Which of them is right?
Will you decide for the rabbi or
For the monk?"

Donna Blanca looked at him,
And, as if thinking, pressed her hands
With interlaced fingers against her forehead
And finally spoke:

"I do not know which one is right—
But it appears to me
That the rabbi and the monk,
They both stink."]

Both Jew and Christian stink! Here the implication of the very choice of the verb is vital, for Heine has not prepared us for quite such a "rank"—to use S. S. Prawer's extraordinarily well-chosen word—conclusion of the poem.[27] The erotic lips of Blanche de Bourbon utter this grotesque and crude conclusion because, indeed, both parties *do* "stink." Heine's synesthesia is striking. For what "stinks" is their rhetoric, especially the disputatious rhetoric of the aggressive disputants.

---

27. Prawer uses this term twice in his discussion of the poem (pp. 194, 199).

The image of the "good" Jew in contrast to the "bad" Jew had begun to be established in the Enlightenment.[28] The good Jew was nondisputatious; he thus avoided confrontation with those who wished to convert him (and who were, by definition, disputatious). He employed only "good" rhetoric, that is, argument within the accepted bounds of the philosophical discourse of Enlightenment. He was clean while the Other was dirty. He created; the Other seemed only to exist. He was accepted into the world of the intelligentsia; the Other was condemned to the irrationalities of scholastic triviality. The Other quickly assumed a specific locus within the world of myth: he was the Eastern Jew. He spoke badly, both in his language and in his rhetoric; he was disputatious, dirty, trapped in his own mode of argument. Here Heine's first impressions of the Eastern European Jew as non-Western Jew were again reified, but within the world of the myth of Spain.

The jarring movement back to the world of the streets, the world of confrontation, rather than the world of the private ritual of "Princess Sabbath," is rooted in the idea of disputation. For it is not just the Jew who is condemned, who "stinks," who is enclosed in the rotting atmosphere of decaying logic, but also the disputatious Christian. This is a pox not merely on both houses, but on the idea of disputatiousness in and of itself. Here the stereotype of the disputatious Jew is extended quite rationally to the image of the aggressive, irrational Christian, and the linkage of the two images is through their odor. The true meaning of the scholastic stench of the Middle Ages is perceived: in their rotting scholasticism Jew and Christian are truly identical. Heine's use of the term "scholasticism" in his very early essay "On Poland" is the leitmotiv of his perception of the corruption of the Eastern Jew. It is the "medieval" rather than the "modern," the non-Western rather than the Westernized Jew who is the link to the barbaric world of myth of the Christian Middle Ages, with its Inquisition and autos-da-fé. Heine's Moses Lump, with his privatized world of liturgical quietude, with his stress on Hebrew poetry and liturgy, is weekly removed from the world of the streets, from the world of the Jew as haggler and scholastic. Heine's world of the myth of the Jew, the world of the "Hebrew Melodies," begins with the odor of the "manure and garbage" (*Kot und Kehricht*) of the streets and concludes with the rank stench of scholasticism. These are aspects of the Otherness of the Jew, an Otherness that Heine wished to exorcise from his own tormented self-image through projection onto the world of myth.

28. See my essay "Moses Mendelssohn und die Entwicklung einer deutsch-jüdischen Identität," *Zeitschrift für deutsche Philologie*, 99 (1980), 506–20.

IV. Similarity and Contradiction

It is the stench of Otherness that the Christian has in common with the Jew. Both reek of the falsity of their textuality. For Nietzsche the communality of the Polish Jew with the early Christian, their common stench, is the cloying nature of their text, of their false mode of argument, of their illusionary and scholastic attempt to disguise the realities of human existence through their text:

> Really, how can one put a book in the hands of children and women which contains that vile dictum: "to avoid fornication, let every man have his own wife, and let every woman have her own husband. . . . It is better to marry than to burn"? And how can one be a Christian as long as the notion of the *immaculata conceptio* christianizes, that is, dirties, the origin of man?
>
> I know no other book in which so many tender and gracious things are said to woman as in the law of Manu; those old greybeards and saints have a way of being courteous to women which has perhaps never been surpassed. "The mouth of a woman"—it is written in one place—"the bosom of a girl, the prayer of a child, the smoke of the sacrifice, are always pure." Another passage: "There is nothing purer than the light of the sun, the shadow of a cow, the air, water, fire, and the breath of a girl." A final passage—perhaps also a holy lie: "All apertures of the body above the navel are pure, all below are impure. Only in the girl is the whole body pure." (KSA, VI, 240)

For Heine it was the disputatiousness of the Christian as proselytizer that created the analogy with the Otherness of the Jew. On the surface these two images seem parallel, and yet they stem from quite disparate sources. Heine sought to link two sources of anxiety that he himself perceived as the Outsider: the aggressive proselytizing of the Christian world, which stressed his position outside the mainstream of European culture even after his conversion; and his need to assign to the Other those negative qualities ascribed to the stereotype of the Jew by this dominant society. This Other then becomes a projection of the qualities that the European anti-Semite viewed as non-Western onto the world of myth. The myth assumes the geographical and religious form of the Eastern Jew even though, of course, it has little or nothing to do with the reality of the Eastern Jew.

Nietzsche begins his confrontation with Heine in seeing him as the classic *farceur*, unable to take anything seriously—and thus as being totally destructive (KSA, VIII, 281). Because Heine was sensitive to the inherently contradictory nature of writing with the rhetorical and linguistic resources of a culture that viewed the Jew as unable to become truly Western, Nietzsche's sense of Heine's destructiveness was quite correct. As Nietzsche himself grew more and more to doubt the values of Western society in its present dress, and as his physical debilities increased (and brought to him, as to the late Heine, the distancing effect of illness), he became more and more alienated from the common rhetoric of Western society (KSA, VI, 286). Nietzsche began to perceive himself as an outsider, but, unlike Heine, he had to create this role for himself: in background and breeding he was quintessentially mainstream. He thus began to project onto his persona the qualities of the outsider. He fashioned himself into the Pole, into the Eastern defender of the Jew (KSA, VI, 268). But all through his argument is the awareness (as opposed to Heine) that he will never truly be the outsider—at least never an outsider to the extent of his double, Heine. Heine's anguish generated a world of myth in which the double image of the "good" and "bad" Jew is seen in part through the eye of the Jew as outsider, and in part through the eye of the European alienated from the culture in which he functions.

Nietzsche's condemnation of the early Christians, especially Paul, thus has a clear, contemporary overlay that can help the reader to understand why the dichotomy between Hellene and Jew is at heart false. For just as Nietzsche's idea of the Greek is permeated with contemporary images having little or nothing to do with classical Greek culture, so too is Nietzsche's understanding of the Jew colored by both his contemporary situation and his literary experience.

XII. Nietzsche and Kierkegaard

Gerd-Günther Grau
(Translated by Wendy Rader)

I. Nietzsche's Idea of Self-Dissolution

1. Thesis and General Conception

One might be tempted to view Nietzsche's passionate attack on Christianity as the result of a highly personal, albeit deeply heartfelt and spiritual, encounter.* As such, this encounter would attain the rank and appeal of a sensitive spirit's intensive rejection of the claims and promises of the Christian faith, which he felt to be totally unsuited to, even fatal to, the solution of the problem of human existence. At the same time, however, the impact of this dissolution of Christianity and the significance of its rejection would be reduced to the personality of the thinker whose vehement attack on traditional values could easily be explained psychologically by the course of his life and sufferings.

This view, expressed often enough by defenders of the faith, overlooks the fact that the philosopher felt his own destiny to be the consequence of a thoroughly disastrous development of the Western spirit. He even considered himself to be a "destiny," in that he saw his vocation as the task of communicating the deeper reasons for such an unfortunate development and introducing a change: "The discovery of Christian morality is an unparalleled event and a genuine catastrophe. Whoever illuminates this matter is a *force majeure*, a destiny. . . ."[1] Thus, Nietzsche's attack on Christianity attains to

---

*This chapter represents a shortened English version of an essay first published in *Nietzsche Studien*, 1 (1972), 297-333. The essay contains a summary of the author's two books, *Christlicher Glaube und intellektuelle Redlichkeit: Eine religionsphilosophische Studie über Nietzsche* (Frankfurt am Main: Schulte-Bulmke, 1958) and *Die Selbstauflösung des christlichen Glaubens: Eine religionsphilosophische Studie über Kierkegaard* (Frankfurt am Main: Schulte-Bulmke, 1963).

1. *Ecce Homo*, "Why I Am a Destiny," sec. 8. All translations from the German are by Wendy Rader.

a general philosophical significance that not only transcends his own personal involvement, but also contains it as an exemplary experience. Nietzsche experiences and learns in Christianity—still the "best part of an ideal life" that he "had ever known,"[2] the representative of an *absolute claim* that is incapable of overcoming the human condition and is doomed to destroy itself.[3] That is, this claim is not destroyed from the outside—as, for example, through the critique of its dogma and values—but rather from an inner "self-destroying" factor: "intellectual honesty," demanded by its own historical development, and even by faith itself. Thus Nietzsche's basic thesis postulates the "self-destruction of all great things" in the sense of a "self-overcoming" of all human, all-too-human assumptions and precepts through a will to truth that increasingly sees through their mere meaning-giving function and, in the end, displays the "ultimate virtue" of intellectual honesty by renouncing them: "All great things destroy themselves through an act of 'self-overcoming': that's the law of life—the law of necessary 'self-overcoming' in the nature of life—the lawgiver himself eventually receives the call: *patere legem, quam ipse tulisti.*"[4]

From this previously overlooked perspective, Nietzsche's confrontation with Christianity contains a general and basically ideological-critical aspect that can, in fact, be extended to every absolute claim. It does this all the more in that it simultaneously takes over, by means of an alternation of historical and systematic views, that methodological Hegelianism—or better, a view of the historical destruction of faith as the explication of its systematic dissolution—which movements based on faith so like to invoke in order to reconcile their total relativizing of earlier currents of history with their own claim to eschatological absoluteness. For, according to Nietzsche's way of thinking, the "coming-to-consciousness of the will to truth" is also historical—although basically by means of its temporal development it merely explicates the systematic "advent of nihilism," which, according to the idea of self-destruction, alone remains and always emerges with particular zeal when mankind has once again "thought through to the end" its absolute values and ideals. "For why is the advent of nihilism *necessary* from now on? Because our previous val-

---

2. Letter to Peter Gast, 21 July 1881.
3. Cf. Gerd-Günther Grau, "Realisierter oder sublimierter Wille zur Macht," *Nietzsche Studien*, 10/11 (1982), 222–53.
4. GM, III, sec. 27.

ues are themselves that which drew the final consequences—because nihilism is the logical conclusion of thinking out our values and ideals to the end."[5]

It is at this point that the comparison of Nietzsche's and Kierkegaard's general philosophy of religion deserves our interest. If we can show that the latter falls victim to the logic of his values on the very issue of a self-dissolution, that is, in the attempt to present a rational confirmation of its claim as well as the historical proof for its validity, then the agreement of the two thinkers would be weighty proof for the inner coherency of Nietzsche's argument. That applies above all to the idea of *self*-destruction which, as the term implies, is released through the self-enforced critical reflection on its foundations and is in no way introduced by an attack from a position outside the system. Christianity, according to Nietzsche's original and genuine theme, would succumb then, not to the ancient and ever-repeated conflict of knowledge and faith, but to the *intellectual honesty* of faith itself—and in such a way that faith has to be increasingly sacrificed to the extent that it is unable to justify itself before the will to truth of knowledge, which faith itself demanded and developed. "We can see what actually triumphed over the Christian God: Christian morality itself, the ever stricter concept of truth, the father-confessor sophistication of the Christian conscience, translated and elevated to a scientific conscience, to intellectual cleanliness at all costs."[6]

The translation, as it were, of this systematic self-dissolution into the historical formation of its development occurs by way of the inevitability of a historical destruction that is plainly the opposite result of ever-renewed restorative efforts to get to a profounder basis of the expression of faith and its practical demands. Every attempt to impede the dissolution of Christianity *in* history has only succeeded in accelerating the self-destruction *through* it, "but what is most curious is that those who have exerted themselves the most to maintain Christianity are the ones who have become its best destroyers—the Germans."[7] Nietzsche speaks of the Germans in this way because he is thinking primarily of the Reformation and the Protestant philosophy resulting from it, in which Christianity "as morality" is supposed to have "expired" at the hands of its "ultimate virtue"—intel-

5. WM, Preface, sec. 4.
6. FW, sec. 357; cf. GM, III, sec. 27.
7. FW, sec. 358.

lectual honesty, to which Nietzsche himself appeals. However, from this standpoint, the Reformation merely draws the consequences of a medieval Catholicism that had already failed "as dogma *because* of its morality"—the moral demand for a foundation based on reason. That this Catholicism tore itself apart from the inside through Scholasticism from Thomas to Duns Scotus and Occam (upon whom the Reformers then based their cause) is clear to see, for example, in the case of Averroes's thesis of a *"double truth"*—a concept that, in Nietzsche's estimation, aptly expressed the intellectual situation of the religious man. In other words, just as "Christianity as *dogma*," that is, as a comprehensible system of interpretation and its corresponding order of life, "collapsed" with the dissolution of medieval Scholasticism, so will contemporary Protestant philosophy also cause "Christianity as morality" to collapse as a result of the absoluteness of its claims to theoretical and practical validity. It is quite possible that one may recognize the final, "strongest inference" of Christian veracity toward itself in the establishment of a secularized cultural and state Protestantism, or even in the "breaking down" of precisely its "strongest souls" in order to demonstrate the genuineness of Christian faith. "In this way Christianity as dogma perished of its own morality: in the same way must Christianity *as morality* also perish. . . . After the truthfulness of Christianity has drawn one inference after another, it must, in the end, draw its most striking conclusion—against itself."[8]

It would fall outside the scope of this essay to point out in detail the cooperation of consciously intended restoration and unconsciously motivated destruction of the Christian faith in history by all the separate thinkers (which could, in fact, be reconstructed from scattered texts of Nietzsche's).[9] Suffice it to say briefly that Leibniz already reveals, with his proposal of a theodicy, an endangered faith, while at the same time the discovery of profound "unconscious ideas" (*Vorstellungen*) makes the inner destruction, which it is supposed to relieve through the rationalization of faith, even more profound.[10] In contrast, Kant's "philosophy of the back doors," in its postulates of practical reason, may nevertheless have opened up afresh a "secret path to the old ideal" for the "Tübinger seminarians," which his theoretical criticism of theological ideas had de-

---

8. GM, III, sec. 27.
9. Cf. the corresponding chapter in the author's *Christlicher Glaube*.
10. FW, sec. 357.

stroyed. However, his criticism, which even in its title indicates destruction, can in fact now only establish transcendentally the Protestant version of the *credo quia absurdum*, which "German logic" had so willingly made use of previously in order to shield its "wishful thinking" from any further criticism. Yet this escape appears too artificial to impede the skepticism of an intellectual honesty that, in the last analysis, cannot be satisfied with "begging the question."[11]

Nietzsche finds the climax and the change from a critical restoration to a destruction-oriented criticism, from the preservation of the moral-Christian claim *in spite of* criticism to a claim *by means of* it, in Hegel—who, ambiguously enough, could guarantee the "preservation" of faith only by absolutizing it through philosophy. At first sight it may even seem that the philosopher had succeeded in making Christianity an absolute according to the principles of reason, "in accordance with the grandiose attempt he made, with the help of the sixth, the 'historical sense,' in the end to convince us of the divine nature of existence."[12] But it is finally only the total relativizing of the absolute *in* history with which faith seeks to hide, rather than to hinder, its ultimate dissolution *by means of* it. "This history, understood in Hegelian terms, has contemptuously been called the sojourn of God on earth—which God, however, is himself first created by history."[13] This ambiguous preservation (*Aufhebung*) of Christianity becomes particularly apparent in the transposition of Christian eschatologically oriented politics, where it reappears in the degenerated form of secular totalitarianism—most notably in socialism. It is no accident, then, that Nietzsche's "madman" simply announces what the young Hegel had already recognized as "the feeling on which is based the religion of modern times, the feeling that God himself is dead."[14]

In the final stages of this development Schopenhauer's honest atheism points the way for Nietzsche's intellectual honesty. For that development, only a transformation of the "pessimism of the weak" into a "pessimism of the strong" was necessary to overcome the last obstacle to insight into the inevitability of nihilism by means of its most extreme radicalization.

---

11. A, sec. 10; G, "Skirmishes of an Untimely Man," sec. 16; GM, III, sec. 25; M, Preface, sec. 3.
12. FW, sec. 357.
13. U, II, sec. 8.
14. Cf. FW, sec. 357, and Hegel's early essay "Faith and Knowledge" (1802).

2. Foundation through the Philosophy of History

Until recently, Nietzsche's interpreters had barely recognized—let alone respected—his obviously fundamental, or at least easily demonstrable, total conception, in their irritation at the aphorismlike arrangement of his texts. Thus, this total conception has never been applied systematically to the understanding of his critique of religion or to his attack on and critique of Christianity. What is of concern here—especially if we undertake the expanded version mentioned earlier and only hinted at by Nietzsche—is one of the most pregnant, because it is one of the most radical, of answers to the *question of the possibility of a Christian philosophy* versus the possible *absurdity* of such a concept and all attempts to realize it, which had been debated since the conscious take-over of Greek philosophical theses by the Christian thinkers of the second and third centuries. On the one hand, Paul hints at a thesis (Rom. 1:2) of the fundamental comprehensibility of the main religious facts and demands, upon which the doctrine of *natural theology* is based and which almost every philosopher from Augustine to Descartes has quoted to maintain and to construct a Christian philosophy. On the other hand, there was never a time that lacked the voices of theology speaking in favor of the second alternative. Tertullian's original formula of the *credo quia absurdum*, which was not so much a paradoxical proof as it was a rhetorically justified paradox, marks the beginning of this tendency and has since been applied again and again, explicitly or implicitly, admittedly or unadmittedly—up to Kierkegaard's paradoxical-dialectical "leap" of faith. To sum up: for Nietzsche the second answer is, in accordance with the historical rather than a purely logical development, the consequence of the experience of failure of the first. Indeed, for him, Christianity as Catholic dogma comes to its end with the Renaissance, only to be revived by Luther as a dialectical theology on the basis of the "German logic" of the *credo quia absurdum*. But just as in the case of the first answer, where the pretension of an intelligible access to "theological truth" is increasingly given up by the Augustinian-Anselmian school of Scholasticism—*credo ut intelligam*—through Scotism and Occamism, and on to Cartesian skepticism, so this development is repeated, as it were, on the basis of the second answer. Nietzsche speaks about this in detail, showing that here—quite unlike the first answer—the pretension of "philosophical truth" is increasingly forced to put restrictions on the inaccessible absolute claims, because it wants to preserve its legitimacy or even to confirm a new one. Here, as with the first answer, it is the religious situation of a "double truth" that escalates the development to a recognition of the thorough discrepancy of their two realms.

A. The Nonappearance of the "Parousia"[15]

With the disclosure of this self-dissolution, seen as the final result of its own criticism, Nietzsche's anti-Christian argument becomes extremely radical as to the question of the possibility of a Christian philosophy. This radicalness lies in his endeavor to prove the negative answer to be the result of a movement that grew out of Christianity itself from an originally opposite intention, in order to show how the impossibility of a Christian philosophy proved the philosophical impossibility of Christianity. This is an impossibility for the intellectual honesty of the philosopher, which cannot allow him to content himself with the religious interpretation of faith projected into everyday life. The impossibility becomes evident for the philosopher likewise in his demonstrated inability to be satisfied with overhasty solutions, the projections of self-assurance, or the compensations of involuntary modesty, and is evident as well in the believer's latent "dissatisfaction with Christianity" that betrays itself in the contorted apologetics, the "stubborn" clinging to the "authority" of its sources. In both cases it is no longer possible at the end of "a two-thousand-year training in truth" to suppress the question in which "the awe-inspiring catastrophe" is fully expressed: "Should you wish, however, to escape this your displeasure with Christianity, then take into consideration the experience of two thousand years of Christianity, which, if clothed in the form of a humble question, would be: If Christ really intended to redeem the world, did he not then fail?"[16]

Yet Nietzsche even goes a step beyond proving the *quid facti* of the failed redemption and offering it as the *quid juris* of his denial, "which ultimately prohibits the lie of believing in God": he wants to know the reasons for this failure insofar as it represents a kind of nihilism—a nihilism not only sprung from a dominant Christian consciousness but, what is more, raised to full consciousness through faith itself. Christianity, far from "abolishing any kind of crisis" or redeeming man externally from his suffering, has instead burdened him additionally with a permanent internal crisis of "sin." As if it

---

15. By which we mean Christ's rising from the dead.
16. MA, II/I, sec. 98.

were not enough that the transcendent meaning of the Christian interpretation of life and the world can in no way be proved or even made comprehensible, the Christian demands themselves are also found to be unprovable and therefore limitless. In this way, however, man, in direct correlation to his honesty, is at the mercy of the ineluctable dialectic of a moral law whose illimitable heights he raises all the higher; faced as he is with the alternative of the nonappearance, or at least the unprovability, of redemption, obedience to the law is, ultimately, his only legitimate religious action for it is the only possible way to break through the irreligious invariability of time, while at the same time each hasty reduction of the demand must arouse the suspicion of being arbitrary self-liberation. Given this point of view, it becomes in turn immediately clear that (and why) for Nietzsche real Christianity is bound to stand under the sign of plain inhumanity if, and insofar as, it has to accept the consequences of its theoretically given, irreconcilable double truth. The philosopher can therefore ultimately accept and take seriously as an opponent only a Christian faith that continues to reiterate its absurd demand arising from a belief that it admits to itself to be paradoxical—in other words, the extreme radical Protestantism (in Kierkegaard's sense) or, at any rate, its Catholic predecessors from Tertullian to Pascal (whose theoretical skepticism tended to produce their moral rigor).[17]

It is well known that Nietzsche attributes responsibility for the tendency inherent in the Christian faith to testify to a Gospel of Bad News ("Dysangelium") rather than Good News ("Evangelium") to the Apostle Paul, while tending to exclude Jesus to a great extent from his attacks and invectives. Nietzsche concedes to Jesus, despite the latter's "morbid" way of thinking and acting, the actual realization of a redemption in the "heavenly kingdom of the heart"—"a new practice," which requires neither an articulated faith nor a law explicating the implicit negation of the world. "What does 'Good News' mean? True life, eternal life, has been found—it is not being promised, it is here, it is in you: as a life in love, without detractions and exclusions, without distance. Everybody is the child of God." In contrast, "formula, law, faith, dogma" become necessary only at the moment where this immediacy has been lost and an interpretation of the world has taken its place, an interpretation to whose establishment and conservation a conceptualized faith and a law expressed as dogma are necessary in their turn. A "psychological symbol redeemed from the concept of time" thus has become the "instrument

---

17. GM, III, sec. 27; A, sec. 62.

of torture" of a realm of theological concepts—concepts like "the life to come," "the last judgment," "immortality of the soul"—as they are required for and explained by the notion of a redemption removed to "the end of time" and a "life beyond" reality. A psychologically intelligible flight from reality, justifiable personally "even today," has intensified and crystallized as an "instinctive hatred of any reality."

This transformation is brought into being—more precisely: is *forced* on us—by the death of Jesus, which, according to Nietzsche, was at least initially totally unexpected by his disciples. This death (which for Jesus rather embodies the "proof of his teaching") gave rise in Paul, attempting an "interpretation" and misinterpreting the temporal "kingdom of the heart" as an actualized "immortality," to the "downright terrible, absurd answer" of the atoning death of a "son of man" who at the end of time would establish the "reign of God"—as a "judgment over his enemies," but also as a promised "reward" for the faithful. With that, however, precisely that concept of "guilt" which Jesus himself had abolished became for the first time the basic principle of Christian life. Moreover, its center of gravity was removed to an afterlife in such a way that instead of a realized blessedness, a realized damnation—ever to be testified to or even to be established by man himself—became the precondition of a faith not only removed from, but hostile to, life: "To live so as to render life meaningless now becomes the 'meaning' of life."[18]

> The thought of eternal pain was totally remote from the early Christians, they thought themselves redeemed "from death" and from day to day awaited a transformation rather than a dying. . . . Paul had nothing better to tell of his redeemer than that he had opened up the access to immortality for everybody—he did not yet believe in the resurrection of the unredeemed . . . , immortality was then only just beginning to open its doors. . . .[19]

> The catastrophe of the gospel was decided by His death, . . . it hung on the "cross". . . . Only His death, this unexpectedly terrible death, . . . only this most awful paradox brought the disciples up against the essential enigma: who was this? what was this?

> From now on, step by step, was added to the type of the redeemer the doctrine of the last judgment and the second coming, the doctrine of [Christ's] death as a death of sacrifice, the doctrine of the resurrection, with which the entire concept of "blessedness," the

---

18. A, secs. 28–42.
19. M, sec. 72.

entire and essential reality of the gospel, is conjured away—in favor of a state after death. . . . Paul made this point of view . . . logical. . . . And suddenly the gospel had turned into the most despicable of all unrealizable promises, the brazen doctrine of a personal immortality. . . . Paul himself taught it as a reward![20]

It is apparent that Nietzsche established the turning of the faith of the early Church to historical Christianity—while dividing the former into the lived practice of Jesus and the theoretical belief of the Apostle, which only after the death of the founder was built up into the believed theory of the latter—at exactly the point at which for Albert Schweitzer the consciousness of a historical Christian faith has to begin if Christianity, carried by precisely the "will towards truth" that enabled the "research into the life of Jesus by the Protestant part of Christianity" to attain its results, is to persist in the face of the "difficulties created for faith by a knowledge of history."

Nietzsche the philosopher was also proud to have been the first to have touched upon "the problem of the origin of Christianity," to have illuminated the *real history* of Christianity," that is, to have uncovered the "misunderstanding" underlying the "word," if this is meant to designate a historical movement and a movement founded for history—a misunderstanding that theologians are unable to explain other than by reinterpreting Jesus' "altogether eschatological" into "Jesus' altogether uneschatological way of thinking." Even if the philosopher's analysis is guided a priori by the opposite tendency of the negation of Christian theology, whose eschatological regeneration implies the desideratum of the negation of its historical legitimation, his intellectual honesty is still akin to that of a theology that ultimately considers itself unequivocally "negative," just as, for example, the destruction of the tradition transmitted through the development of the Christian faith itself appears to be forced on it by its "historical problems": "This picture has not been destroyed from without but has collapsed upon itself, shaken and split by its historical problems. . . ."[21]

B. The Job-Situation

The thesis of a "Parousia," an event repeatedly delayed at first and eventually accepted as definitely not having taken place, is de-

---

20. A, secs. 40f.
21. Albert Schweitzer, *Geschichte der Leben-Jesu Forschung* (1913; reprint, Bonn: Godesberger Taschenbuchverlag, 1966), pp. 42, 31, 620; cf. also A, secs. 24 and 39.

manded altogether compellingly by Nietzsche's analyses and texts—even to the almost literal agreement of Paul's role as an intermediary between Jesus' "Kingdom-of-God piety" and the entirely Hellenistic "piety of redemption."[22] Such a thesis would also appear the only one capable of making intelligible the self-dissolution shown above by an intellectual honesty promoted and developed by faith itself, whose ultimate question concerning the "failed redemption" it would answer directly. For if this failure ultimately is founded in and made apparent by the fact that man is expected to accept, theoretically and practically, the double truth of a redemption that took place and yet cannot be proved, which is given and is ever to be acquired afresh—a redemption that calls into question man's worldly reality without telling him whether his hopes beyond this world can be realized, by referring him to a given meaning without freeing him of the necessity of giving meaning himself in the area at his disposal—then the thesis mentioned above would meet and explain precisely the historical situation of a faith *directed originally toward the sudden end of history* and now referred to an end that is totally unpredictable. Founded in the "tension" of an immediate presence of redemption, a Christianity of Kierkegaard's "instant" would then not be directed toward, and accordingly would not be equipped for, guiding or directing a life in time as either a doctrine or a law. In the existing situation of the early Church any relativization of temporal conditions could unquestionably be defended and any moral restriction undoubtedly considered reasonable, provided that one felt oneself exonerated from an orientation toward and for life on earth, and that one felt one did not have to exist for too much longer with the practical consequences. However, the transformation, so to speak, of the vertical of a finite time into the horizontal of an endless time will cause faith to break down in the face of the very *problem of meaning* for whose solution it has been evoked and sought throughout history.

Ever since Reimarus—whose (albeit politically distorted) analyses, like those of Nietzsche, also move Paul into a position opposite Jesus—and his editor Lessing, for whom "Christ" was no more a historical Christian than he was for Nietzsche, via Nietzsche's contemporaries Strauß and Overbeck, and up to Unamuno, all relevant modern investigations of Christianity that grew out of the intellectual

---

22. See Albert Schweitzer, *Die Mystik des Apostels Paulus*, 2nd ed. (Tübingen: Mohr, 1954); English ed.: *The Mysticism of Paul the Apostle*, trans. William Montgomery (New York: Macmillan, 1955).

honesty of religious endeavor not only emphasized this eschatological "misunderstanding" of the early Church but also based on it the "agony of Christianity" in and through history. This agony, as we may now define it more precisely, manifests itself mainly in such a way that nihilism represents a condition for faith and for a renunciation of that faith as well, while—or because—conversely, the Christian message is always in danger of being felt to be an interpreted lack of an answer rather than an interpreting answer. In any case, however, man is burdened with the load of, as well as the guilt for, a miscarried redemption should he fail to recognize, in the uninterrupted immutability of meaningless events, the demands of a God whom he is not able even to perceive as a discernible being whom he could address.

We have called this situation *the Job-situation of religious thinking* and have characterized it as the state of a redemption that is not so much practically intangible as theoretically unintelligible, and one that man cannot identify as either an affirmative assent or a determining directive. It describes the situation of a historical Job in which Nietzsche, together with the scriptural Job, not only refuses to accept as "guilt" the external "misfortune" of his created being, which is not changed by the Christian message, but is also incapable of recognizing the Christian interpretation of his "suffering" as *God's answer* to his question—"the cry of the question, why suffer?" Nietzsche is angered not by the *fact* of suffering, but by the *meaninglessness* of suffering, culminating in a meaningless death that is not eliminated by Christianity. He doubts the logic of its values only after despairing over the invalidity of its logic.[23]

The idea of God taken to its logical conclusion, by virtue of the attribution of omniscience, makes the notion of an existential test (which in essence belongs to the Old Testament) appear meaningless. If a test with a necessarily foregone conclusion—the notion of proving oneself before an omnipotence whose intervention could easily avoid any failing of such a test—must appear meaningless, then the notion (which belongs to the New Testament) of a plan for redemption that can neither be made factually effective nor even be made unequivocally known in its factuality, or at least unmistakably brought to certainty, must appear completely absurd.

Nietzsche's intellectual honesty asks its ultimate question out of the inescapable recognition of this situation. This insight had already moved Kant, whose attention had been directed by Lavater to the

---

23. GM, III, sec. 28.

only remaining eschatological aspect of death, "to stop short, along with Job, of the crime of flattering God and making inward protestations which perhaps fear had forced and to which the soul did not freely in faith assent."[24] Nietzsche's question is the same as the one asked intrepidly by the scriptural Job, impressed by the "force" of his vulnerability, and taken back only at the very point of Yahweh's answer—a question that in the face of an answerless secular history cannot be held back any longer and cannot forcibly be referred back by its theological interpretation to man's own guilt: the question of "God's honesty."

> The honesty of God. A God who is omniscient and omnipotent and who does not even insure that his intention is understood by his own creatures—is that supposed to be a benevolent God? A God who allows the numerous doubts and reservations to persist, throughout centuries, as if they were immaterial for mankind's salvation, and who yet holds out the prospect of the direst consequences for the violation of truth? Would he not be a cruel God who possessed the truth and were capable of watching mankind agonize over it?[25]

> Know now that God hath overthrown me, and hath compassed me with his net. Behold, I cry out of wrong, but I am not heard: I cry aloud, but there is no judgment. . . . I cry unto thee, and thou dost not hear me: I stand up, and thou regardest me not. . . . Oh that one would hear me! behold, my desire is, that the Almighty would answer me, and that mine adversary had written a book. (Job 19:6–7; 30:20; 31:35)

II. Kierkegaard's Fulfillment of the Self-Dissolution

1. *Personal Development*

Only those who fail to recognize in Nietzsche's arguments the ultimate "failure of all philosophical attempts in the theodicy"[26]—so far as they essentially represent an "answer to Job"[27]—will be able to

---

24. Letter to Johann Caspar Lavater, 28 April 1757.
25. M, sec. 91.
26. Cf. Kant's essay "Über das Mißlingen aller Versuche in der Theodizee" (1791), which contains a reference to Job as "conscious of his intellectual honesty."
27. Cf. C. G. Jung, *Antwort auf Hiob* (Zurich: Rascher, 1952); English ed.: *Answer to Job*, trans. R. F. C. Hull (London: Routledge & Paul, [1954]).

overlook their ultimately religious motivation. Only those who refuse to recognize in Nietzsche's renunciation the dissolution of faith founded on the "immorality of the *deus absconditus*" itself will be able to overlook the deep resignation behind its apparent hubris. Anyone who would deny, however, the fundamental significance of Job's situation for religious thinking would have to ignore not only its implicit recurrence in Nietzsche's texts but also its explicit reiteration by a "religious writer" for whom "Job's significance . . . lies in the fact that the border skirmishes against faith have been fought in him." For Kierkegaard, "Job represents as it were the entire substantial accusation on the part of man in the great case between God and man."[28]

Nevertheless, the author has been heavily criticized, on the part of a committed theology as well as on that of a theologically committed philosophy, for wanting to prove the self-dissolution of Christianity on the basis of Kierkegaard's dialectical struggle for the "genuine essence of Christianity," insofar as this struggle results from the historically unremedied situation of Job and from the faith destroyed by an immanent honesty that is compelled by a reflection of its "historical point of departure," the result of the failed "Parousia." It would be well to mention here that the manifold and often astonishingly literal parallels between the two ancestors of the modern philosophy (and theology!) of existence have long been known and accepted in the academic world, at least since the time of Jaspers's Groningen lectures on "Reason and Existence" and Löwith's early works from the thirties; yet the Danish historians of philosophy and literature respectively, Höffding and Brandes, had already introduced this point by the end of the last century. Brandes even tried to draw Nietzsche's attention to his compatriot—even if too late for a meeting of the minds to be possible—before Nietzsche's illness broke out.

Even so, these early studies only scratched the surface of an understanding of the similarities between Nietzsche and Kierkegaard as regards both the general and the more specific approaches to their philosophical interpretation. Most importantly, these studies failed to take into consideration the significance of the relationship of the

---

28. Kierkegaard citations are taken from the *Samlede Vaerker*, ed. A. B. Drachmann, J. L. Heiberg, and H. O. Lange, 14 vols. (Copenhagen: Gyldendahl, 1901–6), and the Kierkegaard *Papirer*, ed. P. A. Heiberg and V. Kuhr (Copenhagen: Gyldendahl, 1909–48); the Roman numerals indicate volume numbers and the Arabic numerals page numbers. The letters A, B, C refer to sections of the above works, and the indices (for example, X^1) to partial volumes. The reference here is to *Repetition*, III, 243f.

two thinkers as articulators of the religious-philosophical problem of Christianity. This significance becomes clear when we notice how exactly Kierkegaard's explicit desire to have only "honesty" in his faith corresponds to Nietzsche's notion of the "honest Christian"; indeed, it corresponds to the fears that Nietzsche felt for "the one who has come off badly" (as he himself had), should he attempt, with the help of the Christian faith, to face the existential hopelessness that had become especially clear to him. Nietzsche could not have helped but feel supported in his notion of "the birth of Christianity from a movement of resentment" by the existential weakness, be it universally or personally experienced, expressed by a theologian who considered his "thorn in the flesh" the real reason for his faith. And when he, as we have seen, finally became an anti-Christian, driven by that religion of "cruelty against man" which delivers man to the permanent inner state of crisis, how could he have failed to refer to the assertion of his opposite that at times Christianity had seemed to him "the most inhuman cruelty"? If Kierkegaard himself, unsure whether he was an "extraordinary" Christian or even a "Christian" at all, could not determine "if this defense of Christianity taken to such lengths was not just the cunningly clothed form of an attack," then it indeed appears obvious to presume in his argument and interpretation the completed act of self-dissolution, which is finally averted by virtue of the fact that, with the "communication" that has finally become "immediate," even "what is interesting" regarding the possible ambiguity of such a mediation is lost.[29]

It might at first seem that Kierkegaard's confirmation of an "abolition" of Christianity links up with the Christianness of Nietzsche's words "God is dead" only in the secularized form of the "everyday Christian," whom both considered a "pitiable figure"—"assuming there is any faith at all." The actual congruence lies, rather, in the very genuine Christianity of that faith for which arbitrarily caused, or arbitrarily confirmed, nonredemption has become the unique criterion for redemption. To Nietzsche's "modest question" of whether the redemption could perhaps have been a "failure," Kierkegaard would hardly allow for a clear, undialectical answer—not even in the "edifying," then "religious," and finally "Christian discourses," in connection with whose positive content the thinker knew himself to be "without authority," while at the same time their dialectical consistency seemed to betray a "carefully weakened tinge of humor."

---

29. *The Instant*, XIV, 52; *For Self-Examination*, XIII, 564, 576. Cf. WM, sec. 179; *Ecce Homo*, "Why I Am So Wise," sec. 6.

The factual influence of these self-assurances in Kierkegaard's faith, driven to ever-greater rigorousness, was, then, so superficial that Nietzsche, who simply refused to "swallow" the "torment" of a mere "supposition" of the idea of God, would have been hard put to find a better representative for Zarathustra's sayings:

> They would have to sing better songs to make me believe in their Redeemer: his disciples would have to look more redeemed. (Nietzsche)
>
> Given such pain and covertness, it depends on the differences in the individual in which direction he goes, whether this lonely inner suffering finds its expression and satisfaction in the demonic hatred of man and cursing of God, or in their opposite. (Kierkegaard)[30]

It is understandable why one of the experts and important biographers of Kierkegaard, Eduard Geismar, so sharply formulated the dilemma that he saw facing the Christian as a result of the writings of his countryman: "He will scare certain people from Christianity for good. They believe that he has given Christianity the only logical form, and this Christianity is impossible for them to accept. . . . On the other hand, there are people who have found spiritual nourishment in his profound Christian depth . . . and they have, as well as they could, exposed the alleged misleading interpretation. One has to be able to approach this from both sides . . . because in any case it cannot seem very honest for the church-oriented person to appropriate from Kierkegaard what he can use without taking into account how that can be reconciled with the latter's attack on the Church."[31]

Strangely and significantly enough, this alternative has been seen, up till now, only from the Catholic side, which has always recognized in Kierkegaard the representative of the self-dissolution of Protestantism—that is, a Kierkegaard "whose final purgative goal" was to "return to the Mother Church."[32] This line of thought was all the more supported by his inflamed confrontation with the Church, which ended in an open attack on Danish State Protestantism, and his occasionally vehement tirades against the Reformer. Yet despite

---

30. Z, II, "On Priests" (cf. MA, I, sec. 116); *For Self-Examination*, XIII, 566.
31. Eduard Geismar, *Søren Kierkegaard: Seine Lebensentwicklung und seine Wirksamkeit als Schriftsteller*, trans. E. Krüger (Göttingen: Vandenhoeck & Ruprecht, 1929), Introduction.
32. Erich Przywara, *Das Geheimnis Kierkegaards* (Munich/Berlin: Oldenbourg, 1929), p. 76; the same tendency is represented by John Henry Newman and Theodor Häcker.

the fact that he repeatedly praised the merits of Catholicism vis à vis Protestantism and, if not specifically advocating a return to the former, at least encouraged new "respect" for its institutions, he gave from the very outset an unambiguous answer to these ecclesiastical-political speculations: "To join the Catholic Church on that account would be an overhasty step that I would not want to be guilty of, which, however, one might expect since we have entirely forgotten what Christianity means."[33] Once again, then, it is the question of the "essence of Christianity" that determines his attitude and decision. His total agreement with Nietzsche on this point is further confirmed in their common attitude toward the Reformation—not only with respect to the important point of such an irrevocable and irreversible development, but also with respect to the ambiguity of this final "event" in and for the history of Christianity. On the other hand, both thinkers were also very much aware that one could not exactly conclude that a religious position was un-Christian simply because it was "untenable." In fact, it is rather the other way around, for, as we have seen, Nietzsche maintains that "those who have struggled the most to sustain and preserve Christianity have become its best destroyers." This would be the historical self-dissolution not so much of Protestantism as of the Christianity *in it*—which itself had been preceded by the historical failure of Christianity *as* Catholicism.

An important guiding principle in this study is the extraordinary fact that Kierkegaard's Catholic counterparts understood this dissolution in a way opposite to Kierkegaard's own understanding. From the perspective of the Catholics it is primarily an extreme life-denying rigorism that, like the absurd basis of its paradoxical faith, is supposed to reveal the merits of the Catholic system, which is secure against degeneration in both the practical and theoretical spheres. Kierkegaard, on the other hand, considers the actual degeneration of Christianity to be grounded in the Protestant secularization—whereby, to be sure, he overlooks the fact that this is basically but a repetition of the "traffic in indulgences" that had appeared at the end of the Middle Ages, which he had already branded as an expression of the necessary change pursued by the Apostle Paul: from "Christianity in the interests of God, to one in the interests of man." In connection with the erection of a "power-hungry clergy," this generally overlooked criticism of Catholicism had sufficiently revealed to him to what extent Catholicism had represented an actual a

---

33. *The Instant*, XIV, 47.

priori "*offense* against the New Testament" through its concealing, by means of the class division, the necessity for an "imitation of Christ" among the mass of the faithful, while at the same time preserving the possibility for some individuals to demonstrate their "extraordinariness" to the world.

It is through this perspective of an origin-related evaluation of faith that Luther's appearance was at first praised as a renewal of the seriousness of the original Christian claim as well as of evangelical freedom from a Church-instituted religion of laws; in such a way the recovery of the latter was justified by means of the necessary consideration of the historical distance to the early Christian "ideality of the disciple," resulting in the Protestant ideal of "masculinity" having to give *faith priority over any notion of an "imitation of Christ.*" It was merely the deterioration of the historically indispensable Lutheran "*corrective*" into the Protestant "*correction*" of the monastery that brought about Kierkegaard's increasingly violent disapproval; here again, however, he failed to see in this the self-dissolution of his own arguments (the reflection of an inner contradiction of a temporally fixed religion of eternity: "Christ's appearance contained a polemic against existence . . .") and that he is reproaching the Reformer for a "lack of dialectic" when he is in fact the victim of a lack of dialectical faith himself—a faith that commands him to defend himself both against the monastery and against the "riotousness" in Luther's anxious religiosity, insofar as both all too clearly betray, whether externally or internally, the merely compensated-for "insecurity of dread." As a result of this, and out of the fear of betraying the absolute *telos*, he remains no less skeptical of evangelical "sincerity" than he is of Catholic indulgences, and is thus enabled to achieve the dissolution of the notion of the forgiveness of sins.

In this way, Kierkegaard's destruction of historical Christianity gains the dimension of a *historical destruction of Christianity*; in it Luther appears as a "turning point in the development of religiosity," beyond which point Christianity cannot go back—if only because its double destruction in Protestantism was, first and foremost, the result of its destroyed duplication in Catholicism. However, since Protestantism only explains as the "result" that which was clearly implied in the collapse of Catholicism, Kierkegaard has to admit in the end that it was necessary to "eliminate eighteen hundred years" of Christianity completely if the "fundamental confusion" of Christendom was at all to be found in the concept "Church." We remember how Nietzsche posits the basic "misunderstanding" of Christianity in the fact that it places into temporal existence an ideal based upon the end of historical time, which for that very reason cannot fulfill the meaning-giving function that men search for in the historical situation—men who hope in vain that an explanation of their suffering will bring them relief. Hence, it is particularly helpful, and actually the goal of this comparison, to follow up the point of how, for Kierkegaard, this ideal ultimately collapses in its total unverifiability, allowing him to renounce a redemption that is as wrongly placed in the monastery as it is in a religiosity manifested in the concept of "dread"—for, after all, redemption is as little able to be attained in a naturalism legitimized by Catholicism as it is in a secularized Protestantism.[34]

2. The Doctrine of Stages as Proof of the Unfulfilled "Parousia"

What has been thoroughly overlooked is that the *"telos"* of Kierkegaard's "religious movement" was also primarily the solution to the immanent problem of the meaning of human existence; and to protect mankind against the danger of the "aesthetic" nihilism that clearly bears the characteristics of Nietzsche's existential despair, it required a Christian reflection on the transcendent. Indeed, the first "either/or" presented to the reader is the one of a *temporality fulfilled in a Christian way*, culminating in the marriage sanctified by Christianity as the only possibility of "achieving history" (that is, of giving it meaning) and in the temporal fragmentation of the aesthete, who pays for the meager "instants" of fleeting "highs" with a loss of "continuity" or the hesitation to commit himself "ethically" to the experience of his own temporality—in the form of "boredom." Nevertheless, at the end of his journey of faith Kierkegaard will be forced to proclaim this very "instant" Christian as well, and he will have to pay for this regression with the admission that the synthesis of finite and eternal, which had at one time appeared verified to him only in Christian faith, is indeed unattainable.

It would take too much time to detail here the dissolution of the intended synthesis of "absolute" and "relative" *telos* as it is so exactly described in the central work of the writer—his "doctrine of stages."[35] In this doctrine Kierkegaard describes, as we know, the religious development of the individual from "aesthetic" to "ethical," and then to the "religious" stage, from whose division a final

34. Journals, VI, A, 108; VIII, 403; X^2, A, 207; X^1, A, 28, 266, and 305. *Concluding Unscientific Postscript II*, vii, 347ff.; A, XIV, 48 and various catchwords. For a detailed treatment see the author's *Christlicher Glaube*, pp. 176–224.
35. *Concluding Unscientific Postscript II*, vii, 436.

step leads upward to Christian existence. Intermediate between these main stages are "irony" and "humor"—border areas (*confines*) in which continuation in the lower stage, that of aesthetic immediacy or an immediate middle-class morality, is seen to be unthinkable, but in which at the same time doubt exists as to whether existential despair can be overcome through a forced commitment, be it for an ethical immanence or for a religious transcendence. Without question Kierkegaard was thereby presenting, after the fact, the path to becoming Christian (which he had himself passed over) as the necessary result of the gradually deepening insight into the demands of the Christian "ideal." This ideal, in its systematic explanation of the rejection of both religious confessions by means of the duplication of their dialectical method of disputation, not only condemned an aesthetic despair without allowing for an ethical Christianity (middle-class Catholic conservatism), but also endangered a (Protestant-based) Christian ethic through the continuous use of the "teleological suspension" in favor of the absolute commandment.

As already mentioned, the philosopher overlooks (as do all his interpreters) the fact that corresponding to the believer's necessary denial of all religious orientation in and for the world, this "faith movement" is in no way concerned with a strictly goal-oriented development, but is rather one that from the very outset presents a circularity in which the linear destruction of the "ethical" is built into the destructive circle of existence impelled from the aesthetic despair of the moment to the despairing religiosity of the moment. It manifests itself as the *self-dissolution* that against the will and better judgment of the believer, who clearly recognized the danger of a total disavowal of redemption through a Christianity that is its own permanent proof of its unverifiability, is forced upon him by virtue of his intellectual honesty. This development, on the other hand, thereby becomes the historical image of the above-mentioned historical destruction of Christianity, in that it is accomplished through an internalization of *the problem of temporality in religious existence*—an internalization that in the final analysis merely provides for the extension in time of the instant of the immediate expectation of redemption.

This last parallel offers even further concrete evidence for Nietzsche's hypothesis concerning the true origin of historical faith, to the extent that it can be shown fairly conclusively on the basis of personal development *to be the consequence of an unfulfilled divine intervention*. Kierkegaard, indeed, had obviously hoped for the possibility of a "repetition" of his engagement—sanctioned by Christianity—to Regine Olsen as the reward, as it were, for the "obedience" involved in breaking it off. It is the point of his analysis in *Fear and Trembling* of the story of Abraham, who is spared the sacrifice of Isaac, that the "father of faith" had the courage to believe in "*this* life," that is, to expect to receive concrete proof for his faith in the here and now. Only after this failed "absurd intervention" through which Kierkegaard would have been spared the consequences of his paradoxical faith, but which leaves him instead to fall back into unrelieved aesthetic despair, does the intervention of the absurd become the only challenge to an "unending resignation"—earlier viewed literally as only a "surrogate for faith"—that finds itself confronted with the unsolvable paradox that "in the temporal world decisions [have to be] made about the eternal salvation of the individual." Yet this change is the consequence of a reflection of faith—forcing the transition from the dialectical deism of "Religiosity A" to the Christian dialectic of "Religiosity B"—on the basis of a "historical approach" in which "the eternal" could, as Kierkegaard remarks, not only *become*, but in some incomprehensible way also *remain* merely historical *against its own nature*. For if the "repetition" is tantamount to an "imitation" about which the believer must be ready to decide anew at any "instant," then that instant can hardly have had crucial importance for the succeeding history that prohibits man any arbitrary repetition of time. And if that which should originally have held true as a legitimate verification of redemption is suddenly thrown to the winds as "ridiculous anticipation," then the believer must ask himself where faith gets legitimate derivation—a derivation that allows him only to verify his nonredemption, especially considering the fact that the transferral of hope from an intervention of the eternal in history to the beginning of eternity after history remains for its part an anticipation as long as that intervention is constantly contradicted by the unbroken movement of time.[36]

We see that Kierkegaard experienced, in fact, exactly that transformation of faith in the historical situation on whose maxim "to live so as to render life meaningless" Nietzsche, who was himself in need of a timely relief from suffering, based his ultimate rejection of faith—a maxim whose unwilling generation in Kierkegaard again very clearly confirms the historical transformation of faith that is repeated in it. This is the transference of a redemption manifested at the *end* of history—at any rate, historical more in the sense of a psychological

---

36. *Fear and Trembling* in general, especially III, 17ff., 85ff.; *Concluding Unscientific Postscript II*, 504ff. and 435 (revocation of *Fear and Trembling*!).

verification as Nietzsche projects it onto Jesus, or as Kierkegaard expects from heavenly intervention into the "history of his engagement"—to its only theoretically hoped-for realization at the *end* of history. In that Kierkegaard's doctrine of stages anticipates this process by confirming the self-dissolution of the notion of redemption in confrontation with the circle of the unbroken experience of nonredemption, he can be seen as a witness to Albert Schweitzer's thesis of the unfulfilled "Parousia." After all, he himself is more than aware of the difficulty in attempting to capture the genuine "Christ-like life" when "the return of Christ is prophesied as close at hand and yet has not come about." The only thing he does not see in this regard is how much, in fact, this accepted unverifiability of a regenerated faith in the end of history proves the unverifiability of a Christianity that believed itself to be at the end of history. But his admission, "Have you seen anyone among us who, you would say, had the qualities of a Christian? I haven't," corresponds exactly to Nietzsche's view that the actual "misunderstanding" of Christianity is that "there was only one Christian—and he died on the cross."[37]

Kierkegaard too had apparent difficulty in reconciling the impenetrable "incognito" of Jesus, particularly of his suffering and death, with the Christian statement that God had allotted to man the ultimate "condition" if not for actual redemption, then at least for the *understanding* of his lack of redemption. Nevertheless, at the end of one of his *Unscientific Postscripts* he was forced to return to the thesis that subjectivity is the only truth, in order to defend the claim of his faith to objectivity. Thus, the principle of interpretation is never disrupted, the Socratic ignorance is in no way laid aside; the interpretation of sins remains as arbitrary as the invocation of forgiveness, and the "dread" evoked by the nothingness of human existence remains as unmitigated as the fear of its destruction in the *Sickness unto Death*. The appeal to the "instant"—otherwise condemned as the structural instant of a sensual life of pleasure—only points to the circle of an existential surge, showing why often the very person despairing of the *meaning* of his *mortal, temporal* existence cannot escape into faith. Should such a person, like Nietzsche, secretly sense that this religion was really created only for the instant and correspondingly is incapable of guiding a life in time or of directing it by way of commandments? Or, looking at it from the other side, should he have experienced the boredom of his empty existence in time, like Kierke-

---

37. A, secs. 39, 43; Journals, X^1, A, 447; X^4, A, 618.

gaard, so profoundly as to refuse to be deceived by the hopelessness of a repetition of the eschatological situation? ("We destroy eternity through a succession of instants.")[38]

And, on the other hand, should not each interpretation attempt to test precisely how and on what points just this very approach of the philosopher to the question of faith is shattered—an approach whose validity again and again is considered trivial not only as support of, but also as proof for, the necessity of a "theology in the shadow of nihilism?" Perhaps then it would become clear that (and how) this interpretation mistakes the deeper reasons for the lack of resonance of modern nihilism in the face of the Christian message, just as it does the religious unpretentiousness of Christianity—whether theoretical-philosophical, middle-class-practical, or even practical-political—which it alone is capable of proclaiming.

3. The Job-Situation

Our study has now come full circle, in both general and specific terms. If we were initially compelled to introduce a self-reflection of faith on the basis of its own dubiousness as the presupposition for a genuinely religious discussion, indeed for any *Weltanschauung*, then the reflection stimulated by faith itself on the powerlessness of *Christianity to afford an answer*—or any conception of the world based on faith—now becomes apparent as the ultimate precondition for a rejection of it. On the other hand, we have specifically characterized that religious situation which is the common basis for despair in faith and the lack of faith chosen in despair as the *Job-situation in religious thinking*. Indeed, we have seen this as the situation of a *historical* Job in which Nietzsche, like the biblical Job, not only refuses to accept as guilt the external "misfortune" of man's humanity unaffected by the Christian message, but also is unable to accept the Christian interpretation that God's answer is Job's own "inwardness." However, as we have already mentioned, those are the very reasons why, for Kierkegaard, Job is no "hero of faith," but does attain significance in that "the border struggles against faith are fought out in him." Job's argumentation contains, as we have seen, "as it were the entire weighty accusation on the part of man in the great case between God and man."

These words stem from that early work of Kierkegaard in which, parallel to the analysis of Abraham in *Fear and Trembling*, he further

---

38. *The Concept of Dread*, IV, 418.

explores the new concept of "repetition"—whereby we may note that the second document is already very much affected by his own experience of a total unverifiability of that category. In this way the "young writer," incapable of "realizing" his engagements against the conditions of his historically given nature, waits for Job's "thunderstorm"—that is, for some proof, verifiable only in temporal existence, of a possible intervention of the eternal in the natural course of an unvarying history, which will make him able to marry. He must, however, ultimately accept the "thunder" of a forced renunciation, which he later declares to be the actual goal of his faith-filled hope and which he is capable of stylizing as a satisfactory "answer" to his question. He thereby not only renounces his earlier "frankness," with which he felt himself to be called by Job's example, "'in the bitterness of his soul' to stand up and fight against God," but he also refuses, as did Nietzsche, to ascribe his development to his own "guilt," a development as factually unavoidable as it was inexplicable. "If we have to accept existence as it is, wouldn't it be better if we knew how it is? 'Guilt'—what does that mean? Isn't it more or less put upon me? Isn't it all a great coincidence? What kind of power is it that takes my respect and pride from me and in such a senseless way? Who is responsible for this. . . ? Why doesn't anyone *answer*?"

Beyond that, however, the basing of the Job-situation on the unfulfilled Parousia, the grounding of the "quarrel with God" on a guilty verdict, becomes immediately clear, indeed philologically demonstrable. For the indictment of a practically unbroken natural development in time, such a verdict can offer only the penurious "compensation" of a theoretical "elevation" in eternity. If the waiting for the storm reflects clearly enough the anticipation of eternity in the original Christian situation, then in the same way the enthusiasm of the young man for the deepening of his writing shows itself to be entirely a question of mere compensation for the frustration of his original wish. "Or is my compensation that I have become a writer? I forbid myself all compensation; I demand my rights. . . . I didn't pray to become a writer and I don't want to be one at this price."[39]

The dogmatism of Job—which was at the "core" of Kierkegaard's idea that "the passion of freedom is not snuffed out for him nor quieted by an unfortunate expression"—ultimately allows Nietzsche's extremely stringent honesty to turn, in view of the lack of an answer in the "storm" of his mortal existence, to the question of the "honesty of God": "Would he not be a cruel God who possessed the

39. *Repetition*, III, 231ff.

truth and could watch man agonize over it?" This brings us, then, to the crucial point of our comparison of the two antipodal thinkers. At the same time, it is the profoundest proof for the fundamental significance of their kinship when Kierkegaard also ultimately gives vent to his astonishment that it has as yet "not occurred to anyone to complain about God, who as eternal spirit from whom all other spirits derive, should be able to communicate the truth *directly* to these derivative spirits." To be sure, this observation is a significant slip of Kierkegaard's precisely in the above-mentioned "unscientific" reflection about the "offense" that could be caused by a possible "misunderstanding of the instant" in which "the historicity" of the appearance of Jesus was the "occasion" for faith and simultaneously the only thing confirmable about the "absolute fact" on which it supports itself. It is a "paradox" by which the distinction between the "contemporaneous" and the historical "disciple at second hand" is completely canceled, but which thereby conjures up the danger that the intention of God completely fails. He could not have taken on the "form of a servant" "in order to make sport of mankind; his intention cannot . . . be to go about in the world in such a way that not a single man recognizes it." "To grasp the full extent of the matter: Christ's whole life on earth would have become a farce had he gone through it incognito and fully unnoticed—and yet the truth of the matter is: he actually was incognito."[40]

Thus, the project of the *Philosophical Fragments* resolves itself into an attempt to prove that the "coming down" of the "teacher" (instead of raising up the "learners" to his level) is the only way in which God's love can make contact with mankind—insofar as the "learners" are "basically unhappy," not so much because in their lack of similarity "the loving ones cannot possess one another" as for the fact that "they cannot *understand* one another." The young man of the Job-argument must, however, presuppose a minimum of "knowledge," even as regards the validity of the category with whose help Christian dogma seeks to compensate for the loss of the repetition in time through its interpretation as an endlessly repeated *test*. Still, if this category—in its application by Job's theological friends—"aims toward canceling out and suspending all of reality by claiming it to be a test with respect to eternity," such an extension of its scope attests only to the suspension of its actual meaning, which it alone had as a "provisional category" and as which it should have been "canceled" (*aufgehoben*).[41]

40. *Philosophical Fragments*, IV, 218, 163, 222; *For Self-Examination*, XIII, 525.
41. *Philosophical Fragments*, IV, 184ff., esp. 194; *Repetition*, III, 243ff.

Without this cancellation, a dogma remains that exhausts itself in *postulates*, or rather that can only express itself in *that way* and remains only a postulate. Far from protecting man from the crisis of internal and external pressures, it betrays man's "self-defense" just as clearly as it hides the arbitrariness of its formulations through necessary unarbitrariness: "in this way *indeed God becomes a postulate*," but in such a way that the postulate is far from being arbitrary but rather is "self-defense." God is, therefore, not a postulate, but the fact that the existing God postulates—is a "necessity." Yet, the word upon which this necessity metaphysically as well as metaphorically supports itself, functions far more as an interpreted answerlessness than as an interpreting answer. That theological dialectics does not pause even before Job (that is, before the dissolution of his revelation) in its regression from the situation of Job to the Job-situation, is the final mark of its self-destruction. "Therefore the *weak* point in the plan of the Book of Job is that God *reveals* himself in the clouds and at the same time announces himself through his *speaking*."[42]

42. *Concluding Unscientific Postscript I*, vii, 190; *Stages on Life's Way*, VI, 295.

XIII. Language and the Critique of Language in Nietzsche

Josef Simon
(Translated by James C. O'Flaherty)

Philosophy is, from a certain point of view, thinking according to strict concepts by means of which sentences are formed, which in turn are supposed to fit together in a consistent system with the greatest possible coherence. However, even a glance at Nietzsche's writings reveals that there philosophy is not understood in this way. For Nietzsche it is "something childish or even a kind of deception, if a thinker today offers a cognitive whole, a system; we are too well schooled not to respond with the profoundest skepticism concerning the *possibility* of such a whole. It is enough if we agree on a system of *presuppositions concerning method*—on provisional truths, according to whose guidance we intend to operate."[1] That is just as true for the natural sciences as for philosophy. The reason for this is to be found in Nietzsche's reflection on the nature of concepts in general. Concepts are supposed to refer to identical things. It can further be said that one starts from the assumption that certain words are concepts—that is, they always refer to "the same thing," namely, something common to a certain class of things, or they purport to refer to a class of things that can or cannot exist in this manner. Nietzsche interprets this ontological thesis as the moral "demand to see things just this way and not otherwise." For him identity does not subsist in the "essence" of things, but in a "special power of the mind" (WKG, VII-3, 224); it finally derives from a *will* to see things in a certain way, namely, as identical things. Such a will is a will to engage in a *methodical* establishment of things conceptually which do not exist in just that way. For Nietzsche there is no ontologically superior method; such a method is a product of the imagination. The requirements of method are necessarily "one-sided," and

---

1. Friedrich Nietzsche, *Werke: Kritische Gesamtausgabe*, ed. Giorgio Colli and Mazzino Montinari, II (Berlin: de Gruyter, 1967), 128ff. Translations from the German are by James C. O'Flaherty.

precisely in that fact lies their strength. In the "one-sided requirement" of a method for determining identical things the knower is really concerned with his own identity, with his self-assertion, and to this extent the concept of a thing is always an opinion or an interpretation. There are no identical things, and accordingly no *things* at all in the sense of traditional metaphysics, but only *interpretations*. Metaphysical representation, of course, sees a contradiction in this view, for it presupposes that there can be interpretation only if there *is* something to be interpreted. Interpretation is supposed to say *what* something is. It is supposed to make its truth manifest. On the other hand, things *as such* are, in Nietzsche's view, presuppositions *inherent in* the effort of thinking that is designed to make the world comprehensible.

According to Nietzsche, what is true of concepts is also true of their syntactical connection in the form of *judgments* (*Urteile*). "'Knowledge is judgment!' But judgment is *faith* that something is this way or that! And *not* knowledge!" The *legitimacy* of faith in knowledge is always presupposed, just as the "legitimacy of the feeling accompanying a judgment of conscience is presupposed. *Moral ontology* is the *prevailing prejudice* here" (WKG, VIII-1, 273). The ontological claim of the judgment is based, on the one hand, on the identity of concepts, and, on the other hand, on the grammatical *form* presupposed in it, a form in which it unites the concepts. The basic form of this union is that of "subject" and "predicate," and it is ontologically reflected, as Aristotle recognized, in many ways: as the relation of substance and accident or of thing and property, as the relation of thing and species or of species and genus. In such a way the underlying ontological forms or categories are coordinated with the grammatical surface forms. This becomes especially clear if a further distinction is made (as it must be, according to Aristotle) between an accidental property or an accident and a necessary property or a "proprium." What Nietzsche says about concepts is thus confirmed. Just as they spring from a will to interpretation when interpreted as concepts of identical things, so now *language* is *interpreted* as the designation of ontological relations.

The distinction of necessary and accidental properties makes it possible to speak of a "substance" that perdures amid its changes of appearance. According to Nietzsche the concept of substance is "indispensable for logic, although, strictly speaking, nothing real corresponds to it" (WKG, V-2, 150). Nothing that has life, he maintains, can be understood in terms of this category; nevertheless, it is necessary from the *perspective* of a living being. "No living beings would survive if the . . . inclination to affirm rather than to suspend judgment, to err and to engage in fictions rather than to wait patiently, to agree rather than to contradict, to judge rather than to be just, were not cultivated to an extraordinary degree" (ibid.). It is when life is opposed to life in self-assertion that the concept of substance has its *function*; but when Nietzsche says that the concept of substance has its "root . . . in language" (WKG, VII-1, 692), he does not intend to say that "language" as such "seduces" thought (as analytical language philosophers, who would oppose a logical language to language as it is, would argue). Rather, it would be correct in Nietzsche's case to say that the concept of substance results from a specific *interpretation* in the sense of a specific *grammar*. A grammar purports to understand the sequence of words or their aesthetically distinct surface within the framework of a systematic set of rules. It seeks to identify linguistic structures just as the concept seeks to identify things, and to oppose permanent structures to the changing surface appearances. Thinking that involves the category of substance does not simply follow language, nor is it seduced by it, but *wills* to accomplish something with its help. It desires to understand language in a specific sense—for example, to be able to understand itself as substance. "That-which-exists-outside-us" (ibid.) is not interpreted here as something identical, but a language structure is so interpreted in order that "consciousness," in opposition to all "that-which-exists-outside-us" or in opposition to the change of its "contents," can understand itself as identity, and only in that way as "something."

We interpret not only *in* language. We also interpret language when we speak of our speaking, because we interpret this *theme* when speaking *of* something that we allege to ourselves in linguistic form. It is always true that we have only an idea of language as the result of an interpretation in whose justification we "believe." From such an interpretation we derive the categories, including the category of causality. In thinking in terms of this category we are, according to Nietzsche, by no means seeking "for causes, but for what is known" (WKG, VIII-3, 68). If we connect with this assertion of Nietzsche's the further thesis that "the popular belief in cause and effect" is "based on the presupposition that free will is the cause of every effect" (WKG, VII-1, 694), the following idea results: in causal explanations we attempt to attribute what is unknown to what is familiar to us, that is, to *equate* the two in order thus to be able to maintain the interpretation of reality that has hitherto stood the test. The attempt is made to assert that the world as it is already fabricated in our consciousness is the true world. When we do this, consciousness maintains itself in precisely *the* identity in which it *desires* to remain—in "its" identity. It *undertakes* this by means of a particular explanation, that is, one that is *possible for it*, which is always the one that explains something to itself and is also accepted by others *as* an explanation. It is the explanation in which the problematical nature that something poses *for it* is taken care of *at the same time* as its need for the agreement of others, for such is the meaning of the attempt to explain causality (consciousness is "developed in social intercourse" [WKG, VIII-2, 310]).

Thinking in traditional categories, as for example in the categories of substantiality and causality, therefore results not directly from language but from a specific *interpretation* of language that we believe to be justified. This is the "belief in grammar" with which, as is well known, Nietzsche associates belief in God.[2] Whoever "believes" in the ontological relevance of the categories of substantiality and causality will necessarily "believe" in a highest substance of all substances and in a cause of all causes. Nietzsche does not say that this belief is overcome, but he fears we would "not get rid of God, *because* we still believe in grammar" (WKG, VI-3, 72; my emphasis). Grammar is an interpretation of language from which all metaphysics arises, and this is true even of modern natural science as "the most recent of all philosophic methods" (WKG, IV-2, 19). The fact that we believe in grammar makes possible even the belief in "ourselves"—that is, in the idea that we have of ourselves, for example, as an identical consciousness throughout our life. In this concept of ourselves (as "res" or "substantia cogitans") we are something substantial, something perduring; we are the "I think, which must be able to accompany all my representations" (Kant), and are therefore their "subject." To be sure, Kant had seen that this can be only a transcendental presupposition and not a substance in an *objective* sense. But he had also seen that it is a presupposition that we must make, if we are to be at all capable of thinking that the connection of representations in the form of such categories as "substantiality and accidentality," or "cause and effect," is to have *objective* validity.

It was Kant who held that we cannot have objective knowledge of ourselves as a thinking substance, but that we must conceive of ourselves as identity amid all changing representations—and therefore as the unifying element in them—in order that our thought-sequences according to the categories in general can be conceived as

2. Cf. Josef Simon, "Grammatik und Wahrheit," *Nietzsche Studien*, 1 (1972), 1ff.

objective and in this sense as "true" knowledge. One could say with Nietzsche that the "belief" in ourselves as in "something" having identity or substantiality is the basis of the belief in substance and causes in an objective sense, or rather of the interpretive starting-point of the talk about objective truth. By means of the belief in ourselves we maintain the belief in substances and causes. It is a belief that serves life in that it reduces *other* life to objective concepts and thus ignores it as life. Life lives on the fact that it imagines other life according to *its* possibilities, that is, as potentially dead, which is the same as representing to itself life in general. We cannot stop proceeding in this way without ceasing to live ourselves.

This means also that when we speak "of" substances—when we say, for example, that we persist unchanged as speaking substance in all of our speaking—we already have a *definite concept* of language deriving from our belief in a grammar that misrepresents language. These misrepresentations are reductions of language's possibilities to the framework of specific grammatical structures. Language is richer than our consciousness of it is *permitted* to know for its own sake. All categorical thinking is interpretation, and all interpretation is "reductive procedure" or the thought that *simplifies* (WKG, V-2, 182). In such a way language, which to begin with is not "there" only for the individual and his purposes or only for certain interest-groups, can be utilized and made to serve one's own life as opposed to life in general; and thus it becomes an instrument (*Organon*). "An instrument cannot *criticize* its own fitness; the intellect cannot itself determine its limits, not even whether it is in a condition of having turned out well or ill" (WKG, VIII-1, 131). It remains impenetrable to itself, for basically it cannot view itself as a problem.

Nietzsche speaks of rational thought as "interpretation according to a scheme" of thought, "which we cannot throw off" (WKG, VIII-1, 198)—a "final, indiscussible ground." We can just barely imagine *that* we are thinking in terms of a scheme, but even so the scheme is not overcome to the extent that we are moving toward an absolute truth. For a Hegel the insight into this necessity amounted to the liberation from it. Nietzsche, on the other hand, sees in it further a deception that promotes life: "We think that, because something has become transparent for us, it can no longer offer us resistance—and are astonished that we can see through it, but cannot pass beyond it" (WKG, V-1, 274). If we should reflect on the nature of human understanding (as Locke and Leibniz, for example, undertook to do) we are then concerned with imagining this "nature," and if in so doing we obtain results that are enlightening or that can be regarded as "explanations" this occurs from a perspective that, in turn, we cannot determine. All explanations and elucidations are reductive: they follow a scheme, which also holds true for exhaustive reflection *on* the scheme. For every critique of our cognitive powers the judgment must also be made that implies its falsity: to every proposition belongs its counterproposition. *Only in this way* can the scheme be overcome.

Precisely the feeling that something is completely transparent for us is the ground of the deception that makes up our consciousness and that maintains itself in a subjective, imperturbable way primarily by means of a plausible, to say nothing of an evident, concept of itself. Our consciousness universalizes itself in this concept so that it becomes the concept of consciousness in general, and it can imagine itself as an individual only in the negation of this judgment about itself. The positive concept is always the general concept: by conceiving *myself* in terms of it I conceive *all* consciousness in terms of it. I can become clear or transparent to myself only to the extent that, in this generalization, I remove myself from myself, and also from others as individual *persons*. For Nietzsche, therefore, philosophical systems are interesting only as the works of persons. Their generalizations are personal creations whose purpose is to understand themselves and others (as well as everything else possible) *from their own standpoint*, and, if a scheme is necessarily required, to understand themselves as personally fulfilling it. "Of systems that have been refuted only the personal element can still be of interest to us, for that is the eternally irrefutable element" (WKG, III-1, 297). In Nietzsche's sense one may add that even when it is a matter of refuting systems only the personal interest obtains, namely, opposing to their generalizations one's own. What is one's own, what is new, is interesting, especially if it appears as absolute truth to its author. To consider something true is an affect. It is a passion of strong personalities to consider true only what they themselves have thought out; if they do not identify with a rationale opposed to the prevailing ideas in a positive sense, they nevertheless identify *emotionally* with the force behind the project.

To the general grammatical notion, according to which the attempt is made to reduce language in its living function to *concepts*, there is opposed its individual use, which is, for its part, *not* to be reduced to concepts. Speech, in which persons express themselves in a way that cannot be subordinated to semantic or grammatical rules, is, according to Nietzsche, *metaphorical* speech. Every word with which *persons* express themselves is, in its original use, a metaphor; for in expressing themselves in language individuals express something that is not susceptible of *reflection* in concepts, that is, something that cannot be *equated* with other concepts that are considered universally comprehensible. Words are already concepts also, to the extent that every person must make use of ordinary language to express himself: "Every word immediately becomes a concept precisely insofar as it is not supposed to serve simply as a reminder of the unique and entirely individual original experience to which it owes its origin; but rather a word becomes a concept insofar as it simultaneously must fit more or less similar cases—which means, strictly speaking, cases that are never equal, but always unequal. Every concept originates from the equation of unequal things" (WKG, III-2, 373ff.). Here we arrive at the central point of Nietzsche's philosophy of language. In the quotation it is asserted that the word *must simultaneously* fit countless cases; that "must" and that "simultaneously" are the decisive terms for an understanding of this philosophy of language.

First of all it must be said that the word must fit equal cases because it is *supposed* to fit them. Nietzsche speaks of a *making* equal (*Gleichsetzen*). This is an activity of the individual who is capable of expressing himself in the isolated individuality of his "original experience" while also generalizing himself in it. To do this, he must express himself *in such a way* that others not only accept his expression as expression, but also see *truth* in it. Consider poetic expression: Generalization is thus willed *simultaneously* with the expression of the individual experience, in the will to express *oneself* in the common language and to use the concepts of this language so that they serve that purpose. The affect itself aims at it, and individual style is by no means intended to be manneristic as mere idiosyncrasy, but rather to use language in such a way that what is individually experienced *appears* as universal truth. The shift to the universal is intended, for only in that way can anything be asserted over against already existing universal truths.

To this extent the metaphor *must* become a concept. It is meaningful only as a concept *in the making*, that is, when it is understood by others. Its *meaning* consists in its "becoming hard and rigid" (WKG, III-2, 377)! It disrupts the prevailing system of concepts, which define themselves in mutual terms, only by itself becoming a concept that attains to their universal dignity; otherwise, it remains individual and meaningless. A concept "is" only (as meaning) what it is. A metaphor is in that it *becomes* (concept), and "becoming" is, as we know, more than being according to Nietzsche: the meaning of becoming is not implied in being, but in becoming the meaning of being is implied. Whoever is in command of a language as it is, participates, by virtue of that fact, in a definite power (in which he believes). But whoever changes a language gains power *over* this power and thereby also over those who participate in it. Because he is not merely a participant, he brings his individuality to bear on it: not irrationally *over against* the predominant standard, but, rather, making it known *and* recognized by means of that standard. One should therefore not label Nietzsche as the founder of a modern irrationalism, as Lukács has done.[3] We have to do here rather with a rationality that is to be distinguished from a positivism according to which only that is real which can be reduced to allegedly unproblematical "truths" or to evidences that can be "explained."[4]

This view of the metaphor as a concept in the making makes it understandable how Nietzsche can speak of a conceptual scheme that we indeed recognize as a scheme, but that we nevertheless cannot throw off. In using language to express ourselves individually we fulfill the scheme, and we can—and we will to—express ourselves only through fulfillment of the scheme. "*Here is a barrier*: our very thought involves that faith (with its differentiation of substance and accidence, doing and doer, etc.); to abandon it means no-longer-being-able-to-think" (WKG, VIII-1, 325). Belief in the truth of these categories as belief in a deeper *grammar* of language, and therefore in logic as the doctrine of relations between fixed, identical concepts of identical things, is for Nietzsche the same as the "*belief in the ego* as a substance, as the only reality, according to which we ascribe reality to things in general!" (ibid.). One cannot think without it, but it is not therefore true.

We cannot conceive of ourselves apart from willing to fulfill the scheme in question, that is, we attain to a consciousness of ourselves, to self-consciousness, only *by* expressing in language "the unique and entirely individualized original experience" *in such a way* that it appears merely a particular instance of something universal. Otherwise there is no consciousness of ourselves. We must think of ourselves as something universal, as "ego," as that which *all* designate themselves, if we are to think of ourselves *at all*; and if we

3. Cf. Georg Lukács, "Nietzsche als Begründer des Irrationalismus der imperialistischen Periode," in *Die Zerstörung der Vernunft* (Neuwied: Luchterhand, 1954), chap. 3.
4. Cf. further Alfred Schmidt, "Über Nietzsches Erkenntnistheorie," in *Nietzsche*, ed. Jörg Salaquarda, Wege der Forschung, no. 521 (Darmstadt: Wissenschaftliche Buchgesellschaft, 1980), pp. 124–52.

would be conscious of ourselves as speaking beings, we must think of ourselves as interchangeable speakers of a language that has become concrete for us as a *specific* language by way of its conceptual version in a grammar. In other words, only by sacrificing individuality can an individual express himself in language and come to *consciousness* of himself. Only in this self-abandonment *is self-consciousness realized*, and only in this way does it gain power over others who do not have the courage necessary for it. One can say further: it is realized only insofar as it is realized for others and only insofar as it understands how to express itself in language so that others *likewise* see its "truth." It has power over others to the extent that it makes itself the subject of a determination in which they *likewise* appear simply as instances of something universal, as poetic users of language in which *all* individualities disappear in a universal aesthetic "agreement" exhibiting the *same* mood. Only in this activity does it assert itself in contrast to others who are passive. It *determines* itself as an instance (*Fall*) whereas the others are determined as instances or rather allow themselves to be so determined without contradiction.

Nietzsche criticizes the equation of man with his consciousness. He speaks of a "ridiculous overestimation and misunderstanding of consciousness," which to be sure has "resulted in the great usefulness . . . that its all-too-rapid cultivation has been *prevented*" (WKG, V-2, 57). Thus the human being could become accustomed to the consciousness of *being* "consciousness." He could cling to that idea, despite the fact that consciousness is only a superficial part of him. It does not, in Nietzsche's view, "really belong to the individual existence of the human being" (WKG, V-2, 274), and it is allied to thought insofar as it is expressed in language: "The development of language and the development of consciousness (*not* of reason, but only the becoming-self-conscious of reason) go hand in hand" (ibid.). To that extent, consciousness is an achievement of its self-expression in language. One cannot say, according to Nietzsche, that man *is* a "subject"—he only appears as a subject to the extent that he successfully expresses in language a *theory* of himself as a subject *in such a way* that it appears to others as a veridical theory of the humanness of *all* human beings and is therefore accepted by them. Thus it is not a matter of the truth of this theory in an absolute sense, but of whether others also subsume themselves under it, believing that in so doing they come to an understanding and certainty of themselves. Like the originator of the theory, they *believe* that they become thereby transparent to themselves, which means indeed to become *conscious*. Consciousness and self-consciousness relate thus to the universal concept of the human species, as "theoretical concepts" in a theory accepted as definitive, with the aid of which man distinguishes himself, for example, from the animals. It follows from the status of this theory of consciousness that there cannot be simply *one* theory that accomplishes this task: it is not its truth that is decisive, but only the historical fact that men believe that they become conscious of themselves by virtue of it. As individual persons men remain "impenetrable" for themselves and others *precisely by virtue of that fact*—as Hegel also sees.[5]

Hegel and Nietzsche agree to a great extent in their philosophical evaluation of consciousness. Hegel states the matter thus: "Only pure knowledge, the spirit, which has freed itself from its appearance as consciousness, has also free, pure being as its beginning."[6] Only this spirit is no longer bound to the representation of *being* "consciousness" according to a definite image of itself. It is open to its *own* (unconscious, impenetrable) being. But for precisely that reason it will have to create a conscious picture of itself again and again in order even to attain to a conception of itself *as the element of a theory of knowledge*, according to which it can defend itself against skepticism or be certain of its capacity for truth. When it has freed itself "from its appearance as consciousness" it becomes aware of the necessity of this appearance and of its falsity, and then it can express in language other dimensions of itself—for example, itself as instinct and affect or as something else, and over against the self-consciousness of being "conscious" as something new. It regains the capacity for becoming and for the renewal of its concept of itself, on the basis of which it had indeed even earlier understood itself *as* "consciousness." Theories of the significance of the "unconscious" are, for example, a result of such possibilities as have been opened up, but even they are naturally not "truer" than the older theories just because they are newer. Only an individual mind (*Geist*) expresses itself anew in language, but precisely in a language in which it immediately transforms itself into concepts again. Even a theory concerning the significance of the unconscious in comparison to the restricted area of consciousness renders its content *conscious*.

In this connection there appears immediately the contradiction of the form in relation to the intended content, and one must be

---

5. G. W. F. Hegel, *Wissenschaft der Logik, Gesammelte Werke*, ed. Johannes Hoffmeister, XII (Hamburg: Meiner, 1968), 236.
6. Ibid., XI, 34.

warned against "allowing himself to be deceived" (WKG, VIII-1, 217). Only in this way can one see through the lack of seriousness of such a new science—of which its originator must have been aware, when he was able to free himself from the traditional axioms in general and to arrive at these new perspectives. Only a knowledge that can free itself from identification with its "appearance" (*Erscheinung*), for example, from the appearance of being consciousness, and that has freed itself from its assumed identity, is enhanced in the "will to power." But there must also be renewed faith in the new perspectives as if they were the absolute method of attaining truth. The new theory must announce its absolute claim to truth and must will to become universal. After the lack of seriousness prevailing during the period of transition, the new values must again be taken seriously; otherwise, they are no values. Any contradiction of form and content regarding them makes no difference; their strength derives from the fact that they perdure. For all consciousness is a contradiction in that it considers itself to be true consciousness of things outside us, about which it actually has knowledge only insofar as they are present in consciousness as "appearance."

According to Hegel only the spirit that has *freed* itself "from its appearance as consciousness" is a free spirit. That is the spirit which no longer identifies itself with what is ordinarily considered to be "identity of consciousness" beyond life or through life; it is the freedom to understand even itself differently, for example, as nonidentity of consciousness. In that case identity is freed from its conceptualization, or rather, man no longer understands himself under the aspect of an identity persisting throughout life in the sense that one can *say* anything about it in terms of a theory. According to Hegel, but also according to Nietzsche, the concept of freedom is to be understood along this line: being free from a fixed, positive *concept* of oneself or of "what" one should be and according to which one should orient himself in order to fulfill his concept.

This concept of freedom from a fixed, positive concept of oneself must, as such, always be a general concept. According to Kant it must even be the most general concept of man, under which *all* men can subsume themselves (or have already done so) by virtue of having presupposed themselves to be "rational" only. Whatever is thereby considered rational can no longer be an object of possible differences of opinion. Therefore it must constitute the supreme rule of rational thought itself, that is, the freedom from contradiction in the moral concept of itself, *if* it is generalized in an unlimited way. According to Nietzsche, however, the test of freedom from contradiction is not without presupposition: it presupposes identical concepts. But because we can only act as if we had identical concepts—for we are not acquainted with their actual usage in the language of all peoples, certainly not beyond the limit of individual languages—this presupposition amounts to the assumption that all men use words with the same meanings as our own, and that even we always use them with the same meanings. We return here to Nietzsche's point of departure: whoever *introduced* the concepts used them really as an individual. Others subsume themselves under this usage, that is, they exert themselves to act in accordance with it in that they "form" or "conduct" themselves within this framework.

Kant's "categorical imperative" is thus called into question on the basis of a critique of language. The attempt to formulate a *universally* binding concept of humanness is revealed as the flash of originality of an individual who so formulates his subjective maxim of behavior that it can be elevated to the level of universal legislation without thereby becoming involved in contradiction. In so doing he proceeds on the basis of how *he himself* understands his maxim. The whole background experience of his individual life is involved here, from which he arrives at the formulation of his maxim that he now desires to test. If the maxim is: Thou shalt not kill, he necessarily starts from what he himself understands by "killing"; likewise from what he himself understands by "life," which would be terminated by this "killing." At this point it is necessary to determine when life begins and ends, and further, whether only human life is meant, whether borderline cases such as self-defense are supposed to fall in this category, and so on. One can only expect that others will agree or "concur," for without the presupposition of the fixed identity of the concepts present in the maxim there is no way of testing whether it can be generalized into a universal law without contradiction.

Freedom in Nietzsche's view is primarily the dispensing with such uncertain presuppositions, and, what is more, for reasons arising from his critique of language. If the concurrence of others is not considered necessary, owing to the lack of fixed linguistic usage or equivalent concepts, but is a "presumption" arising out of one's own subjective conviction, even Kant would speak of an *aesthetic* condition. Now Nietzsche takes this step in that he concedes to a morality that understands itself in this way the subjective *appearance* of truth, but not the moral absoluteness that it claims. "Only as an *aesthetic phenomenon* are existence and the world eternally *justified*" (WKG, III-1, 43). Whereas Kant regarded religion only as morally justified, Nietzsche employs the theological concept of "justification" consciously for the notion that claims to truth "get stuck," as it were, at the aesthetic level. They are, he maintains, always mere *fictions* by which we orient ourselves, words *claiming* to represent concepts, while in reality they only take the place of concepts. Therefore all systems possess only an *apparent* freedom from contradiction, and the consciousness oriented in them can only be "appearance," that is, it too can only be understood as an aesthetic phenomenon. Supposedly logical distinctions obtain only as illusion (*Schein*) by the grace of aesthetic distinctions—that is, as a result of the fact that individuals understand one another as such, or are so well acquainted with the language that, without recourse to the rules, they can express themselves so that others give assent. The goal of all speech is the other individual, and the temporal or even epoch-making illusion of "fundamental" truths (e.g., concerning the nature of human consciousness as the basis of all other truths) is actually due to the assent of the individual. According to Nietzsche there are, in reality, no privileged concepts: the fact that "a metaphor becomes hard and rigid is by no means a guarantee of its necessity and exclusive justification" (WKG, III-2, 378). The condition in which all metaphors are still possible, and in which the success of a certain one means nothing regarding the success of further metaphors or extensions of the language, is the free aesthetic condition. In that condition the possibility of expressing something in language does not depend on the fact that something distinctly different could be expressed in language. For in that case one would be already caught up in foundational thinking, that is, thinking in terms of substantiality. Consciousness would then be understood as the principle of the unconscious.

But how is this freedom of the aesthetic condition to be more precisely determined? We have already noted that for Nietzsche all causal explanation as reduction of the unknown to the known has its real basis in the idea "that the free will is the cause of every effect" (WKG, VII-1, 694). Thus an *assumption* is involved. The free will becomes the cause of every effect by virtue of the fact that it is the cause of all causes: it is that which allows something to be regarded *as* a "cause" by virtue of the fact that it accepts that something as such, if the explanation or naming of the cause seems to make the matter sufficiently clear. Otherwise there would be further inquiry. The "substantiation" depends on its appearing to be true for the one who had inquired about it, not on its being true. For only if one knew everything, could he call something a cause with a good conscience. The presupposition that free will is the final cause of calling something a cause is the same as the insight that one can only think in terms of a scheme. To be sure, one can relativize consciousness by, for example, attempting to explain all conscious processes as effects of physiological processes. Even Nietzsche considers progress in this regard possible. But he also says that even the complete success of this attempt would not eliminate the presupposition of free will—for even such an "explanation" of consciousness would be an achievement of the (free) will. It would then indeed constitute the truth about "consciousness," but not the absolute truth; it too would be only a successful theory, that is, another interpretation.

The fact that there is no final truth for Nietzsche, but only interpretations that are considered to be true, is identical with the inescapable presupposition of freedom. It results from the experience that we can, without further explanation, put our "selves" or "what" we are in the place of physiological causes, for example, when we crook a finger. We are free in that we assume as a cause nothing other than ourselves, and that is to say literally nothing that is qualitatively or conceptually definite. For then we take the responsibility for it ourselves without backing off from it "by way of explanation" and ascribing it to something else *outside of us*. In that case we remain for ourselves that which is simply unexplained. But we are also responsible for all *theories* in which we explain something other than ourselves as the cause of anything. Strength in Nietzsche's view consists essentially in enduring this responsibility as the renunciation of "true" explanations. That is his positive interpretation of nihilism.

The interplay of aspects of the word *as concept and metaphor* is the basic thought of Nietzsche's philosophy of language. It is not a matter of a juxtaposition of words that are concepts and other words that one would have to call "metaphors" because of some image-content, but of two views of the same thing: a word is a concept when it is to be understood as a name for a species of identical things; a word with which an individual *attempts* to express himself or "a completely individual original experience" (*Urerlebnis*), is a metaphor. Because whatever is individual is "ineffable" as long as the expression of it fails to signify anything for others also—that is, it fails to make such an impression on others that they recognize themselves in it, and also find themselves expressed in it—the linguistic expression of an individual "original experience" above all amounts only to an exerting-oneself for expression or for a language not yet existing, but in the making; it is uncertain whether the expression is understood. What Nietzsche calls a metaphor is in Hamann's language "a confluence of ideas and sensations," syntactically understood, a "group of small islands for whose community life the bridges and ferries of method" are lacking.[7] It is a *venture* in language as over an unstable bridge to another individuality, a venture in which there still exists no normative binding force of language so that individuals are aware of a *mutual freedom* in it.

In the moment of acceptance when the expression signifies "something" to others, the common object in question is constituted, "about" which it is possible to speak further. Here belong primarily the basic concepts of philosophy such as "substance," "idea," etcetera, all of which were once *introduced* into philosophical language by someone (for example, by Aristotle or Plato) with the intention of being able to say "something" in this way which, if they had not been introduced, could not have been said. Because these "neologisms" were accepted by the philosophers' guild, they became concepts representing "something," about which it was possible to discourse further, as something "given," even if they had meaning only in the language of philosophy. At the moment of their acceptance there arose the idea of something existing (*das Seiende*), *for* which they were supposed to stand. Later, from about the time of Descartes, the concept of consciousness was added. Previously it had, as "consciencia," only the meaning of conscience; if it was now to signify consciousness, it was primarily a matter of "transferred meaning," hence a metaphor. But as soon as it was accepted in philosophy and then also in other fields with the new meaning, even consciousness had *become* "something," namely, something like a human characteristic or capacity. One could now say all sorts of things "about it" and establish whole sciences dealing with it, and people believed that they had or even were "such a thing": they understood themselves now as a composite of body and consciousness. Earlier models of human self-understanding were displaced by this one, and belief in the truth of these representations of "identical things," all of which were to be subsumed under the concept of consciousness, was so strong that one would have been regarded as insane if he had ventured to deny that he "had consciousness." *Having consciousness* seemed, *from now on*, as natural as having a head. Precisely this example makes it plain that even we, for the most part, continue to cling to this entrenched belief. As a consequence, Nietzsche's warning against the "overestimation" of consciousness (WKG, V-2, 40) hardly impresses us, even though modern anthropologists assign

---

7. Johann Georg Hamann, *Sämtliche Werke*, ed. J. Nadler, II (Vienna: Herder, 1950), 61.

to the concept only a stopgap function, while awaiting future progress in brain research. Belief in consciousness is so firmly entrenched that it seems unworthy of us to deny it; to do so would seem a violation, as Nietzsche would say, of a "moral ontology"—although, as we know from the history of philosophy, the need for a concept of consciousness was not even felt before the modern period. "Soul" means something different, and it is chiefly the supplanting of the concept of the soul by the concept of consciousness that makes it so difficult for modern man "still" to comprehend statements about the "soul," its immortality, and so forth. In this connection the idea of the necessity of consciously being-also-present inevitably suggests itself as a *consciously* experienced identity of the self.

The historical view of the matter caused Nietzsche to say that such instances of the hypostatizing of concepts as basic concepts of human thought about the world and about itself have always had "their time," and will probably continue to have their limited time. He maintains, for example, that the idea "that a kind of adequate relation obtains between the subject and the object—that the object is something which, *seen from within*, constitutes the subject—is a pleasant invention, which according to my notion has had its time" (WKG, VIII-2, 299). The subject-object relation, in whose validity we also, to judge by our language, continue to believe, is called "a pleasant invention." On the other hand, Nietzsche asks whether it is not permissible "by this time to be a bit ironical concerning subject as well as predicate and object? May not the philosopher rise above faith in grammar? All respect for the governesses, but isn't it time for philosophy to renounce faith in governesses?" (WKG, VI-2, 50). The *epistemological* subject-object relationship is derived from the *grammatical*. As a matter of fact, the concept of "hypokeimenon" ("the substratum of matter or essence" [Webster]), which is oriented to the subject of a sentence, has, since Aristotle, been a "given" in philosophical language; it is only in the modern period that the subject-object antithesis has obtained.

In the passage quoted above Nietzsche also considers "the time" of *this* basic orientation of thought to be over. That which has passed during this time for the concept of "something" is again to be seen in its merely linguistic character as the expression of a time that is itself, in a certain sense, also something individual. We must again recognize that these apparent "concepts of something" were *originally* metaphors. Thus, as concepts they are again immersed in their origins and lose their absolutized meaning. But can one still say that they lose their "meaning"? Or hasn't the concept of "meaning" also come under fire? Even that, according to Nietzsche, must be a question of the times. It appears as if precisely this is a question for *our* times, which seems to be posing a crisis for philosophy. In agreement with Nietzsche one can say, in any case, that a crisis threatens *all* concepts, and that new ones will take their place. The *universal* insight that the history of ideas is the ossuary of philosophical concepts, and indeed of any concepts affording a world-view, is of no avail here. One can also say that it does no harm. The recognition of change makes no difference: we are and remain dependent on such basic orientation in our thought, if we will to think at all, and if we *will* to think, we also will to believe in the validity of such concepts. We cannot cast off any schema, if "the time" for discarding it is not ripe. No thought can extricate itself from "its time." Nietzsche always includes here his own position at any given time: "And therefore! Therefore! Therefore! Oh, do you understand me, my brothers? Do you understand this new law of ebb- and floodtide? We too have our time" (WKG, V-2, 46.) *Everything* that, in his language, is to be understood as the expression of truth, has "its time," and cannot, even as a result of insight into this "law of ebb- and floodtide," of coming into being and perishing, escape its time—for to do so it would have to lose its individuality. The threefold "therefore" underscores the full consequence of this basic concept of Nietzsche's. This "law," remaining eternally the same and eternally repeating itself, is demonstrated in the sensibility of the aesthetic insofar as it is not yet reduced to identical concepts. It is demonstrated by the concrete word, which in being used shifts from *one* meaning to *another*, and which is understood precisely in so doing, that is, without a general rule. It is understood precisely by virtue of the fact that it loses "its" meaning in individual usage, which, as an isolated concept, it may have reflected.

It is all the more certain, therefore, that there can be no "highest" concepts. That a concept attains in any philosophy the rank of highest concept is due to a linguistic construction with which an individual has *attempted* to express *his* "dominant thought" (WKG, VI-1, 77), and in which other individuals also found themselves expressed. When that is no longer the case—that is, when such conceptuality is no longer useful in confirming others in their consciousness of what they themselves are—the concept loses its meaning. From this particular standpoint Nietzsche could not really have objected to proofs of the existence of God. But proofs, he could have argued, presuppose faith in the reality of certain concepts, and such faith always endures for a limited time. No time-mysticism can, however, be derived from this position. "The time into which we are thrown" (*geworfen*) is the "time of great decline, growing ever worse. . . . Collapse, hence uncertainty, is the characteristic of this age: nothing stands on a firm footing and certain faith in itself" (WKG, VII-2, 8). As far as its orienting concepts are concerned, a strong faith obliterates the feeling of living in a certain *time*; whenever it is self-conscious, it knows itself to be anchored in eternity. Only insecure ages of transition give rise to the feeling of temporality and of being-thrown-into-the-world (*Geworfenheit*); accordingly, they spawn relativistic and decadent philosophies, whose contradictions are obvious—whereas strong philosophies are aware of no contradiction. In the case of theories that are actually believed in, ideas have the potential of being interpreted in such a way that they do not contradict one another, as long as men have not lost the strength for such an interpretation.

However much the individual is identified with his time, that time is also precisely "his" time, that is, that which he, in an age of declining belief, is capable of experiencing as an *individual* who participates in that decline. "Being" and "time" are, according to Nietzsche, related to each other in such a way that time reveals the *difference* of being (*Sein*) from existence (*das Seiende*), which is supposed to correspond to concepts, while time itself is *present* as a countermove to the "truth" of concepts or as the quintessence of the nothingness of that which is comprehended in them. That everything has its time, which (according to concepts) is "something" *definite*, means that everything that we are able to grasp in *concepts* has its end—rather than just that which was originally, according to its *concept*, conceived as "something finite." Thus, even that which is conceived as true, as infinite, has "its time," precisely because of its nature as conception; language passes beyond it, times change.

From this vantage point one can also determine what "criticism" means in terms of Nietzsche's philosophy. Nietzsche cannot mean being able to criticize "the times" or the *Zeitgeist* from any sort of "higher" or truer standpoint, for that would presuppose the subject-object antithesis all over again. Only that which belongs to a past time can really be criticized, that is, decadence that manifests signs of decline *in and of itself*. Such signs are: waning *faith* in itself, and corresponding attempts at apology—above all as attempts to ground itself on logic or as *reflection* on the "conditions" of its own possibility. Such attempts, as indeed all "epistemological critiques," in Nietzsche's view, have something absurd about them: precisely as attempts at self-justification, they reveal their inherent contradiction.

"How can the instrument criticize itself, if it can only make use of *itself* for such criticism?" (WKG, VIII-1, 103). "One doesn't write the critique of a world-view at all, but one simply comprehends it or not.... Anyone who doesn't smell the fragrance of a rose will certainly not be able to criticize it; and when he smells it—*à la bonheur!* Then he will have no desire to criticize it" (to Paul Deussen).[8] One comprehends a world-view insofar as one has it, that is, insofar as one adopts the perspective that renders it harmonious. In that case one can gloss over its contradictions without losing the "pleasure" in doing so; one discovers contradictions in the positions of *others*, but then out of "malice," so to speak. One refutes these positions to the extent that they themselves no longer possess the strength to set anything in opposition. This strength is not something conscious: "... it is our strength that has the mastery of us" (WKG, VII-2, 258); it expresses itself, for example, in the "pleasure" of criticizing alien positions. Like all strength that expresses itself in language, criticism is always emotionally tinged and not a purely theoretical matter.

Nevertheless it is possible to speak of signs or indeed of a logic of *decline* to which criticism can address itself. This logic is the logic of the imagined world of things subsisting in themselves. Here belong all forms of *reflection* upon the *absolute foundations* of one's own thought in their inherent contradictoriness, and therefore all logical attempts at establishing and justifying them. The hallmark of *decadence* consists in the fact "that life no longer resides in the whole. The word becomes sovereign and springs out of the sentence; the sentence encroaches upon and obscures the meaning of the page; the page takes on life at the expense of the whole—the whole is no longer a whole" (WKG, VI-3, 21). That means that there is no longer a will behind it which is certain of itself. The transmutation into *concepts*, that is, into words taken to be significant in their own right, and therewith the transmutation into the representation of *things* subsisting in and of themselves as the objective correlates of the words themselves, has already taken place. *Logic* is now supposed to hold together the whole in a way that is *universally* established and is divorced from the will. This cohesion is to be rendered universally transparent or validated purely theoretically, although precisely this position presupposes an unquestioned *faith* in the objective relevance of a *particular* language with its historically developed references to reality. It has to do with a language that no longer has any confi-

---

8. Friedrich Nietzsche, *Briefwechsel*, ed. Giorgio Colli and Mazzino Montinari, I-2 (Berlin: de Gruyter, 1975), 328.

dence in its own historical rudiments and therefore tries to give itself the *appearance* of unconditioned universal validity. According to Wittgenstein's grounding of logic in the *Tractatus Logico-Philosophicus*, one must, in order to presuppose at all that individual sentences have a specific value of truth, that is, for the sake of the basic presupposition of formal logic, assume that "the world divides into facts."[9] This "atomism" was already for Nietzsche the chief characteristic of a logic of decay. Formal-logical argumentation relates per se to a logic that expresses decadence and, to that extent, touches upon an aesthetic question of style.

In order not to misunderstand this as irrational, however, we must remember that even for Nietzsche one cannot think without logic. But he maintains that it is a question of whether one *wills* to think, and if one wills it, of whether it is willed in a consistent way. It is also necessary to allow sufficient mobility to concepts to enable a discourse to appear consistent in the face of criticism, that is, to give to words the meaning that a particular context justifies, and not to yield to a "universal" meaning, divorced from the acts that give them their significance. The alleged universal meaning of a word is always and necessarily a *specific* one. It is always the one *given* in a particular usage, and it is only a question of *whose* will to expression governs the dialogue. Of course, a mode of exposition is not, in Nietzsche's view, to be criticized because it is logical, but because the logical element is the factor that is supposed to validate its truth. By virtue of that fact, it essentially criticizes itself.

One must add that the listener accepts a particular expression as formulated by a speaker because he also sees himself expressed in it. He accepts it necessarily in his own sense; even the allowing-something-to-be-said-to-oneself is an individual and productive attitude. There can be no criterion by which to judge whether two human beings understand "the same thing" when hearing it. According to Wilhelm von Humboldt,[10] all language belongs "necessarily to two" —and that two people understand anything in the "same" way, can never be more than an experimental, hypothetical presupposition. One must, of course, always make such a presupposition when speaking with another, but to every "risked" attempt of this kind a "new one" must, according to Humboldt, be joined.[11] Finally, the

---

9. Ludwig Wittgenstein, *Tractatus Logico-Philosophicus* (London: Routledge & Kegan Paul, 1958), p. 30, I.2.
10. Wilhelm von Humboldt, *Gesammelte Schriften*, ed. Königliche Preussische Akademie der Wissenschaften (Berlin: Behr, 1903–36), VI, 180.
11. Ibid., p. 160.

question remains open as to whether the *presupposition* of identical meaning is realized or not. The idea of a realized presupposition is an axiomatic condition of linguistic *science* upon which the talk of a fixed relationship between a sign and "its" meaning is based, and without which there would not be the smallest linguistic units.

Such reflections are not foreign to Nietzsche, according to whom there "belongs to every soul a different world; for every soul, every other soul is an afterworld" (*Hinterwelt*; WKG, VI-1, 268). Indeed, as we have seen, everyone is, as an individual, opaque *even to himself*. "The individual is something absolute, all actions completely *his* own. . . . At least the interpretation of the formulation is personal, even though he creates none; as *interpreter* he is always acting creatively" (WKG, VII-1, 705). With this evaluation of the individual, Nietzsche actually stands within the Christian tradition, as opposed to the platonizing (i.e., in his view, moral-ontological) interpretation. But above all he proceeds from the idea that one "soul" wills to prevail over the other, and that each attempts to become for the other that which is universal and sovereign. Each one raises *a claim to the truth on his own authority*. But would he not, in Nietzsche's view, be compelled out of philosophical insight to raise this claim as if he were not raising it? If one knows that even his own doctrine has its "time," then the will to generalization that should prevail over all other individuality seems to be repressed, at least as subjective will.

Nevertheless, the Nietzschean concept of the will can no longer be understood as "subjective" will. It can only be thought of along with the counterconcept to the *concept* of a subjective will, that is, along with the "tragic" concept of the hopelessness of conceptual thinking. Individuality is no longer "subjectivity." It remains *without concept*— that is, as "something absolute" in its value, inestimable and infinite from the standpoint of "universal" moral and ontological representations and judgments. It has the absolute right to posit itself over against moral demands. Therein consists the *justice* that, "in its geniality," "avoids" everything "that blinds and confuses the judgment of things; it is therefore an *opponent of convictions*, for it desires to render to each his own, and to this purpose it must understand it in a cleanly manner [i.e., without a moral representation of what it *should* be]; therefore, it places everything in the best light. Finally it will grant even to its opponent, blind and shortsighted conviction, whatever belongs to conviction—for the sake of truth" (WKG, IV-2, 373f.). This justice vis à vis the truth of individuality is also called "love with seeing eyes, which bears not only all punishment, but also all guilt," and which "absolves everyone except those who judge" (WKG, VI-1, 84). The Christian overtones are obvious. But they are opposed to the moralizing features of Christianity, which subsume the individual under universal moral claims.

This justice is decisive even for Nietzsche's *concept of language*. True speech allows the other to be free in *his* understanding; it thereby allows "justice" to be done to him, as especially Lévinas has emphasized from the standpoint of the Jewish tradition. For Lévinas, "language" *is* "justice."[12] Heidegger, on the other hand, has always seen in Nietzsche's concept of justice the "lawgiving, authoritative ground" of the "imperious character," of "human knowledge," and of the "fictional character of human reason"[13] as "the highest kind of the will to power." "All representations of justice stemming from Christian, humanistic, enlightened, bourgeois, and socialistic morality" are to be ruled out in understanding this concept.[14] Certainly all these *moral* representations of justice are to be ruled out, and therefore also the Christian *moral representation*. But justice is the will to power insofar as *even the moral representation of power*, by which power wills to set itself above other individuality with a claim to universality, cancels itself. It is the will that "wills" only individuality, its own as well as that of others, and thereby allows itself and others *to be* free or *to be* as opposed to whatever they are *supposed* to be on the basis of any universal representations or authoritative claims. Nietzsche's concept of justice is "absolving" justice. It entails no "imperious character," but the recognition of the individuality of the other as the absolute spirit of human speech.

12. Emmanuel Lévinas, *Totalité et Infini* (The Hague: Nijhoff, 1965), p. 188.
13. Martin Heidegger, *Nietzsche* (Pfullingen: Neske, 1961), I, 647.
14. Ibid., II, 325.

XIV. The Intuitive Mode of Reason in *Zarathustra*

James C. O'Flaherty

Herbert W. Reichert in memoriam

"My concept of the 'Dionysian' was here realized as the *supreme deed*."
—Ecce Homo

According to Nietzsche there are essentially two ways in which the will to power may impose cognitive order on the chaos of the universe: the rational and the intuitive.* Thus, in his early, unfinished treatise *On Truth and Lie in a Nonmoral Sense*, he writes: "There are ages in which the rational man and the intuitive man stand side by side, the one in fear of intuition, the other with scorn for abstraction. The latter is just as irrational as the former is inartistic. *They both desire to rule over life* . . ." (my emphasis).[1] In its purest form rationality—that is, abstract or discursive reason—issues in scientific discourse, intuitive reason in myth. The two modes of reason are never, of course, present in their pure form in any philosophy or worldview. Nevertheless, one or the other usually predominates in any plausible philosophy. Rationality, however, may function in one of

---

*The present chapter is a fuller and somewhat modified version of a paper read at the North American Nietzsche Society, 26 March 1982, in Sacramento, California, and published in *International Studies in Philosophy*, XI-2 (Summer, 1983), 57–66.

1. "On Truth and Lie in a Nonmoral Sense," in *Philosophy and Truth: Selections from Nietzsche's Notebooks of the Early 1870s*, trans. and ed. Daniel Breazeale (Atlantic Highlands, N. J.: Humanities Press; Sussex: Harvester Press, 1979), p. 90. Cf. *Friedrich Nietzsche, Sämtliche Werke: Kritische Studienausgabe*, ed. Giorgio Colli and Mazzino Montinari, I (Berlin: de Gruyter, 1980), p. 889. Most quotations from Nietzsche will be from this edition, hereafter referred to as KSA with the volume and page number. Unless otherwise indicated, all translations are my own.

two ways, the one involving low-degree abstraction, the other high-degree abstraction,[2] and herein lies a crucial distinction. We may, *with certain important qualifications*, equate what Nietzsche calls the "Dionysian" element in knowledge with intuition or intuitive reason, and what he calls the "Apollonian" and the "Socratic," taken together, with rationality.

In regard to rationality, however, a very important distinction must be made at the outset: in its Apollonian function reason is creative and may unite creatively with the Dionysian element,[3] but in its Socratic function reason suffers from "a superfetation of logic" (KSA, I, 90), which renders it analytical, critical, and uncreative, and hence incapable of uniting with the Dionysian (KSA, I, 82, 90). Further, since it is parasitical upon life,[4] it cannot create genuine order. Its proper discourse is the syllogism,[5] and in its most refined form it becomes mathematico-logical symbolism.[6] Since we are dealing with a text that Nietzsche himself characterized as quintessentially Dionysian, we are justified in excluding Socratism as a basic category here, however important it may be from another perspective.[7] The fact that we are then left with a dyadic rather than a triadic set of categories should not be surprising, for Nietzsche is uncomfortable with

---

2. Nietzsche refers to "the highest concepts" as "the most general, the emptiest concepts" (KSA, VI, 76); in discussing Kant's philosophy he castigates the worship of "the Moloch of abstraction" (KSA, VI, 177). Cf. Jörg Salaquarda, "Der Antichrist," in *Nietzsche Studien*, 2 (1973), 133.

3. KSA, I, 139-40. Dionysus may learn to speak in the idiom of Apollo and vice versa, but Dionysus may never learn to speak in (Socratic) syllogisms!

4. Socratism is seen as a "life-consuming" force (KSA, I, 153). Its embodiment is the "Alexandrian man," who is "the eternal starveling, the critic without joy and strength . . . basically a librarian and proofreader, miserably blinding himself with the dust of books and typographical errors" (KSA, I, 120; cf. KSA, VI, 265). For an epistemological approach to the problem of Socratism, see my "The Concept of Knowledge in Hamann's 'Socratic Memorabilia' and Nietzsche's 'Die Geburt der Tragödie,'" *Monatshefte*, 64 (1972), 334-47; rpt. in abbreviated form in *Studies in Nietzsche and the Classical Tradition*, University of North Carolina Studies in the Germanic Languages and Literatures, no. 85 (Chapel Hill: University of North Carolina Press, 1976; 2nd ed., 1979), pp. 134-42. See John T. Wilcox, *Truth and Value in Nietzsche* (Washington, D.C.: University Press of America, 1974), for an excellent study of Nietzsche's epistemology in general.

5. KSA, I, 94; cf. ibid., 101.

6. Thus he repudiates "that hocus-pocus of mathematical form with which Spinoza armored and masked his philosophy as if in iron . . ." (KSA, V, 19).

7. Nietzsche saw in Socratism a world-historical force (albeit an unfortunate one), however contradictory it may seem that feckless "Alexandrian man" could so function (KSA, I, 97, 100).

triadic thinking, and rapidly shifts perspective when it suits him in order to introduce a new pair of conceptual opposites.[8]

However, the later Nietzsche not only assimilates Apollo to Dionysus, but also, when he comes to create his countermyth to the Gospels, *Also sprach Zarathustra*, largely abandons his professed ideal of a "fraternal union" or *communicatio idiomatum* between Apollo and Dionysus.[9] For *Zarathustra* is cast in a form that is Semitic rather than Hellenic, biblical rather than Greek (whether Sophoclean or even Platonic). In a fragment from the *Nachlaß* Nietzsche writes: "The language of Luther and poetic form of the Bible as the basis of a new German *poetry*—that is *my* invention! Imitation of the ancients, rhyming—all false, and does not speak *profoundly* enough to us, nor even the alliteration of Wagner" (KSA, XI, 60). His claim to this "invention" is of course not valid because both Hamann and Herder had anticipated him, and many of their ideas had long since been realized in the literature of the *Sturm und Drang*. Since my concern in the present study is to demonstrate the operation of a mode of reason, the emphasis is primarily epistemological; but since the demonstration involves the analysis of a literary work, the method is hermeneutical. The combination of these usually disparate approaches —required by the underlying philosophy of language—will be seen to offer important advantages.

Zarathustra, though couched in poetic form, is essentially a philo-

---

8. The dualities vary greatly, depending on Nietzsche's perspective at a given time. In addition to the well-known and definitive opposites—Dionysus-Apollo, Dionysus-Socrates, Dionysus-The Crucified—there are numerous others. *The Birth of Tragedy*, in particular, teems with antitheses of varying degrees of clarity and importance. All in all, I have identified over forty of them that may be categorized under the rubrics of metaphysics, epistemology, literature, art, politics, and ethics, but that by no means exhausts the list. In any event, Nietzsche's thought is essentially dialectical whatever the antithesis adopted. Cf. Alfred Schmidt, "Über Nietzsches Erkenntnistheorie," in *Nietzsche*, ed. Jörg Salaquarda, Wege der Forschung, no. 521 (Darmstadt: Wissenschaftliche Buchgesellschaft, 1980), p. 125.

9. In Nietzsche's later works the Apollonian is subsumed under the Dionysian or simply drops from view. Cf. Walter Kaufmann, *Nietzsche: Philosopher, Psychologist, Antichrist*, 3rd ed. (Princeton: Princeton University Press, 1968), pp. 281–82, 410; also Arthur Danto, *Nietzsche as Philosopher* (1965; reprint, New York: Macmillan, 1970), p. 64. The abandonment of the Apollonian may, however, not be complete, for, as Eric Blondel says: ". . . Dionysus without Apollo would lead to nothingness" ("Nietzsche: Life as Metaphor," in *The New Nietzsche: Contemporary Styles of Interpretation*, ed. David B. Allison [New York: Dell, 1977], p. 162). Undoubtedly Nietzsche has given us clues as to how the Apollonian may be *unconsciously* present in the Dionysian in the *Nachlaß* of the early years—but this is not the place to pursue that subject.

sophical work. Since that is true, it must perforce be informed by reason.[10] However, it is clear that it is *not* informed by discursive reason. The question arises then as to what mode of reason characterizes it, and the answer to this question can be found by identifying the method of reasoning that Kant once imputed to Hamann, namely, "anschauende Vernunft" or "intuitive reason,"[11] a method that the latter consciously derived from the Bible.[12] Before proceeding to demonstrate the use of this mode of reason in Zarathustra it is necessary to specify the linguistic categories that are its hallmarks. We shall see that *all* of these categories are utilized to varying degrees in the work. Not only do they inform Zarathustra but they also constitute the means by which Nietzsche imposes a kind of order on the work.

The distinction between the two disparate kinds of reason with which we are concerned actually revives an age-old tradition in Christian theology, namely, the distinction between *ratio superior* and *ratio inferior* made by Peter Lombard[13] and Meister Eckhart[14] in the

---

10. That Nietzsche characterizes the intuitive individual as "irrational" (quotation on p. 274 above) should not mislead one into acceptance of such an ambiguous term. Cf. his statement that Dionysus and other "gods also *do philosophy*" (my emphasis; KSA, V, 238).

11. Kant once asked Hamann's help in interpreting a passage from Herder, requesting, however, that the reply be "if possible, in human language. For I, poor mortal, am not at all organized for the divine language of *intuitive reason* (anschauende Vernunft). What can be spelled out for me in common concepts according to logical rules I can understand well enough" (Kant's emphasis; letter, 6 April 1774: *Johann Georg Hamann, Briefwechsel*, ed. W. Ziesemer and A. Henkel, 3 [Wiesbaden: Insel, 1957], 82). Although Kant is here engaging in a bit of raillery, the term *anschauende Vernunft* is a felicitous one to describe Hamann's mode of thought.

12. The categories are derived from the thought of J. G. Hamann, but freely adapted. See my "Language and Reason in the Thought of Hamann," in *Creative Encounter: Festschrift for Herman Salinger*, ed. L. R. Phelps and A. T. Alt, University of North Carolina Studies in the Germanic Languages and Literatures, no. 91 (Chapel Hill: University of North Carolina Press, 1978), pp. 86–103, or my *Johann Georg Hamann*, Twayne World Authors 527 (Boston: Hall, 1979), chap. 5.

13. Peter Lombard taught that *ratio superior* characterized Adam, and *ratio inferior*, Eve. *Ratio superior* involves thinking in concepts, that is, logically; *ratio inferior* involves thinking in images, and is associated with a "sensual impulse of the soul" (*sensualis motus animae*). He held further that "the higher part of reason is suited for contemplation or consultation of the eternal reasons; the lower part is turned aside toward governing temporal things." The Fall resulted from Adam's failure to use his more logical reasoning and allowing himself to be persuaded by Eve's kind of reasoning. Peter Lombard, *Sententiarum liber* II, distinctio xxiv, cap. 6, 7.

14. See Benno Schmoldt, *Die deutsche Begriffssprache Meister Eckharts* (Heidelberg: Quelle & Meyer, 1954), esp. pp. 18–19, 22, 79.

Middle Ages, and taken up by Lessing in the eighteenth century.[15] But none of these thinkers gives us the full set of linguistic criteria by which the two modes of reason may be clearly distinguished. Both Hamann and Nietzsche, of course, reverse the traditional evaluation of the two modes: for them, reasoning in images is not *ratio inferior*.

Nietzsche makes it quite clear that only a poetic style is really appropriate for expressing his vision of the world. Commenting on *The Birth of Tragedy* many years after its appearance, he wrote: "It should have *sung*, this 'new soul'—and not spoken. What I had to say then —too bad that I did not venture to say it as a poet . . ." (KSA, I, 15). In accordance with this principle, when he set about to compose his most important work he did adopt a poetic form. Despite the unfolding of his thought in the years between the appearance of *The Birth of Tragedy* and that of *Zarathustra*, his world-view did not essentially change. What did change was his decision to adopt a different style, to couch his philosophy in poetic language. This fact has implications of fundamental importance for his thought.

The categories that we may identify are six in number, and each has its counterpart in the abstract or discursive mode of reason. They are all derived from language, not from empirical thought (Aristotle) or pure thought (Kant).

From the following table we see that abstract reason, after making its initial assumption, alters course, so to speak, and proceeds to deal in nonmetaphorical (logical) terms as far as possible; intuitive reason, however, does not alter course but continues to deal in metaphor (analogy) as far as possible. For abstract reason, initially assumed metaphors are mere crutches to be dispensed with as soon as possible; for intuitive reason, however, they are of the essence. Thus, to say that the physical or abstract sciences are also intuitive is to assert a partial truth, whereas to say that poetry is intuitive is to assert a whole truth. In any case, wherever the six linguistic categories are present, one may assume that a particular mode of reason is at work. The language of "B" in the table may always be transformed into mathematico-logical symbols, and even reduced to the binary scale of computers; the language of "A" may not. Or, in Nietzschean terms, we may say: the Apollonian may "superfetate" as extreme Socratism; the Dionysian may not (cf. KSA, I, 485–86).

---

15. Jürgen Schröder maintains that Lessing accepted Peter Lombard's distinction, agreeing with him that there is a moral obligation to heed *ratio superior* rather than *ratio inferior* (*Gotthold Ephraim Lessing: Sprache und Drama* [Munich: Fink, 1972], pp. 82ff.).

Categories of Intuitive and Abstract Reason as Reflected in Language[16]

A. Intuitive Reason	B. Abstract Reason
Principle of Unconscious Selection*	Principle of Conscious Selection*
I) Image (description)	I) Concept
II) Metaphor (analogy)	II) Logic
III) Paradox (cf. oxymoron)	III) Nonparadoxical language
IV) Multivalence (cf. *Quadriga*)	IV) Univalence
V) Parataxis (coordination)	V) Hypotaxis (subordination)
VI) Affective language	VI) Nonaffective language

Notes on A.*	Notes on B.*
1) Underlying the intuitive mode is either the *oneiric* or the *organic* root-metaphor.	1) Underlying the abstract mode is either the *architectonic* or *mechanistic* root-metaphor.
2) Discourse *nonreductive*.	2) Discourse *reductive*.
3) Open to the infinite (since there is no limit to what things may be likened).	3) Observes *limits* (since we delimit when we define).
4) Results in *open form* (cf. Romanticism).	4) Results in *closed form* (cf. Classicism).
5) Characterizes the structure of *myth*.	5) Characterizes the structure of *scientific* discourse.
6) Equivalent of Peter Lombard's *ratio inferior*.	6) Equivalent of Peter Lombard's *ratio superior*.

1. Image (*Bild*)

In Nietzsche's view the image represents a closer approximation to reality than does the abstract concept.[17] Thus in *The Birth of Tragedy* he writes: ". . . we must understand Greek tragedy as the Dionysian chorus that constantly discharges itself anew in an Apollonian world

---

16. Principles and annotations marked with an asterisk are not explicit but implicit in Hamann's observations on language.

17. As Harold Alderman trenchantly says: "For Nietzsche, the world is more like a metaphor (i.e., indefinite and soft-edged) than it is like a logical theorem (i.e., definite and hard-edged)" (*Nietzsche's Gift* [Athens, Ohio: Ohio University Press, 1977], p. 15).

of images" (KSA, I, 62). These lines are crucial to an understanding of Nietzsche's use of imagery in *Zarathustra*. Although the "image" belongs essentially to the "Apollonian world" of plastic art as opposed to the intangible, nonimagistic world of music, Dionysus *must, if he would speak at all, appropriate such images as his primary linguistic medium* (cf. KSA, I, 139–40). Nietzsche makes this abundantly clear in another case: that of Archilocus and lyric poetry in general, where "an unequal and irregular image-world" prevails. Though it is a (Dionysian) image-world "basically in opposition to the Homeric" (KSA, I, 49), it is just as dependent on its particular use of imagery as is the Apollonian epic, where the poet is described as merely "absorbed in the pure contemplation of images" (KSA, I, 44) and therefore as having the deeper purpose of neither the lyricist nor the philosopher. A failure to note carefully Nietzsche's shift of perspective from the world of the plastic arts and music to the world of literature would lead one hopelessly astray. In other words, the Dionysian-Apollonian duality means one thing in the nonverbal realm of art and another thing in the verbal realm of literature. We shall see that Nietzsche's "unequal and irregular image-world" of the Dionysian lyricist is also a felicitous phrase to describe the style of *Zarathustra*.

It is important in our discussion to distinguish between the image as description and the image as metaphor (*Gleichnis*). It is unfortunate that Nietzsche himself does not do this, especially in *The Birth of Tragedy*, where the basic outlines of his subsequent thought are laid down or at least anticipated. Undoubtedly this is one of the areas where, as he confessed years later, the work suffers from a lack of "logical cleanliness" (KSA, I, 14). His characterization of *Zarathustra* in *Ecce Homo* is, however, not necessarily at odds with the distinction between the two functions of imagery: "What is closest to us and most everyday, here speaks of unheard-of things . . . the most powerful capacity for metaphors [*Gleichnisse*] that has existed so far is poor and only child's play compared with this return of language to the nature of imagery [*Bildlichkeit*]" (KSA, VI, 344). It is thus important that his analogies be as replete with the imagery of everyday human experience as possible. If one substitutes, in the passage just quoted, for the word "metaphors" the term "analogies" or "parallels," the statement poses no problem. That the distinction between the two functions of images is basic we shall also see in our discussion of multivalence. It is true that Nietzsche held, in another context, that *all* language is metaphorical, but a discussion of the problem posed by that idea does not fall within the scope of this study, where his practical distinction between metaphor and concept is basic.[18]

It must also be noted that there are two types of descriptive imagery: pure or straightforward imagery, and metonymy. Although the latter is a trope, it does not involve analogy, and is therefore fundamentally different from that most important of tropes, the metaphor.[19] In *Zarathustra* Nietzsche employs the metonym or synecdoche much less frequently than pure description, and more often than not his usage in the narrative passages is commonplace. Occasionally Nietzsche's metonymical expressions are striking—as when Zarathustra, having been rebuffed by the people of the marketplace, says to himself: "I am not the mouth for these ears,"[20] or when we are told that "for a long time Zarathustra slept, and not only dawn passed over his face but the morning too" (25)—but most, if not downright commonplace, are not far from it: the jester's leap over the tightrope "made every mouth dumb and every eye rigid" (21); he confides "to his heart" that he will carry off and bury the corpse of the tightrope walker (23); "whoever still has ears for the unheard-of—his heart shall become heavy with my happiness" (27); "the higher you ascend, the smaller you appear to the eye of envy" (81); on his sea-voyage "eventually his own tongue was loosened" (197). Although Nietzsche uses metonymy most sparingly its function is important, for, in combination with his impressionistic use of imagery, it lends a poetic quality to his descriptions and matter-of-fact statements. In such a way he avoids a breach of style in the work as a whole.

Imagery as pure description occurs, of course, in the narrative passages of *Zarathustra*, but, like the narrative framework itself, it is exceedingly meager. Thus we know: that the younger Zarathustra's eyes were "pure" (12); that there was no disgust about his mouth (12); that he walked like a dancer (12); that the town he entered after ten years lay on the edge of a forest (14); that the jester in the mar-

---

18. KSA, I, 878ff. Suffice it to say the following: to show that an abstract term is a dead metaphor proves something *etymologically*, but does not eliminate the functional (and fundamental) difference between the metaphor and the concept.

19. The effective exploitation of this difference in another area is well illustrated by the structural anthropologists. Cf. Claude Lévi-Strauss, *The Savage Mind*, trans. George Weidenfeld (Chicago: University of Chicago Press, 1968), esp. pp. 204–8, 212–13, et passim.

20. I have cited Walter Kaufmann's translation (*Thus Spoke Zarathustra* [New York: Viking, 1966]), but have changed "overman" to "superman" as a rendering of "Übermensch." References to KSA, IV, appear parenthetically in the text (here, 20).

ketplace was dressed in "motley clothes" and had an "awe-inspiring voice" (21); that moss grew under the tree in which Zarathustra placed the dead man (25); that there was a stone before his cave (300); that the two kings he met in the woods were "adorned with crowns and crimson belts and colorful as flamingoes" (304); that the last pope was "a tall man in black, with a gaunt face" (321); that at noon one day Zarathustra came to an old, crooked, knotty tree that was entwined by a grapevine with abundant yellow grapes (342); that "the ugliest man" once adorned himself with a crown and two crimson belts borrowed from the two kings (346); that his lion was a mighty animal with a thick warm mane (406); that doves sat on Zarathustra's shoulders and caressed his white hair (407); that the lion kept licking up the tears on his hands, and roared and growled bashfully (407); that Zarathustra left his cave glowing and strong like the sun coming out of dark mountains (408).

Obviously some of the descriptions cited could also be construed as symbolic, as for instance the last one. Conceivably, each of them might under certain circumstances be so interpreted. But it must be borne in mind that even the sparest of narratives cannot dispense entirely with imagery as pure description. In other words, one must find descriptive imagery somewhere in a given literary work if there is to be a narrative at all. *Zarathustra* is so replete with imagery in general that the thought becomes difficult to follow, but it is imagery as metaphor that causes the difficulty, not imagery as description.

2. Metaphor (*Gleichnis*)

The metaphor or parable ("Gleichnis" denotes both) is based on analogical reasoning despite the fact that its grammatical form, unlike that of the simile, tends to mask the underlying analogism. If the descriptive imagery of *Zarathustra* is minuscule in comparison with the metaphorical imagery, it is because this is a philosophical, not a dramatic or epic, work. Metaphors never move the action forward, but are intended to illuminate their context (i.e., to convey meaning). The metaphors of *Zarathustra* may for our purposes be divided into two classes: those that constitute symbols conveying the basic ideas of the work, and those that illuminate various lesser aspects of Nietzsche's thought. Some of the metaphors that rise to the level of important symbolism are: the sun = man's relation to superman and eternal recurrence (11–12); bridge = man (16–17); eagle = pride (27); serpent = wisdom (27); camel = learner (28); lion = overturner of conventional values (30); dragon = guardian of values (30); child = a new beginning (31); tarantulas = secretly vengeful preachers of equality (128); the leech = scholarly specialization by the conscientious in spirit (311). Lesser symbols are also quite striking: adder = enemy who unintentionally does one good (87); ropemakers = the old who, ripe for death, are living in the past (94); the devil's face in a mirror = Zarathustra's teaching distorted (105); cork = friend who keeps Zarathustra's dialogue with himself from sinking into the depths (71); bitch = hidden sensuality of the chaste (69); gravediggers = pedantic scholars (234). Since the work teems with metaphors, one could make an exceedingly long list of them. Further, in an aesthetic analysis of the work, one could identify the tropes that are simple metaphors, effective mixed metaphors, similes, allegories, personification, synesthesia, etcetera. But the important fact here is that they are all based on analogy, and that the plethora of metaphors in *Zarathustra* establishes it as a prime example of analogical reasoning in concrete terms.

Nowhere is the affinity of *Zarathustra* with the method of Jesus' discourse more evident than in the use of metaphor and parable. Matthew reports of Jesus' teaching that "without a parable spake he not unto them" (Matt. 13:34). In his discourse "On the Gift-Giving Virtue" Zarathustra says to his disciples: "All names of good and evil are parables: they do not define, they merely hint. A fool is he who wants knowledge of them. Watch for every hour, my brothers, in which your spirit wants to speak in parables: there lies the origin of your virtue. There your body is elevated and resurrected; with its rapture it delights the spirit so that it turns creator and esteemer and lover and benefactor of all things" (98–99; cf. 128). Thus it is characteristic of both Jesus and his archenemy Nietzsche-Zarathustra that they do not say what the most important values *are* but what they are *like*. It is the *tertium comparationis* of metaphor and parable, not the unfolding of the syllogism, that is at work here. And between the indirect, nonapodictic knowledge yielded by analogy and the direct, apodictic knowledge yielded by logic there is a great gulf.

3. Paradox

The very first hallmark of intuitive reason encountered in *Zarathustra* is the paradox. Already in the subtitle of the work we encounter the paradoxical description: "A Book for All and None." Indeed, the work is studded with paradoxes. One investigator has identified approximately three hundred such formulations;[21] others will find more or less, depending on the criterion adopted. Here again the Bible, particularly the New Testament, is the primary model. A few examples will suffice: "I give no alms. For that I am not poor enough" (13); "I love those who do not know how to live except by going under, for they are those who cross over" (17); "I love the great despisers because they are the great reverers . . ." (17); "One virtue is more than two" (17); "I love him who chastens his god because he loves his god . . ." (18); "Living companions I need, who follow me because they want to follow themselves—wherever I want" (25); "Your very commanding should be an obeying" (59); "Physician help yourself; thus you help your patient too" (100); "To be the child who is newly born, the creator must also want to be the mother who gives birth and the pangs of the birth-giver" (111); "Deeply I love only life—and verily most of all when I hate life" (140); "It is the good war that hallows any cause" (307); "Man must become better and more evil" (359).

Despite its appearance of contradiction we intuitively accept the paradox—and its contraction, the oxymoron—in ordinary language as quite meaningful, provided we are aware of the context. This is true to an even greater degree in poetic and religious language. If, on the other hand, the contradiction is stated in the univocal language of discursive reason, we do not accept it as meaningful but seek to resolve the contradiction. In the former case, we have the so-called literary paradox,[22] and in the latter case the genuine antinomy. With paradoxes of the latter type we are here not at all concerned. Nietzsche's paradoxes belong to the tradition of literary or, more specifically, religious paradoxes, whose genealogy is ancient and impressive—as exemplified most prominently in the language of the Apostle Paul, of the German mystics of the Middle Ages, of Jacob Böhme, of Angelus Silesius, and of Luther, as well as in the quasi-religious paradoxes of the essay "Die Natur," which is traditionally ascribed to Goethe. Nietzsche's motivations in employing paradoxical language in *Zarathustra* are several: to parody the teachings of Jesus; to provide a shock effect; to invite reflection on the double meaning involved. However, we are concerned neither with the psychological motivation for his usage nor with the aesthetic reasons for

21. Karl Groos, "Der paradoxe Stil in Nietzsches Zarathustra," *Zeitschrift für angewandte Psychologie und psychologische Sammelforschung*, 7 (1913), 472.
22. See Rosalie L. Colie, "Literary Paradox," in *Dictionary of the History of Ideas*, 3 (New York: Scribners, 1973), 76–81.

it; nor are we concerned with the question of whether his use of the paradox means that he was basically a paradoxical thinker, for, as Karl Groos reminds us, there are thinkers whose teachings are paradoxical but whose language is not.[23] Rather, we are concerned here only with the fact that Nietzsche has employed his literary device so prominently in an essentially philosophical work.

4. Multivalence

Multivalence in language is of course closely related to the metaphorical aspect, since it is based on the fundamental distinction between the literal and figurative use of words.[24] But its distinctiveness lies in the fact that the metaphorical level is not introduced simply to clarify the literal meaning of a statement, but to shift the statement to another level of meaning, thereby conveying a different but parallel idea. The number of levels may vary widely, from merely two to almost any number in the case of fanciful exegesis. Thus, "the Talmud, which is often Kafka's archetype, refers to the forty-nine levels of meaning which must be discerned in a revealed text."[25] Medieval biblical exegesis was generally limited to the so-called *Quadriga*, that is, the fourfold sense of Scripture. One readily recognizes that Zarathustra is characterized by various levels of meaning, which is to say it may be read from different perspectives. Because the form of the work is quasi-biblical, one can expect it to be informed by considerable multivalence. Despite the fact that the so-called allegorical method of Scriptural interpretation has been rejected by scholarly biblical critics since the eighteenth century—and that Nietzsche was always ready, whenever it suited his purpose, to use their findings *against* Christianity—we may have no qualms about applying it to the mythical, and hence multilayered, *Zarathustra*.

In speaking of the literal level of a work one must distinguish between the immanent literal level, as intended by the author, and an extraneous literal level represented by hidden allusions to persons or events (as, for example, in a *roman à clef*). Although Nietzsche chose the name "Zarathustra" for his prophetic mask, it has little, if any-

23. "Der paradoxe Stil," p. 476.
24. It is obviously quite important at times to determine whether Nietzsche is speaking literally or figuratively, as for example when Zarathustra praises war (KSA, IV, 58–60), or when Nietzsche speaks of the notorious "blond beast" (KSA, V, 275 et passim).
25. George Steiner, *After Babel* (London: Oxford University Press, 1977), p. 66.

thing, to do with the historical Zoroaster.[26] Therefore, the literal level in the immanent sense may be ruled out, and insofar as this is true, we are dealing with pure myth. For pure myth is in no way dependent on a literal historical level for its validity. Here a similarity to the gospels is lacking, since they purport to be literal history. Nevertheless, if we identify Zarathustra with Nietzsche, the work can then be said to have a literal level, for it can be shown to be somewhat autobiographical. Further, there are covert allusions to friends and acquaintances of Nietzsche's in the work.

Recently Richard Hayman has sought to demonstrate a surprising number of autobiographical references in *Zarathustra*.[27] For instance, Zarathustra's initial withdrawal to the mountains is a withdrawal not simply from men in general but specifically from Lou Salomé and Paul Rée (Hayman, p. 255). In the section "On Self-Overcoming" the reader is confronted, according to Hayman, with the "cross-fire of Nietzsche's battle against himself" (p. 264). Or, again, in "The Dancing Song" he is declaring, albeit obliquely and perversely, his love for Lou (p. 266). His nausea and weariness are symbolized by the snake-episode in "On the Vision and Riddle" (p. 271). Zarathustra's disappointment at not having better disciples in "On the Higher Men" is a symbol of Nietzsche's own disappointment at not having any disciples (p. 279). The autobiographical character of the book is certified, Hayman tells us, by Nietzsche himself: it "contains the most sharply focused image of me," he wrote to Overbeck, "as I am *after* I have fully unburdened myself" (p. 256); in a letter to Gast about six months later he declared that in the book there is "an incredible amount of personal experience and suffering, intelligible only to me. Many pages are bloodstained" (p. 266). On the other hand, Hayman observes that "Nietzsche must have been nervous that his friends would recognize themselves in the new book" (p. 286).

The text of the "The Magician" in the fourth part of *Zarathustra* provides an instructive example of multivalence. The "magician" refers not only to Nietzsche, but also to Richard Wagner; on another level, he is an allegorical figure for the artist who may imagine himself to be like that which he creates. The song of the magician is intended as the lament of both Nietzsche and Wagner, and also, as we know from extraneous sources, of Cosima Wagner. If we take into consideration the later version of the song, "Ariadne's Lament," yet another dimension is manifested, namely that of the Greek myth

---

26. It has recently come to light that Ralph Waldo Emerson's reference to "Zarathustra" (Zoroaster) probably prompted Nietzsche to adopt the name (KSA, XIV, 279).

27. Richard Hayman, *Nietzsche: A Critical Life* (New York: Oxford, 1980).

involving Dionysus's love for Ariadne. There is nothing on the surface of this section, however, to lead one to suspect the presence of references beyond that to the allegorical "magician." If the *Quadriga* as formulated by Nicholas of Lyre[28] in the fourteenth century, involving the literal, allegorical, moral, and anagogical senses of Scripture, is applied to the exegesis of the term "superman," we find that it does indeed throw light on the matter. To be sure, the sparse information that Nietzsche gives on the nature of the superman is scattered throughout the text; however, the important fact is that whenever the term "superman" is used, it means all those things at once. On the literal level, Zarathustra flatly denies that the superman has ever existed: "Never yet has there been a superman. . . . Verily the greatest I found all too human" (119). On the second level, that of allegory—which, according to the *Quadriga*, concerns belief —the superman accepts the death of God and the consequent necessity for a transvaluation of values (30–31). On the third, or moral, level, which proclaims what one should do, the superman is one who overcomes himself and becomes a creator of new values (90). Finally, despite Zarathustra-Nietzsche's denial of transcendence, the anagogical level, which has to do with the ultimate destiny of man, is very much present: for the superman is able to embrace wholeheartedly the idea of eternal recurrence,[29] indeed to cherish the idea of *amor fati* (291). Thus the anagogical level constitutes the metaphysical aspect of the work, and is the bearer of the doctrine that is of equal importance with the idea of the superman.

Nietzsche's use of the verb "untergehen" and its related noun, "Untergang," is also a prime example of multiple levels of meaning in *Zarathustra*, and again the *Quadriga* furnishes a convenient means of distinguishing the levels. Although the word occurs throughout the book with different meanings, all four levels can readily be discerned in a few passages of Zarathustra's "Prologue." Thus, when he apostrophizes the sun, saying: "Like you I must go under," he is referring to the literal setting or going down of the sun as well as to his literal descent from the mountains into the nearby town. In his words: "I love those who do not first seek behind the stars for a

---

28. Nicholas of Lyre (Lyra), d. 1340, is credited with the following lines: "*Littera gesta docet, quae credas Allegoria, / Moralis quid agas, quo tendas Anagogia*" (quoted in Frederic W. Farrar, *History of Interpretation* [Grand Rapids, Mich.: Baker, 1961], p. 276).

29. See Bernd Magnus, *Nietzsche's Existential Imperative* (Bloomington and London: Indiana University Press, 1978), pp. xiii, 32–38, for an enlightening discussion of the superman's relation to eternal recurrence.

reason to go under and be a sacrifice, but who sacrifice themselves for the earth, that the earth may some day be the superman's" (17), he has in this one assertion touched on both the allegorical and moral meanings of the word—for he esteems those who no longer believe in a transcendent world, but who are willing to sacrifice for the superman, "the meaning of the earth." The former attribute is termed "allegorical," because it involves belief; the latter is termed "moral," because it involves what one should do, namely, sacrifice himself for the sake of the superman. An earlier statement in the "Prologue" points to the anagogical or metaphysical level: "I love those who do not know how to live, except by going under, for they are those who cross over" (17). As becomes clear in the latter half of the book, "crossing over" can only refer to that substitute for transcendence: the eternal return of the same. Followers of Zarathustra here are characterized, in a striking metaphor, as "arrows of longing for the other shore" (17).

It is interesting to note that, whereas David Friedrich Strauß attempted to demolish the credibility of the gospels precisely by demonstrating their mythic character, for Nietzsche myth is the form par excellence for conveying truth. If in traditional biblical exegesis the whole superstructure of the fourfold sense of Scripture rested on the firm basis of the literal account of historical events, and was believed to stand or fall on the soundness of that basis, Nietzsche, in depicting the superman, ironically subverts that idea, for he is explicit that the superman has never existed. For the traditional believing Christian, the idea that Jesus never existed, that he is merely an ideal, is utterly inadmissible.

In calling attention to the multivalent character of *Zarathustra*, we should also stress that Nietzsche vehemently repudiates this method of exegesis when practiced by "the philology of Christianity" (KSA, III, 79). He severely indicts the priest's "incapacity for philology" (KSA, VI, 233); here he is making common cause with the rationalistic biblical critics of his own day who rejected the allegorical interpretation of Scripture in the interest of scientific philology: "The way in which a theologian, whether in Berlin or Rome, interprets 'a verse of Scripture' or an event—for example, a victory of the armies of the fatherland, in the higher light of the Psalms of David—is always so audacious that a philologist can only despair" (ibid.). But even when one concedes the abuse involved in such extravagant use of the so-called allegorical method of biblical interpretation with its resulting fantastications, the fact remains that analogical reasoning is at the bottom of it, and insofar as a meaningful *tertium comparationis* is actually present, the method may be justified. It is ironic that Nietzsche, who, in *The Dawn* and *The Antichrist*, aligns himself with the rationalistic biblical critics who insist in effect that language must be univalent, nevertheless chooses a vehicle for the expression of his most important thoughts that, though essentially lacking the literal level, is otherwise characterized by multivalence.

5. Parataxis

In the strict sense parataxis involves the *coordination* of clauses in a sentence, and is contrasted with *hypotaxis*, which involves the *subordination* of clauses. In the present discussion, however, both terms have not only their technical syntactical meaning but also an extended meaning. Thus, not only a single sentence may be characterized as paratactic or hypotactic, but also larger literary units such as paragraphs, or even whole works. In the extended sense, Nietzsche's literary "forms of eternity" (KSA, VI, 153), the aphorism and the apothegm, are essentially paratactic. Further, the two terms may be understood as referring to two different kinds of order, the intuitive and the rational. Parataxis may be said to refer to the kind of order in which the parts agree with the whole, but not necessarily with each other; hypotaxis, on the other hand, may be said to refer to the kind of order in which the parts agree with the whole and necessarily with each other, and such order lies at the basis of all systems. The first kind of order may be termed "intuitive," the second, "rational." Intuitive order is characterized by what Nietzsche calls "law in the strife of the manifold" (KSA, I, 831; cf. VI, 152). We may further regard intuitive order as essentially Dionysian—and biblical; rational order, as essentially Apollonian—and Hellenic.

It is necessary to make a distinction between two kinds of both parataxis and hypotaxis as they appear in literature. Although the former is universally characteristic of folk-literature,[30] one may not conclude that it always bespeaks a primitive mentality: it may be employed by quite sophisticated writers. On the other hand, hypotaxis may not always bespeak the predominance of rationality in a belletristic work: rather the opposite is true where its purpose is primarily rhetorical. Paradoxically, except in *Zarathustra*, Nietzsche's prose at its best is apt to be characterized, as shown by Stefan Son-

---

30. Wolfgang Kayser, *Das sprachliche Kunstwerk*, 9th ed. (Bern and Munich: Francke, 1963), p. 143.

deregger, by a balance between parataxis and hypotaxis, the latter being employed for its rhetorical effect.[31] In that case there is some justification for asserting hypotaxis to be a "Dionysian" characteristic of Nietzsche's style. In the present usage, however, hypotaxis is regarded as essentially Apollonian, that is, as evidence that the *ratio* is at work, whether in *belles lettres* or in scientific prose; parataxis, on the other hand, is regarded as essentially Dionysian, that is, as evidence that intuition is at work.

In view of Nietzsche's earlier extravagant praise for the union of Apollonian with Dionysian elements in all great art, it is surprising that, in creating his masterpiece, he all but eliminates the Apollonian element, and is therefore left with essentially Dionysian form, a form that also turns out to be Semitic. But the shift is not simply due to a difference in the taste of the ancients and moderns—the former being aurally, the latter visually, oriented (that this cultural difference did indeed obtain is no doubt true, as Nietzsche maintains [KSA, V, 190]). Rather, the matter has to do with the nature of the language that reflects an underlying world-view.[32] The language of the Bible and of a Luther not only conveys ideas, but "grows into" the heart (KSA, V, 191). In *Zarathustra* Dionysus speaks almost entirely alone, and parataxis is his natural mode of speech. As Otto Olzien says: "In *Zarathustra* there is scarcely one example of a complex periodic sentence."[33] Its aphoristic (hence, essentially paratactic) style is not only the hallmark of the work but also a warrant of its immortality (KSA, VI, 153).

Nietzsche's style in *Zarathustra* is paratactic not only in the narrower sense but also in the broader. This fact contrasts strangely with

---

31. Stefan Sonderegger, "Friedrich Nietzsche und die Sprache," in *Nietzsche Studien*, 2 (1973), 26.

32. Thorleif Boman has compared the Hebrew and Greek modes of thought as reflected in their languages: the former he considers psychological, the latter logical. Cf. also Claude Tresmontant: "From the very start Greek categories and the Hebrew forms of thought are heterogeneous"; Hebrew thought implies the metaphysics of the sensible (*A Study of Hebrew Thought*, trans. M. F. Gibson [New York: Desclee, 1960], p. 141). One writer suggests that the deconstructionist's approach may be helpful here. Thus, Herbert N. Schneidau asserts that in "aligning Derrida and the Bible, we open the possibility of reviving the Hebraic-Hellenic distinction . . ." ("The Word against the Word: Derrida on Textuality," *Semeia: An Experimental Journal for Biblical Criticism*, 23 [1982], 14). Incidentally, Derrida's ideas are quite in harmony with Hamann's idea of abstractions as "mere relations"; cf. my *Unity and Language: A Study in the Philosophy of Hamann*, University of North Carolina Studies in the Germanic Languages and Literatures, no. 6 (Chapel Hill: University of North Carolina Press, 1952; reprint, 1966), pp. 48–51.

33. Otto Olzien, *Nietzsche und das Problem der dichterischen Sprache*, Neue deutsche Forschungen, no. 32 (Berlin: Junker und Dünnhaupt, 1941), p. 121.

his idealization of Greek tragedy's fusion of Dionysian and Apollonian elements. Although he praised the ability of the Greek writers, especially the dramatists, to "dance in chains" (KSA, II, 612), the fact that he held up French neoclassical tragedy as a model is even more revealing.[34] But it should be remarked that, whereas Racine strove to achieve *clarity* with the least Apollonian means, Nietzsche strove to achieve *depth* with the least Dionysian means.

The structure of *Zarathustra* is anything but architectonic. It may be, as Nietzsche maintained and others have confirmed, the analogue of a musical composition.[35] In any case, the parts rarely follow any causal or logical sequence. Apart from the sketchy biography of Zarathustra, the proclamation of the doctrine of the superman early in the work, the will to power, and eternal recurrence later, there is scarcely any discernible structure. Many of the sections could be interchanged without damage to the whole. Further, many passages could be deleted. As Walter Kaufmann has said, the work "cries out to be blue pencilled."[36]

Despite its lack of formal structure, *Also sprach Zarathustra* nevertheless possesses a kind of unity. The work is not decadent in Nietzsche's sense.[37] There is no "anarchy of atoms"; the individual word, sentence, or aphorism never becomes "sovereign," but always remains subordinate to the principal theme or themes. Where there is any discord, it is between the parts. Just as in the case of the Bible, where the diversity and disharmony of the parts is sometimes very great, one nevertheless intuits an underlying unity.

6. Affect

The most pervasive of all the categories we have considered is that of affect. Nothing strikes the reader quite so forcefully from beginning to end as the fact that one is confronted with a text that, though

---

34. See Kurt Weinberg, "The Impact of Ancient Greece and of French Classicism on Nietzsche's Concept of Tragedy," in *Studies in Nietzsche and the Classical Tradition* (above, n. 4), pp. 89–108.

35. *Ecce Homo*, KSA, VI, 335. Cf. Friedrich von der Leyen, "Friedrich Nietzsche: Die Sprache des 'Zarathustra,'" *Literaturwissenschaftliches Jahrbuch*, ed. Hermann Kunisch, Neue Folge, 3 (1962), 238.

36. *Thus Spoke Zarathustra*, p. xvii.

37. KSA, VI, 27. For my criticism of Nietzsche's idea of decadence, see "Eros and Creativity in Nietzsche's *The Birth of Tragedy*," in *Studies in German Literature of the Nineteenth and Twentieth Centuries: Festschrift for F. E. Coenen*, University of North Carolina Studies in the Germanic Languages and Literatures, no. 67 (Chapel Hill: University of North Carolina Press, 1970), pp. 98–100.

primarily philosophical, is couched in a prose of extraordinary emotional power. Its dithyrambic nature is such that one is not at all aware of any *Stilbruch* when the prose suddenly flows into pure poetry, as in, for example, "The Song of Melancholy," "Among the Daughters of the Wilderness," "The Drunken Song," and others. This lyrical aspect is counterbalanced by the dramatic, but, as Fritz Martini says: "If the pure form of either genre had been realized, it would have excluded the other. The mean between the extremes is prose, whose elasticity can embrace the lyric as well as the dramatic elements."[38] With a hitherto-unheard-of virtuosity Nietzsche makes use of rhetorical and musical—especially rhythmical—means, combining them with a verbal playfulness that at times only obscures his meaning. Illuminating studies of the language of *Zarathustra* have appeared for a number of years,[39] and doubtless will continue to appear, for, like any great work of art, the perspectives from which it can be viewed are innumerable.

Here, however, we are concerned with the Zarathustran style not as an aesthetic matter but as the instrument of intuitive reason. Therefore we must exclude the aspects of Nietzsche's language that serve as purely rhetorical devices employed to heighten the pathos or emotional appeal to the reader—such as interjections, exclamations, imperatives, anaphoras, parallelisms, etcetera—many, of course, in imitation and parody of the Bible. Only those devices which are clearly basic instruments of intuitive reason are relevant to our purpose. Nietzsche's uses of the categories we have so far considered all contribute, in a sort of synergistic effect, to heighten the emotional impact of his language on the reader.

In conclusion, however much Nietzsche in his early phase praised the "fraternal union" of Dionysus and Apollo (or, in our present terms, the fruitful union of intuitive and abstract reason), and however much some commentators may maintain that the Apollonian is not abandoned by the later Nietzsche, but only subsumed under the concept "Dionysian," the fact remains that *conscious* Apollonianism plays no part in *Zarathustra*. In *Ecce Homo* he wrote concerning that work: "My concept of 'the Dionysian' was *perfectly realized* here" (KSA, VI, 343). Dionysus has now ceased to speak the language of

---

38. Fritz Martini, *Das Wagnis der Sprache* (Stuttgart: Klett, 1956), p. 16.

39. Ferruccio Masini has compiled a thorough bibliography of such studies: see "Rhythmisch-Metaphorische 'Bedeutungsfelder' in 'Also sprach Zarathustra,'" *Nietzsche Studien*, 2 (1973), 276–77n.

Apollo, even though Nietzsche's earlier concept of the highest art required, as it were, a *communicatio idiomatum* of the two deities. Now Zarathustra speaks only the language of the biblical prophets, of the psalmist, of Jesus, and of the despised Apostle Paul. It is significant that the categories explicated in this study were originally derived by Hamann from the *form* of the biblical revelation, and that form may also, in Nietzsche's own words, be described as Dionysian. Nietzsche-Zarathustra has now learned to reason in the Semitic or Hebraic mode as the one in which he believed the will to power to be most effectively expressed. In his prose writings Nietzsche is a Greek, in *Zarathustra* he has become a Jew.[40] However much or little the Hebraic mode of thought requires a historical element, it is essentially mythic—and "myth is not," says Nietzsche, "the expression of a thought as the children of an overrefined culture imagine, *but is itself a mode of thought*";[41] moreover, it is absolutely "disparate" in relation to the theoretical sphere (KSA, I, 485).

Nietzsche chose the biblical style for *Zarathustra* because of its power to move the *inner* man, for in it deep calls to deep. But the mode of reason that informs the Bible is authoritative only because it is the vehicle of revelation: its authority stems from the "Deus dixit." Lacking that authority, Nietzsche's work is, from one point of view, only philosophy expressed poetically, and, from another point of view, only poetry with philosophical import. However intellectually convincing as philosophy, and however aesthetically pleasing as poetry, it is unable to create values and to move men in the manner of the sacred literature of the Bible or the Koran. For "God is dead" and it is only Zarathustra who "speaks." As a literary and philosophical experiment, however, and as the expression of Nietzsche's own highly individual will to power, *Also sprach Zarathustra* is a most remarkable achievement; apart from the hyperboles he heaped upon it, Nietzsche was certainly correct in his judgment of its uniqueness.

Ironically, Nietzsche has done his great adversary, Christianity, a notable service by vindicating its conception of the proper role of

---

40. Nietzsche relegated his straight prose writings (where the Dionysian and the Apollonian are balanced) to second place in regard to *Zarathustra*. In a letter to Franz Overbeck, 7 April 1884, he wrote: "On reading the *Morgenröte* and *Fröhliche Wissenschaft*, I happened to find that hardly a line there does not serve as introduction, preparation, and commentary to . . . *Zarathustra*. It is a *fact* that I did the commentary *before* writing the text" (*Selected Letters of Friedrich Nietzsche*, ed. and trans. Christopher Middleton [Chicago and London: University of Chicago Press, 1969], p. 221). Even his post-*Zarathustra* treatises may be so regarded.

41. My emphasis; KSA, I, 485; cf. ibid., 58.

reason as exemplified in its Scriptures. For, as our analysis of *Zarathustra* has shown, he has demonstrated paradigmatically the salient features of biblical or Dionysian reason. Too long has the conflict between faith and (discursive) reason in Western Christianity obscured the nature and perennial power of another kind of reason, a kind that also issues, in the words of Lévi-Strauss, in the "science of the concrete." It is further quite ironic that a rationalistic exponent of Christian morality like Lessing, who demythologizes Scripture in order to salvage its essential teachings,[42] may unwittingly do more to undermine its authority than even a Nietzsche—for Nietzsche and the biblical writers are at one in accepting the mythic form as the only authoritative one for the most important affairs of human life. On one occasion Zarathustra taught his disciples: "But if you have an enemy, do not requite him evil with good, for that would put him to shame. *Rather prove that he did you some good*" (my emphasis; KSA, IV, 87). Though the follower of Jesus could not accept this inversion of the Saviour's teaching as binding, he might—with some irony—accept it in the case of Nietzsche's obeisance to the gospels in *Zarathustra*: for that work is not simply a parody of the gospels but an unsurpassed vindication of the mode of thought that informs them. By adopting that mode Nietzsche has demonstrated what no other "literary" philosopher has. *Zarathustra* thus proves to be—however unwittingly—a powerful ally in the unequal contest that has long prevailed in the West between discursive reason and *anschauende Vernunft*, which is as congenial to Dionysian wisdom as it is to religious faith. This fact in no way diminishes Nietzsche's irreconcilable hostility to Judaism and especially to Christianity, but simply throws it into a new and illuminating perspective.

42. In his *Education of the Human Race* Lessing essentially equates the unfolding of revelation in the Bible with progress from metaphorical or mythic thinking to conceptual thinking, that is, from the scholastic *ratio inferior* to *ratio superior*, thus betraying a profound distrust of intuitive reason.

XV. Jesus, Christianity, and Superhumanity

Bernd Magnus

In this paper I shall not be concerned with the emergence, development, and modifications of Nietzsche's opinions about Christianity and the Judaeo-Christian tradition.* I shall concentrate instead on certain conceptual/structural features of Nietzsche's critique of Christianity and the religious impulse generally, features that motivate not only his antichristianity, in my opinion, but his critique of morality and metaphysics as well. Put briefly, I am attempting to understand, however indirectly, Nietzsche's suggestive remark in *Beyond Good and Evil* that "Christianity is Platonism for 'the people' (*für's 'Volk'*)."[1] To accomplish this I shall have to say something about his understanding of Jesus of Nazareth, "original" Christianity, Paul, and later Christianity, before attempting to relate that discussion to other themes in Nietzsche's philosophical arsenal of which I believe his religious discussion to be only one expression. Superhumanity, *Übermenschlichkeit*, shall serve as the contrast term for this attempt.

The first important contrast to be marked concerning Christianity is Nietzsche's insistent separation of Jesus the evangel from the Pauline Christ. Put more generally, this distinction becomes roughly equivalent to his contrast between Jesus and Christianity. Although he himself may have put this contrast most pithily, as when he wrote, for example, ". . . in truth there was only *one* Christian and he died on the cross,"[2] Nietzsche was scarcely alone among the prescient nineteenth-century thinkers for whom this contrast is so basic—the names of Kierkegaard and Dostoevsky spring immediately to mind. Nor was Nietzsche's often violent prose rhetorically more extreme or severe than, say, that of Kierkegaard. Consider the in-

---

*This paper was made possible through the support of the Academic Senate of the University of California, Riverside; the National Endowment for the Humanities; and the John Simon Guggenheim Memorial Foundation. I am grateful to each institution.

1. *Beyond Good and Evil*, Preface. Whenever possible I will refer to the title, section, and/or aphorism number when I quote Nietzsche, for the reader's convenience. Only in the troubling case of material from the *Nachlaß* will this procedure be abandoned.

2. *The Antichrist* (hereafter "A"), sec. 39.

295

flammatory lines written by Kierkegaard on the occasion of the succession of Bishop Martensen as Primate of the Church of Denmark. Bishop Mynster, the previous Primate of the Danish Church, had died only recently, and then-*Professor* Martensen had delivered the funeral oration, in which he referred to Bishop Mynster as "a genuine witness to the truth." That phrase was to prove to be more than Kierkegaard could bear; for it deprived the notion of its martyrdom and apostolic purity. To be sure, Bishop Mynster had been a respected, successful prelate; he had received every conceivable honor; he had been a learned humanist; but he was also a man of means, comfortable in and with the world. For Kierkegaard, to call such a person a witness to the truth mocks Christianity, slanders and usurps the Gospels; so he waited several months until Professor Martensen had in his turn succeeded Bishop Mynster as Church Primate, and then he seized the moment and published these remarks —extreme even for him—in the year before his own death: "A witness to the truth is a man who bears witness in destitution, in poverty, in disgrace and humiliation, a man despised, detested, insulted, outraged, flouted; a man who is beaten, tortured, dragged from prison to prison, and then at last . . . crucified, decapitated, burnt at the stake, or roasted on a grille, and thrown on the trash heap by the executioner, without burial. . . . In truth, there is something more contrary to Christianity than any heresy or any schism— and that is to play at Christianity, to scamp its dangers. . . ."[3]

If Nietzsche's often polemical hostility toward what passes for Christianity displays a marked resemblance to Kierkegaard's, as quoted above, his reasons for rejecting Christianity and any religious tradition generally are at a far remove from Kierkegaard's. Kierkegaard's indictment of Christianity is rooted in the contrast between the unconditional acceptance of the incomprehensible absurdity that is required of the knight of faith on the one hand—the leap of faith stripped of any taint of comfort or assurance—and the genteel social-club security sought by typical Christian "believers," on the other hand. The primordial content of the religious experience had been buried and forgotten, Kierkegaard certainly thought; but it would never have occurred to him to challenge its absolute validity. Hence Kierkegaard's contemptuous dismissal of the shallow religious institutions and practices of his contemporaries. Yet it is precisely the unconditional validity of this primordial content, which Kierkegaard

3. Denis de Rougemont, *Love Declared* (New York: Random House, 1963).

accepts, that Nietzsche rejects equally unconditionally—and this difference makes all the difference between the two thinkers.

Nietzsche's perception of Jesus of Nazareth and Christianity is complex, therefore, and requires some explanation. For Nietzsche seems to reject wholesale the Pauline invention "Christ" and the institutions of Christianity that this fabrication made possible. His attitude toward Jesus the evangel is more bivalent, on the other hand: there is a sense, Nietzsche acknowledges, in which Jesus' teaching and *praxis* of unconditional love does represent a successful attempt to overcome priestly domination, does represent a successful challenge to the ritualistic dependence upon law and theologico-juridical norms generally; but it remains a flawed attempt, in the final analysis, one unalive to its own origins in the phenomenon of *ressentiment*, in reactive resentment.

Jesus and Paul: Evangel and Dysangel

Perhaps the clearest image of Jesus unburdened by Pauline trappings to be found in Nietzsche's writings occurs in sections 28 to 35 of *The Antichrist*. "This 'bringer of glad tidings' died as he had lived, as he had taught—*not* to 'redeem men' but to show how one must live. This practice is his legacy to mankind . . . to resist not even the evil one—to *love* him."[4] Nietzsche insists repeatedly that what the historical Jesus bequeathed to humankind was not a doctrine of redemption, and certainly not salvation after death, but love as the unconditional form of life:

> It is not a "faith" that distinguishes the Christian: the Christian *acts*, he is distinguished by acting *differently*. . . . He broke with the whole Jewish doctrine of repentance and reconciliation; he knows that it is only in the *practice* of life that one feels "divine," "blessed," "evangelical," at all times a "child of God." Not "repentance," not "prayer for forgiveness," are the ways to God: *only the evangelical practice* leads to God, indeed, it *is* "God"! The deep instinct for how one must *live*, in order to feel oneself "in heaven," to feel "eternal," while in all other behavior one decidedly does *not* feel oneself "in heaven"—this alone is the psychological reality of "redemption." A new way of life, *not* a new faith.[5]

4. A, sec. 35.
5. A, sec. 33.

Everything one has typically come to identify with Christianity—God as person, the son of God, the kingdom of heaven, salvation, the trinity, the immortality of the soul, sin, guilt, repentance, faith, and the power of prayer—all are for Nietzsche alien to the life and legacy of Jesus of Nazareth. So it follows for Nietzsche that

> The concept of "the son of man" is not a concrete person who belongs in history, something individual and unique, but an "eternal" factuality, a psychological symbol redeemed from the concept of time. The same applies once again, and in the highest sense, to the *God* of this typical symbolist, to the "kingdom of God," to the "kingdom of heaven," to the "filiation of God." Nothing is more unchristian than the *ecclesiastical crudities* of a god as person, of a "kingdom of God" which is to come, of a "kingdom of heaven" beyond, of a "son of God" as the second person in the Trinity. All this is—forgive the expression—like a fist in the eye—oh, in what an eye!—of the evangel—a *world-historical cynicism* in the derision of symbols.[6]

But if "father" and "son," "the kingdom of heaven," and "the kingdom of God" are not the crude ecclesiastical symbols they have generally been taken to be, what *are* they symbols of? What *do* they symbolize for the historical Jesus? Here, too, Nietzsche speaks unequivocally, speaks with a direct voice:

> ... the word "son" expresses the *entry* into the over-all feeling of the transfiguration of all things (blessedness); the word "father" expresses *this feeling itself*, the feeling of eternity, the feeling of perfection. ... The "kingdom of heaven" is a state of the heart—not something that is to come "above the earth" or "after death." The whole concept of natural death is lacking in the evangel: death is no bridge, no transition; it is lacking because it belongs to a wholly different, merely apparent world, useful only insofar as it furnishes signs.[7]

Perhaps Nietzsche's most startling but significant subtraction from the more standard picture is the elimination of the concepts of guilt and punishment from the psychology of the evangel as well:

> In the whole psychology of the "evangel" the concept of guilt and punishment is lacking; also the concept of reward. "Sin"—any dis-

---

6. A, sec. 34.
7. Ibid.

tance separating God and man—is abolished: *precisely this is the "glad tidings."* Blessedness is not promised, it is not tied to conditions: it is the only reality—the rest is a sign with which to speak of it. . . .[8]

True life, eternal life, has been found—it is not promised, it is here, it is *in you*: as a living in love, in love without subtraction and exclusion, without regard for station.[9]

It would be a mistake to infer, however, that Nietzsche's attempt to liberate the historical Jesus from subsequent ecclesiastical trappings is motivated by admiration. For Nietzsche, Jesus remains decadent. Indeed, in discussing the psychology of the Redeemer-type, he suggests that Jesus' psychology is governed by an instinctive hatred of reality. Just as there is a pathological tactile state characterized by shrinking from physical contact of any kind, including grasping solid objects, so Nietzsche suggests that "One should translate such a physiological *habitus* into its ultimate consequence—an instinctive hatred of every reality, a flight into 'what cannot be grasped,' 'the incomprehensible,' an aversion to every formula, to every concept of time and space, to all that is solid, custom, institution, church; a being at home in a world which is no longer in contact with any kind of reality, a merely 'inner' world, a 'true' world, an 'eternal' world. 'The kingdom of God is *in you*.'"[10] Indeed, Nietzsche summarizes what he calls the two physiological realities out of which the doctrine of redemption arose in a very suggestive aphorism, number 30:

> *The instinctive hatred of reality*: a consequence of an extreme capacity for suffering and excitement which no longer wants any contact at all because it feels every contact too deeply.
> *The instinctive exclusion of any antipathy, any hostility, any boundaries or divisions in man's feelings*: the consequence of an extreme capacity for suffering and excitement which experiences any resistance, even any compulsion to resist, as unendurable *displeasure* . . . and finds blessedness (pleasure) only in no longer offering any resistance to anybody, neither to evil nor to him who is evil—love as the only, as the *last* possible, way of life. These are the two *physiological realities* on which, out of which, the doctrine of redemption grew.[11]

8. A, sec. 33.
9. A, sec. 29.
10. Ibid.
11. A, sec. 30.

Nietzsche's image of Jesus, then, is almost that of Dostoevsky's Prince Myshkin—the "idiot" with whom Nietzsche identifies Jesus in aphorism 29 of *The Antichrist*—and Nietzsche expresses his regret "that a Dostoevsky did not live near this most interesting of all decadents—I mean someone who would have known how to sense the very stirring charm of such a mixture of the sublime, the sickly, and the childlike."[12]

Nietzsche's observation that even a deecclesiasticized, deconstructed Jesus remains decadent is not argued for in *The Antichrist*. It is merely asserted there; and we shall have to look elsewhere to find Nietzsche's justification for such an ascription, justification for the view that despite its contrast with historical Christianity, original, apostolic Christianity too is nihilistic. Yet Nietzsche hints at the basis for such an evaluation quite early in *The Antichrist*:

> I have drawn back the curtain from the *corruption* of man. So much so that I experience this corruption most strongly precisely where men have so far aspired most deliberately to "virtue" and "godliness." *I understand corruption, as you will guess, in the sense of decadence: it is my contention that all the values in which mankind now sums up its supreme desiderata are decadence-values.* . . . Where the will to power is lacking there is decline. It is my contention that all the supreme values of mankind *lack* this will—that the values which are symptomatic of decline, *nihilistic* values, are lording it under the holiest names.[13]

The following points need to be stressed here in a preliminary sort of way, since they will be mentioned again later: Nietzsche, like Marx, really seems to have believed sincerely that his talk about decadence, corruption, nihilism, and the like is intended to be morally neutral. The justification for that claim will emerge later; for now, however, it may be worth pointing out that Nietzsche seems to have believed that his corruption-talk is nonnormative, much as Marx seems to have believed that much of his talk about oppression, capitalist plunder, shackles, chains, and exploitation is also descriptive and, hence, not a rhetorical condemnatory device. A further point to observe is that Nietzsche identifies corruption with decadence, and identifies both with humankind's highest values. Neither Jesus nor Christianity is picked out for exclusive censure; rather, the sustaining and informing values of humankind have all been deca-

12. A, sec. 31.
13. A, sec. 6; my italics.

dence-values, Nietzsche asserts here. The history of our highest aspirations is the history of nihilism. Finally, one should not take lightly Nietzsche's identification of nihilism with a sublimated instinct of self-destruction, nor his conclusion that the loss of an instinctual vitality reappears as a counterfeit "under the holiest names." The highest values hitherto—identified elsewhere by Nietzsche as "the ascetic ideal"—have been thanatological values dressed up in life-affirming disguise.

If Jesus of Nazareth, the deconstructed "idiot," is defined in part by an instinctive hatred of reality, he is also a "holy anarchist"—he is nevertheless a solution to the problem of the rule of the priestly class, of rabbinic domination:

> Jesus has been understood, or *misunderstood*, as the cause of a rebellion; and I fail to see against what this rebellion was directed, if it was not the Jewish church. . . . It was a rebellion against "the good and the just," against "the saints of Israel," against the hierarchy of society—*not* against its corruption, but against caste, privilege, order, and formula; it was the *disbelief* in the "higher man," the No to all that was priest or theologian. . . .
>
> That holy anarchist who summoned the people at the bottom, the outcasts and "sinners," the chandalas within Judaism, to opposition against the dominant order . . . was a political criminal insofar as political criminals were possible at all in an absurdly unpolitical community.[14]

If "that holy anarchist," that impertinent and unintentional champion of the rabble against all forms of authority, was to have a lasting impact, however, his life—which *was* his "glad tidings"—had to be remythologized. The apostolic anticleric had to be transvaluated if "Christianity would become master over *beasts of prey*."[15]

In a clever series of steps Nietzsche argues that the notion of a "moral world order" had to be invented to reinstate priestly authority: "From now on all things in life are so ordered that the priest is indispensable everywhere; at all natural occurrences in life, at birth, marriage, sickness, death, not to speak of 'sacrifices' (meals), the holy parasite appears in order to denature them—in his language: to 'consecrate.' "[16] And the most powerful instruments for the reascendancy of the priest are the notions of sin and guilt: "the

14. A, sec. 27.
15. A, sec. 15.
16. A, sec. 26.

priest rules through the invention of sin."[17] "Psychologically considered, 'sins' become indispensable in any society organized by priests: they are the real handles of power. The priest *lives* on sins, it is essential for him that people 'sin.' Supreme principle: 'God forgives those who repent:—in plain language: those who submit to the priest.' "[18] Indeed, as Nietzsche reads post-Nazarene Christianity, the entire scaffolding of its ideology, the entire redemptive drama, is designed to retain the power of the priestly class, born of *ressentiment*: " 'Last Judgment,' 'immortality of the soul,' and 'soul' itself are instruments of torture, systems of cruelties by virtue of which the priest became master, remained master."[19] So the history of Christianity, Nietzsche argues, is the history of an error—a misunderstanding in which the original symbolism of Jesus becomes transvaluated into a crude ecclesiastical tale, a tale that becomes as vulgar as the slave's mentality that seeks revenge in and through it: "the history of Christianity, beginning with the death on the cross, is the history of the misunderstanding, growing cruder with every step. . . . The destiny of Christianity lies in the necessity that its faith had to become as diseased, as base and vulgar, as the needs it was meant to satisfy were diseased, base, and vulgar. In the church, finally, *diseased barbarism* itself gains power."[20]

The figure most responsible for the emergence and triumph of Christianity as "diseased barbarism" is Paul, of course; and "Paul was the greatest of all apostles of vengeance,"[21] says Nietzsche, for "in Paul the priest wanted power once again—he could use only concepts, doctrines, symbols with which one tyrannizes masses and forms herds."[22] Of course, the soil had been prepared for Paul's revaluation by Jesus' disciples. Jesus' death on the cross—a punishment typically reserved for "the rabble"—presented his disciples with the suspicion that Jesus' manner of death constituted a refutation of their cause. Since "a disciple's love knows no accident,"[23] as Nietzsche says, Jesus' life and death became transfigured in a world-historical misunderstanding. Nietzsche states the case nicely as follows:

17. A, sec. 49.
18. A, sec. 26.
19. A, sec. 38.
20. A, sec. 20.
21. A, sec. 45.
22. A, sec. 42.
23. A, sec. 40.

Evidently the small community did *not* understand the main point, the exemplary character of this kind of death, the freedom, the superiority over any feeling of *ressentiment*. . . . After all, Jesus could not intend anything with his death except to give publicly the strongest exhibition, the *proof* of his doctrine. But his disciples were far from *forgiving* this death—which would have been evangelic in the highest sense—or even from offering themselves for a like death in gentle and lovely repose of the heart. Precisely the most unevangelical feeling, *revenge*, came to the fore again. The matter could not possibly be finished with this death: "retribution" was needed, "judgment". . . . Once more the popular expectation of a Messiah came to the foreground; a historic moment was envisaged: the "kingdom of God" comes as a judgment over his enemies.[24]

Jesus, as Nietzsche deconstructs him, had set aside notions of guilt, sin, and atonement; but the ludicrous image of Jesus crucified required, step by step, notions of sin and atonement once again, and of the doctrine of resurrection, above all. And Paul seizes on this resurrection requirement above all else. "Paul, with that rabbinical impudence which distinguishes him in all things, logicalized this conception . . . in this way: '*If* Christ was not resurrected from the dead, then our faith is vain.' And all at once the evangel became the most contemptible of all unfulfillable promises, the *impertinent* doctrine of personal immortality."[25]

Thus, through Paul, Jesus the evangel is transvaluated, becoming the Redeemer, the dysangel. "On the heels of the 'glad tidings' came the *very worst*: those of Paul. In Paul was embodied the opposite type to that of the 'bringer of glad tidings'. . . . *How much* this dysangelist sacrificed to hatred! Above all, the Redeemer: he nailed him to *his own* cross . . . he *invented his own history of earliest Christianity* . . . he falsified the history of Israel that it might appear as the prehistory of *his* deed. . . . At bottom, he had no use at all for the life of the Redeemer—he needed the death on the cross *and* a little more."[26] The "little more" Paul needs to gain supremacy is the notion of the potential immortality of each and every soul, ultimate democratization of and through the spiritual realm:

24. Ibid.
25. A, sec. 41.
26. A, sec. 43.

That everyone as an "immortal soul" has equal rank with everyone else, that in the totality of living beings the "salvation" of *every* single individual may claim eternal significance . . . such an intensification of every kind of selfishness into the infinite, into the *impertinent*, cannot be branded with too much contempt. And yet Christianity owes its triumph to this miserable flattery of personal vanity: it was precisely all the failures, all the rebellious-minded, all the less favored, the whole scum and refuse of humanity who were thus won over to it. The "salvation of the soul"—in plain language: "the world revolves around *me*."[27]

Many commentators have observed, quite rightly, that for Nietzsche democracy and socialism—as well as nationalism and world wars—would have had a different etiology without the triumph of Christianity as a Pauline invention. And throughout *The Antichrist* Nietzsche remarks repeatedly on the political consequences of the triumphal slaves' morality. For example, "The aristocratic outlook was undermined from the deepest underworld through the lie of the equality of souls; and if faith in the 'prerogative of the majority' makes and *will make* revolutions—it is Christianity, beyond a doubt, it is *Christian* value-judgments, that every revolution simply translates into blood and crime."[28] Further, Christianity ultimately undermines any distinction in rank or merit through a "tarantula" morality in which the base inveigh against nobility. "Christianity is a rebellion of everything that crawls on the ground against that which has *height*: the evangel of the 'lowly' *makes* low."[29] And, "The poison of the doctrine of 'equal rights for all'—it was Christianity that spread it most fundamentally . . . out of the *ressentiment* of the masses it forged its chief weapon against *us*, against all that is noble, gay, high-minded on earth, against our happiness on earth. 'Immortality' conceded to every Peter and Paul has so far been the greatest, the most malignant attempt to assassinate *noble* humanity."[30]

Flattered, self-congratulatory conceit born in and nurtured by resentment finds expression in Pauline Christianity, mocks noble values and converts the "noble" into the "evil" ones. But this self-congratulatory conceit veils itself as modesty, as humility, argues Nietzsche. "What really happens here is that the most conscious *conceit of being chosen* plays modesty: once and for all one has placed oneself,

27. Ibid.
28. Ibid.
29. Ibid.
30. Ibid.

the 'community,' the 'good and the just,' on one side, on the side of 'truth'—and the rest, 'the world,' on the other."[31] In *The Antichrist* the distinction between life-affirming, noble, nondecadent values, on the one hand, and life-denying, base, decadent values is couched in the language of a contrast between "aristocratic" and "chandala" moralities. This contrast, in substance and form, mirrors Nietzsche's earlier contrast between "base" and "noble" moralities, adumbrated in *Beyond Good and Evil* and in *Toward the Genealogy of Morals*. As is well known, Nietzsche's portrait of the rise of moral valuations painted a "twofold early history of good and evil."[32] This theme of Nietzsche's, that there is such a twofold early history of morals—and two fundamentally opposed moral perspectives that correspond to and arise out of this history—is basic. Mention of the two primary types of morality that he had discovered was first made explicit by Nietzsche in *Beyond Good and Evil*: he called them "master morality and slave morality."[33]

The bare sketch of master and slave moralities presented in *Beyond Good and Evil* is amplified in *Toward the Genealogy of Morals*, where the concepts are deepened and rendered more systematic. For one thing, the notion of resentment, *ressentiment*, is given prominent display and functions as just precisely the sort of explanatory tool that is needed to account for moral attitudes and beliefs. The concept of resentment is then also used to explain why Christianity is slave morality sanctioned and incarnate.

Nietzsche begins with two types, the aristocratic master and the servile slave, in a secular context. The master is, and his morality extols, autonomy, independence, power, self-control, pride, spontaneity, and passion. The self-directed master derives his values not from the community, not from "the herd," but from the abundance of his own life and strength. The slave, however, fears the strength and power of the master. He despises him. He is dependent, powerless, without self-direction, discipline, or self-control. To seize control over his own psychic destiny, the slave must curb and tame his master; he must displace him, in a sense. And the method of "overcoming" the master and his morality, the means to his displacement, is to render the values of the herd absolute and universal: "The revolt of the slaves in morals begins with resentment becoming creative and giving birth to values."[34] The revolt of the slave in moral

31. A, sec. 44.
32. MA, I, sec. 45.
33. J, sec. 260.
34. GM, I, sec. 10.

matters is indeed creative and resentful. Powerless to effect a fundamental change in his condition, he wreaks vengeance against the master by converting the master's attributes into vices. And while master morality sanctions coexistence with inferior types and morals—so long as the baser ones keep their assessments to their own kind—the resentment of the slave yearns for universality. Nothing may escape its moral clutches alive. Nietzsche does not suggest, of course, that the slave's resentment of and revenge against the master is either direct or conscious. Far from it.

It is in this context, the context of moral-psychological imperialism, that the slave's resentment is to be understood. Since the slave cannot displace the master in reality, he avenges himself symbolically, mythically. Enter the religion of the slave—Christianity. Whatever else Christianity may be for Nietzsche—and as I have argued above we should not forget that it *is* many things besides—it is first of all the ideology of slave morality. It expresses the slave's resentment against the attributes of master morality by vilifying them. The virtues of the master become "sin." In place of power, it is said that the meek are to inherit the earth. Pride is sin. Humility is virtue. Charity, chastity, and obedience displace self-reliance, spontaneity, and autonomy. And it is said that it will be easier for a camel to pass through the eye of a needle than for a "rich" man to pass into the kingdom of heaven.

The resentment of slave morality that finds expression in Christianity is at once virulent and fateful: virulent, because its moral imperialism is of unprecedented scope. Its "moral" dictates are meant to cover all men at all times. Denied the actual gratification of supremacy over the master, it condemns him symbolically—but for eternity. He is condemned to hell. The scope of the sanction is "eternity." Apart from its virulence, Christian slave morality is fateful—in that it introduces into the Western psyche something virtually ineradicable: consciousness of sin and guilt.

Superman: Ideal or Attitude?[35]

Many commentators have observed that Nietzsche's rejection of Jesus and Christianity in *The Antichrist* presupposes what it needs to

---

35. The discussion that follows appears in modified and enlarged form in my "Perfectibility and Attitude in Nietzsche's Übermensch," forthcoming in *The Review of Metaphysics*.

Jesus, Christianity, and Superhumanity 307

show: that an instinctive hatred of reality coupled with a sublimated will to power lies at the root of both phenomena. This is particularly troublesome in the case of Jesus, as Nietzsche deconstructs him, because the ascription of decadence is never argued for. Thus many commentators, Walter Kaufmann for example,[36] have attributed to Nietzsche the view that Jesus' Myshkin-like innocence is simply naive, a flight from reality in its fulsome and sometimes painful aspects. Jesus is typically contrasted unfavorably with Socrates: in such a scenario Socrates becomes health embodied, and an object of Nietzsche's unequivocal admiration.

I find this view unhelpful; and I propose instead that we take Nietzsche's image of the superman as the contrast term, rather than Socrates. Thus, Nietzsche's failure to argue for his vision of "health" in *The Antichrist* before vivisecting Jesus and Christianity is a consequence both of the fact that Nietzsche's image of nonnihilistic human beings is presupposed, and of the further assumption that Nietzsche always thought of his writings in contexts, thought that his readers would connect theses advanced in one book with those previously advanced in another.

Let us approach the contrast between Nietzsche's Jesus and superman obliquely, then, by looking now at the notion of the superman, just as we concentrated on Jesus above.

The standard construal of Nietzsche's superman has a long, sometimes lurid, history; only a few paradigm expressions of the "ideal type" reading—the reading that sees Nietzsche's superman as a human ideal, as the image of human perfectibility—need be cited here as a way of assembling reminders. And it may also be well worth remembering at the outset that Nietzsche himself entered an acerbic barb in *Ecce Homo* against those who would construe the concept denoted by the term *Übermensch* as the embodiment of a type of higher species of human being:

> The word "Übermensch," as the designation of a type of supreme achievement, as opposed to "modern" men, to "good" men, to Christians and other nihilists—a word that in the mouth of a Zarathustra, the destroyer of morality, becomes a very thoughtful word—has been understood almost everywhere with perfect innocence in the sense of those very values whose opposite Zarathustra was meant to represent—that is, as an "idealistic" type of a higher kind of man, half "saint," half "genius". . . . Those to

---

36. Walter Kaufmann, *Nietzsche: Philosopher, Psychologist, Antichrist* (Princeton: Princeton University Press, 1950, 1969, 1974).

whom I said in confidence that they should sooner look even for a Cesare Borgia than for a Parsifal, did not believe their own ears.[37]

Yet despite Nietzsche's own cautions, the superman has generally been construed as a heroic ideal, as a higher type who must be bred by all-too-human humankind, as the great man, the superior individual whose self-perfection—half genius, half saint—places him at a far remove from the mediocrity and stagnation of the crowd, the rabble, "the herd"; he has also been understood as the nonconforming immoralist, and as the value-legislator whose values express his own authentic self-possession.

Very early, indeed during Nietzsche's lifetime, he was beset by those who would breed a superman. His sister, for example, gives us the following account of her brother's intention, in her own 1906 introduction to *Thus Spoke Zarathustra*:

> The phrase "the rearing of the *Übermensch*" has very often been misunderstood. By the word "rearing," in this case, is meant the act of modifying by means of new and higher values—values which, as laws and guides of conduct and opinion, are now to rule over mankind . . . a new table of valuations must be placed over mankind—namely, that of the strong, mighty, and magnificent man, overflowing with life and elevated to his zenith—the *Übermensch*, who is now put before us with overpowering passion as the aim of our life, hope, and will. And just as the old system of valuing, which only extolled the qualities favorable to the weak, the suffering, and the oppressed, has succeeded in producing a weak, suffering, and "modern" race, so this new and reversed system of valuing ought to rear a healthy, strong, lively, and courageous type, which would be a glory to life itself. Stated briefly, the leading principle of this new system of valuing would be: "All that proceeds from power is good, all that springs from weakness is bad." This type must not be regarded as a fanciful figure . . . it is meant to be a possibility which men of the present could realize with all their spiritual and physical energies, provided they adopted the new values.[38]

---

37. *Ecce Homo*, "Why I Write Such Good Books," sec. 1. This reference to Cesare Borgia has often been taken out of context to argue that Nietzsche admired the Borgias, even that he regarded (some of) them as supermen. Attention to context, of course, renders such claims dubious. Nietzsche's point here is that, among all of the *implausible* candidates, a Parsifal-like character is even more implausible than a Cesare Borgia. This is consistent with Nietzsche's view that there is no point in commending involuntary eunuchs for their celibacy, or cowards for their restraint.

38. Elisabeth Förster-Nietzsche, Introduction to *Thus Spake* (sic) *Zarathustra* in *The Philosophy of Nietzsche* (New York: Random House, 1927), p. xxi.

Jesus, Christianity, and Superhumanity 309

It might seem trivial to quote these lines of the thoroughly discredited Elisabeth Förster-Nietzsche; but we ought to remind ourselves that such an interpretation of the superman—as a power-monger who legislates new values to humankind—is scarcely a thing of the past. Consider, for example, J. P. Stern's recent influential appraisal:

> He (i.e., Nietzsche) seems unaware that he is giving us nothing to distinguish the fanaticism that goes with bad faith from his own belief in the unconditioned value of self-realization and self-becoming—that is, from his own belief in the superman. We for our part are bound to look askance at this questionable doctrine. We can hardly forget that the solemn avowal of this reduplicated self—the pathos of personal authenticity—was the chief tenet of fascism and National Socialism. No man came closer to the full realization of self-created "values" than A. Hitler.[39]

Prof. Stern's reading of Nietzsche as presented in his 1978 Modern Masters series Penguin book did not change when his 1979 Cambridge University Press publication appeared: in *A Study of Nietzsche* he repeats these lines verbatim.[40] The Nietzsche who emerges from the latter monograph is a preacher of a doctrine of "heroic commitment," of existential self-realization, of self-assertion without moral restraint or inhibition, and all this in opposition to the inherited Judaeo-Christian ontology and moral philosophy. Most distressing of all, perhaps, the Nietzsche here depicted is a proto-fascist ideologist (unwitting, to be sure)—the very distortion that Walter Kaufmann's pioneering work had successfully debunked. Consider, lamentably: "If there is anything in the recent 'Nietzschean' era that comes close to an embodiment of 'the will to power,' it is Hitler's life and political career."[41] And then the *coup de grace*: "Indeed, the 'power' which is the will's goal need not be conceived in any such barbaric ways as the Italian and French fascists and the German national socialists conceived of it (*though it cannot be denied that the intellectual superstructure of these political movements is as inconceivable without Nietzsche's ideas as these movements are without their superstructure*)."[42] While I read and reread these elusive and yet profoundly regressive lines, the image of Adolf Eichmann in the docket at Jerusalem—blurting out a vulgarized version of *Kant's* moral philosophy as his self-justifica-

---

39. J. P. Stern, *Friedrich Nietzsche* (Middlesex: Penguin, 1978), pp. 85–86.
40. Approximately two-thirds of J. P. Stern's *A Study of Nietzsche* (London: Cambridge University Press, 1979) is a verbatim repetition of the 1978 Penguin book, *Friedrich Nietzsche*.
41. Ibid., p. 120.
42. Ibid., p. 122; my italics.

tion—haunted me like a shadow. The point is that reading Nietzsche's writings as the perhaps unwitting superstructure for fascist ideologies and practice has once again descended upon us, and not only in publications of distinguished university presses. If there remains any doubt about this I recommend that you look at what sometimes passes for journalism these days: as in the 8 June 1981 issue of *Der Spiegel*, for example, where editor Rudolf Augstein has written a lengthy article on Nietzsche and Hitler. The magazine's cover depicts Nietzsche in the pose of Rodin's "The Thinker" with Hitler rising from his head brandishing a pistol. The upper left-hand corner carries the thematic article lead "Recurrence of a Philosopher"; the lower right-hand corner conveys the point in large, bold italics: "Doer Hitler, Thinker Nietzsche."

To be sure, there is a strain in Nietzsche that invites such readings. The apocalyptical facade and rhetoric of much of Nietzsche's peroration about the superman does indeed appear menacing, especially when taken out of context, a fact with which more scholarly and sensitive commentators have had to contend. Consider, for instance, the tenor of this note from the *Nachgelassene Fragmente* from the period 1885–86:

> From now on there will be more favorable preconditions for more comprehensive forms of domination, whose like has never yet existed. And even this is not the most important thing, the possibility has been established for the production of international racial unions (*Geschlechts-Verbänden*) whose task will be to rear a master race (*Herren-Rasse*) the future "masters of the earth";—a new, tremendous aristocracy, based on the severest self-legislation, in which the will of philosophical men of power and artist-tyrants will be made to endure for millennia—a higher kind of man who, thanks to their superiority in will, knowledge, riches, and influence, employ democratic Europe as their most pliant and supple instrument for getting hold of the destinies of the earth, so as to work as artists upon "man" himself. Enough: the time is coming when politics will have a different meaning.[43]

And in a note penned earlier, in 1884, one finds:

> I write for a species of man that does not yet exist: for the "masters of the earth. . . ." In Plato's *Theages* it is written: "Each one of

---

43. *The Will to Power*, trans. Walter Kaufmann and R. J. Hollingdale, ed. Walter Kaufmann (New York: Random House, 1967), n. 960.

us would like to be master over all men, if possible, and best of all God." This attitude must exist again.[44]

The above passages are not cited to lend credibility to any right-wing reading; as a rule, appropriate attention to the status (published or *Nachlaß*) and context of Nietzsche's notes is sufficient to dispose of such interpretations. They are referred to primarily in order to remind myself that what I am calling the "ideal type" reading of Nietzsche's superman need not always be benign. After all, monstrous crimes against humanity are, to my knowledge, never understood in such terms by their perpetrators. Rather, as Stanley Cavell has observed, "someday, if there is a someday, we will have to learn that evil thinks of itself as good, that it could not have made such progress in the world unless people planned and performed it in all conscience."[45] And that may perhaps be the most telling point against understanding the superman as a value-legislator who simply embodies a new, albeit a "higher," morality. For Nietzsche is not primarily intent upon erecting a new morality, a new set of values upon the ashes of the old tablets; rather, his philosophizing beyond good and evil means to deny not only morality but with it the basis for a contrast with *immorality* as well. To put this differently: it is the moral perspective itself, the foundation upon which distinctions between good and evil may be said to rest noncontextually, that Nietzsche has deconstructed. For Nietzsche denies morality much as he denies alchemy—not saying that there are no alchemists or that there have never been alchemical motives, but calling into question the presuppositions that make alchemy possible. And so it is with "morality." In the second book of *Morgenröte* (*The Dawn*) Nietzsche writes:

> Thus I deny morality just as I deny alchemy; that is, I deny their presuppositions; however, *not* that alchemists have existed who believed these presuppositions and behaved in terms of them. I also deny immorality: *not* that countless men *feel* themselves to be immoral, but rather that there be a foundation in *truth* that one should feel this way. I do not deny that which is self-evident—presuming that I am no fool—that many acts which are called immoral are to be avoided and fought against, and that many which are called moral are to be done and encouraged. I do mean: *the*

---

44. Ibid., n. 958. It has long been agreed that *Theages* was written not by Plato but by an imitator of Plato.
45. Stanley Cavell, *Must We Mean What We Say? A Book of Essays* (New York: Charles Scribner's Sons, 1969), p. 136.

one, as well as the other, but on other grounds than before. We must learn to transform our thoughts (*umzulernen*), in order at last, perhaps very far from now, even more to reach the point at which we transform our feelings (*umzufühlen*).[46]

Fortunately, by no means all "ideal type" readings have stressed the alleged political consequences of *Übermenschlichkeit*, of what it is like to be a superman. Perhaps the most popular interpretation of the superman is the one articulated so successfully in the English-speaking world by the late Walter Kaufmann:

> The unphilosophic and inartistic mass remain animalic, while the man who overcomes himself, sublimating his impulses, consecrating his passions, and giving style to his character, becomes truly human or—as Zarathustra would say, enraptured by the word *über*—*super*human.[47]
>
> The *Übermensch* . . . is the "Dionysian" man who is depicted under the name Goethe at the end of the *Götzendämmerung* (IX, 49). He has overcome his animal nature, organized the chaos of his passions, sublimated his impulses, and given style to his character—or, as Nietzsche said of Goethe: "he disciplined himself to wholeness, he *created* himself" and he became "the man of tolerance, not from weakness but from strength," "a spirit who has *become* free."[48]

This construal of the superman as creative self-perfection has also been endorsed by philosophers of markedly differing temperaments and orientations. Consider the following assessment from Arthur Danto's pen: "The *Übermensch*, accordingly, is not the blond giant dominating his lesser fellows. He is merely a joyous, guiltless, free human being, in possession of instinctual drives which do not overpower him. He is the master and not the slave of his drives, and so he is in a position to make something of himself rather than being the product of instinctual discharge and external obstacle."[49]

But precisely this reading of *Übermenschlichkeit*, of what it is like to be a superman, defeats Nietzsche's originality in its triumph. For what we are left with is a most unoriginal formula of sorts:

---

46. M, sec. 103.
47. Kaufmann, *Nietzsche*, p. 312.
48. Ibid., p. 316. Kaufmann's pioneering work has, ironically, only now been translated into German, by the Nietzsche scholar Jörg Salaquarda.
49. Arthur C. Danto, *Nietzsche as Philosopher* (New York: Macmillan, 1965), pp. 199–200.

A sultry heart plus a cool head, minus the human-all-too-human. But this, divorced from the extravagant language and the rushing cadences of Zarathustra's singing, turns out to be a bland and all-too-familiar recommendation, rather squarely in a moralistic tradition. It says only that we should seek to keep our passionate as well as our intellectual life in our command, not to deny one at the price of the other, and that we should not be petty and "merely" human. It is something of an irony that Nietzsche is least original where he has been most influential. Here is an ancient, vaguely pagan ideal, the passions disciplined but not denied, in contrast with the life and attitude of guilty celibacy which has been an official moral recommendation until rather recent times.[50]

If we were to insist upon construing the superman as an ideal type, and at the same time wished to rescue Nietzsche from the charge of having overdramatized a cliché—namely, Aristotle's megalopsychic man—we could of course assimilate *Übermenschlichkeit* to the notion of authenticity. While there may be something to recommend this maneuver, one suspects that everything depends upon how the notion of "authenticity" gets spelled out. For, after all, Heidegger's own early political perception of authentic individuals is scarcely helpful.

The main contrast I wish to mark in this section is between the "ideal type" reading and the attitudinal or diagnostic reading of the superman. This contrast is not as sharp, nor is it as clear, as one should like it to be; nor is it an all-or-nothing affair. But what I have in mind when I refer to the attitudinal interpretation is that it does *not* necessarily emphasize the superman as an ideal of human perfectibility, an ideal that could be realized if only we were to do something or other—such as to sublimate our impulses, consecrate our passions, spiritualize our instincts, give style to our character, or live authentically—assuming all the while, of course, that we would know how to begin to *do* any of these things. Instead, I take the superman to be the *nonspecific* representation, the underdetermined embodiment if you will, of a certain attitude toward life and world—the attitude that finds them worthy of *infinite* repetition. On this reading, then, the frequently voiced lament that the superman is left vague by Nietzsche and is never portrayed adequately is not a defect: it is, rather, the necessary consequence of the fact that what is being portrayed is not a set of character traits nor an algorithm telling us how, what, and when to choose. Indeed, if the concept of the super-

50. Ibid., p. 199.

man can be read usefully at all as a *diagnostic* rather than a prescriptive concept, one would expect its embodiment to be radically underdetermined, just as a description of a Rorschach inkblot inevitably would be.

This diagnostic reading has been defended in some detail, especially in my *Nietzsche's Existential Imperative*.[51] Perhaps one need repeat here only the minimum that is necessary in order to spell out the internal connection between the superman notion and eternal recurrence. Allow me, therefore, to repeat one thrust of the thesis concerning Nietzsche's remarks about eternal recurrence. Eternal recurrence, in its principal sense, is offered by Nietzsche as an illustration of the attitude of *Übermenschlichkeit*, of what it is like to be a superman: it illustrates the being-in-the-world—the basic attunement—of the *Übermensch*. I do not mean to suggest that it is one possible attitude among many possible ones; it is *the* attitude *simpliciter* that Nietzsche wishes to portray if passive and active nihilism are to be overcome. This attitude toward life is the opposite of decadence, decline of life, world-weariness. It is the attitude of affirmation, of overfulness; the attitude that expresses ascending life, life as celebration, life in celebration.

If the thought of eternal recurrence is called into service to tell us what a certain attitude is like, what celebrating life *feels* like, we must not forget Nietzsche's other point—that attitudes toward life are to be read as symptoms of the condition of the person having the attitude. Attitudes toward life are self-reference clues. This is stated with exceptional force and clarity in the frequently cited portion of *Twilight of the Idols* that deals with "The Problem of Socrates," especially section 2: "Judgments of value, concerning life, for or against it, can, in the end, never be true: they have value only as symptoms, they are worthy of consideration only as symptoms . . . *the value of life cannot be estimated.*" It is difficult to overestimate the importance of this point for Nietzsche, or at least for my reading of him. Increasingly for me *everything* depends on reading Nietzsche bifocally: as committed to no *particular* world-version, or vision of human perfectibility, in his metaphilosophical critique of philosophy, while at the same time urging particular versions and visions, and attacking particular idols. If one takes seriously Nietzsche's suggestion that the value of life cannot be estimated and that assessing it is, therefore, to be read only as a symptom, one gets both levels at once, I think.

---

51. Bernd Magnus, *Nietzsche's Existential Imperative* (Bloomington and London: Indiana University Press, 1978).

What Nietzsche affirms and denies is always radically historically conditioned, variable in principle on this reading—and self-referring; but the larger self-referential thesis is itself not variable in principle. Thus the attitude toward life captured in the eternal-recurrence vision is the expression of nihilism already overcome. The ecstatic attitude expressed is the attitude toward life captured by the superman. Simply put, again, eternal recurrence expresses the attitude of *Übermenschlichkeit* and is the being-in-the-world of supermen.

Concerning this question of attitude, then, one might usefully construe diagnostically Nietzsche's statement that his teaching says the task is to live in such a way that one must wish to live again. Notice that Nietzsche does not appear to say or imply that recurrence should be thought of as true in order that we may accept our proper task. Live in such a way that you must wish to live again, he tells us simply. Whether or not one's life is worthy of infinite repetition here seems to become Nietzsche's principle of selection and redemption. But there are no spectators to decide these matters: I cannot tell you whether what you are and do is such that you must wish to be it and do it again, nor can you be my judge. Here, perhaps, the strongest divergence from Kant's categorical imperative surfaces. A central point of the Kantian thrust is to subsume judgments about individual actions under rational, moral law; the moral law speaks no private language. Yet Nietzsche's eternal recurrence seems to be deliberately pluralistic: "My teaching declares: the task is to live in such a way that you must wish to live again—you will *anyway*! To whom striving gives the highest feeling, let him strive; to whom rest gives the highest feeling, let him rest; to whom ordering, following, obedience give the highest feeling, let him obey. *May* he only become aware of *what* gives him the highest feeling and spare no means! Eternity is at stake!"[52] On the "ideal type" construal of *Übermenschlichkeit*, what it is like to be a superman, to judge something or someone worthy of *infinite* repetition, is to prize and praise a specific something, a certain way of living, a specific trait or form of life. But Nietzsche does not seem to say that. Become aware of that which is worthy of infinite repetition in your life, whether that be striving or reposing, ordering or obeying, he tells us. The important thing is to become aware of what is worthy of infinity in our lives. And about these things we surely will differ.

There is of course a sense in which Nietzsche's existential impera-

---

52. WKG, V-2, 403; aphorism II [164]. This note was penned at about the time that the "discovery" of eternal recurrence occurred, in August 1881.

tive—live in such a way that you must wish to live again—*does* choose among types, does choose among lives and what have recently come to be called life-styles. For even if we cannot distinguish life-affirmers from life-deniers by looking at what they affirm or deny, *they* may nevertheless be able to see *whether* they affirm or deny. Recall, if you will, Nietzsche's first published aphorism concerning eternal recurrence, from *The Gay Science*:

> *The greatest stress.* What if one day or night a demon were to sneak after you into your loneliest loneliness and say to you, "This life as you now live it and have lived it, you will have to live once more and innumerable times more; and there will be nothing new in it, but every pain and every joy and every thought and sigh and everything immeasurably small or great in your life must return to you—all in the same succession and sequence. . . ." Would you not throw yourself down and gnash your teeth and curse the demon who spoke thus? Or have you once experienced a tremendous moment when you would have answered him, "You are a god, and never have I heard anything more godly." If this thought were to gain possession of you, it would transform you, as you are, or perhaps crush you. The question in each and every thing, "Do you want this once more and innumerable times more?" would weigh upon your actions as the greatest stress. Or how well disposed would you have to become to yourself and to life to *crave nothing more fervently (um nach nichts mehr zu verlangen)* than this ultimate eternal confirmation and seal?[53]

It is easy to see from this aphorism's hypothetical diction ("what if . . .") why the normative interpretation of Nietzsche's thought of eternal recurrence should have gained widespread currency. From a modified perspective, however, we need primarily to emphasize the *conclusion* of this aphorism. How well disposed would we have to become, have to *be*, toward life, toward our lives and the world, in order to affirm eternal recurrence? How life-affirming indeed would one have to be to crave *nothing* more fervently than eternal recurrence?

On a superficial level, of course, it may be easy to say Yes to Nietzsche's demon. After all, given the alternative—death with no afterlife—who would hesitate? I think the right answer is that virtually all of us would or should give pause. For how many persons can assert without self-deception that they crave nothing more fervently

---

53. FW, IV, sec. 341.

than the eternal recurrence of each and every moment of their lives? Moreover, to affirm, to appropriate eternal recurrence would not only require a nonselective affirmation of one's existence—present and past[54]—but by implication would commit its affirmer to preferring his or her life to any and all other possible lives. To crave *nothing*, absolutely nothing, more fervently than the ultimate confirmation and seal of eternal recurrence for one's life seems to exclude preferring the life of another. And my hunch is that just as each of us would affirm the eternal recurrence of our lives only selectively—omitting this or that pain, regret, or humiliation—virtually none of us would fervently prefer our lives to all other possible lives. Who, for example, would not prefer to be God, if he were still alive?

The point of these remarks may now be clearer. A superman—and only a superman—would be so well disposed to himself and the world that he would crave *nothing* more fervently than the eternal repetition of his life, not even the life of God or the gods. What it would be like sincerely, non-self-deceptively, and nonpathologically to have such an attitude only supermen (and perhaps Nietzsche) know. I certainly don't. However, this confession should not be taken as a sign of paralysis, an indication that something has gone wrong with our analysis. For although we may not know what it is like to have the attitude of a superman as our most basic and defining disposition, and even though we cannot easily infer *Übermenschlichkeit* from another's behavior, most of us have in fact experienced that tremendous moment of which Nietzsche's demon speaks in "The Greatest Stress." Virtually all of us have at one time or another experienced a tremendous moment whose repetition we would will unto eternity were this within our power, and for the sake of which we would exchange our lives for no other. Artists at work in every medium have been known at one time or another to experience that enormous satisfaction when their work achieves (their standard of) perfection, when they would not trade places with gods. The mystical literature of East and West is full of descriptions of yearned-for ecstatic states that are perceived as the unique and irreplaceable goal of human longing. Less esoterically, it is said that the agony of the long-distance runner is sometimes replaced—after "the wall" has been "hit"—by an incredible sense of euphoria, well-being, and achievement, for which no other experience is an adequate substitute. Most mundane of all, perhaps, human sexual satisfaction can

---

54. The most forceful statement may be found in Z, II, "On Redemption" (*Von der Erlösung*).

sometimes be so intense and rewarding that one would will its eternal repetition, and exchange lives with none at that instant.

These illustrations are tricky, to be sure. Some may be inclined to argue that artistic, religious, athletic, and sexual peak experiences—or "highs," if you prefer—are seldom if ever without self-deception or pathology. We need not enter that debate here, however; for the burden of the remark is not that we know what it is like to achieve *Übermenschlichkeit*, to achieve superhumanity, but only that we may on rare occasions perceive it as through a glass darkly.

One thing is clear, however. If the value of life cannot be estimated, if, that is to say, estimates of life's ultimate value and significance function as the conceptual equivalent of the psychologist's Rorschach tests, then systematic world-views—religious, moral, metaphysical—must also be read as symptoms of the condition of the person who articulates cosmic estimates. And Nietzsche never doubted that the Christian prescription, when viewed in this self-referring light, is incapable of the joyous self-affirmation of the superman, because its dualism is born of resentful decadence.

XVI. The Dionysian Theodicy

Georges Goedert
(Translated by Robert M. Helm)

Since Leibniz, the term "theodicy" has denoted the justification of divine goodness in the face of arguments that deny it in giving an account of evil in the world.* Of course, Nietzsche had no intention of justifying a supraterrestrial being. For him, it was a matter of justification of life, of life in all its aspects, including the most frightful and the most depressing. Heinz Heimsoeth writes in this connection:

> For some time, it can no longer have been a question of theodicy for Nietzsche. But now there arose, in those years of the development of his philosophy on the basis of his new thinking on the Greeks and Heraclitus, a metaphysical-existential need in Nietzsche for a positive evaluation of concrete being (*das Seiende*), a will to affirmation passionately pressing its way through and working in opposition to his life-threatening tendency toward negation of the world. And with that, *cosmodicy* became a new concern for him.[1]

There are, nevertheless, four reasons why we prefer the term "theodicy" to "cosmodicy." (1) Nietzsche himself, as we shall see, uses that expression in important passages. (2) He thus raises a major problem of German philosophy. Heimsoeth writes:

> Justification of becoming, the world "eternally justified," that is a new sound. It proceeds from the language of theodicy, in particular of that of the century and a half of German speculation from Leibniz to Hegel, interrupted only by the quickly forgotten objec-

---

*The present chapter is from Georges Goedert, *Nietzsche, critique des valeurs chrétiennes* (Paris, Editions Beauchesne, 1977).

1. Heinz Heimsoeth, *Metaphysische Voraussetzungen und Antriebe in Nietzsches "Immoralismus"* (Wiesbaden: F. Steiner, 1955), p. 525. (Translator's note: Translations from the works of German writers are my own. Professor Goedert is responsible for italicization of words and phrases in the quotations from Nietzsche's writings, with the exception of a few that appear in the German text.)

tion of the late Kant, a period in which a metaphysical optimism with regard to the world (the claim to embrace all of nature, the human condition, and, finally, universal history) became established on the basis of the postulate of the absolute goodness of God. It is precisely this transfiguration of the world, this "justification," that Schopenhauer had rejected to the end, seeing in it a "wicked" misunderstanding and a disfiguring disguise of the true character of life and of the whole world.[2]

(3) In reality, the term "cosmodicy" is also in part inadequate to Nietzsche because, according to him, the universe is not a rationally ordered "cosmos," but a chaos. (4) The works of Nietzsche by no means exclude the possibility of making this chaotic becoming, justified in all its manifestations, appear as a sort of new divinity. Thus we read, for instance: "You call it the self-destruction of God. But it is only his moulting. He is shedding his moral skin. And we are going to see him again, beyond good and evil."[3] It is only the God of Christian theology who is dead: "God suffocated from theology and morals from morality."[4] This parallel between theology and morality is highly interesting. Has not Nietzsche in effect developed a new morality on the ruins of the old? Why should he not at least have envisaged the elaboration of a new concept of God?[5]

The problem is this: How can one legitimate life in the face of those who, like Schopenhauer, maintain that the negative element predominates in it and that, for this reason, it is preferable to deny the will to live?

It may be maintained that the tragic wisdom of Nietzsche, after *The Birth of Tragedy*, entails a justification of life. Life is at the same time growth and decay, and where it is most thriving, it must also commit the greatest number of destructions. Also, for man, power is augmented in proportion to suffering. It is in that fact that the latter finds its justification.

Nietzsche thinks that in nature, man has encountered evil under a triple aspect: "the accidental, the uncertain, the sudden."[6] In human-

---

2. Ibid.
3. GOA, XII, 329.
4. Ibid.
5. Concerning the analogy between various ideas of Nietzsche and the theology called "negative," in particular that of Saint Augustine, cf. Eugen Biser's work, "*Gott ist tot*": *Nietzsches Destruktion des christlichen Bewußtseins* (Munich: Kösel, 1962), pp. 293f.
6. WKG, VIII-2, 133.

ity's attitude toward evil, he distinguishes three phases: (1) Man defends himself against evil by conceiving it "as reason, as a power, even as a person": so he gains the possibility of putting it in some way under contract. Or indeed, "one interprets the consequences of the accidental, of the uncertain, of the sudden, as the result of *good intentions*, as full of meaning. . . ." Their evil and noxious character becomes, because of that, illusory. Or, indeed, one finally justifies evil by conceiving it as a chastisement. It is, then, a matter of three different ways of submitting to evil. And the writer adds: ". . . every moral and religious interpretation is only a form of submission to evil—the belief that evil has a beneficial import amounts to giving up fighting it."[7] (2) After the development of civilization, men learn to be satisfied with the moral and religious interpretation of evil: thanks to rational thought, indeed, they come to combat evil thereafter by abolishing it. But for Nietzsche, this stage could not be final. Indeed, the elimination of evil would mean, above all, the abolition of suffering as well: thus one would lose the indispensable ingredient of creative activity, the most important stimulus for anyone who creates. We know that already, in *The Birth of Tragedy*, Nietzsche had rejected the optimism inherent in Socratic intellectualism because he took it for a symptom of "decadence." At that time, then, he had already interpreted the belief in the value of reason as a way of escaping suffering. On the other hand, however, he demonstrated in the same work that Socratic rationalism can be legitimated from the moment one believes that he takes thought to the frontiers where, illuminated by new experiences, it finds the gateway to Dionysian wisdom. This surpassing of rational thought can also result, in fact, in man's beginning quite simply to have enough of the feeling of security in which he revels as a result of the progress of rational knowledge. "Yes, it is possible," says Nietzsche, "to come to a feeling of security, to a belief in laws and calculability, which produce in the consciousness a state of *satiety;*—one sees then the rising into view of the *relish for the accidental, for the uncertain, for the sudden*, appreciated as a stimulant. . . ."[8] (3) The third phase commences at the moment when, suddenly, man acquires a taste for evil and recognizes that it constitutes a source of his greatest power. In the eyes of Nietzsche, this taste for evil is a "symptom of *very* high culture." The philosopher calls it the *"pessimism of strength."*[9]

7. Ibid., p. 132.
8. Ibid., p. 133.
9. Ibid.

Thenceforth, it is no longer evil, but good, that requires legitimation. Such a change of tack clearly cannot surprise us from the moment we understand Nietzsche's judgment concerning "respectable people." Now good is legitimated by the fact that, in its essence, it belongs to evil. Likewise the philosopher sanctions the conservation of virtues in the traditional sense, and particularly the Christian virtues, because he recognizes in them "a refinement, a subtlety, a love of gain and power."[10] He sees in them, then, manifestations of a will to power! It does not matter that this is possessed by the weak. That does not keep it from serving as an adversary to the higher man.

The philosopher writes: "This *pessimism of strength* leads . . . to a *theodicy*, that is to say, to a total *affirmation* of the world, but for the same reasons that had formerly served to deny it: and in that way, to a conception of this world as the *effective realization of the highest ideal*."[11] Schopenhauer had denied the world because of the sufferings and conflicts inherent in it. Nietzsche wished to approve the world in its totality for the same reasons, that is to say, because the world includes conflicts and sufferings, because he judged that these are indispensable to the type of superior humanity.

This theodicy constitutes the supreme and definitive rejection of Schopenhauer and of compassion. The pessimism of the strong consists in the fact that they do not fly from evil with the suffering it brings on, but that, on the contrary, they seek it. That was already the lesson of *The Birth of Tragedy*. Suffering is too precious for one to combat it by altruism, charity, pity. Nietzsche writes:

> For *us*, it is not pity that opens the doors of the most distant and strangest kinds of being and culture. On the contrary, our openness and lack of prejudice, far from "sympathizing," delight in a hundred things that formerly caused suffering (that revolted or agitated, or were regarded with hostility or indifference). Suffering in all its nuances is now interesting to us: we are certainly *not* sympathizers any more, even if the sight of suffering moves us so profoundly that the tears flow:—we are therefore, completely indisposed to be helpful.[12]

And nevertheless, the Dionysian theodicy of Nietzsche involves also the legitimation of the existence of a philosophy like Schopenhauer's—and then, of course, the existence of Christianity as well. In

10. Ibid.
11. WKG, VIII-2, 133–34.
12. Ibid., p. 191.

the end, Nietzsche says yes even to the followers of nihilist philosophy and religion. In fact, if decay is indispensable to life, if there is no new growth without the will to nothingness, then it is proper to take Christianity and its virtues of "decadence" seriously because of the function they fulfill in life. Accordingly, Dionysian affirmation not only involves a yes with regard to the most powerful and perfect phenomena of life, but also approves even the phenomena of "decadence." Without "decadence" and nihilism, the idea of the superman would be nonexistent. That ideal is rightly, then, the justification of life in all its forms and of all judgments of value, these latter being always and everywhere the product of a fixed type of living beings for whom they serve as a means to the acquisition of power.

So we arrive at a paradox that, at first sight, must appear incredible: the understanding that, in the end, the superman justifies Christian values as well. Dionysus ends by rallying to his cause the Crucified One too. Paul Wolff writes on this subject: "Nietzsche opposes Dionysus to the Crucified One, but he would like, nevertheless, to save the Crucified One for Dionysus, to see the Crucified One in the service of Dionysus."[13] And this writer also speaks of "the immensity of the enterprise to which Nietzsche puts his hand. *Vanquished, but not annihilated,* Christian values have to serve Dionysus."[14]

The approval of life is more passionate in Zarathustra than in Nietzsche himself. Zarathustra proclaims: "But I myself am a blesser and a yea-sayer . . . into all abysses I carry still my yea-saying which blesses. / I am become a blesser and a yea-sayer: and for that I fought for a long time and was a fighter so that I might one day get my hands free to bless."[15] Nietzsche knows that his Zarathustra approaches more closely than he himself to the ideal of the superman. In fact, at the place in the *Genealogy of Morals* where he speaks of the "man of the future" who will free reality from "the anathema hurled against it by the ideal that has been in circulation up to now," he adds: "But what am I saying? Enough! Enough! At this point I ought to be silent: else I violate that to which only someone younger has a right, someone 'who belongs more to the future,' someone stronger than I am—*Zarathustra, Zarathustra the godless.*"[16]

Nietzsche's work involves the ruthless struggle against moral philosophy and metaphysics, in short, against the whole Western tradi-

---

13. Paul Wolff, "Dionysus oder der Gekreuzigte," in Wolff, *Denken und Glauben* (Trier: Paulinus Verlag, 1963), p. 94.
14. Ibid.
15. Z, III, "Before Sunrise."
16. GM, II, sec. 25.

tion. This polemic is indispensable to the definition of a new ideal. But it constitutes only one side of Dionysian wisdom—necessary, to be sure, but not the most important. In that wisdom, the approval of life in all its forms would seem to represent the essential element.

In *Ecce Homo*, Nietzsche properly asserts that, in *Zarathustra*, his "concept of the 'Dionysian' became . . . *a splendid achievement.*"[17] There he places the supreme affirmation of life, as he says, in the mouth of "someone younger." He feels himself still too marked by the "degenerating, self-doubting present,"[18] in which he lives and in which it is important first of all to free himself from the burden of the old ideal. That is why he is obliged to be more fighter than blesser.

Nietzsche expresses the meaning of "Dionysian" briefly in this way:

> . . . a desire for unity, a surpassing of one's self, of daily life, of society, of reality, an abyss of oblivion, a passionate and painful overflowing that is poured out in darker, fuller, more flowing conditions, an ecstatic affirmation of existence in its wholeness, equal to itself across all changes, equally powerful, equally blessed; the great pantheistic participation in every joy and every pain, which, from the depth of an eternal will to procreation, to fecundity, to eternity, approves and sanctifies even the most dreadful and most enigmatic qualities of life: as a sentiment of the necessary union between creation and destruction.[19]

The "participation . . . in every pain" recalls the "tragic compassion": it is a matter of participation in the sufferings of all living beings, conceived as an ingredient of the joy that creative activity bestows.

The Dionysian affirmation of life does not retreat before the vital forms and manifestations that, elsewhere, Nietzsche rejects and fights because he sees in them phenomena of "decadence." In this, there is no contradiction. In fact, it is only thanks to the Dionysian affirmation that the struggle against "decadence" fully finds its meaning and its justification. In this affirmation, the intuition triumphs that life is made up of contradictions and that it would not be able to perpetuate itself if the contradictions were not maintained. Nietzsche says that it is in the "accessibility of what is most contradictory" that Zarathustra experiences himself "as the supreme type of all beings."[20]

17. *Ecce Homo*, "Why I Write Such Good Books": Thus Spoke Zarathustra, sec. 6.
18. GM, II, sec. 24.
19. WKG, VIII-3, 16.
20. *Ecce Homo*, "Why I Write Such Good Books": Thus Spoke Zarathustra, sec. 6.

In *Ecce Homo*, we read also: "the psychological problem posed by the type of Zarathustra is how he who denies to an unheard-of degree, in word and *action*, everything to which yes has so far been said can at the same time be the opposite of a nay-saying spirit. . . ."[21] In the same work, Nietzsche also writes: "I contradict as no one has ever contradicted before and am nevertheless the opposite of a nay-saying spirit. I am a *joyous messenger* such as there has never yet been. . . ."[22] Nietzsche at the same time says yes and no to Christianity. He combats the Christian virtues of "decadence" in the name of an ideal of strength, but he recognizes that at the time in which he lives, Christianity is the adversary without which he would not feel himself impelled to search for a better ideal. The yes and the no complete each other and reciprocally justify each other. The affirmation of life, as well as the affirmation of Christianity, is possible only through the struggle against Christian values; for the legitimation of the struggle contains also the justification of the adversary without which the struggle would not take place. The Nietzschean affirmation of life presents an eminently tragic character.

At the highest rung, Nietzsche's Dionysian wisdom is highly reminiscent of Hegel. In a posthumous fragment, we read: "The meaning of German philosophy (Hegel): to invent a *pantheism* in which evil, error, and suffering *will not* be felt as arguments against Divinity."[23] It can be seen that the Hegelian theodicy interested Nietzsche. Hegel had actually conceived his philosophy as a "theodicy." He was looking for a reconciliation of Spirit with evil, chiefly on the level of his philosophy of history. He conceived universal history as a "rich production of creative reason," while declaring that it is precisely in history that "all the mass of the concrete manifestations of evil is spread out before our eyes." According to him, the thinking spirit has here the possibility of reconciling itself with the existence of evil "by coming to understand the affirmative, in which the negative disappears as something subordinate and overpowered, by the consciousness, on the one hand, of what is in truth the final goal of the world and, on the other, by the consciousness that the final goal has been realized in the world and that the evil alongside it has not ultimately become effective."[24]

Hegel appears, then, as a philosopher who affirms life in the same way as Nietzsche. But it is well to take into account that the relation-

21. Ibid.
22. *Ecce Homo*, "Why I Am a Destiny," sec. 1.
23. WKG, VIII-1, 111.
24. Georg Wilhelm Friedrich Hegel, *Sämtliche Werke*, 3rd ed. (Leipzig: F. Meiner, 1930), VIII, 24f.

ship between the two philosophers is only superficial. In general, it can be maintained that, despite a certain number of points in common—which it is clearly important not to underestimate—Nietzsche is in disagreement with Hegel on the fundamental matters. To the writers who interpret the affinity between Nietzsche and Hegel in too positive a manner, we oppose three arguments that appear to us decisive: (1) Hegel made the "logos" the very principle of becoming. For Nietzsche, on the contrary, reason is no more than one element among others, sprung from a profoundly irrational ground. It is a product of universal unreason. Those who believe in the values of reason—must we be reminded?—he takes for decadents. He holds that the true philosopher, one who is also a really strong man, conceives becoming as a chaos, destitute of rational order. Of course, like Hegel, he admits that contradiction performs its function as much on the ontological plane as on the level of human thought, but the significance that he attributes to it goes beyond the logical sense that Hegel conferred on it.[25] (2) Hegel speaks of a final end of the eternal wisdom, whereas Nietzsche, as did Spinoza before him, rejects, for the natural world, all idea of finality. (3) Nietzsche reproaches Hegel for having been, with Kant and Schopenhauer, "of moral origin."[26] Karl Löwith pertinently writes that Nietzsche saw Hegel as an "artful theologian,"[27] and he maintains that the former differs from the latter "by his radical criticism of Christian morality and philosophy, of which he recognizes the dominant influence also in the Hegelian philosophy of history."[28] Indeed, one might say that, in assigning to religion an important place on a level with the manifestations of Absolute Spirit, Hegel had as his end not only the preservation of Christianity, but even the restoration of vigor to it.

---

25. In any case, Walter Kaufmann is wrong in calling Nietzsche a "dialectical monist." In general, Kaufmann greatly exaggerates the influence of Hegel on Nietzsche. He writes: "Nietzsche's position is best elucidated by comparing it not with Schopenhauer's, as has generally been done, but with Hegel's" (Walter Kaufmann, *Nietzsche: Philosopher, Psychologist, Antichrist* [Princeton: Princeton University Press, 1950], p. 206). The French philosopher Gilles Deleuze also has rightly recognized "the resolutely antidialectical character of Nietzsche's philosophy"; but we cannot agree with him when he adds: "Anti-Hegelianism runs through Nietzsche's philosophy like the thread of aggressiveness" (Gilles Deleuze, *Nietzsche et sa philosophie* [Paris: Presses Universitaires de France, 1962], p. 9)—Nietzsche's philosophy is not directed in the first place against Hegel, but against Schopenhauer.

26. WKG, VIII-1, 142.

27. Karl Löwith, *Von Hegel zu Nietzsche*, 2nd ed. (Stuttgart: Kohlhammer, 1950), p. 193. Cf. Erich Rothacker, who maintains that the German idealism of Kant and Hegel is as apparent in Schopenhauer as in Nietzsche as "a camouflaged theology" (Erich Rothacker, *Poètes et penseurs* [Paris: Sorlot, 1941], p. 27).

28. Löwith, *Von Hegel zu Nietzsche*, p. 197.

Now in the matter of his total legitimation of becoming, Nietzsche had another precursor in Germany much more important than Hegel. This precursor was Goethe. At the outset, however, he formulated with regard to Goethe a certain number of critical reservations. "But," Löwith writes, "when, later, Nietzsche had attained in the *Zarathustra* a sort of perfection, he silenced the reservations of his youth in order to appreciate Goethean existence all the more resolutely."[29] Moreover, it is necessary to remember that it was for the most part the reading of Schopenhauer that, in great measure, succeeded in inspiring in Nietzsche his veneration of Goethe. Ernst Bertram writes on this subject: "And it is, above all, Schopenhauer's position on Goethe that determined almost wholly and for a long time Nietzsche's attention and attitude. We know how personal association for such a short time with the poet of color theory contributed to Schopenhauer's education and to an allegorical clarification of his thought; how his conception of genius, his cult of genius, indeed, almost his inner experience of genius always oriented him toward Goethe with proud and respectful regard."[30]

It is interesting to note that, during his third period, Nietzsche attributes to the Goethe of the classical epoch some truly Dionysian traits. What he admires in him is "a return to nature . . . an effort to *lift* himself to the naturalness of the Renaissance. . . ."[31] Goethe also would have affirmed life in all its forms: "Such a *liberated* spirit stands at the center of the universe in a joyous and confident fatalism with

---

29. Ibid., p. 195.
30. Ernst Bertram, "Nietzsches Goethebild," in *Festschrift für Berthold Litzmann*, ed. Carl Enders (Bonn: Friedrich Cohen, 1920), p. 320. Here again, Walter Kaufmann remains much too superficial when he writes: "Nietzsche's repudiation of Christian morality cannot be understood any more than can his critique of romanticism unless one keeps in mind that his own positive conception of the Dionysian was derived from Goethe's classical ideal—and not from the German Romantics" (Kaufmann, *Nietzsche*, p. 333). Nietzsche discovered his Dionysian ideal above all as a result of his study of the Greeks. However, he did not always greatly respect historical truth. As Alfred Bäumler pertinently declares, Nietzsche himself acknowledged having invented Dionysus (Alfred Bäumler, *Bachofen und Nietzsche* [Zurich: Verlag der Neuen Schweizer Rundschau, 1929], pp. 33f.). It is the same with the antagonism between the Dionysian and Apollonian elements in *The Birth of Tragedy*: that opposition "is of a general order, it is not specifically Greek, and today, it is everywhere applied in that way" (ibid., p. 35). It was strongly marked by the Schopenhauerian distinction between will and idea (cf. Aloys Riehl, *Friedrich Nietzsche. Der Künstler und der Denker*, 4th ed. [Stuttgart: Frommann, 1901], p. 49). We repeat also what we have persisted in bringing to light throughout our study: Nietzsche conceived his Dionysian ideal as the exact opposite of the Schopenhauerian ethic of the negation of the will to live. That said, we shall not fail to recognize that Goethe himself also influenced Nietzsche. But the importance of that influence must not be exaggerated.
31. G, "Skirmishes of an Untimely Man," sec. 49.

the *faith* that only that which exists in isolation is loathsome, and that everything is redeemed and affirmed in the whole. *He no longer denies*. . . . But such a faith is the highest of all possible faiths. I have baptized it with the name of *Dionysus*."³² Nietzsche in some way associates Goethe with his Dionysianism. Bertram expresses this relationship in his own way: "The classical Goethe becomes the companion of fortune to the Dionysian Zarathustra. The Roman-German joins himself to the 'South'-German, the enemy of revolution to the hater of democracy, the adversary of romanticism to the enemy of Wagner, the 'decided non-Christian' to the Antichrist, the pupil of the Greeks to the disciple of the Greeks."³³ There is, properly speaking, no contradiction if, on the one hand, the philosopher continues to present himself as the fiercest adversary of Christianity, as the "Antichrist," while, on the other hand, legitimating, in his Dionysian perspective, the existence of that against which he struggles with such fierceness. According to Nietzsche, the feeble and impotent themselves also aspire to power, and it is of the greatest importance that they remain powerful enough to be able to serve as adversaries to the strong. In a posthumous fragment, he writes:

> I have declared war on the anemic ideal of Christianity (and everything related to it), not with the intention of destroying it, but only to put an end to its *tyranny* and to get a place free for new ideals, for *more robust* ideals. . . . The *persistence* of the Christian ideal is among the most desirable things there are: and even for the sake of the ideals that want to make themselves effective beside it and perhaps over it—they must have adversaries, *strong* adversaries, to become *strong*.³⁴

With regard to the values of the weak, the philosopher likewise says: "It is senseless to set forth the hypothesis that all this *victory of values* is antibiological: One must try to explain it by reference to an interest of life. . . . the *maintenance* of the 'human' type through this method of assuring the *supremacy* of the weak and the disinherited. . . ." The "*elevation* of the type" may be "inauspicious for the *conservation of the species*." History shows us in fact that "the strong races *decimate* one another reciprocally," that they waste their powers rapidly and afterwards become, in consequence, "feebler, more apathetic, more unreasonable than the average of the weak." Nietzsche

---

32. Ibid.
33. Ernst Bertram, *Nietzsche: Versuch einer Mythologie*, 7th ed. (Berlin: Bondi, 1929), pp. 202f.
34. WKG, VIII-2, 189.

thinks that it may even be proven that the victory of the weak permits the achievement of a "richer production of value" than that of the brief existence of prodigal races. He says: "We are in the presence of a problem of economy. . . ."[35] He even goes on to declare: "The *shrinking* of man must for a long time serve as the only goal: because a broad base must first be established on which a *more vigorous* sort of man can stand."[36] In a similar perspective, there would evidently no longer be a question of condemning "decadence" in the same way as the nihilism that it conveys. In another posthumous text we read: "Waste, decay, rubbish, are not condemnable in themselves: they are a necessary consequence of life, of the increase of life. The phenomenon of *decadence* is as necessary as any other phenomenon of the ascent and advance of life. We do not have the power to suppress it. Reason, on the contrary, demands that we *render it justice*."[37]

Nietzsche often complains that the will to nothingness propagates itself more and more, that men become ever "smaller." But, he asks himself at this point, is it not precisely there that the guarantee lies that one day the superman will be born?

> The *instincts of decadence* have become master over the instincts of ascent. . . .
> the *will to nothingness* has become master over *the will to live*. . . .
> —is it true? is there not perhaps a greater guarantee of life, of the species, in this victory of the weak and mediocre?
> —is it perhaps only a means to the total movement of life, a slackening of pace? a defense against something yet worse?
> —assuming that the *strong* were to become master in everything, even in value-judgments: may we draw out the consequences with regard to what they would think of sickness, suffering, sacrifice? A contempt of the *weak for themselves* would be the result; they would seek to disappear and be obliterated . . . and would this perhaps be *desirable*? . . .
> —and would we really like a world lacking in the traits shown by the weak, their delicacy, their kindness, their spirituality, their *adaptability*?[38]

It appears, in fact, that the weak have at their command qualities that the strong do not possess—or at least not in the same degree—qualities in the service of their will to power. In their turn, the strong

---

35. This and the previous quotations, WKG, VIII-3, 161–62.
36. WKG, VIII-2, 10.
37. WKG, VIII-3, 47–48.
38. Ibid., pp. 115–16.

would also have developed these qualities in order so much the more to exercise their dominion. The author writes: "*The values of the weak* are preponderant because the strong have adopted them in order to *direct* the others."[39]

In the very important posthumous writing entitled "Why the Weak Prevail," Nietzsche enumerates the traits that constitute the strength of the weak. He cites first compassion: "the sick and the weak have more *compassion*, are more 'human.' "[40] Next, he mentions their "spirit," and asserts that they have "more spirit."[41] They are more astute and artful than the strong.[42] "One must have need of spirit," he says, "in order to come to have spirit."[43] In addition, they "have more *fascination* for one another, they are *more interesting* than the healthy...."[44] Then, in the same text, Nietzsche specifies that every man is in part a decadent. "And as for *decadence*," he says, "everyone who does not die too early puts himself in that situation in almost every sense ... he also knows then from experience the instincts that belong there ... : for *nearly half his life*, every man is decadent."[45] Every human being ages from a certain moment on, and, from a physiological point of view, aging is decadence. Besides, Nietzsche believes that it is, above all, women—quite half, to be sure, of humanity—who incarnate weakness and sickness: "*Half of the human race* is feeble, essentially sick, changeable, unstable; woman has need of strength, in order to hold fast to it—and of a religion of weakness that glorifies as divine *debility*, love, humility...."[46] To that, the writer adds, moreover, that the progress of civilization entails the growth of a number of morbid elements. Among them appear the "artiste" (*der Artist*), in whom he sees a "hybrid species":

> ... the *artiste* [he says] removed from criminal action by the weakness of his will and his fear of society, not yet ripe for a lunatic asylum, but with his antennae stretched inquisitively in both spheres: this specific plant of civilization, the modern artist, painter, musician, above all, novelist, who uses for his manner of being the highly improper word "naturalism". . . .

39. Ibid., p. 249.
40. Ibid., p. 157.
41. Ibid.
42. WKG, VIII-3, 96.
43. G, "Skirmishes of an Untimely Man," sec. 14.
44. WKG, VIII-3, 158.
45. Ibid.
46. Ibid.

The mad, the criminals, and the "naturalists" increase in number: signs of a growing and swiftly *progressing* civilization—that is to say, rubbish, waste, excrements gain in importance. . . . The downward tendency *sets the pace*. . . .[47]

Finally, the writer makes the *"social mishmash"* responsible for the victory of the weak. He sees there the "consequence of revolution, of the institution of equal rights, of the superstition of 'the equality of men.' " That brings about prejudice against the elite: "There results a collective instinct against the *select*, against *privileges* of every sort, of such power and certainty, hard and cruel in practice, that in fact the *privileged* themselves soon submit to it."[48]

But the strength of the weak also springs quite especially from their morality. We have seen that the energy of which this is evidence springs essentially from resentment. But given that superior men need to find a strong adversary facing them, they too have an interest in having the morality of the weak powerful. The philosopher writes: "So we immoralists need the *strength* of *morality*: our instinct for self-preservation demands that our *adversaries* remain strong—demands only to *become master* over them."[49] He also writes more especially on the subject of the herd morality: "Beyond good and evil,—but we shall demand absolute respect for the herd morality. / We shall reserve for ourselves many sorts of philosophy which it will be necessary to teach; under certain conditions, pessimism in the guise of a hammer; might not a European Buddhism perhaps be indispensable?"[50]

The usefulness of morality resides equally in the fact that it propagates the practice of a certain discipline, of a certain askesis,[51] thus constituting a barrier against "letting go." Besides, morality would have been indispensable at a determined moment of the evolution of humanity *"in order that* man might triumph in the struggle with nature and the 'wild beast.' "[52] Nietzsche then can speak of "the profoundest recognition of everything that morality has done up to the present," but he adds that *"at present,* it is *only a constraint,* which could become fatal! *It itself,* as honesty, forces the denial of morality."[53] Thus, we encounter afresh the theme of the "self-destruc-

---

47. WKG, VIII-3, 158–59.
48. Ibid., p. 159.
49. WKG, VIII-2, 189.
50. W, III, 450.
51. Cf. WKG, VIII-2, 218 and 310; J, sec. 188.
52. WKG, VIII-1, 212.
53. Ibid., p. 210.

tion of morality," developed already in the course of the second period. Nietzsche conceives his immoralism as being still founded in part on Christian morality. It is to Christian morality that he would attribute the honesty that leads to the critique of morality, a critique that could be considered, by virtue of that fact, as a phenomenon of the self-surpassing of morality. We read: "Honesty—supposing that this is the virtue from which we cannot free ourselves, we free spirits—let us cultivate it with all our malice and love and not grow tired of 'fulfilling' ourselves in *our* virtue, the only one left us. . . ."[54] If Nietzsche is maintaining that what is at stake is the only "virtue" of free spirits, the term "virtue" must be understood in the traditional sense. Finally, the struggle of morality against the instincts of life would also have some importance in the fact that it bears witness to the universal immorality: "the history of the *struggle of morality against the fundamental instincts of life* is in itself the greatest immorality that has appeared on earth up to this day."[55]

It is precisely the lessening of man that necessitates the instauration of a new ideal. The nausea that this spectacle arouses in superior men awakens new forces: "There is wisdom in the fact that many things in the world smell bad; even nausea creates wings and dowsing-powers! / Even in the best there is still that which nauseates; and the best is still something that must be surpassed."[56] This nausea can be conquered only by the aspiration toward a new ideal and, besides, by the recognition of the function fulfilled by the "little people," which is precisely to make necessary the instauration of new values. The "little people" are indispensable also because it is through comparison with them that the ideal of the superman will have to acquire the attraction that it needs to have.

According to Nietzsche, life will not end in nothingness, for it evolves in a cycle that will renew itself eternally. Everything that has once existed will recur eternally. This idea of eternal recurrence is the highest expression of the affirmation of life. It means that even that which is small, feeble, miserable, is going to come back eternally. This last part is for Nietzsche the heaviest to bear. The chapter of *Zarathustra* entitled "The Convalescent" shows that it leads him dangerously into Schopenhauer's waters and the negation of the will to live. Zarathustra has fallen ill because of this idea: "Alas! Man comes back eternally! The small man comes back eternally!"[57] Messer

54. J, sec. 227.
55. WKG, VIII-2, 93.
56. Z, III, "Of Old and New Law Tables," sec. 14.
57. Z, III, "The Convalescent," sec. 2.

writes: "It is that experience which visibly made Nietzsche suffer most. It was the harshest temptation in his pursuit of the ideal. And, indeed, that experience whispers to us in effect: What is the use of all the aspirations, all the struggle with its privations and victories over the self: all that is truly good for nothing; men cannot be helped; they always remain the same!"[58] The danger of falling prey through compassion and disgust to the lure of practical pessimism attains here its culminating point. But, because the danger is so great, one is then witness also to an enormous growth of contrary forces: courage and toughness surpass every human norm at present. The same author continues: "In the eternal recurrence of little people is included, so to speak, the problem of theodicy in the idea of the superman. Why aspire to that if the small always returns?" Messer gives Nietzsche's solution, formulated in abstract terms, as follows: "because only in the struggle with the small can the great be achieved, because only through opposition to nonvalue can value truly be actualized for us."[59] The idea of "the eternal recurrence even of the smallest"[60] becomes thus an indispensable stimulus for the creation of new values. Far from inciting to inertia, it is the ingredient with which no one who creates can dispense. Thus, the notions of "superman" and of "eternal recurrence" become truly correlative. Belief in the eternal recurrence of everything that exists is necessary in order that superman may be born, while the idea of superman, in return, permits the creative spirit to bear—without falling into the practical negation of the will to live—the idea that everything, absolutely everything, even that which is quite small, will recur eternally. Practical pessimism is thus surmounted by men who, like Nietzsche, have enough strength to endure that highest suffering through the justification conferred on it by the supreme ideal.[61]

58. August Messer, *Erläuterungen zu Nietzsches Zarathustra* (Stuttgart: Strecker und Schröder, 1922), p. 102.
59. Ibid., p. 103.
60. Z, III, "The Convalescent," sec. 2.
61. The idea of "eternal recurrence" is therefore perfectly compatible with that of the "will to power." Alfred Bäumler was wrong to reject the eternal recurrence because of the will to power. He writes: "It [the eternal recurrence] has no affinity with the concept of 'will to power'; indeed, if one took it seriously, it would shatter the unity of the philosophy of the will to power" (Alfred Bäumler, *Nietzsche, der Philosoph und Politiker*, 3rd ed. [Leipzig: Reclam, 1937], p. 80). Heidegger, so far as he is concerned, does not see any contradiction between the two ideas (Martin Heidegger, "Wer ist Nietzsches Zarathustra?" in *Vorträge und Aufsätze* [Pfullingen: Neske, 1954], pp. 116f.). Cf. also on this subject: Jean Granier, *Le problème de la vérité dans la philosophie de Nietzsche* (Paris: Editions de Seuil, 1966), pp. 611–28; Karl Löwith, "Heideggers Vorlesungen über Nietzsche," in *Aufsätze und Vorträge* (Stuttgart: Kohlhammer, 1971).

The eternal recurrence is conceived also as the supreme expression of universal necessity—of a necessity that, however, does not exclude creative liberty but, on the contrary, favors it. Each moment is, in fact, a new beginning of futures that are repeated forever. Nietzsche writes in the *Dithyrambs of Dionysus*:

> Buckler of necessity!
> Highest star of Being!
> —which no desire attains,
> which no negation defiles,
> eternal yea of Being,
> eternally I am thy yea:
> *for I love thee, O
> eternity.*[62]

Thanks to this affirmation, man is totally integrated into nature. He is the yea of nature, that is to say, the manifestation of its eternal will to power. The affirmation of life, at its highest level, is the affirmation of eternity. This represents what is most contrary to the Schopenhauerian ethic of negation of the will to live.

There are evidently truths here that transcend logical forms. The "pessimism of strength" is suited to a culture of the highest level, which permits man to renounce the support of reason. It is no longer a question here of combatting evil by means of reason. Man "savors evil (*Übel*) pure and raw and finds *absurd* evil most interesting. If he formerly had need of a God, what delights him now is a world-disorder without God, a world of accidents, the essence of which includes the terrible, the ambiguous, the seductive. . . ."[63]

Reason, a crutch for the use of the weak! Belief in the rationality of existence, a symptom of "decadence"! For Nietzsche, all rationalism is fundamentally nihilistic and, like the Christian religion, contributes to the nihilistic condition into which modern man is plunged. We read: "*The belief in the categories of reason* is the cause of nihilism— we have measured the value of the world according to categories *that apply only to a purely fictitious world*."[64] In the same way as happiness and traditional virtue, reason is, for Zarathustra, "poverty and ordure and wretched contentment."[65]

Dionysian wisdom is fundamentally irrational. Nietzsche conceives the real as a chaotic evolution, not as a rationally ordered

62. WKG, VI-3, 403.
63. WKG, VIII-2, 133.
64. Ibid., p. 291.
65. Z, Prologue, sec. 3.

cosmos. It is precisely therein that a new mark of strength must be seen: strong men are able to dispense with the convenience offered by order; they crave the difficulties that disorder entails. Chaos gives them pleasure, and confrontation with it augments their greatness. Zarathustra proclaims that "one must still have chaos in oneself in order to be able to give birth to a dancing star."[66] It is necessary for the rational categories not yet to have dissolved disorder completely in the human spirit! This is the first of the preliminary conditions for the realization of a superior humanity. The creation of the new ideal from chaos is opposed to rational aspirations just as much as the will to power of the strong is opposed to the powerlessness of "decadence."

In his study on the meaning of "chaos" in Nietzschean thought, the French philosopher Jean Granier shows how the disagreement between Nietzsche and the Western tradition is crystallized in this concept. He writes:

> To risk the formidable thought: the real is a chaos with no common measure with human requirements; it is necessary, then—we conjecture—to have traversed the desert of nihilism, to have experienced its agonies, its fears, its poignant deception. It is necessary to be disillusioned, like a dreamer who awakens in an implacable world. It is, indeed, "the death of God," the destruction of metaphysical idealism that frees the attention for the lucid contemplation of a tragic reality to which only our courage can raise a challenge.[67]

Chaos is life, while reason is paralysis and death.

It may be interesting here to establish a comparison with the distinction made by Henri Bergson between "vital order" and "geometric order." In the "geometric order" of the universe, according to him, only reason is competent; it even represents the expression of the universe on the plane of thought. The "vital order," on the contrary, can be apprehended only through intuition. Intuition is the mental expression of that "vital order" which, in its most elevated manifestations, in man, becomes a "spiritual order." Matter and intelligence—for Bergson the concept of "intelligence" is almost synonymous with "reason" in the traditional sense—represent forms of paralysis of life. They are an obstacle to life, but also constitute, at

---

66. Ibid., sec. 5.
67. Jean Granier, "La pensée nietzschéene du chaos," *Revue de Métaphysique et de Morale*, 2 (1971), 129–66. With regard to the meaning attributed by Nietzsche to chaos, cf. also Martin Heidegger, *Nietzsche* (Pfullingen: Neske, 1961), I, 349ff.

the same time, a support for its evolution. Bergson speaks of a shock that would emanate from matter and intelligence and would act as a stimulant on the activity of life and intuition.

For Nietzsche, the conception of reason and the rational is similar to Bergson's. He too affirms that life in its profoundest aspects transcends reason. He considers, on the one hand, that reason is a product of "decadence," and because of that he finds himself at first sight in the service of the nihilist movement; on the other hand, however, he claims that "decadence" is not only useful but even indispensable for life. Therefore, according to Nietzsche, reason exercises a function analogous to that which Bergson attributes to it. In the strong, the will to power makes use of reason as of a driving-bolt, in order to soar up toward a greater perfection. The tragic affirmation of life is realized only in confrontation with the forms of its negation. For Nietzsche, as for Bergson, reason is at the same time an obstacle and a support for the expansion of life.

One might object that there is, all the same, a difference between the Nietzschean concept of "decadence" and the Bergsonian notion of matter. To this it is proper to reply, however, that in reality the difference is far from being great. In fact, we read in Bergson: ". . . with this image of a *creative act that unmakes itself* we shall already have a more exact representation of matter. And we shall see then, in vital activity, that which subsists of the direct movement in the inverted movement, *a reality that is making itself in one that is unmaking itself.*"[68] Is matter not presented here as a sort of fall-out of the "élan vital," comparable to "decadence" as Nietzsche conceived it?

According to Nietzsche, it is chance that reigns in the chaotic process that is life. This does not mean the absence of all law, but only of a determined kind of law. The laws established by reason do not succeed in expressing in an exhaustive fashion the relations existing among the different facts and phenomena of life. Here again, one might have the impression that the Bergsonian philosophy expounds in systematic summary what Nietzsche's philosophy includes in germ. According to Bergson, we speak of chance when we are in the presence of facts that relate to the "vital order" while we expect to encounter the "geometric order," and vice versa. There exists no chance in the absolute sense. All change takes place in the framework of one or the other of these two orders.[69] For Nietzsche too, chance is a phenomenon that is answerable to the vital order; ac-

---

68. Henri Bergson, *L'évolution créatrice*, 86th ed. (Paris: Presses Universitaires de France, 1959), p. 248.
69. Ibid., pp. 234–36.

cordingly, we are incapable of explaining and foreseeing it by means of rational categories. For purpose and efficient cause are categories with the aid of which it is impossible to apprehend life. And what is true of life is true also of the value-judgments to which it gives birth. These last are to be considered and treated as vital phenomena. In a passage of *Philosophy in the Tragic Age of the Greeks*, let us recall, Nietzsche said: ". . . the expression of every profound philosophical intuition, by dialectic and scientific reflection, constitutes without doubt, on the one hand, the sole means of communicating the content of intuition, but it is a poor means, indeed, in the last analysis, no more than a metaphorical transference, quite inadequate in a different sphere and language."[70] Once again, what a resemblance to Bergson! For him too, "intuition" is the kind of knowing by means of which man succeeds in penetrating the very essence of life. And when Nietzsche speaks of "a transference . . . quite inadequate in a different sphere and language," does that not recall that, according to Bergson, "intelligence," as a mental expression of "geometric order," can give only a quite inadequate explanation of vital phenomena?

Moreover, Nietzsche's irrationalism can, if one wishes, be inferred in part from Schopenhauer's ideas of genius and from the difference that they establish between "concept" and "idea," just as between science and art. The "concept," according to Schopenhauer, is accessible to all beings endowed with reason; by contrast, to know the "idea," it is necessary ". . . to have raised oneself above all willing and all individuality to the state of a pure knowing subject; thus, it is attainable only by the genius, and thus by one who, motivated generally by works of genius, has attained an exalted state of mind by increasing his power of pure knowing."[71] Concepts are no more than simple instruments of science, which has phenomena as its exclusive object and obeys the principle of reason. Art, by contrast, is *"the mode of contemplation of things, independent of the principle of reason; it is opposed therefore to the mode of knowledge properly subject to that principle which leads to experiment and science."*[72] The essence of genius consists in the aptitude for the contemplation of "ideas." "It is only by this contemplation, pure and completely absorbed in the object, that ideas are conceived, and the essence of *genius* consists precisely in an eminent aptitude for such contemplation."[73] It may

---

70. GOA, X, 25.
71. Arthur Schopenhauer, *Die Welt als Wille und Vorstellung*, vol. I of the *Sämtliche Werke* (Munich: Piper, 1924), 276.
72. Ibid., I, 218.
73. Ibid.

seem that, on this point, Bergson and Nietzsche both allowed themselves to be inspired by Schopenhauer.[74]

Zarathustra, in his poetic style, admirably illustrates Nietzschean irrationalism:

> Indeed, it is a benediction, not a blasphemy when I teach: "Over all things stand the heaven accident, the heaven innocence, the heaven chance, the heaven playfulness."
>
> "By chance"—that is the oldest nobility in the world, and this I restored to all things; I liberated them from servitude to purpose.
>
> This freedom and celestial serenity I placed over all things like an azure bell when I taught that over them and across them no "eternal will"—wills.
>
> This playfulness and folly I put in the place of that will when I taught "In everything one thing is impossible—rationality!"
>
> A *little* reason, to be sure, a seed of wisdom dispersed from star to star—this leaven is mixed in with all things: for the sake of folly, wisdom is mixed in with all things!
>
> A little wisdom is indeed possible; but I found this blessed certitude in all things: that on the feet of chance they prefer—*to dance*.
>
> O heaven over me, pure and high! To me that is now thy purity, that there does not exist any eternal spider-reason or spider web of reason:
>
> —that thou art to me a dance floor for divine accidents, that thou art to me a divine table for divine dice and dice players!—[75]

This text recalls to us the profound admiration that Nietzsche, during his first period, had already evinced for Heraclitus. Existence, a game that the gods play. Gods with human visages or men with divine faces?

Even poetic expression does not suffice to communicate the extreme richness of the interior vision. Zarathustra says:

> . . . in truth, I am ashamed that I am *obliged* still to be a poet!
>
> Where all becoming seemed to me to be a dance of gods and the playfulness of gods and the world seemed free and boisterous and as if returning to itself:—

---

74. In his work *Die schaffende Natur* (Leipzig: Quelle & Meyer, 1919), J. Reinke challenges the idea that Bergson depends on Schopenhauer, but he maintains that the latter could not have remained unknown to the French philosopher. He undertakes to show "a certain number of planes on which Schopenhauer and Bergson are near to each other" (p. 130).

75. Z, III, "Before Sunrise."

—as an eternal fleeing of one another and seeking of one another afresh of many gods, as the happy contradicting of one another, hearkening again to one another, and belonging again to one another of many gods:—

Where all time appeared to me to be a happy scorning of moments, where necessity was freedom itself, playing happily with the sting of freedom:—[76]

And in addition, Zarathustra, making allusion anew to the eternal recurrence and to the theodicy implied by belief in it, continues:

Where I too found again my old devil and archenemy, the spirit of gravity, and everything that he created, compulsion, rule, necessity, and consequence and purpose and will and good and evil:—

For *must* there not be that *over* which one dances and dances away? Must there not for the sake of the light, the lightest—be moles and grave dwarfs?[77]

The "spirit of gravity" must exist in order that it may be possible for the strong to surpass themselves in dancing! In this symbol of the dance are expressed the lightness and freedom that characterize superior men. Let us recall that in *The Birth of Tragedy*, dance was presented, along with music, as a Dionysian art! Zarathustra sees, then, in the "spirit of gravity," his "ancient devil and archenemy." What is thus alluded to here is "decadence" with all its works and nihilistic manifestations. It is, in the first place, a matter of the Schopenhauerian philosophy, toward which, for a brief period, Nietzsche once felt himself attracted after reading *The World as Will and Idea*. We may say that the attraction toward Schopenhauer's ethic remained latent in Nietzsche, a little in the manner of a permanent temptation that, from time to time, he had to overcome afresh.

But the theodicy inherent in the idea of the eternal recurrence constitutes the culminating point of Nietzsche's opposition to Schopenhauer. One could not go farther "beyond good and evil." Besides, "beyond good and evil" is a formula the full sense of which one does not grasp without having understood that it is, from the very first, opposed to Schopenhauer and his moralistic conception of existence. According to Schopenhauer, existence means shortcoming and punishment. To that, Nietzsche opposes the innocence of becoming, the legitimation of becoming in all its forms. But if all the vital phe-

---

76. Ibid., "Of Old and New Law Tables," sec. 2.
77. Ibid.

nomena are justified, this means that the "spirit of gravity" also has his approval: it is approved to the extent that the new freedom is the result of the fight against it, when, without that fight, it would be unrealizable. Thanks to the belief in the eternal recurrence, man is truly free, for, having bowed to universal necessity, he participates henceforth in the free play of the world.[78]

As a posthumous note indicates, play is "the ideal of one overflowing with strength."[79] That is the reason why the higher man becomes like a child. In the chapter entitled "Of the Three Metamorphoses," Zarathustra recounts that he has first been a "camel," that he was then transformed into a "lion," and that finally he has become a "child." The "camel" symbolizes the period when he was still under the control of morality and, in general, of the old tradition. Then there comes the phase when he is a "lion," when, with the strength of a lion, he fights against the values of yesteryear. At length, he attains a still more elevated state, that of approval of existence in all its forms, which alone permits him to engage fully in the play of the world. The creation of new values is a part of that game which, eternally, builds and destroys. Zarathustra says:

> Innocence is the child and forgetfulness, a beginning again, a game, a self-rolling wheel, a first movement, a holy yea-saying.
>
> Yes, for the game of creation, my brothers, there is need of a holy yea-saying: The spirit now wills its own will; He who is lost to the world now wins his own world.[80]

This creative game is Dionysus himself.

---

78. From the time of his youth, Nietzsche was interested in the antinomy between determinism and free will, between "fatum" and freedom (cf. in particular Heimsoeth, *Metaphysische Voraussetzungen* [above, n. 1], pp. 512ff.). It may be maintained that Dionysian play, in abolishing the separation of necessity from freedom, constitutes the highest expression of his idea of "fatum" conceived so much earlier.
79. WKG, VIII-1, 127.
80. Z, I, "Of the Three Metamorphoses."

XVII. Nietzsche: What Christians and Non-Christians Can Learn

Hans Küng
(Translated by Edward Quinn)

I

Certainly Christians do not need to accept all that Nietzsche produces by way of criticism.* And with all due respect for his passion for truth, Nietzsche's truths are often half-truths. His knowledge of theology and Church history does not come up to the seriousness of his charges. Many passages, especially in the historically and exegetically oriented *Antichrist*, are more like pamphlets than records of cool investigation: Nietzsche's indignant and contemptuous language is meant to wound. His slips are sometimes embarrassing, generalizations and labels abound, anti-Christian fanaticism clouds his judgment. Even his compliments on the antidemocratic order of precedence of the Roman hierarchy, their will to power and their aristocratic, lordly manners, and even on Jesuits, celibacy, and confession, are questionable. Particularly questionable are his invectives against Luther as the corrupter of the pagan Renaissance, the plebeian and hooligan, the most eloquent and most presumptuous peasant in Germany, who approached all cardinal questions of power short-sightedly, superficially, and recklessly: "Luther, this calamity of a monk, restored the church and, what is a thousand times worse, Christianity, at the very moment *when it was vanquished.*"[1] What is to be said about all this? Detailed refutations would fill volumes and yet would not be worthwhile. For it is a question not of details but of the whole. Isolated positive statements on the Church and priests simply do not count by comparison with Nietzsche's wholly destructive criticism of Christianity as it has come to be.[2]

---

*The present chapter consists of an excerpt from Hans Küng, *Does God Exist? An Answer for Today*, trans. Edward Quinn (New York: Doubleday, 1980), pp. 405–15, reprinted by permission of the publisher.

1. *Ecce Homo*, "The Case of Wagner," sec. 2; W, II, 1148.

2. The positive statements are stressed—perhaps overstressed—by Karl Jaspers, *Nietzsche und das Christentum*, 2nd ed. (Munich: Piper, 1952), pp. 8–10.

Here in any case is a decisive rejection of Christianity, but surprisingly enough we find respect for him whose person and cause Christianity invokes: *Jesus of Nazareth*. Certainly he, too, in the end is rejected by Nietzsche as the—admittedly "most interesting"—*decadent*, but without the tirades of hate and feelings of disgust usually linked with matters of Christianity. In his attempt at a critique of the Gospels, Nietzsche thought he could establish a fundamental contradiction: Here we have "the mountain, lake, and field preacher, whose appearance strikes one as that of a Buddha on a soil very little like that of India"[3] and on the other hand "the aggressive fanatic, the mortal enemy of theologian and priest."[4] Nietzsche thinks that this fanatic type only later "overflowed on to the type of the Master" as a result of Christian propaganda.[5]

What really interests Nietzsche about Jesus is "the problem of the *psychology of the redeemer*."[6] Concepts such as "hero" and "genius" do not suit him: "a quite different word would, rather, be in place here: the word idiot."[7] There is an odd agreement here with Dostoevsky's interpretation of Christ, and Nietzsche had perhaps read Dostoevsky's novel *The Idiot*. "Idiot" means "instinctive hatred of *every* reality, as flight into the 'ungraspable,' into the 'inconceivable,' as antipathy towards every form, every spatial and temporal concept, towards everything firm, all that is custom, institution, Church."[8] For the "good news" of this "bringer of glad tidings" consists in the fact that there are no longer any antagonisms. The barriers have fallen between Jews and non-Jews, foreigners and natives, even between God and man. Such concepts as guilt, punishment, and reward do not exist: "Blessedness is not promised, it is not tied to any conditions: it is the *only* reality—the rest is signs for speaking of it."[9] The kingdom of heaven of this "great symbolist" is "a condition of the heart—not something that comes 'upon the earth' or 'after death'. . . . It is everywhere, it is nowhere."[10] Hence it is practice, not belief, that distinguishes Christians: no resistance to evil, no defense of one's rights despite calumny and scorn, passive acceptance of everything that happens. That is why this Jesus of Nazareth died on the

3. A, sec. 31; W, II, 1192.
4. Ibid.; W, II, 1193.
5. Ibid.
6. Ibid., sec. 28; W, II, 1190.
7. Ibid., sec. 29; W, II, 1190–91. Cf. A, sec. 27; W, II, 1189.
8. Ibid., sec. 29; W, II, 1191.
9. Ibid., sec. 33; W, II, 1195.
10. Ibid., sec. 34; W, II, 1196–97.

cross as he lived: "he entreats, he suffers, he loves *with* those, in those who are doing evil to him. . . . Not to defend oneself, *not* to grow angry, *not* to make responsible. . . . But not to resist even the evil man—to *love* him. . . ."[11]

This is not an unsympathetic picture of Jesus of Nazareth. It is clear to Nietzsche that the message of such a "symbolist *par excellence*"—who spoke only of innermost reality, of life, truth, light, and for whom all other reality had value only as a sign or a parable—cannot be reduced to formulas, dogmas, and doctrines. It is clear too that the disciples understood him only when they could fit him into the well-known categories: prophet, Messiah, future judge, moral teacher, miracle man. But even that was a distortion, a misunderstanding. And the whole history of Christianity, which became increasingly vulgarized, barbarized, absorbed the doctrines and rites of all the subterranean cults of the Roman Empire, turned out to be the history of "progressively cruder misunderstanding of an *original* symbolism."[12] Jesus' living practice was turned into a faith and this faith into a doctrine. Think, for instance, of what Christians (especially Paul) have made of the cross. In the sign of this cross—which, for Jesus, was precisely the most severe test of his love—revenge, retribution, punishment, justice, were preached and the glad tidings turned into tidings of woe. It was now that the type of Jesus the fanatic was created: "Now all that contempt for and bitterness against Pharisee and theologian was worked into the type of the Master—one thereby *made* of him a Pharisee and theologian."[13]

Is this a picture only in black and white? Certainly from the present-day standpoint we must judge critically this style of historiography and exegesis. But is it not more important for Christians—who see themselves in the light of their Christ Jesus—to note with what respect the person, the message of Jesus Christ is brought out here, even though we cannot agree with the picture as a whole? In individual features—to the shame of many Christians—is not the message perhaps more credibly proclaimed by this atheist and nihilist than it is by these Christians themselves? How many Christians even ask about the authentic, original Christianity? The main charge brought by Nietzsche deserves all our attention: "I shall now relate the *real* history of Christianity.—The word 'Christianity' is already a misunderstanding—in reality there has been only one Christian,

---

11. Ibid., sec. 35; W, II, 1197.
12. Ibid., sec. 37; W, II, 1198.
13. Ibid., sec. 40; W, II, 1202.

and he died on the Cross. The 'Evangel' died on the Cross. What was called 'Evangel' from this moment onwards was already the opposite of what *he* had lived: 'bad tidings,' a *dysangel*. It is false to the point of absurdity to see in a 'belief,' perchance the belief in redemption through Christ, the distinguishing characteristic of the Christian: only Christian *practice*, a life such as he who died on the Cross *lived*, is Christian. . . ."[14] And we may hear and wonder at the words in *The Antichrist*: "Even today such a life is possible, for certain men even necessary: genuine, primitive Christianity will be possible at all times."[15] Are not Christians challenged here continually to compare their claim critically with reality, to make theory and practice coincide credibly, to judge themselves by the source, by Jesus himself?

The Antichrist is obviously more anti-Christian than anti-Christ: a provocation for Christians which can be salutary. We need only recall some typical headings to find sufficient material for critical reflection.

First: How much is true in Nietzsche's *critique of the Church*? Church as power structure over men's souls, a kind of pseudo-state? Church in opposition to the gospel of Jesus and to honest, straightforward humanity? Church in conflict with all human greatness, intent on making itself indispensable? Church as a center of psychological forgery, devaluing the natural virtues of life and intruding into people's private life? Churches as sepulchers of God, estranged from life, immobile, rigid . . . ?

Secondly: How much is true in his *critique of the priesthood*? Priests as the great haters in world history? The smartest, conscious hypocrites? Poisoners of life, parasites who live on men's sins, feelings of fear, and feelings of guilt? Who fear both sensuality and science, suppress both liberty and life? Priests—far too long wrongly regarded as the supreme type, the ideal, of man . . . ?

Thirdly: How much is true in Nietzsche's *critique of the idea of God*? That idea of God which is born out of resentment and plebeian morality, the one above this pitiful loafer morality of good and evil? That idea of God from which all that is strong, brave, heroic, proud, has been eliminated and which has made God into a God of the weak, sick, and decadent, a poor man's God, a sinner's God, a sick man's God? How much is true in the critique by Friedrich Nietzsche, who sees an abuse of divine dexterity in all talk of "grace," "providence," "experience of salvation"? Who finds "absurd" a God who cures a cold at the right time or gets us into the cab at the very moment of an

---

14. Ibid., sec. 39; W, II, 1200.
15. Ibid.

outbreak of heavy rain? A God, that is, who is more of a "servant," "postman," "Santa Claus": when all is said and done, a word for the most stupid kind of all coincidences? Must it not be admitted that this critique of God is made for man's sake: to protect human identity against a paralyzing knowledge, a petty moral supervision, an oppressive love of God? Did Nietzsche not get rid of God for man's sake: godlessness not as an end in itself but as a precaution against a belief in God that depreciates human existence? Cannot the immediacy of human existence be threatened by an alienation brought about by religious influences?

Nevertheless, something more has to be said: If Christianity really *were* as Nietzsche saw it, then it could be and would have to be rejected today, and for good reasons;
if "God" were merely the counterconcept to life, and in it everything detrimental, poisonous, slanderous, the whole mortal enmity to life, were brought into a horrible unity;
if the concept "beyond" or "true world" had been invented in order to devalue the only world that exists, in order to have no goal, no reason, no function left for this earthly reality;
if the concept "soul" or "spirit" or, still more, "immortal soul" had been invented in order to despise the body, to make it sick, "holy," in order to approach with an appalling superficiality all the things that deserve to be taken seriously in life, that is, the questions of sustenance, a place to live, treatment of the sick, cleanliness, weather;
if, instead of health, "salvation of the soul" were sought, as a manic-depressive condition, a *foile circulaire*, alternating between spasms of penance and redemption hysteria;
if both the concept of "sin" and that of "free will" had been invented in order to confuse the instincts and to make mistrust of these into a second nature;
if the mark of real decadence were involved in the concept of the "selfless" or of "self-denial";
if self-destruction were made into a stamp in general use, into a "duty," into "holiness," into the "divine" in man;
if, finally, the concept of the "good man" implied taking the side of all the weak, the sick, the failures, all those suffering from themselves, against the people who say Yes, who are certain of the future, who are guaranteed the future;
if, then, all that were Christian morality,[16]
then—yes, then—we would have to subscribe along with Nietzsche

---

16. Cf. the description in *Ecce Homo*, "Why I Am a Destiny," sec. 8; W, II, 1158–59.

to Voltaire's *Ecrasez l'infâme*! Then—yes, then—we would have to be with "Dionysus versus the Crucified."[17] Then it would no longer be possible to be Christian, but only anti-Christian.

But how often has Christianity—in certain forms of Protestantism and Catholicism—actually been presented as it was seen by Nietzsche, who had gotten to know Christianity mainly in a Protestant parsonage, a Christian boarding school, and through Schopenhauer's philosophy? And how often is it preached, commended, lived, in this way even today in the churches?

All that we can say here is that Christianity does not have to be seen in this way. Indeed, it cannot be seen in this way if Jesus Christ is rightly understood. For in this light it is impossible to be a Christian without being human, to be a Christian at the expense of being human, to be a Christian alongside, above or below being human. Being a Christian must be radically, truly humanly being human, so far—that is—as it can fully incorporate the human, all-too-human in all its negativity.[18]

II

Non-Christians? Can even non-Christians learn from Nietzsche? The question might surprise anyone who was far too sure of knowing where he stood with Nietzsche. The question should surprise anyone who is not clear about the consequences of getting involved with Nietzsche. Nietzsche pierced through to the foundations of human knowledge and questioned them as no one had done before him. No one has equaled him in the acuteness, depth, and radicalness of his thought: not Feuerbach, not Marx, and not even Freud; at most, Pascal. Ought not the consequences particularly of the nihilism analyzed by Nietzsche to have been considered at the opportune time?

After all we have had to say about Nietzsche's struggle against Christianity, one thing is crystal clear. With all the passion that was in him, Nietzsche opposed a particular kind of human being: the sick, suffering, inferior, mediocre human being. The latter is the type of decay, disintegration, and weakness. At this very point, therefore, we have a revaluation of values, the will to power. Nature, seen from the Darwinian standpoint, is the model on which Nietzsche bases his picture of man: "The grandiose prototype: man in nature—the

---

17. This is how *Ecce Homo* ends; W, II, 1159.
18. Cf., on the whole subject, my work *On Being a Christian* (New York: Doubleday, 1976), especially D: "Practice."

weakest, shrewdest creature making himself master, subjugating the stupider forces."[19]

As we have seen, Nietzsche nowhere saw the type he despised more fully realized than in Christianity, with its "God on the Cross," where "everything that suffers, everything that hangs on the Cross" is declared "divine."[20] And who would say—particularly as a Christian—even today that this picture by Nietzsche of a suffering, guilty, inferior, feeble "typical" Christian is merely a caricature? Of course Christians, too, have learned something. Even within Christianity, today, there is no question of building up the hypocritical, the weakly, the mediocre, the frustrated, the guilty. But—and this question must in turn be put to Nietzsche—what of the opposite type, which—after the publication of *Zarathustra*—he never tired of propagating, commending, celebrating as an alternative: the superman? Is it, then, the superman or at least the man of power who should be sought and bred today? Who despises the mob and counts himself among the physically and mentally strong, the distinguished, aristocrats, privileged? Who, while certainly also ruthless toward himself, wants to exterminate whatever is mediocre and to cultivate whatever promises hardness and cruelty? Who as a beast of prey with the motto "live dangerously" pursues his interests regardless of the victims, if this only feeds power, is useful to life, is of service to the rulers? Who simply withstands his destiny right up to pointless extinction?

In the second half of the twentieth century, this type of man has become only too well known: men without God, whose relationships with one another are concretized even into the private sphere, determined by functional and practical values, guided by power interests, the weak everywhere being the victim of the stronger, superior, less scrupulous. The horizon of meaning is in fact effaced, there are no longer any supreme values, reliable guiding principles, absolute truth. In practice, does this not mean that a nihilism of values is determining human behavior? Has that not come to pass which Nietzsche foresaw—more clearsightedly than many before him? But it is often a mild, concealed, unemotional nihilism, without the passion of a Zarathustra but no less dangerous. Many today are distrustful toward a loud, public nihilism, and no politician, anyway, could afford to indulge in it. But people permit themselves a mild, private nihilism, often guilelessly, innocently, perceiving the consequences only at a very late stage. For, after so many taboos were broken in

---

19. *Nachlaß* (WM), sec. 856; W, III, 491.
20. A, sec. 51; W, II, 1217.

the war years and subsequently, so many traditions disappeared, conventions were dropped, humanisms were emptied of meaning, despite all the prosperity and better education, in many families parents no longer know to which values, guiding principles, ideals, norms, to which truth, they should cling and to which they should educate their children: devaluation (often without any revaluation) of values, the loss of which can then be noted, but can be canceled only with difficulty. In education, culture, economy, science, politics, "an incomplete nihilism" lived in a middle- or upper-class style, feeble and only half affirmed: "we live in the midst of it."[21]

Sometimes, however, more is involved. Nihilism presents many faces, from bored, intellectual skepticism to brutal political anarchism. Undoubtedly it is not only because of a whole packet of social factors but in the last resort also because of a nihilistic lack of orientation and lack of norms, that there has been an alarming increase in the number of thefts, robberies, crimes of violence, murders, by children, young people, students (more and more of them female), that the number of drug addicts, dropouts, suicides has risen tremendously in the past decade, that susceptibility to ideologies has often amounted to mania. The "meaning deficit" and "meaning vacuum" in the Western affluent society, for a long time now, has not only provided the middle classes with intellectual titillation in the "theater of the absurd" of an Ionesco or a Beckett, has not only been diagnosed and deplored by psychotherapists and psychiatrists.[22] It is beginning to be a political fact.

Has Nietzsche, then, been proved right? As we saw, in many ways certainly with his analysis. Was Nietzsche right? Not with his alternative. For just as the weakling type, of Christian provenance—as Nietzsche saw him—cannot be, may not be, the model for being truly human, neither can the superman, of secular provenance. These are not true alternatives. Can weakness be overcome only by hardness? Are there no intermediate hues, no gradations, no mean? Are compassion, goodness, mercy, indulgence, fellowship, love, something that can only be denounced as weakness? Is there not also a mercy that comes from strength, a compassion from fullness, a goodness from the greatness of a man? Indeed, is not this perhaps the very goal that men should seek today, precisely as Christians, precisely in the light of belief in God? If not moralism,

---

21. *Nachlaß* (WM), sec. 28; W, III, 621.
22. Cf. section C. III. 3 of *Does God Exist?* ("The Importance of Religion for Jung, Fromm, Frankel").

then perhaps morality? If not idealism, then perhaps ideals? If not sanctimoniousness, then perhaps religion.

The devastating crisis of meaning today not only affects the individual but has also gripped society and its institutions: marriage and family, school and university, even the state itself. The question may occur to some people: What has all this to do with a "permissive society," in which nothing is true and everything is allowed, in which no deeper meaning can be seen, in which everyone may be permitted everything? On the other hand, public discussion of human rights, of fundamental values, of commercial and political morality, shows that now, as before, there is undeniably a genuine need of norms, values, orientation, meaning. In this respect, of course, Nietzsche had developed his own sociological ideas.

"Temporary preponderance of the social value-feelings comprehensible and useful: it is a question of creating a *foundation* upon which a *stronger* species will ultimately be possible.—Standard of strength: to be able to live under the reverse evaluations and to will them again eternally. State and society as foundation: world-economic point of view, education as *breeding*."[23] Three important aspects of Nietzsche's picture of society are combined in this note: education as breeding, the world-economic point of view of a total society, social value-feelings useful as precondition of the creation of a stronger species of man.

Nietzsche attached little importance to *education*. For education means being concerned with the mediocre, with human beings *en masse*, raising them up to a higher level. He wants nothing of this: the gulf between the species must be widened; "establish distances"—this is the solution.[24] The lower species is the base on which the higher stands, on which alone the higher can perform its task. And what is due to the higher is nothing for the lower. "That which is available only to the *strongest* and most fruitful natures and makes their existence possible—leisure, adventure, disbelief, even dissipation—would, if it were available to mediocre natures, necessarily destroy them—and actually does. This is where industriousness, rule, moderation, firm 'conviction' have their place—in short, the 'herd virtues': under them this intermediate type of man grows perfect."[25]

Where education is not desired, *breeding* must take its place. What

---

23. *Nachlaß* (WM), sec. 903; W, III, 562.
24. Ibid., sec. 891; W, III, 610.
25. Ibid., sec. 901; W, III, 554.

Nietzsche wrote about this became the prescription followed by the National Socialist ideologists, blinded by their biology of race, fifty years later: "A question constantly keeps coming back to us. . . . Is it not time, now that the type 'herd animal' is being evolved more and more in Europe, to make the experiment of a fundamental, artificial, and conscious *breeding* of the opposite type and its virtues? And would it not be a kind of goal, redemption, and justification for the democratic movement itself if someone arrived who could make use of it—by finally producing beside its new and sublime development of slavery (that is what European democracy must become ultimately) a higher kind of dominating and Caesarian spirits who would stand upon it, maintain themselves by it, and elevate themselves through it? To new, hitherto impossible prospects, to their own prospects? To their own tasks?"[26] These ideas of Nietzsche were not disposed of when National Socialism came to its disastrous end. They are again relevant today in view of microbiological discoveries concerning the manipulation of genes.

When such a doctrine of contempt for man is preached, it is not difficult to *justify war*, the sacrifice of the many, endurance at all costs: "One must learn from war: (1) to associate death with the interests for which one fights—that makes *us* venerable; (2) one must learn to sacrifice *many* and to take one's cause seriously enough not to spare men; (3) rigid discipline, and to permit oneself force and cunning in war."[27]

In the present century, we have seen all these ideas exploited in the most cruel, albeit one-sided fashion, particularly when a real "superman" finally appeared. In the person of a German, which was not exactly what Nietzsche had expected. For Nietzsche was an antinationalist and European, despiser of German philistinism, squareness, beeriness, nationalistic blustering, and at the same time an admirer of Latin form, French wit, and Mediterranean mentality. Allowing for all this, Nietzsche must still be described as one of the—involuntary—precursors of National Socialism (and Italian Fascism, which people like to forget today), which—understanding and misunderstanding—put into practice essential ideas of Nietzsche.[28]

It was clear that Nietzsche could not think anything of *democracy* or parliamentary government, nor could he think anything of social-

---

26. Ibid., sec. 954; W, III, 505–6.
27. Ibid., sec. 982; W, III, 432.
28. For early evidence of this, see Hermann Rauschning, *Hitler Speaks. A Series of Political Conversations with Adolf Hitler on His Real Aims* (London: Thornton Butterworth, 1939).

ism. The people? From the time of his early preoccupation with the Greeks, Nietzsche was fascinated by the idea of the elite, now with the power elite. The Revolution? For him it had only one good aspect: it produced Napoleon. Otherwise the result was a *"social hodgepodge"*: "the establishment of equal rights, of the superstition of 'equal men.' "[29] Universal suffrage, parliamentary government? For Nietzsche, this is the tyranny of mediocrity, the rule of inferior human beings. All that could so long be kept under now comes to the top: "the slave instincts, the instincts of cowardice, cunning, and *canaille* in those orders that have long been kept down."[30] Walter Jens is right when he says: "While Kant and Hegel, Goethe and Heine, knew the age in which they lived and expected from the French Revolution or the Prussian court, from America or the republican spirit, influences that characterized their epoch . . . while they were contemporaries, exchanging ideas with kindred spirits and opponents, Nietzsche lived alone, by himself, in a no-man's-land, in a realm of shades: blind not only in a physical sense. No Marx ever encountered him. The manner in which he describes socialism—'tyranny of the stupid,' 'the herd animal itself as master,' 'a hopelessly sour affair'—displays pure ignorance. Nietzsche—it must be said—did not know what he was talking about."[31]

Also, did Nietzsche know what he was talking about when he compared the practical value of men—of the inferior men, it should be noted, not of the superior men—with the function of a machine? "The task is to make man as useful as possible and to approximate him, as far as possible, to an infallible machine: to this end, he must be equipped with the virtues of the machine (he must learn to experience the states in which he works in a mechanically useful way as the supremely valuable states; hence it is necessary to spoil the other states for him as much as possible, as highly dangerous and disreputable)."[32] Did Nietzsche know what he was talking about when he demanded "the production of a synthetic . . . man for whose existence this transformation of mankind into a machine is a precondition, as a base on which he can invent his *higher form of being*"?[33] Did he know what he was talking about when he preferred to express his

---

29. *Nachlaß* (WM), sec. 864; W, III, 708.
30. Ibid.
31. Walter Jens, "Friedrich Nietzsche. Pastor ohne Kanzel," *Frankfurter Allgemeine Zeitung*, 6 February 1974; reprinted in his collected articles, *Republikanische Reden* (Munich: Kindler, 1976), pp. 101–12.
32. *Nachlaß* (WM), sec. 888; W, III, 630.
33. Ibid., sec. 866; W, III, 629.

contempt for inferior human beings in a metaphorical language of industrial technology: "Lunatics, criminals, and 'naturalists' are increasing: sign of a growing culture rushing on precipitately—i.e., the refuse, the waste, gain importance—the decline keeps pace."[34] There is no doubt that we have here an anticipation of what Fritz Lang, in his famous film of the twenties *Metropolis*, evoked in expressionistic imagery, and Aldous Huxley, in *Brave New World*, in the early thirties, developed in the shape of a negative Utopia: The mob has to function in the style of a machine, the rule of an aristocratic-technocratic elite has been set up, the superman created.

And Nietzsche himself? What a contrast between this man and his work, this message and this messenger. It must be made quite clear that here is someone who proclaims a philosophy of world-historical import with great visionary force, with the passion of a world-surveying prophet and the gestures of the founder of a religion—and is himself an unknown retired professor of ancient philology, traveling restlessly from place to place, barely managing to live in modest rooms of a hotel or bakehouse. Here is someone who proclaims the message of absolute hardness, ruthless cruelty, and the extermination of all that is ailing and weak—and has himself been a sick man since his student days, needs the help of the very people he despises, depends on the compassion of the very people he opposes, is continually troubled about his food and mode of life, following planned diets, drawing up climatological graphs and even forging medical prescriptions. Here is someone who proclaims the doctrine of the superman, of light and of life—and never comes out of his own shadowy world, lives unsuccessfully remote from the reality of his time, conversing only with hotel guests and especially with his books. What a contrast! An essentially tender, vulnerable, rather timid, effusive person, whom everyone—even the most simple people—found agreeable. And yet this hatred for people, particularly the weak and inferior. An absolutely intellectually honest thinker. And yet he prefers to adopt an aristocratic, upper-class manner and to talk about his supposed descent from a noble Polish family, instead of admitting his origin from a Protestant pastor's family. A divided personality? Yet, in many respects: thinker, psychologist, rhetorician, preacher, but also actor in the grand manner, all in one person, whose thought is challenging in its radicality, whose destiny is shattering in its severity, whose teaching, however, is alarming in its consequences.

---

34. Ibid., sec. 864; W, III, 708.

XVIII. Humanity without the Fellow-Man: Nietzsche's Superman and Christian Morality

Karl Barth
(Translated by G. W. Bromiley)

I

We have to rule out the possibility of a humanity without the fellow-man.* Hence we must not discuss it. But it will be worth our while to consider briefly what we are ruling out, what conception of man we are passing by without discussion. We may begin by admitting that it is not self-evident that it should be ruled out in this way, and thus passed by without discussion. In doing this, we follow the higher right of theological necessity. But on behalf of the rejected humanity which is either without or against the fellow-man, or pays him only casual attention, it may be argued that it is not only infinitely more appealing but even self-evident on a nontheological view.

If we bracket the Christian judgment, does not the word "man" immediately and at bottom definitively conjure up a being which is basically and properly for itself, so that although it may be vaguely recognized in others it can be and is seen immediately and directly only in the self? According to this constantly victorious conception humanity consists in the fact that I am, that I am for myself, and neither from nor to others. In certain circumstances this "I am" can have a powerful radius. And it is not to be subjected to a moralistic judgment and condemnation as limitation or self-seeking. For after all, it will somewhere embrace others as well. The only trouble is that basically and properly it is without them or against them or only secondarily and occasionally with them and for them.

"I am"—this is the forceful assertion which we are all engaged in

---

*The present chapter consists of an excerpt from Karl Barth, *Church Dogmatics*, ed. G. W. Bromiley and T. F. Torrence, 5 vols. in 14 (Edinburgh: T. & T. Clark, 1936–77), III-2, 229–42, reprinted by permission of the publisher.

making and of which we are convinced that none can surpass it in urgency or importance; the assertion of the self in which we can neither be replaced by any nor restrained by any. "I am" means that I satisfy myself even in the sense that I have to do justice to myself, that I am pressingly claimed by myself. "I am" means that I stand under the irresistible urge to maintain myself, but also to make something of myself, to develop myself, to try out myself, to exercise and prove myself. "I am" means further, however, that in every development and activity outwards I must and will at all costs maintain and assert myself, not dissipating and losing myself, but concentrating even as I expand, and getting even as I give. It means that I must and will acquire and have personality. But the radius is even wider than this. "I am" means that I may and must live; that I may and must live out my life in the material and spiritual cosmos, enjoying, working, playing, fashioning, possessing, achieving and exercising power; that I may and must in my own place and within my own limits—and who is to say where these are to be drawn?—have my share in the goods of the earth, in the fullness of human knowledge and capacity, in the further development of human technique and art and organization.

These are powerful projections of the "I am" outwards into space and time and its truth and poetry or rather its poetry and truth, its myth and history. And to these projections there certainly belongs the fashioning of a relationship to what is called "heaven" in the Bible and "God," "the gods," or "the divine" elsewhere; the construction of a positive or negative, believing or skeptical, original or conventional position with reference to the ultimate limits and mystery of life, the incomprehensible which will finally confront all our comprehension. And inevitably in this onward progress of the "I am" the encounter with fellow-men will have its own specific and determinative part; the burning questions whether this or that person is important or indifferent to me, whether he attracts or repels me, whether he helps and serves or obstructs and harms me, whether he is superior to me or I can master him and am thus superior to him. To these projections there also belong the dealings with him, with all the selection and rejection, the conflict, peace and renewal of conflict, the constant hide-and-seek, the domination and dependence, the morality and immorality which these dealings inevitably involve and without which life would certainly be much easier and simpler but also much poorer and duller. The only thing is that here too we have a projection of the "I am" outwards. Even the many forms of our fellows are ultimately elements in our own myth or history, not found but invented and decked out by us, and merely speaking the words which we put on their lips. There are merely more or less serviceable or unserviceable figures in our own play, drawn into ourselves to the extent that we have in some way transformed them into something that belongs to us. In their genuine otherness and particularity they are without like in the rest of the cosmos.

Originally and properly within I am still alone by myself: in my freedom in relation to the whole cosmos; with my poetry and truth; with the question of my needs and desires and loves and hates; with my known and sometimes unknown likes and dislikes; with my capacities and propensities; as my own doctor, as the sovereign architect, director, general, and dictator of the whole, of my own earth and heaven, my cosmos, God, and fellow-men; as the incomparable inventor and sustainer of myself; in first and final solitude. Within this total conception there is naturally an infinite range of colors and contours, of nuances and emphases, to the final and apparently self-exclusive extremes. It is a unity only in general. In detail the variations are so great as to make the common features almost unrecognizable. It never repeats itself. It constantly takes on new forms not only in the different ages and cultures, not only in the distinction of individuals, but also within their own specific development, in youth and maturity and age, in the changing stations and circumstances of life. But we should not be misled. The "I am" may often be less powerfully at work as the basis and beginning of all things. We may not always see that in everything else we really have projections of this I. Our fellows in their otherness and particularity may often be more forcefully and obstinately and pertinently at work than our depiction suggests. Yet the overwhelming unity of the whole remains— of an attempted humanity in which the fellow-man has no constitutive function. And, if for a moment we suspend our Christian judgment, we at once recognize that it is the most obvious thing in the world to answer the question of humanity with perhaps a more profound and purified and convincing modification of this view. We have to realize what it means that theological anthropology cannot grasp this most obvious of all possibilities, but must reject it *a limine*.

II

By way of illustration we may refer to Friedrich Nietzsche. We do this for two reasons. He developed this conception of humanity with unequaled logic and perspicacity. And in his refusal to evade its deepest root and supreme consequence, in his enthusiastic acceptance of them, he resolutely and passionately and necessarily rejected, not a caricature of the Christian conception of humanity, but in the form of a caricature the conception itself. He shows us how necessary it is that we for our part must less violently but no less resolutely reject the conception of humanity of which he is a classical exponent.

In 1888 Nietzsche wrote his *Ecce Homo*, which was published in 1908. This is an autobiography, of the same genre as Augustine's and Rousseau's *Confessions*, but with no admission of mistakes, and constituting an unequivocal final testimony for the future interpretation of the author. Shortly after writing it, Nietzsche was declared to be afflicted with an incurable mental sickness. It was understandable that Franz Overbeck, one of his closest friends, should at first prevent its publication. But he was not justified on material grounds, for whether Nietzsche was already ill or not when he wrote this book there can be no doubt that in it he rightly perceived and summed up the final intentions of his purposes and work as they had marked him from the very first.

On the first page of *Ecce Homo* we read in heavy type the statement: "Hear me, for I am he; do not at any price mistake me."[1] And even more menacingly on the final page, again in heavy type: "Am I understood?—Dionysus against the Crucified. . . ."[2] The first saying is a bizarre but genuine form of the first and final proposition of humanity without the fellow-man. Nietzsche liked to see it represented in the form of the ancient Greek god Dionysus. The second is the repudiation of Christianity self-evident on the basis of this humanity.

"Hear me, for I am he; do not at any price mistake me." We shall first try to see what this means. Goethe too, whom Nietzsche usually although not always mentioned respectfully as a precursor, wanted to be regarded and estimated as "he," with a certain solemnity and joyous reverence making himself and his way and culture and work the theme of special consideration and explanation, and having an obvious consciousness of himself. But Nietzsche was basically and properly self-consciousness and nothing more. His angrily uncertain: "Do not at any price mistake me" and later his eager: "Am I understood?" would have been quite unthinkable on the lips of Goethe. Goethe was on the same path as Nietzsche, an exponent of the

---

1. *Ecce Homo*, Preface, sec. 1.
2. Ibid., "Why I Am a Destiny," sec. 9.

same "I am," but he knew when to stop, and said certain ultimate things about this beginning and end either not at all or very seldom and with great caution. He knew how often and not unjustly he was praised for keeping to the golden mean. He could do so, and necessarily, because his self-consciousness was continually filled with the most attentive and deeply interested world-consciousness. The quiet fulfillment of almost uninterrupted work in the world outside gives to his picture, and his occasional self-portraits, the character of a cheerful sanity in which he could not be tempted by any anxiety lest he should be confused with others, because he was far too worldly-wise even to make this a matter of debate. But Nietzsche was the prophet of that humanity without the fellow-man. He did not merely reveal its secret; he blabbed it out. He was in a nonclassical form what Goethe was in a classical. Apollo did not content him, it had to be Dionysus. Was he no longer sure of himself, as Goethe so obviously was? He once described himself as a victim of decadence, an example of the decline of the human type which he thought to be perfect and sometimes found to be represented and actualized in certain respects in Goethe. Did he perhaps really speak the final word of this humanity? At any rate, he had to cry out something which was in Goethe, and to which he occasionally gave expression, but which he wisely preferred to keep to himself—the fact that in a last and deepest isolation he and he alone was the eye and measure and master and even the essence of all things. What Goethe quietly lived out Nietzsche had to speak out continually with the nervous violence of ill-health.

Basically, when he was not engaged in polemics but spoke positively, Nietzsche never spoke except about himself. If we study him, it constantly strikes us how little he deals with material and objective problems. What he himself was not, if it did not repel him and he it, interested him only as a paradigm and symbol, or, to use his own expression, a projection of himself. And even when he repelled, and was repelled, it was only because the object concerned either could not be used as a paradigm of himself (like Christianity), or could no longer be put to this service (like the later Wagner). Nietzsche was originally a Greek philologist, but he no longer needed Greek philology when he had discovered Dionysus as "the one root of all Greek art," as "the philosophizing god," and this Dionysus was none other than himself, Friedrich Nietzsche. For a while he devoted himself with fiery energy to natural science under the banner of evolution, but when, probably in this sphere, he had discovered the "will to power" as the supreme and proper form of human existence—and this, of course, as an unmistakable but impressive symbol of his own will—the subject did not present him with any further interest or problems. He wrote concerning "Schopenhauer as Educator," but the instructive Schopenhauer was admittedly he himself. And he magnified Wagner so long as he could find and represent in him himself and his own paganism—which was no longer possible after the personal injury done him by Wagner's *Parsifal*, in which he discerned a pilgrimage to Canossa.

"Delight in things, it is said, but what is really meant is delight in oneself through the medium of things"[3]—this is something which Goethe could never have admitted. Nietzsche did not merely admit it; he openly championed it as a maxim. In fact, he never really had any other. And so Zarathustra too—and there was little need for the pride with which Nietzsche expressly assures us of the fact—is none other than he himself, and this time the true Nietzsche. Nietzsche admits that by his ophthalmic affliction he had been redeemed from "the book" and had not read for many years—"the greatest benefit which I have ever experienced."[4] For to read as the scholar reads is not to think but simply to answer to an attraction, to react. "I call it criminal that at the crack of dawn, in all the youth and freshness of his powers, the scholar—a decadent—should read a book."[5] There is apparently only one exception: "As I see it, it is one of the most singular distinctions that anyone can evince to take up a book of my own:—I myself will guarantee that he will take off his shoes, not to speak of boots. . . . When Doctor Heinrich von Stein once honestly complained that he could not understand a word of my Zarathustra, I told him that this was quite usual. To have understood, i.e., experienced six sentences of it is to be lifted on to a higher mortal plane than 'modern' men can reach."[6]

Nietzsche was of the opinion that with his Zarathustra he had given humanity a greater gift than any so far given.[7] He declared that in comparison with it the rest of human activity was poor and limited; that a Goethe or a Shakespeare could not last a single moment in this atmosphere of tremendous passion and exaltation; that face to face with Zarathustra Dante was merely a believer and not one who creates truth, a masterful spirit, a destiny; that the authors of the *Veda* were priests and unworthy to unloose the shoes of a

---

3. MA, I/I, sec. 501.
4. *Ecce Homo*, "Why I Write Such Good Books": Human, All-Too-Human, sec. 4.
5. Ibid., "Why I Am So Clever," sec. 8.
6. Ibid., "Why I Write Such Good Books," sec. 1.
7. Ibid., Preface, sec. 4.

Zarathustra. And this is only the least to be said concerning it, giving no conception of the distance, the "azure isolation" of the work. "The spirits and qualities of all great souls put together could not produce a single speech of Zarathustra."[8] Naturally this sounds disordered. But it is the position which Nietzsche indicated, to the representation of which he dedicated his life's work. And what is this position but the "I am" of humanity without the fellow-man, except that this time it is adopted without condition or restraint, in all its nakedness? I am—in "azure isolation."

Nietzsche often thought that he lived in indescribable wealth in this isolation, and these were the moments when he could beseechingly and yet also angrily point to the fact that he had infinite things to give, that infinite things were to be received from him. But then he had to contradict himself, for how could he give wealth and life and joy in this isolation? On the contrary, "when I have given myself for a moment to my Zarathustra, I walk up and down the room for half an hour, unable to master an unbearable spasm of sobbing."[9]

The desert grows: woe to those who fight it,
Stone grates on stone, the desert gulps and swallows,
And dreadful death looks gleaming brown
And cowers—life is a cowering . . .
Forget not man, hired out to pleasure,
Thou art the stone, the desert, thou art death.[10]

And how is Zarathustra to be anything for others or give anything to them? If there were others, he would not be Zarathustra. "First give thyself, O Zarathustra."[11] But he cannot do this even if he desired now that it has been and is his necessity and triumph to be "6,000 feet beyond man and time."[12] "The whole fact of man lies at a dreadful distance below him."[13]

Alone!
And who would dare
To be a guest,
Thy guest? . . .[14]

---

8. Ibid., "Why I Write Such Good Books": Thus Spoke Zarathustra, sec. 6.
9. Ibid., "Why I Am So Clever," sec. 4.
10. "Dionysos-Dithyramben": "Unter Töchtern der Wüste"; WKG, VI-3, 385.
11. Ibid., "Von der Armut des Reichsten"; WKG, VI-3, 407–8.
12. *Ecce Homo*, "Why I Write Such Good Books": Thus Spoke Zarathustra, sec. 1.
13. Ibid., Preface, sec. 4.
14. "Dionysos-Dithyramben": "Zwischen Raubvögeln"; WKG, VI-3, 387.

To whom is he, the superman, the absolute "I am," to give himself? And if there is someone, will he thank him for this or any gift?

> Who can love thee,
> The unattainable?
> Thy blessing makes all dry
> And poor in love
> —a thirsty land. . . .[15]

To this very day Nietzsche has been much admired and honored and loved. But he had no use for the fact; he could not love in return. Nothing is more striking than that he had no use at all for women. "They all love me," he could say, but without any satisfaction. He can only ignore them or heap upon them scorn and his choicest invective. And in his very rejection of them he regards himself as "the first psychologist of the eternal-feminine."[16] Yet in addition he cannot repay or be faithful to even the best and most sincere of his male friends. "At an absurdly early age, when I was only seven, I knew that no human word would reach me, but has this ever caused me any obvious concern?"[17] "An extreme candor towards me is for me a necessary condition of existence; I cannot live in conditions of insincerity. . . . This means that my intercourse with men constitutes no little problem of patience; my humanity does not consist in fellow-feeling with men, but in restraint from fellow-feeling. . . . My humanity is a continual self-conquest."[18] It is also to be noted, of course, that Nietzsche described the contempt for man, misanthropy, as his greatest danger, and one from which he thought that he had finally redeemed himself. But how? By fleeing to a height "where there are no companions to sit at the well" and drink with him.

> On the tree of the future we build our nest;
> Eagles will bring us solitary ones food in their beaks.
> Not food which the unclean may eat,
> For they would think they were eating fire,
> And burn their mouths.
>
> We have no homesteads here for the unclean,
> To their bodies and spirits our fortune
> Would be an icy cavity,

---

15. Ibid., "Von der Armut des Reichsten"; WKG, VI-3, 407.
16. *Ecce Homo*, "Why I Write Such Good Books," sec. 5.
17. Ibid., "Why I Am So Clever," sec. 10.
18. Ibid., "Why I Am So Wise," sec. 8.

And we shall live over them like strong winds,
Neighbors of the eagles and the snow and the sun,
Like strong winds.[19]

In this way Zarathustra is lord even of misanthropy. But how? "Man is for him something unshaped, material, an ugly stone which needs the sculptor." His only impulse toward man is that of the hammer to the stone.

Oh, ye men, in the stone there sleeps a picture,
The picture of all pictures!
Oh that it must sleep in the hardest and ugliest stone!
My hammer rages furiously against its prison,
And pieces fly from the stone,
But what care I![20]

Has he ever been obviously concerned that man is either unattainable or attainable only in such a way as to cause a repugnance from which he must seek that lofty refuge with the eagles and strong winds? And yet Zarathustra does frequently seem to be very greatly troubled by this inaccessibility. It is intrinsic to the superman, to Dionysus, to Zarathustra to be almost torn asunder by sorrow at having to be the superman, Dionysus, Zarathustra.

The world—a door
To a thousand deserts silent and cold!
Who has lost
What thou lost, can find no rest.

Thou standest pale
Condemned to winter wandering
Like smoke
Always seeking the cold heavens.

Fly, bird, rasping
Thy song like a wilderness-bird!—
Conceal, thou fool,
Thy bleeding heart in ice and disdain!

The crows cry
In whirring flight to the city.
—Soon it will snow
And woe then to him who has no home![21]

19. Ibid.
20. Ibid., "Why I Write Such Good Books": Thus Spoke Zarathustra, sec. 8.
21. "Mitleid hin und her (Vereinsamt)"; WKG, VII-3, 37.

The only thing is that he soon rises up again like the eagle, scorning himself for his weakness, and finding joy and exultation and self-glory in the very thing which pains him:

> Yea, I know whence I derive!
> Insatiable as the flame,
> I burn and consume myself.
> All I touch is light,
> And what I leave a cinder.
> I am indeed a flame![22]

Which prevails—the complaint or the rejoicing? "I know my fate. The memory of something dreadful will be linked with my name, of an unparalleled crisis, of the most profound clash of conscience, of a decision conjured up against everything that has so far been believed and demanded and held sacred. I am no man; I am dynamite."[23] Is this complaint, or rejoicing, or both? In the same breath Nietzsche can call himself both the incomparable bearer of good news and the "destroyer *par excellence*." "I am easily the most terrible man there has ever been, but this does not mean that I am not also the greatest benefactor." He promises that only because of him are there renewed hopes. And yet he prophesies: "There will be wars such as never were on earth. Only after me will there be high politics on earth."[24] According to view or inclination, we can be deaf to his true message, rejecting or believing either the one or the other, the *evangelion* or *dysangelion*, but his real place is beyond good and evil, not merely like that of a Hercules choosing between the two, but genuinely as the place of the superman, who conjoins good and evil and evil and good in himself, and is thus, like Voltaire, "a *grandseigneur* of the spirit,"[25] "the first true man."[26] It is thus that Nietzsche is he, and declares the fact, proclaiming himself and refusing to be mistaken. "I am the first immoralist."[27] Immoral does not mean nonmoral. There is no point in making him a bogeyman in this sense. His immoralism consists in the fact that he has the question of morality behind him, that like God he is without "tables," that he "invents" his own categorical imperative,[28] that he is his own table. With the conclusion of

22. FW, "Joke, Cunning, and Revenge," sec. 62.
23. *Ecce Homo*, "Why I Am a Destiny," sec. 1.
24. Ibid., secs. 1 and 2.
25. *Ecce Homo*, "Why I Write Such Good Books": Human, All-Too-Human, sec.1.
26. Ibid., "Why I Am a Destiny," sec. 1.
27. Ibid., "Why I Write Such Good Books": The Untimely Ones, sec. 2; "Why I Am a Destiny," secs. 2 and 5.
28. A, sec. 11.

the *Götzendämmerung* in the same year, 1888, there followed indeed a "seventh day; the stroll of a God along the Po."[29] The one who strolls in this way along the Po is the great "he" whom Nietzsche proclaims and whom he will not have mistaken for any other.

A clever man of our own day has called Nietzsche "the greatest horse-dealer of any age." It cannot be questioned that we have here a genuine short circuit, a genuine deception and self-deception. But I should hesitate to accept that severe judgment because it would apply to too many things and people whose last intentions are merely represented with less restraint and we might almost say with greater honesty by Nietzsche. Goethe, Hegel, Kant, and Leibniz would come under the same condemnation, and not just a specifically German spirit, but the spirit of all European humanity as fashioned and developed since the sixteenth century.

Outside Germany it has become customary today to represent and castigate Nietzsche as one of those who must bear responsibility, and even primary responsibility, for preparing and making possible National Socialism. There is something in this. But it must not be forgotten that Nietzsche directed his most scathing terms against the German nationalism of his age, the age of Bismarck, so that any contribution he made to its development was highly indirect. More positively, dismissing Germany as the "plain" of European culture, he liked to remember that he was half-Polish by descent, and valued no literature or culture more highly than the French. And was he not the man who at the very height of the age of Bismarck expressed the view that it would be worth looking for a time to Switzerland to escape the opportunist outlook prevailing in Germany? And, like so many others, he praised Italy, and historically the Italian Renaissance, as his true home, perversely maintaining that he found his superman most adequately portrayed in its most notorious representative, Cesare Borgia. But the Italian Renaissance was the mother and model not merely of Italian but of all European humanity in the modern age. And so Nietzsche-Zarathustra emphatically wished to be understood as a European, as the best and only and final European. If his representation of humanity is "horse-dealing," the same is true at root—a hidden and suppressed, but very real root—of a number of others as well. And if Nietzsche prepared the ground for National Socialism, the same may be said with equal justification of other manifestations and expressions of the European spirit during the last centuries. It is thus a very serious and responsible undertaking

---

29. *Ecce Homo*, "Why I Write Such Good Books": Twilight of the Idols, sec. 3.

genuinely to oppose the humanity which he represented. The same consideration holds good in respect of his mental ill-health. If it was only as one who was mentally ill that he was capable of this representation, or conversely, if he became mentally disordered in the course of it, the question who was really deranged amongst them may be seriously asked in relation to many who were perhaps healthy in mind, or seemed to be so, only because they did not or would not see that to be a consistent champion and representative of this humanity is necessarily to be or to become mentally sick. The current affirmation and accusation are so serious that there is every reason to hesitate before making them.

We now turn to the other saying: "Am I understood—Dionysus against the Crucified."

At a first glance, it does not seem as if the book will finally lead to this antithesis, or that Nietzsche all the time wishes it to be taken in the sense of this antithesis. Prior to the last five pages of the *Ecce Homo* we are not directly prepared for it even by the occasional flashes which anticipate this conclusion. Its pregnancy and violence do not seem to stand in any real relationship to the polemic of the book or of the life-work of Nietzsche summed up in it. Nietzsche was an indefatigable fighter. Proclaiming that existence on high, he could hardly be otherwise. He was always against what others were for. "I am the anti-donkey *par excellence*, and therefore a monster in world history." The continuation is, of course, as follows: "In Greek, and not only in Greek, I am the Antichrist." And under this title Nietzsche wrote a whole book in 1886. Yet we cannot conclude from the book that this was more than one of the many fronts on which he was active as "anti-donkey." Nietzsche attacked the philosophy, morals, art, science, and civilization of his own and most earlier times, and in none of these spheres did he fail to leave dead and wounded behind him. Often rather sketchily in detail, but always with a sure intuition for essentials, for true correspondence and opposition, he attempted with equal taste and ruthlessness in all these fields a "transvaluation of all values" in the light of the superman and his will to power. It was only natural, therefore, that he should also attack Christianity. But that as "anti-donkey" he should supremely and decisively be "Antichrist," that everything should finally become a formal crusade against the cross, is not immediately apparent, but has to be learned and noted from a reading of Nietzsche. Yet it must be learned and noted if we are to understand him.

The strange culmination in the *Ecce Homo* is no mere freak. For the book about Antichrist was not just one among many. Nietzsche did not fight on all fronts in all his books. And yet there is not a single one of them, so far as I can see, in which he did not have whole sections or notable individual statements devoted to Christianity and directed in more or less violent polemic against it. And the polemic gained in weight and severity with the passage of time. We might describe this conflict as a swelling base accompanying the others and finally overwhelming and taking them up into itself, until finally there is only the one theme: "Dionysus against the Crucified."

But a second point has also to be learned and noted. The Antichrist has a definite and concrete sense. If he opposes Dionysus to the Crucified, according to the last five pages of the *Ecce Homo* this means that he opposes him, or rather himself, to what he calls Christian morality. Already in the sphere of morals as such it might have been said that this was not just one of Nietzsche's foes but like Christianity itself the great enemy which he always had in view when he fought the philosophy, art, science, and civilization of his time. From the very outset Nietzsche was concerned about ethics, and it was for this reason and in this sense that he was an "immoralist." And morality and Christianity finally coalesced for him in a single detestable form, so that wherever he encountered morality he thought that he could see and deplore and attack Christianity. The last five pages of the *Ecce Homo* begin with the words: "But in a very different sense as well I have chosen the word immoralist as my banner, my badge of honor; I am proud to have this word as a mark of distinction from humanity. For no one previously has experienced Christian morality as something beneath him. For this there was required a hardness, a perspective, a hitherto unheard-of psychological depth and radicalness. Christian morality has previously been the Circe of all thinkers—they stood in its service. Who before me has descended to the depths from which there gushes out the poison of this kind of ideal —of world-renunciation?"[30] And then he continues: "Am I understood?—What separates and marks me off from the rest of humanity is that I have discovered Christian morality." Discovered it as that which has corrupted humanity! "Not to have seen this before seems to me to be the greatest stain which humanity has on its conscience . . . an almost criminal counterfeiting *in psychologicis*. Blindness in face of Christianity is the crime *par excellence*, a crime against life itself. . . . Millennia and nations, first and last, philosophers and old

---

30. Ibid., "Why I Am a Destiny," sec. 6.

wives—apart from five or six moments of history, and myself as the seventh—have all been equally guilty in this respect."[31] And again: "Am I understood? . . . The discovery of Christian morality is an event without parallel, a veritable catastrophe. Whoever sheds light on it is a *force majeure*, a destiny, breaking the history of humanity into two parts. One either lives before him or after him. . . . The lightning of truth shatters that which formerly stood completely secure. Let him who understands what is destroyed see to it whether he has anything still in his hands."[32] Nietzsche means that which must now be destroyed (it is not yet destroyed) on the basis of this epoch-making discovery. He thus concludes with Voltaire: *Ecrasez l'infâme*. And this is what leads him to his final word: "Am I understood?—Dionysus against the Crucified."

It is not self-evident that Nietzsche's general offensive should finally be against Christianity in this sense and under this sign. Again, in the *Ecce Homo* itself and the earlier writings there seems at first to be a certain discrepancy of polemical standpoint. The offense of modern man is primarily at the incredible fact of the past reaching from remote ages into the present in the form of Christianity. "When on a Sunday morning we hear the old bells sounding, we ask ourselves: Is it really possible? This all has to do with a crucified Jew of two thousand years ago who said that he was the Son of God."[33] The Greek in him is offended at the "non-Greek element in Christianity."[34] The philologist is offended at the exegetical and historical methods of the apostle Paul: "All these holy epileptics and seers did not possess a thousandth particle of the integrity of self-criticism with which a modern philologist reads a text or tests the truth of a historical event. . . . In comparison with us, they are moral cretins."[35] He is also incensed at the imprudence, impatience, and crudity of modern Christian theologians which drive the philologist in him almost to frenzy.[36] Again, the aesthete in him experiences "a kind of inexpressible aversion at contact with the New Testament": little, bad-mannered bigots who quite uncalled-for try to speak about the deepest problems; a quite undistinguished type of man with the swelling claim to have more and indeed all value; something of *foeda*

31. Ibid., sec. 7.
32. Ibid., sec. 8.
33. MA, I/I, sec. 113.
34. Ibid., sec. 114.
35. WM, sec. 171.
36. A, sec. 52.

superstitio; something from which we withdraw our hands in case of defilement.[37] "We would no more choose to be 'early Christians' than Polish Jews. . . . They have a nasty smell. I have looked in vain even for one redeeming feature in the New Testament. It does not contain anything free or generous or open or sincere. Humanity has not even made its first beginning at this point."[38] Arguments are also used which show that it was not for nothing that Nietzsche was the friend of F. Overbeck. The greatest witness against Christianity is the pitiable figure of the everyday Christian, whose complacency—he has no thought of seeking his salvation with fear and trembling—is a clear demonstration that the decisive assertions of Christianity are of no importance.[39] It is the Church, which is the very thing against which Jesus preached and taught His disciples to fight, embodying the triumph of that which is anti-Christian no less than the modern state and modern nationalism.[40]

It is to be noted that the fact that Nietzsche will have nothing to do with God is so self-evident that it plays no part at all in his arguments against Christianity. In the *Ecce Homo* he said that he knew atheism neither as an experience nor as an event, but by instinct. "God is dead"—there is no need for heat or polemics. But is he quite so sure about this? The Dionysus-dithyrambs of 1888 show that he must have had some misgivings on the point. An "unknown God" obtrudes his obviously dangerous being in the speeches of a curious opponent of Zarathustra, and he is not a complete stranger to Nietzsche himself, this hunter, thief, robber, bandit, this great enemy, this executioner-God, etc., who tries to penetrate into his heart, his most secret thoughts.[41] But we need not pursue this aspect. Nietzsche's heart was not in contesting the existence of God, or in the other arguments to which we have referred. His central attack, into which he flung himself with all his force, was upon what he called Christian morality. All his other assaults upon Christianity derive their secret strength, and are initiated and directed, from this point. Even in the *Antichrist* this motif has become the *cantus firmus*, suppressing all the others.

But what is the absolutely intolerable and unequivocally perverted element which Nietzsche thinks that he has discovered, and must

37. WM, sec. 175.
38. A, sec. 46.
39. MA, I/I, sec. 116.
40. WM, secs. 168 and 213.
41. "Dionysos-Dithyramben": "Klage der Ariadne"; WKG, VI-3, 397.

fight to the death, in Christian morality, and in this as the secret essence of all morality? Why is it that he must finally act in this matter as if there were no other foe upon earth, and no more urgent task than to vanquish it? The answer is given by Nietzsche himself with a hundred variations and nuances the complicated pattern of which we cannot follow, but the content of which is perfectly clear. It is because Christianity is not really a faith, and is not really "bound to any of its shameless dogmas," and does not basically need either metaphysics, asceticism, or "Christian" natural science, but is at root a practice, and is always possible as such, and in the strict sense has its "God" in this practice,[42] that Nietzsche encounters it as the last enemy on his own true field. For he himself is finally concerned about a definite practice; he is decisively an ethicist. And he encounters it as an enemy because it opposes to Zarathustra or Dionysus, the lonely, noble, strong, proud, natural, healthy, wise, outstanding, splendid man, the superman, a type which is the very reverse, and so far has managed to do this successfully with its blatant claim that the only true man is the man who is little, poor, and sick, the man who is weak and not strong, who does not evoke admiration but sympathy, who is not solitary but gregarious—the mass-man. It goes so far as to speak of a crucified God, and therefore to identify God Himself with this human type, and consequently to demand of all men not merely sympathy with others but that they themselves should be those who excite sympathy and not admiration. "The neighbor is transfigured into a God . . . Jesus is the neighbor transposed into divinity, into a cause awakening emotion."[43]

"The absurd residuum of Christianity, its fables, concept-spinning, and theology, do not concern us; they could be a thousand times more absurd, and we should not lift a finger against them. But this ideal we contest."[44] Nietzsche contests it as the greatest misfortune of the human race thus far. For it was the practical victory of a religion and morality of slaves, of failures, of those who go under, of the colorless, the mistaken, the worthless, the under-world, the ghetto, the variegated mass of abjects and rejects, those who creep and crawl on the earth revolting against all that is lofty.[45] It was "typically Socialist teaching." "What I do not like at all about this Jesus of Nazareth and His apostle Paul is that they put so many things into the heads of little people, as though their modest virtues were of some

42. A, sec. 39; WM, sec. 212.
43. WM, sec. 176.
44. WM, sec. 252.
45. A, secs. 22, 43, and 51.

value. The price was too high; for they have brought into disrepute the far more valuable qualities of virtue and manhood, opposing a bad conscience to the self-esteem of the excellent soul, and betraying even to self-destruction the noble, generous, bold, excessive inclinations of the strong."[46] And this pernicious ideal is Christianity both in kernel and in substance right up to the present day. It has been able to insinuate itself into the whole of Western culture, philosophy, and morality to their great detriment, namely, at the price of the surrender of their Greek inheritance and their surreptitious and flagrant barbarization. And apart from six or seven upright figures no one has ever even noticed the fact right up to the present time. "God has chosen what is weak and foolish and ignoble and despised in the eyes of the world, is how the formula ran, and *décadence* conquered *in hoc signo*. God on the cross—do we still not understand the terrible background significance of this symbol?—Everything that suffers, everything that hangs on the cross, is divine. We all hang on the cross and therefore we are all divine. . . . We alone are divine. . . . Christianity was a victory, and a more excellent way went down before it—Christianity is the greatest misfortune of the human race thus far."[47]

This was what Nietzsche discovered as Christian morality, and this was his attack against it: the attack in which all his onslaughts on Christianity finally have both their origin and issue; the attack which finally emerged in *Ecce Homo* as the common denominator of his whole Dionysian offensive. What happened to the man that he had finally to burst out in this frenzied way and to give to his whole lifework the stamp of this outburst: Dionysus against the Crucified?

If we are to understand what took place, we must again draw some comparisons. Goethe, too, had no great time for Christianity. Nor did he merely repudiate the enthusiasm of his friend Lavater and similar contemporary manifestations of Christianity, but there lived and reverberated in him something of the Greek to whom the cross is foolishness, and we may even suspect that he was personally a far more obstinate pagan than Nietzsche. But his repudiation remained cool and good-tempered and mild. For what are the occasional slights which he allowed himself, as in his famous juxtaposition of the four annoyances, "tobacco-smoke, bugs, garlic, and [†]"? As he was content to be Apollo or preferably Zeus, as he did not think of dramatizing himself and his Hellenism in the form of Diony-

---

46. WM, secs. 209 and 205.
47. A, sec. 51.

sus (he finally rejected this possibility in his Tasso, who is certainly no Dionysus), so he never even dreamed of compromising himself by explicitly and passionately opposing Christianity as Nietzsche did. And the same is true of the great philosophical Idealists of the time, of Kant, Fichte, Schelling, and Hegel. If they could not make much of the Christianity of the New Testament, they were restrained and cautious and sparing in their criticisms, trying to interpret it as positively as possible within the framework of their systems, within the limits of their own understanding. They did not oppose to it any Zarathustra. Among them there was indeed a Herder and a Schleiermacher, with their strange but subjectively quite seriously meant attachment to Christianity and the Church. It is a little different with the heirs and disciples of this classical period. We undoubtedly have to say of a Feuerbach or a Strauß that—more akin to Nietzsche—they suffered all their lives from Christianity, and made it their main task to combat it. But on poor Strauß Nietzsche looked down as from a tower and laughed. He did not even remotely see himself as in the same class. And he was right. What was their critical philosophy and philosophy of religion to him, their biblical and dogmatic criticism, their contesting of Christianity in the name of modern reason and the modern view of things? Strauß certainly could not have introduced a Dionysus-Zarathustra (any more than Martin Werner in our own day), and certainly not the friend of nature, Feuerbach.

The new thing in Nietzsche was the fact that the development of humanity without the fellow-man, which secretly had been the humanity of the Olympian Goethe and other classical figures as well as the more mediocre, reached in him a much more advanced, explosive, dangerous, and yet also vulnerable stage—possibly its last. The new thing in Nietzsche was the man of "azure isolation," six thousand feet above time and man; the man to whom a fellow-creature drinking at the same well is quite dreadful and insufferable; the man who is utterly inaccessible to others, having no friends and despising women; the man who is at home only with the eagles and strong winds; the man whose only possible environment is desert and wintry landscape, the man beyond good and evil, who can exist only as a consuming fire. And so the new thing in Nietzsche's relationship to Christianity necessarily consisted in the fact that this pressed and embarrassed him in a way which the others had not seen, or at most had only sensed. On this view Christianity seemed to be so incomparably dreadful and harassing, presenting such a Medusa aspect, that he immediately dropped all the other polemics which he needed to proclaim his Zarathustra in favor of the necessary battle against this newly discovered side of Christianity, and all the other attacks on it, whether in the form of the dignified rejection of Goethe, the speculative reinterpretation of the classical Idealists, or the rational objections of their successors, necessarily seemed to him to be irrelevant, stupid, and even—and especially—frivolous. These predecessors had not seen how serious the matter was or how much was at stake. They could not do so, because on the positive side they did not go far enough and were not consistent enough. At bottom, they really knew nothing of the "azure isolation" of the superman. They had been left far, far behind by Zarathustra. They still crept along the ground, having only an inkling of the proximity of the eagles and strong winds in which alone real man can breathe. How could they see the true danger in Christianity? How could they fail either to reach a frivolous compromise with this enemy, or, if they knew and attacked it as such, to commit the serious error of leaving it intact where it was really dangerous? Nietzsche, however, was consistent on this positive side. He trod the way of humanity without the fellow-man to the bitter end. And this enabled him, and him alone, to see the true danger at this point.

And the true danger in Christianity, which he alone saw at the climax of that tradition, and on account of which he had to attack it with unprecedented resolution and passion—and with all the greater resolution and passion because he was alone—was that Christianity—what he called Christian morality—confronts real man, the superman, this necessary, supreme, and mature fruit of the whole development of true humanity, with a form of man which necessarily questions and disturbs and destroys and kills him at the very root. That is to say, it confronts him with the figure of suffering man. It demands that he should see this man, that he should accept this presence, that he should not be man without him but with him, that he must drink with him at the same source. Christianity places before the superman the Crucified, Jesus, as the Neighbor, and in the person of Jesus a whole host of others who are wholly and utterly ignoble and despised in the eyes of the world (of the world of Zarathustra, the true world of men), the hungry and thirsty and naked and sick and captive, a whole ocean of human meanness and painfulness. Nor does it merely place the Crucified and His host before his eyes. It does not merely will that he see Him and them. It wills that he should recognize in them his neighbors and himself. It aims to bring him down from his height, to put him in the ranks which begin with the Crucified, in the midst of His host. Dionysus-Zarathustra, it says, is not a God but a man, and therefore under the cross of the Crucified and one of His host. Nor can Dionysus-Zarathustra redeem himself, but the Crucified alone can be his Redeemer. Dionysus-Zarathustra is thus called to live for others and not himself. Here are his brothers and sisters who belong to him and to whom he belongs. In this Crucified, and therefore in fellowship with this mean and painful host of His people, he has thus to see his salvation, and his true humanity in the fact that he belongs to Him and therefore to them. This Crucified is God Himself, and therefore God Himself is only for those who belong to His host. They are then the elect of God. And Dionysus-Zarathustra can be an elect of God only if he belongs to them. Away, then, the six thousand feet, the azure, the isolation, the drinking from a lonely well! Everything is back to disturb and destroy the isolation. The fellow-man has returned whom Zarathustra had escaped or to whom he merely wanted to be a hammer, and he has returned in a form which makes escape impossible (because it embodies something which even Zarathustra cannot escape) and which makes all hammering futile (because in this form of suffering man there is nothing really to hammer).

This was the new thing which Nietzsche saw in Christianity and which he had to combat because he found it so intolerable, wounding, and dangerous. It was for this reason that in the last resort his "anti-donkey" meant Antichrist. And it was only perhaps a relic of the frivolity of which he accused others that sometimes he could act as if Christianity were mere donkey-dom and he could meet it with the corresponding attitudes and measures. We might well ask how it was that all their life long even Strauß and Feuerbach found it necessary to keep hammering away at what they declared to be so bankrupt a thing as Christianity, especially in a century when it no longer cut a very imposing figure outwardly, and the battle against it had long since ceased to be a heroic war of liberation. But we have certainly to ask why Nietzsche was guilty of the Donquixotry of acting in the age of Bismarck as if the Christian morality of I Cor. 1 constituted the great danger by which humanity necessarily found itself most severely imperiled at every turn. Yet the fact remains that Nietzsche did take up arms against Christianity, and especially the Christianity of I Cor. 1, as if it were a serious threat and no mere folly. And he had to do so. We cannot explain this necessity in purely historical terms, which in this context means psychological and psycho-pathological. That Nietzsche became deranged in this attack, or that he was deranged to undertake it, merely throws light on the fact; it does not alter the necessity. The one who as the heir, disciple, and prophet of the Renaissance and its progeny discovered the superman was quite unable—irrespective of historical and psychological circumstances—to overlook the fact that in Western culture, in face of every repudiation, reinterpretation, or assault, persisting in spite of every evacuation, there existed at least in the form of the Greek New Testament such a thing as Christianity, so that from the pages of the New Testament he was inevitably confronted by that figure, and could only recognize in that figure the direct opposite of his own ideal and that of the tradition which culminated in him, and was forced to protest and fight against it with the resolution and passion which we find in Nietzsche, not as against asininity, but with the final resolution which is reserved for a mortal threat.

Naturally there is an element of caricature in his depiction. Those who try to fight the Gospel always make caricatures, and they are then forced to fight these caricatures. Nietzsche's caricature consists in his (not very original) historical derivation of Christianity from a revolt on the part of slaves or the proletariat, for which Paul and other mischievous priests provided a metaphysical foundation and superstructure, and which thus became an incubus on the unhappy West. We all grasp at such aids as are available. And the nineteenth century had tried to bolster up Christianity with historical interpretations of this kind. Nietzsche was undoubtedly conditioned by his age when he thought that he could regard Christianity as typical Socialist teaching and contest it as such; for there did not lack those who in his own time thought that they should praise and commend it as typical Socialist teaching, or at least find a positive place for it as a transitional stage. At this point Nietzsche was perhaps loyally and sincerely a little class-conditioned. According to the Marxist analysis, he belonged to the middle class, although in a form worthy of Zarathustra. In this respect he was at one with D. F. Strauß, to whom the moderate Social Democratic teaching of the period was as a red rag to a bull. But this is not really essential. The caricature which he served up was itself an element in his resistance and attack. And of this attack we have to say that it was well aimed, that it centered on the point which was vital for Nietzsche as the most consistent champion and prophet of humanity without the fellow-man. It is another matter, and one that objectively considered is to the praise of Nietzsche, that he thus hurled himself against the strongest and not the weakest point in the opposing front. With his discovery of the Crucified and His host he discovered the Gospel itself in a form which was missed even by the majority of its champions, let alone its opponents, in the nineteenth century. And by having to attack it in this form, he has done us the good office of bringing before us the fact that we have to keep to this form as unconditionally as he rejected it, in self-evident antithesis not only to him, but to the whole tradition on behalf of which he made this final hopeless sally.

Contributors

Max L. Baeumer—Professor of German and Permanent Member of Institute for Research in the Humanities, University of Wisconsin. Author: *Das Dionysische in den Werken Wilhelm Heinses* (1964); *Heinse Studien* (1966); editor and contributor to *Toposforschung* (1973); *W. Heinse: Ardinghello* (1975); articles on Nietzsche, Luther, Hamann, Winckelmann, Hölderlin, and others.

Karl Barth (d. 1968)—Formerly Professor of Theology, University of Bonn (where he refused to take the oath of allegiance to Hitler), later University of Basel. The most important Christian theologian of the twentieth century. Among his numerous and epoch-making publications are: *Der Römerbrief* (1918); *Das Wort Gottes und die Theologie* (1928); *Credo* (1935); and *Die Kirchliche Dogmatik* (1932–62), from which his chapter in this book is excerpted.

Diana Behler—Professor of German and Comparative Literature and Chairman, Department of Germanics, University of Washington. Author: *The Theory of the Novel in Early German Romanticism* (1978); articles on Nietzsche, Lessing, Herder, Fr. Schlegel, Thomas Mann, and Henry Crabb Robinson. She is a collaborator on the forthcoming English edition of Nietzsche's works based on the Colli-Montinari *Studienausgabe*.

Eugen Biser—Professor of Christian Thought and the Philosophy of Religion, University of Munich. Author: *"Gott ist tot": Nietzsches Destruktion des christlichen Bewußtseins* (1962); *Theologische Sprachtheorie und Hermeneutik* (1970); *Theologie und Atheismus* (1972); *Glaubensverständnis: Grundriß einer hermeneutischen Fundamentaltheologie* (1975); numerous articles in his field.

Brendan Donnellan—Lecturer, University of Tübingen. Author: *Nietzsche and the French Moralists* (1982); articles on Nietzsche and the history of ideas.

Israel Eldad (Scheib)—Lecturer in Humanities, Haifa Technion. Author: *Ma'aser Rishon* (1953), memoirs of the underground; *Hegyonot Mikra* (1958), philosophy of the Bible; *The Jewish Revolution: Jewish*

Statehood (1971). Editor of *Sullam*. He received the Tschernikovsky Prize for his translation of Nietzsche's works into Hebrew; he has also translated Walter Kaufmann's *Nietzsche: Philosopher, Psychologist, Antichrist* into Hebrew.

Sander L. Gilman—Professor and Chairman, Department of German Literature, Cornell University. Author: *Form und Funktion: Eine strukturelle Untersuchung der Romane Klabunds* (1971); *The Parodic Sermon in European Perspective* (1974); *Bertolt Brechts Berlin* (1976); *Nietzschean Parody* (1976); *Wahnsinn, Text und Kontext. Die historischen Wechselbeziehungen der Literatur, Kunst und Psychiatrie* (1981); numerous articles on Nietzsche and others in his field.

Georges Goedert—Professor of Philosophy, Centre Universitaire, Luxembourg. Author: *Albert Camus et la question du bonheur* (1969); *Nietzsche critique des valeurs chrétiennes* (1977), a chapter of which appears in the present volume in translation; articles on Nietzsche, Schopenhauer, and Camus.

Gerd-Günther Grau—Professor of Philosophy, University of Hannover. Author: *Christlicher Glaube und intellektuelle Redlichkeit: Eine religionsphilosophische Studie über Nietzsche* (1958); *Die Selbstauflösung des christlichen Glaubens: Eine religionsphilosophische Studie über Kierkegaard* (1963).

Robert M. Helm—Worrell Professor of Philosophy, Wake Forest University. Author: *The Gloomy Dean: The Thought of William Ralph Inge* (1962); co-editor and contributor, *Studies in Nietzsche and the Classical Tradition* (1976, 1979); co-author, *Meaning and Value in Western Thought*, Vol. 1 (1981).

Hans Küng—Professor of Ecumenical Theology, University of Tübingen. Author of many books, including: *Freiheit der Christen* (1971); *Wozu Priester?* (1971); *Fehlbar? Eine Bilanz* (1973); *Christsein* (1974); *Jesus in Widerstreit: Ein jüdisch-christlicher Dialog* (1976); *Existiert Gott?* (1978); *Wegzeichen in die Zukunft* (1980); *Kunst und Sinnfrage* (1980); and numerous articles in his field.

Charles Lewis—Associate Professor of Philosophy, Wake Forest University. Author of articles on logic and religious belief, also of studies of Karl Barth and D. Z. Phillips.

Bernd Magnus—Professor and Chairman, Department of Philosophy, University of California, Riverside. Co-founder with Walter Kaufmann of the North American Nietzsche Society, of which he is Executive Secretary. Co-author: *Cartesian Essays* (1969); author: *Heidegger's Metahistory of Philosophy* (1970); *Nietzsche's Existential Imperative* (1978); and numerous articles in his field. He is an editor of the forthcoming English edition of Nietzsche's works based on the Colli-Montinari *Studienausgabe*.

Harry Neumann—Professor of Philosophy and Government, Scripps College and Claremont Graduate School. Author: articles on the philosophy of history, Nietzsche, Plato, and Socrates. Director, Scripps Association for the Study of Freedom.

James C. O'Flaherty—Professor of German, Wake Forest University. Member, at the invitation of Walter Kaufmann, Organizing Committee, North American Nietzsche Society. Among his books: *Hamann's Socratic Memorabilia* (1967); editor and contributor, *Studies in Nietzsche and the Classical Tradition* (1976, 1979); *Johann Georg Hamann* (1979). Articles on Nietzsche and others in his field.

Jörg Salaquarda—Professor of Theology, Johannes Gutenberg University, Mainz. Editor-in-chief of *Nietzsche Studien* (1972–); *Nietzsche* (1980); author of articles on Nietzsche's view of Christianity and myth as well as the will to power.

Timothy F. Sellner—Associate Professor of German, Wake Forest University. Co-editor and translator, *Studies in Nietzsche and the Classical Tradition* (1976, 1979); editor and translator, Theodor Gottlieb von Hippel's *On Improving the Status of Women* (1979); articles on Schiller and Tieck.

Josef Simon—Professor of Philosophy, University of Tübingen. Author: *Das Problem der Sprache bei Hegel* (1966); *Hamann: Schriften zur Sprache* (1967); *Sprache und Raum* (1969); *Philosophie und linguistische Theorie* (1971); *Wahrheit als Freiheit* (1978); *Sprachphilosophie* (1981); numerous articles in his field.

Joan Stambaugh—Professor of Philosophy, Hunter College. Author: *Nietzsche's Thought of Eternal Return* (1972); she has also written on the philosophical significance of music as well as articles on Nietzsche and Heidegger. She is a collaborator on the forthcoming English edition of Nietzsche's works based on the Colli-Montinari *Studienausgabe*.

Index

The Index includes the essays of all contributors, but not the Introduction.

Abraham (Bible), 67, 77
    (character in Kierkegaard) 246, 248
Adam, 41, 65, 68, 184, 277
Alderman, Harold
    Nietzsche's Gift, 279n.
Alexander II (Tsar), 208
Alkabets, Salomon, 217
Alt, A. Tilo (ed.), 277n.
Angelus Silesius (Johannes Scheffler), 284
Anselm of Canterbury, 24
    Proslogion, 24, 85n.
Anstett, Jean-Jacques (see Behler, Ernst)
Antiochus (Epiphanes), 216
Apollo, 58, 113, 276, 292, 293, 357, 369
Archilocus, 280
Arendt, Hannah
    Men in Dark Times, 193n.
Ariadne, 96n., 287
    "Ariadne's Lament," 92, 96, 286, 367n.
Aristotle, 253, 266, 278
    Metaphysics, 84n.
    Physics, 39n.
Arnold, Matthew, 213
Ashton, E. B. (trans.), 159
Ashtoreth, 66
Augustine (Aurelius Augustinus), 91, 109, 171, 231, 320n.
    De libero arbitrio, 24
Averroes, 229

Baal, 66
Baeumer, Max
    "Lutherfeiern und ihre politische Manipulation," 147n., 160
Baker, J. A. (trans.), 75n., 77n.
Barth, Karl
    Church Dogmatics, 353n.
Barton, Dorothea (trans.), 77n.

Bathsheba, 51
Bauer, Bruno, 149
Bäumler, Alfred
    Bachofen und Nietzsche, 327
    Nietzsche, der Philosoph und Politiker, 333n.
    Nietzsche in seinen Briefen (ed.), 16n.
Beckett, Samuel, 348
Beethoven, Ludwig van, 150
Behler, Diana
    "Nietzsche and Lessing: Kindred Thoughts," 178n.
    "Lessing's Legacy to the Romantic Concept of the Poet-Priest," 185n.
Behler, Ernst (ed. with Jean-Jacques Anstett and Hans Eichner) *Kritische Friedrich-Schlegel Ausgabe*, 180n.
Benz, Ernst, 101, 159
    Nietzsches Ideen zur Geschichte des Christentums und der Kirche, 101n., 145, 150n., 158, 159n.
Bergson, Henri, 335, 336, 337, 338
    L'évolution créatrice, 336n.
Bernoulli, Carl Albrecht, 62, 116n.
    Franz Overbeck und Friedrich Nietzsche: Eine Freundschaft, 63n., 103n., 167n.
Bertram, Ernst, 102, 159, 328
    "Nietzsches Goethebild," 327n.
    Nietzsche: Versuch einer Mythologie, 102n., 148n., 159, 328n.
Best, Otto
    "Noch einmal: Vernunft und Offenbarung," 199n.
Biser, Eugen
    "Das Desiderat einer Nietzsche-Hermeneutik," 17n., 88n.
    Die Gleichnisse Jesu, 24n., 26n.
    "*Gott ist tot*": *Nietzsches Destruktion des christlichen Bewußtseins*, 24n.,

26n., 88n., 320n.
Der Helfer: Eine Vergegenwärtigung Jesu, 86n.
"Der Leidensgefährte," 96n.
"Nietzsches Kritik des christlichen Gottesbegriffs und ihre theologischen Konsequenzen," 18n., 24n., 27n., 97n.
"Nietzsche und Dante. Ein werkbiographischer Strukturvergleich," 87n.
Theologie und Atheismus: Anstöße zu einer theologischen Aporetik, 90n.
Theologische Sprachtheorie und Hermeneutik, 24n.
Bismarck, Otto von, 148, 150, 151, 153, 157, 363, 372
Blondel, Eric
"Nietzsche: Life as Metaphor," 276n.
Bluhm, Heinz, 145, 159
"Das Lutherbild des jungen Nietzsche," 145n., 148n., 149n., 150n., 159n.
"Nietzsche's Final View of Luther and the Reformation," 145n.
"Nietzsche's Idea of Luther in *Menschliches, Allzumenschliches*," 145n.
"Nietzsche's View of Luther and the Reformation in *Morgenröte* and *Fröhliche Wissenschaft*," 145n.
Böhme, Jacob, 284
Bohnenstädt, Elisabeth
(ed.) Nicholas of Cusa, *De visione Dei*, 93n.
Boman, Thorleif
A Study of Hebrew Thought, 290n.
Borgia, Cesare, 308, 363
Bothe, B., 177n.
Bouchard, Donald F. (trans.), 191n.
Brahma, 53
Brandes, Georg, 89n., 110n., 161n., 239
Friedrich Nietzsche, 143n.
Breazeale, Daniel (trans. and ed.), 274n.
Brentano, Franz, 87, 88
Die Lehre Jesu und ihre bleibende Bedeutung, 87n.
"Nietzsche als Nachahmer Jesu," 87n.
Bromiley, G. W. (ed.), 353n.

Brummack, Jürgen (ed.)
Heinrich Heine: Epoche—Werk—Wirkung, 219n.
Brutus, 87
Buber, Martin, 86n.
Zwei Glaubensweisen, 86n.
Buchanan, Emerson (trans.), 75n.
Buddha, 342
Bultmann, Rudolf, 27
Theologie des Neuen Testaments, 105n.
"Zum Problem der Entmythologisierung," 27n.
Burckhardt, Jakob, 25n., 87
Buri, Fritz
Kreuz und Ring. Die Kreuzestheologie des jungen Luther und die Lehre von der ewigen Wiederkunft in Nietzsches "Zarathustra," 144-45n.
Buttrick, George Arthur
The Interpreter's Bible (ed.), 77n.

Cain, 65
Calvin, John, 109
Chadwick, Henry (trans.), 193
Chater, A. G. (trans.), 143
Christ (see Jesus)
Cicero, Marcus Tullius, 118n.
Circe, 22
Colie, Rosalie L.
"Literary Paradox," 284n.
Colli, Giorgio, 188
(ed. with Mazzino Montinari), *Kritische Gesamtausgabe*, 100n.
Courberive, J. de
Génies dévoyés, Luther-Nietzsche-Hitler, 144n.

Dannhauser, Werner
Nietzsche's View of Socrates, 206n.
Dante Alighieri, 87, 109, 358
Danto, Arthur
Nietzsche as Philosopher, 276n.
David, 47, 50, 51, 56, 122, 216, 288
DeLaura, David J.
Hebrew and Hellene in Victorian England, 213n.
Deleuze, Gilles
Nietzsche et sa philosophie, 326n.
Denifle, Heinrich, 145
Descartes, René, 231

Deussen, Paul, 270
Devil, 191
Dibelius, Martin
    "Der 'psychologische Typ des Erlösers' bei Friedrich Nietzsche," 107n.
Diogenes, 216
Dionysus (Dionysos), 25, 47, 48, 51, 58, 68, 94, 97, 111, 112, 113, 114, 116, 127, 136, 189, 190n., 276, 277n., 290, 323, 327n., 328, 340, 356, 357, 361, 364, 365, 368, 369, 370, 371, 372
Dostoevsky, Fëdor Mikhailovich, 87, 98, 106, 107, 161, 187, 295, 300, 342
Drachmann, A. B. (ed.), 239n.
Duns Scotus, 229
Dürer, Albrecht, 102

Eckhart, Meister, 277
Eichner, Hans (see Behler, Ernst)
Eichrodt, Walter
    "Einfluß der Rasse auf pathologische Erscheinungen," 209n.
    Theology of the Old Testament, 75n., 77n.
Eli, 56
Elijah, 66
Elster, Ernst (ed.), 213n.
Engels, Friedrich, 155 (see also Karl Marx)
    "Der deutsche Bauernkrieg," 155n.
Eros, 90
Esau, 77, 80
Eve, 184, 277n.

Fadiman (trans.), 134
Fairweather, Eugene R.
    A Scholastic Miscellany: Anselm to Ockham (ed.), 85n.
Farrar, Frederic W.
    History of Interpretation, 287n.
Faustus, 87
Feuerbach, Ludwig Andreas, 69, 149, 346, 370, 372
Fichte, Johann Gottlieb, 370
Fittbogen, Gottfried, 178n.
Förster, Bernard, 210, 211n.
Förster-Nietzsche, Elisabeth (see Nietzsche, Elisabeth)
Foucault, Michel
    Language, Counter-Memory, Practice, 191n.
Francis of Assisi, St., 187
Freud, Sigmund, 346
    "Friedrich Nietzsche über die Juden!" (anon.), 207n.
Friedrich Wilhelm IV, 146
Fritsch, Theodor, 211
    Handbuch der Judenfrage, 211n.

Gans, Eduard, 214n.
Gast, Peter (Heinrich Köselitz), 128, 145, 227n.
Geismar, Eduard, 241
    Søren Kierkegaard: Seine Lebensentwicklung und seine Wirksamkeit als Schriftsteller, 24n.
Gilman, Sander L.
    "The Image of the Black in the Works of Hegel and Nietzsche," 210n.
    Introducing Psychoanalytic Theory (forthcoming) 210n.
    "Moses Mendelssohn und die Entwicklung einer deutsch-jüdischen Identität," 223n.
    Nietzschean Parody, 213n.
    Seeing the Insane, 210n.
Goedert, Georges
    Nietzsche, critique des valeurs chrétiennes, 319n.
Goethe, Johann Wolfgang von, 146, 150, 156, 157, 161, 284, 327, 328, 351, 356, 357, 358, 363, 370, 371
    Faust, 41
Goeze, Johann Melchior, 193, 197, 198
Gogol, Nikolai Vasilyevich, 209
Golffing, Francis (trans.)
    The Birth of Tragedy and the Genealogy of Morals, 177n.
Granier, Jean, 335
    "La pensée nietzschéene du chaos," 335n.
    Le problème de la vérité dans la philosophie de Nietzsche, 333n.
Grau, Gerd-Günther
    Christlicher Glaube und intellektuelle Redlichkeit, 206n., 226n., 244n.
    "Realisierter oder sublimierter Wille zur Macht," 227n.

Grimm, Reinhold
  (ed. with Jost Hermand), *Deutsche Feiern,* 147n.
Grisar, Hartmann, 145
Groos, Karl
  "Der paradoxe Stil in Nietzsches Zarathustra," 284n., 285n.
Gutzkow, Karl Ferdinand, 214
  Rückblicke auf mein Leben, 214n.

Ha'am, Achad
  "Nietzscheanismus und Judentum," 207n.
Häcker, Theodor, 241n.
Hahn, Ferdinand
  Christologische Hoheitstitel. Ihre Geschichte im frühen Christentum, 88n.
Haman, 216
Hamann, Johann Georg, 265, 276, 277, 278
  Briefwechsel, 277n.
  Sämtliche Werke, 266n.
Händel, Georg Friedrich, 53
Harvey, John W. (trans.), 75n.
Hayman, Richard, 286
  Nietzsche: A Critical Life, 286n.
Heftrich, E., 177n.
Hegel, Georg Wilhelm Friedrich, 69, 124, 256, 261, 262, 319, 325, 326, 327, 351, 363, 370
  "Faith and Knowledge," 230n.
  Sämtliche Werke, 325n.
  Wissenschaft der Logik, 261n.
Heiberg, J. L. (ed.), 239n.
Heiberg, P. A. (ed.), 239n.
Heidegger, Martin, 273
  Nietzsche, 39n., 43n., 273n., 335n.
  Vorträge und Aufsätze, 333n.
  "Wer ist Nietzsches Zarathustra?" 333n.
Heimsoeth, Heinz
  Metaphysische Voraussetzungen und Antriebe in Nietzsches "Immoralismus," 319n., 340n.
Heine, Heinrich, 18, 23, 87, 213, 351
  The Baths of Lucca, 215
  "Disputation," 219, 222
  Die Harzreise, 220
  "Hebrew Melodies," 218, 219, 223

"On Poland," 214, 223
"On Religion and Philosophy in Germany," 18n., 23-24
"Princess Sabbath," 217, 218, 221, 223
Romanzero, 219
Sämtliche Werke, 213n., 215n., 216n., 221n.
Shakespeare's Girls and Women, 213
Heisenberg, Werner, 27n.
Heller, Yom Tov Lipmann, 221
Helm, Robert M. (ed.), 275n.
Henke, Dieter
  Gott und Grammatik: Nietzsches Kritik der Religion, 180n.
Henkel, Arthur (ed.), 277n.
Heraclitus, 121, 189, 338
Herder, Johann Gottfried, 276, 370
Hermand, Jost (see Grimm, Reinhold)
Hick, John, 83
  Evil and the God of Love, 83n.
Hildebrandt, Kurt, 159
  Wagner und Nietzsche. Ihr Kampf gegen das neunzehnte Jahrhundert, 159n.
Hilpert, Konrad
  "Die Überwindung der objektiven Gültigkeit," 181n.
Hirsch, Emanuel
  Lutherstudien II, 145n., 150n.
  "Nietzsche und Luther," 145, 148n.
Hitler, Adolf, 42, 144, 158, 160, 309, 310
Hitzig, Julius Eduard, 218
Höffding, Harald, 239
Hoffmeister, Johannes (ed.), 261n.
Hofmiller, Josef
  "Nietzsche," 95n., 96n.
Hölderlin, Friedrich, 87
Holdheim, William W. (trans.), 84n.
Homer, 50, 122, 216
Honecker, Erich, 160
Hosea, 55
Hultsch, Gerhard
  Friedrich Nietzsche und Luther, 144n.
Humboldt, Wilhelm von, 271
  Gesammelte Schriften, 271n.
Hume, David, 39
Huss, John, 152
Huxley, Aldous
  Brave New World, 352

Ionesco, Eugène, 348
Isaiah, 49, 54, 55
Jacob, 57, 77, 80
Jacobi, Ruth L.
 Heinrich Heines jüdisches Erbe, 213n.
Jacobs, Louis
 Essay in *Religion and Morality*, 83n.
Jacolliot, Louis
 Les législateurs religieux. Manou-Moïse-Mahomet, 100n.
Jahn, Friedrich Ludwig, 215
Jankolowitz, Samuel
 "Friedrich Nietzsche und der Antisemitismus," 207n.
Janssen, Johannes
 History of the German People, 145
Jaspers, Karl, 87, 89, 92, 98, 101, 104, 159, 181n.
 Nietzsche: An Introduction to the Understanding of His Philosophical Activity, 70n.
 Nietzsche und das Christentum, 159n., 341n.
 "Reason and Existence," 239
Jean Paul (Johann Paul Friedrich Richter)
 "Rede des toten Christus vom Weltgebäude herab, daß kein Gott sei," 27n.
Jehovah (see Yahweh)
Jehuda ben Halevy, 217, 218
Jens, Walter, 351n.
Jeremiah, 36, 67
Jesus = Christ, 24, 33, 34, 35, 36, 37, 40, 43, 46n., 48, 50, 54, 57, 59, 60, 63, 72, 73, 77, 81, 86, 87, 88, 89, 91, 92, 93, 94, 95, 97, 98, 104, 105n., 106, 107, 108, 111n., 112, 116, 117, 119, 120, 170, 176, 182, 183, 185, 186, 187, 189, 190n., 196, 197, 198, 199, 232, 233, 235, 247, 276, 282, 293, 294, 295, 297, 298, 299, 300, 303, 307, 342, 343, 344, 368, 371
Job, 67, 79, 80, 235, 237, 238, 239, 248, 249, 250
Jülicher, Adolf
 Die Gleichnisreden Jesu, 26n.
Jung, Carl G.
 Antwort auf Hiob, 238n.
Jüngel, Eberhard
 "Deus qualem Paulus creavit, dei negatio. Zur Denkbarkeit Gottes bei Ludwig Feuerbach und Friedrich Nietzsche. Eine Beobachtung," 114n.

Kafka, Franz, 87
Kanowsky, Walter
 Vernunft und Geschichte, 214n.
Kant, Immanuel, 24, 116n., 122n., 184n., 187, 237, 255, 262, 275n., 277, 278, 309, 315, 320, 326, 351, 363, 370
 "Über das Mißlingen aller Versuche in der Theodizee," 238n.
Kastil, Alfred
 (ed.) Franz Brentano, *Die Lehre Jesu und ihre bleibende Bedeutung*, 87n.
Kaufmann, Walter, 47, 48, 63, 101, 143n., 206n., 281n., 291, 307, 309, 312, 326n.
 Basic Writings of Nietzsche, 47n., 70n., 177n.
 The Birth of Tragedy and the Case of Wagner, 177n.
 Thus Spoke Zarathustra, 177n.
 The Will to Power (with R. J. Hollingdale), 50n., 69n., 70n., 177n.
Kayser, Wolfgang
 Das sprachliche Kunstwerk, 289n.
Kierkegaard, Søren, 68, 87, 136, 194, 195, 197, 199, 231, 233, 248, 295
 Concept of Dread, 248n.
 Concluding Unscientific Postscript, 179n., 180n., 194n., 197n., 198n., 244n., 246n., 247, 251n.
 Fear and Trembling, 246, 248
 For Self-Examination, 240n., 250n.
 The Instant, 240n., 242n.
 Journals, 244n.
 Papirer, 239n.
 Philosophical Fragments, 250
 Repetition, 239n., 249n., 250n.
 Samlede Vaerker, 239
Kircher, Hartmut
 Heinrich Heine und das Judentum, 213n., 214n., 216n.
Kirchhoff, Jochen
 "Zum Problem der Erkenntnis bei Nietzsche," 181n.
Kirchhoff, Theodor, 209
 Handbook of Insanity, 209n.
"Klage der Ariadne" (see "Ariadne's La-

ment")
Kleist, Heinrich von, 205, 209
Klopstock, 146
Kluckhohn, Paul (ed.), 188n.
Kolb, Jocelyne
  "Literary Decorum or the Absence of Taste," (unpublished talk), 220n.
  "Wine, Women, and Song: Sensory References in the Works of Heinrich Heine" (diss.), 220n.
Koopmann, Helmut
  "Heines 'Romanzero': Thematik und Struktur," 219n.
Köster, Peter
  "Nietzsche Kritik und Nietzsche-Rezeption in der Theologie des 20. Jahrhunderts," 75n., 181n.
  Der sterbliche Gott. Nietzsches Entwurf übermenschlicher Größe, 113n.
Kraepelin, Emil, 209
Krafft-Ebbing, Richard, 209
Krailsheimer, A. J. (trans.), 161n.
Kraus, Eberhard
  "Wie Friedrich Nietzsche über das Judentum urteilte," 207n.
Krüger, E. (trans.), 241n.
Kuhr, V., 239n.
Küng, Hans
  Does God Exist? 341n.
  "The Importance of Religion for Jung, Fromm, Frankel," 348n.
  On Being a Christian, 346n.
Kuttenkeuler, Wolfgang (ed.)
  Heinrich Heine: Artistik und Engagement, 219n.

Lafuma, Louis, 161n.
Lagarde, Paul de, 149
Lang, Fritz, 352
  Metropolis (film), 352
Lange, H. O. (ed.), 239n.
Lavater, Johann Caspar, 237, 238n., 369
Leeuw, Gerardus van der
  Religion in Essence and Manifestation, 75n., 76n.
Leibniz, Gottfried Wilhelm, 229, 256, 319, 363
Leopardi, Giacomo, 209
Lessing, Gotthold Ephraim, 236, 278, 294
  "Anti-Goeze," 198n.

  Axiomata, 197, 198n.
  "The Christianity of Reason," 200
  Eine Duplik, 197n.
  The Education of the Human Race, 185n., 191, 192, 193, 198n., 199, 200, 202, 203n., 294n.
  Nathan the Wise, 178, 194
  Rejoinder, 193
  "Die Religion Christi," 198n.
  "The Religion of Christ," 198
  Sämtliche Schriften, 193n.
Lessing, Karl, 193
Lévinas, Emmanuel
  Totalité et Infini, 273n.
Lévi-Strauss, Claude
  The Savage Mind, 281n., 294
Levy, Oscar
  The Complete Works of Friedrich Nietzsche (ed.), 50n., 144n.
Lewis, Charles
  "Divine Goodness and Worship Worthiness," 83n.
Leyen, Friedrich von der
  "Friedrich Nietzsche: Die Sprache des 'Zarathustra,' " 291n.
Lichtenberg, Georg Christoph
  "Über Physiognomik," 118n.
Locke, John, 256
Lombard, Peter, 277, 278n.
  Sententiarum liber II, 277n.
Low, Alfred D.
  Jews in the Eyes of the Germans, 207n.
Löwith, Karl, 239, 326, 327
  "Heideggers Vorlesungen über Nietzsche," 333n.
  Von Hegel zu Nietzsche, 326n.
Lubac, Henri de
  Die Tragödie des Humanismus ohne Gott, 18n.
Lüdemann, Hermann, 104-5, 106, 117n., 118n.
  Die Anthropologie des Apostels Paulus und ihre Stellung innerhalb seiner Heilslehre, 105n.
Lukács, Georg, 259
  "Nietzsche als Begründer des Irrationalismus der imperialistischen Periode," 259n.
Luther, Martin, 53, 101, 109, 118, 143, 144, 145, 146, 147, 148, 149, 150, 151,

152, 153, 154, 155, 156, 157, 158, 159, 160, 197n., 231, 243, 276, 284, 290, 341

Machiavelli, Niccolò, 178
MacIntyre, Alasdair
  (with Paul Ricoeur) *The Religious Significance of Atheism*, 79n.
Magnus, Bernd
  Nietzsche's Existential Imperative, 38n., 129n., 181n., 287n., 314
  "Nietzsche's Mitigated Skepticism," 181n.
  "Perfectibility and Attitude in Nietzsche's Übermensch" (forthcoming), 306n.
Maimonides, 217
Malachi, E. R.
  Mekubolim in Eretz Israel, 217n.
Mann, Otto, 177n.
Mann, Thomas, 87, 93
  "Nietzsches Philosophie im Lichte unserer Erfahrung," 93n., 99n.
Manu, 53, 55, 100, 122, 210, 211, 224
Martensen, Hans Lassen, 296
Martin Heidegger zum 80. Geburtstag von seiner Heimatstadt Meßkirch, 44n.
Martini, Fritz, 292
  Das Wagnis der Sprache, 292n.
Marx, Karl, 43, 149, 155, 300, 346, 351
  (with Friedrich Engels) *Werke*, 155n.
Mary, 104
Masini, Ferruccio
  "Rhythmisch-Metaphorische 'Bedeutungsfelder' in 'Also sprach Zarathustra,' " 292n.
McGovern, William M.
  From Luther to Hitler: The History of Fascist-Nazi Political Philosophy, 144n., 158n.
Mephisto, 41
Messer, August, 93, 333
  Erläuterungen zu Nietzsches Zarathustra, 93n., 333n.
Michal, 51
Middleton, Christopher (ed. and trans.), 293n.
Mirabeau, 87
Mishna, 221
Mohammed, 53, 87
Montgomery, William (trans.), 236n.

Montinari, Mazzino (see also Colli, Giorgio), 105n.
Moses, 34n., 36, 37n., 56, 63, 67, 68, 87
Most, Otto
  Zeitliches und Ewiges in der Philosophie Nietzsches und Schopenhauers, 180n.
Mühlhaupt, Erwin
  Der Kölner Dom im Zwielicht der Kirchen- und Geistesgeschichte, 153n.
Müller-Lauter, Wolfgang
  Nietzsche. Seine Philosophie der Gegensätze und die Gegensätze seiner Philosophie, 120n.
Mynster, Jacob Peter, 296

Nadler, Josef (ed.), 266n.
Napoleon, 147, 351
Nathan (Lessing), 200
Nathan (Prophet), 51, 56
Nebuchadnezzar, 216
Nelson, Donald F.
  "Nietzsche, Zarathustra and *Jesus redivivus*," 212n.
Neumann, Harry
  "The Beginning of Wisdom" (forthcoming), 38n.
  Review of Bernd Magnus, *Nietzsche's Existential Imperative*, 38n.
Newman, John Henry, 241n.
Nicholas of Cusa, 27
  De visione Dei, 27n., 93n.
Nicholas of Lyre, 287
Nietzsche, Elisabeth (Elisabeth Förster-Nietzsche)
  Das Leben Friedrich Nietzsches, 167n.
  "Nations and Fatherlands," 207
Nietzsche, Friedrich (works only)
  "Aftersong. From High Mountains," 16n.
  "An Spinoza," 35n.
  The Antichrist, 21n., 29, 30, 31, 33n., 34n., 35n., 56n., 72, 74, 78, 79, 81, 87, 89, 90n., 92n., 94, 95n., 98, 100, 101, 102, 103, 106, 107, 108, 110, 111, 112, 113, 116n., 117n., 122n., 127, 133, 157, 158, 160, 166, 169, 179, 180, 181, 184, 186, 187, 188, 192, 197, 200, 208, 210, 211, 230n., 233n., 235n., 289, 295n., 297, 298n., 299n., 300, 301n.,

302n., 303n., 304, 305, 306, 307, 328, 341, 344, 347, 362, 366n., 367, 368, 369
"Ariadne's Lament," 92, 96, 286, 367n.
"Attempt at a Self-Criticism," *The Birth of Tragedy* (1886 ed.), 96, 113n.
"The Attitude of Germans to Morality," 153
"Before the Crucifix," 93
Beyond Good and Evil, 21n., 26n., 29n., 32n., 33n., 72, 83, 84, 94, 111, 114, 116n., 120, 122n., 124n., 155, 168, 178, 207, 295n., 332n.
"Beyond Good and Evil," 17n., 26n.
The Birth of Tragedy, 22n., 39n., 96, 113, 147, 148, 159, 185, 189, 190, 276, 278, 279, 280, 320, 321, 327n., 339
"The Birth of Tragedy," *Ecce Homo*, 113n., 114n., 128n.
The Case of Wagner, 120n.
"The Case of Wagner," *Ecce Homo*, 133n., 157n., 158, 341n.
"Critique of Religion," 69
The Dawn = *The Dawn of Day*, 50n., 56n., 60n., 67, 73, 90, 109, 116, 117, 126, 127n., 128, 152, 164, 166, 167, 168, 172, 173, 230, 234n., 238n., 289, 311, 312
Dithyrambs of Dionysus, 334
Ecce Homo, 17, 21, 68, 86, 90, 94, 96, 97, 98, 99, 110, 111, 114, 116, 151, 157, 161, 187, 291n., 292, 307, 324, 346n., 356, 364, 366, 367, 369
"Excelsior," 98n.
"Exhortation to the Germans," 151
"The Four Great Errors," 29n., 79, 168
The Gay Science = *The Joyful Wisdom*, 17, 24, 30n., 31n., 32n., 33n., 35n., 44n., 57n., 66n., 69, 72, 76, 89, 94, 98n., 101n., 104, 115n., 122n., 154, 161, 173, 191, 195n., 228n., 229n., 230n., 316
"Genealogie der Moral," 91n.
Genealogy of Morals = *Toward the Genealogy of Morals*, 16, 18, 19n., 22, 23n., 36n., 44n., 47n., 69, 70, 71, 72, 74, 81n., 82, 90, 101, 104n., 109n., 122n., 123n., 124n., 156, 166, 170, 172, 173, 184n., 201, 203, 227n., 229n., 230, 233n., 237n., 305, 321, 324n.
Human, All-Too-Human, 17, 19n., 56n., 58n., 59n., 65n., 94, 119n., 144, 145, 152, 153, 163, 165, 172, 173, 183, 232n., 305n., 358n., 366n., 367n.
"Human, All-Too-Human," 151, 358n., 362n.
"The 'Improvers' of Mankind," 100n.
"Joke, Cunning, and Revenge," 362
"Journey to Hades," 161
Literary remains (see *Nachlaß*)
"Maxims and Arrows," 65n., 74
"Mitleid hin und her (Vereinsamt)," 361n.
"Morality as Anti-Nature," 59n., 109n., 122n.
"Eine Musik ohne Zukunft," 53n.
Nachlaß = *Nachgelassene Fragmente* (literary remains), 18, 23, 87, 101n., 102n., 104, 105, 106n., 108n., 109n., 110, 112n., 113n., 114n., 115n., 116n., 119n., 122, 123n., 125n., 128n., 129n., 276n., 295n., 310
"The Natural History of Morals," 120n.
"New Education of the Human Race," 203
Nietzsche contra Wagner, 133n.
"On the Future of Our Educational Institutions," 21, 147
"On Truth and Lie in an Extra-Moral Sense" = "On Truth and Lie in a Nonmoral Sense," 20, 274
Philosophy in the Tragic Age of the Greeks = *Die Philosophie im tragischen Zeitalter der Griechen*, 121n., 337
"Preface," *Ecce Homo*, 110n., 111n., 358n.
"The Problem of Socrates," 108n., 118n., 314
" 'Reason' in Philosophy," 74, 121n.
Revaluation of All Values, 106

"Schopenhauer as Educator," 358
"Skirmishes of an Untimely Man," 30n., 59n., 69n., 230n., 327n., 330n.
"Star Friendship," *The Gay Science*, 98
Thus Spoke Zarathustra, 18, 63, 67n., 128, 138, 141, 156, 167, 173, 201, 211-12, 308, 323, 327, 347, 358, 359, 361
  "At Noon," 140
  "Before Sunrise," 139n., 323n., 338n.
  "The Convalescent," 332n., 333n.
  "The Cry of Distress," 45n.
  "The Leech," 22n.
  "Of the Bestowing Virtue," 21n.
  "Of Old and New Law Tables," 332n., 339n.
  "On Child and Marriage," 35n.
  "On the Famous Wise Men," 22n., 38n.
  "On Free Death," 95n.
  "On the Great Longing," 138n.
  "On Immaculate Perception," 33n.
  "On Priests," 98n., 241n.
  "On Redemption," 137n., 317n.
  "On Those Who Are Sublime," 45n.
  "On the Thousand and One Goals," 30n.
  "On the Three Metamorphoses," 34n., 46n., 204, 340n.
  "Prologue," 334n.
  "The Soothsayer," 45n.
  "Tarantulas," 78
  "The Ugliest Man," 24n., 27n., 96n.
  "Thus Spoke Zarathustra," 128n., 324n., 359n., 361n.
Twilight of the Idols, 19, 25n., 110n., 312, 363
  "The Twilight of the Idols," 25n., 363n.
Die Unschuld des Werdens, 17n., 22n., 23n., 51n., 87n.
"Unter Töchtern der Wüste," 359n.
Untimely Meditations = *Thoughts out of Season*, 17, 146, 149, 151
  "The Untimely Ones," 21n., 67n., 362n.
"Von der Armut des Reichsten," 359n.
"Wagner in Bayreuth," 150
"We Fearless Ones," 149
"What I Owe to the Ancients," 113n., 128n.
"Why I Am a Destiny," 97n., 111n., 115n., 226n., 325n., 345n., 356n., 362n., 365n.
"Why I Am So Clever," 18n., 138n., 358n., 360n.
"Why I Am So Wise," 134n., 240n., 360n.
"Why I Write Such Good Books," 21n., 22n., 97n., 308n., 324n.
"Why the Weak Prevail," 330
The Will to Power, 16n., 20n., 22n., 23n., 32n., 33n., 35n., 36n., 39n., 43n., 44n., 50n., 51n., 52, 53n., 55n., 61n., 69n., 70n., 72, 78, 85, 91n., 95n., 96n., 100, 104n., 106, 108, 119, 125n., 136n., 143n., 165n., 168, 170, 171, 173, 228, 240n., 310n., 338, 347, 348n., 351, 366, 367n., 369n.
"Wir Philologen," 202n.
"Wishing Perfect Opponents for Oneself," 167
"Zwischen Raubvögeln," 359n.
Nimrod, 67
Novalis (Friedrich Leopold Freiherr von Hardenberg), 130, 188, 201
  "Die Christenheit oder Europa," 185n.
  Schriften, 188n.

Occam, William of, 229
Oedipus, 65
O'Flaherty, James C.
  "The Concept of Knowledge in Hamann's 'Socratic Memorabilia' and Nietzsche's 'Die Geburt der Tragödie,'" 275n.
  "Eros and Creativity in Nietzsche's *The Birth of Tragedy*," 291n.
  Johann Georg Hamann, 290n.
  "Language and Reason in the Thought of Hamann," 277n.
  Studies in Nietzsche and the Classical Tradition, 275n.

Unity and Language, 290n.
Okochi, Ryogi
    "Nietzsches Amor fati im Lichte von Karma des Buddhismus," 128n.
Olsen, Regine, 245
Olzien, Otto, 290
    Nietzsche und das Problem der dichterischen Sprache, 290n.
Otto, Rudolf
    The Idea of the Holy, 75n.
Outka, Gene H.
    (with John P. Reeder, Jr.) Religion and Morality (eds.), 83n.
Overbeck, Franz, 63, 101, 105n., 110n., 236, 293n., 356, 367
    Christentum und Kultur, 101n.
Overbeck, Ida, 167n.
Ovid, 216

Paquier, Jules
    Le protestantisme allemand, Luther-Kant-Nietzsche, 144n.
Parsifal, 308, 358
Pascal, Blaise, 87, 116n., 161, 162, 163, 164, 165, 166, 167, 168, 169, 170, 171, 172, 173, 174, 175
    Apology, 169
    Pensées, 161n., 163, 164, 165, 166, 169, 173, 174, 175
Paul (Apostle), 34, 35, 54, 57, 60, 72, 77, 78, 80, 81, 91, 92, 100, 101, 102, 103, 104, 105n., 106, 107, 108, 109, 110, 111, 112, 114, 115, 116, 117, 118, 119, 120, 123, 124, 125, 126, 127, 128n., 159, 170, 171, 182, 183, 184, 187, 191, 208, 225, 231, 234, 235, 236, 242, 284, 293, 295, 302, 303, 304, 368
Pericles, 50, 56, 122
Peter, 100, 104, 304
Peters, H. F.
    Zarathustra's Sister, 207n.
Pfeffer, Rose
    Nietzsche: Disciple of Dionysus, 111n., 114n.
Phelps, Leland R. (ed.), 277n.
Pilcz, Alexander, "Geistesstörungen bei den Juden," 209n.
Plato, 38, 50, 51, 56, 84, 87, 114, 116n., 122, 136, 161, 206, 266
    Epinomis, 84n.
    Laws, 84n.
    Republic, 33n., 39n., 40n., 84n.
    Symposium, 180n.
    Timaeus, 84n.
Podach, Erich
    Nietzsches Werke des Zusammenbruchs, 107n.
Poe, Edgar Allan, 209
Pons, Georges, 178n.
Prawer, S. S.
    Heine, The Tragic Satirist, 216n., 218n., 222
Prince Myshkin, 300
Przywara, Erich
    Das Geheimnis Kierkegaards, 241n.
Pütz, Peter, 87
    "Thomas Mann und Nietzsche," 87n.
Pythagoras, 189

Racine, Jean, 291
Rad, Gerhard von
    Deuteronomy, 77n.
    Old Testament Theology, 77n.
    Studies in Deuteronomy, 77n.
Rauschning, Hermann
    Hitler Speaks, 350n.
Reagan, Charles E. (ed. with David Stewart)
    The Philosophy of Paul Ricoeur, 190n.
Rée, Paul, 286
Reeder, John P., Jr. (see Outka, Gene H.)
Rehm, Walther
    Jean Paul—Dostojewski. Eine Studie zur dichterischen Gestaltung des Unglaubens, 27n.
Reichert, Herbert W.
    (ed. with Carl Schlechta) International Nietzsche Bibliography, 144n.
Reimarus, Hermann Samuel, 179, 193, 197, 198, 199, 200, 236
Reinke, J.
    Die schaffende Natur, 338n.
Renan, Joseph Ernest, 106, 107, 187
Richter, Johann Paul Friedrich (see Jean Paul)
Ricoeur, Paul, 75n., 190n.
    "Religion, Atheism, and Faith," 79n.
    (with Alasdair MacIntyre), The Religious Significance of Atheism, 79n.

The *Symbolism of Evil*, 75n., 79n.
Riehl, Aloys
  Friedrich Nietzsche, 327
Ries, Wiebrecht
  Friedrich Nietzsche, 206n.
Rietschel, Ernst, 146
Robespierre, Maximilien Marie Isidore, 197n.
Rohde, Erwin, 63, 150, 156
Rohrmoser, Günther, 178n.
Romundt, Heinrich, 151
Rosenthal, Ludwig
  Heinrich Heine als Jude, 213n., 218n.
Rothacker, Erich
  Poètes et penseurs, 326n.
Rougemont, Denis de
  Love Declared, 296n.
Rousseau, Jean Jacques, 59, 164, 197n.
  Confessions, 356
Runestam, Arvid
  "Nietzsches Übermensch und Luthers freier Christenmensch," 144n.

Sachs, Michael, 218
St.-Simon, Claude Henri de, 197n.
Salaquarda Jörg
  "Der Antichrist," 124n., 183n., 275n.
  "Dionysos gegen den Gekreuzigten: Nietzsches Verständnis des Apostels Paulus," 100n.
  (ed.) *Nietzsche*, 100n., 105n.
  "Umwertung aller Werte," 126n.
  Review of Bernd Magnus, *Nietzsche's Existential Imperative*, 129n.
  Review of Rose Pfeffer, *Nietzsche: Disciple of Dionysus*, 111n.
Salomé, Lou (Lou Andreas-Salomé), 128
  Friedrich Nietzsche in seinen Werken, 128n.
Salomon, Ibn Gabirol, 217
Samuel, 51, 56
Samuel, Richard (ed.), 188n.
Sandvoss, 87
Sauder, Gerhard
  "Blasphemisch-Religiöse Körperwelt," 219n.
Saul, King, 50, 51, 56, 122, 184
Savonarola, Girolamo, 197n.
Scheler, Max, 84n.

Ressentiment, 84n.
Schelling, Friedrich Wilhelm Joseph von, 135, 370
Schiller, Johann Christoph Friedrich von, 146, 150, 205
Schilson, Arno
  Lessings Christentum, 177n., 198n.
Schlechta, Karl (See Reichert, Herbert W.)
Schlegel, Friedrich, 180n.
Schleiermacher, Friedrich Daniel Ernst, 370
Schmidt, Alfred
  "Über Nietzsches Erkenntnistheorie," 259n.
Schmidt, Hermann Josef
  Nietzsche und Socrates. Philosophische Untersuchungen zu Nietzsches Socratesbild, 108n.
Schmitt, Carl
  The Concept of the Political, 33n, 34n.
Schmitz, Frederick J. (trans.), 70n.
Schmoldt, Benno
  Die deutsche Begriffssprache Meister Eckharts, 277n.
Schneidau, Herbert N.
  "The Word against the Word," 290n.
Schneider, J., 177n.
Schopenhauer, Arthur, 53, 64, 114, 149, 162, 168, 171, 326, 327, 332, 337, 338, 339, 358
  Die Welt als Wille und Vorstellung, 337n.
  The World as Will and Idea, 339
Schrattenholz, Josef
  Anti-Semiten Hammer, 207n.
Schröder, Jürgen
  G. E. Lessing: Sprache und Drama, 278n.
Schubert, Franz, 19
Schulz, Bernhard
  "Die Sprache als Kampfmittel. Zur Sprachform von Kampfschriften Luthers, Lessings und Nietzsches," 144n., 158
Schwab, George (ed., trans.), 33n.
Schweitzer, Albert, 235, 247
  Geschichte der Leben-Jesu Forschung, 235n.
  Die Mystik des Apostels Paulus, 236n.

(trans. *The Mysticism of Paul the Apostle*), ibid.
Sellner, Timothy F. (ed.), 275n.
Shakespeare, William, 150, 358
Shestov, Lev, 87
Shylock, 29, 214
Simon, Sherry (trans.), 191n.
Sinclair, E. M. (trans.), 36n.
Socrates, 38, 39, 41, 42, 43, 44, 46, 50, 51, 52, 87, 108, 109, 114n., 118n., 121, 122, 125, 178, 276n., 307
Sokel, Walter H., 87
Soloviev, Vladimir, 88
   "Short Story of the Antichrist," 88
Sonderegger, Stefan, 289-90
   "Friedrich Nietzsche und die Sprache," 290n.
Sophocles
   Oedipus at Colonus, 132n.
Spencer, Herbert, 87
Spenlé, Jean-Edouard
   La penseé allemande de Luther à Nietzsche, 144n., 158n.
Spinoza, Baruch, 36, 37, 43, 44, 59, 87, 94, 130, 131, 132, 135, 141, 142, 161
   Ethics, 131n.
   Political Treatise, 36n.
   Theological-Political Treatise, 31n., 32n., 34n., 36n., 39n., 44n.
Stalker, D. M. G. (trans.), 77
Steffen, Hans
   Nietzsche, Werk und Wirkungen, (ed.), 87n.
Stein, Heinrich von, 358
Steiner, George
   After Babel, 285n.
Sterling, Amelia Hutchinson
   Review of trans. of Baruch Spinoza, *Ethics*, 133n.
Stern, J. P., 309
   A Study of Nietzsche, 206n., 309
Stewart, David (see Reagan, Charles E.)
Stirner, Max, 206n.
   The Ego and Its Own, 39
Stolzing, Josef
   "Friedrich Nietzsche und Judentum," 207n.
Strauß, David Friedrich, 149, 236, 288, 370, 372, 373
Strauss, Leo
   Spinoza's Critique of Religion, 36n., 44n., 45n.
Strindberg, Johann August, 110n.

Tabak, Israel
   Judaic Lore in Heine, 213n.
Tertullian, 231, 233
Thielecke, Helmut, 177n.
Titus, 216
Tolstoy, Lev (Leo) Nikolaevich, 106
Torrence, T. F. (ed.), 353n.
Tosefot Yom Tov, 221
Träger, Claus, 199
   "Lessing—Kritik und Historizität," 199n.
Turner, J. E. (trans.), 75n.

Unamuno, Miguel de, 236
Unnik, Willem Cornelis van
   Evangelien aus dem Nilsand, 86n.
Uriah, 51

Vaglia, 87
Veda, 358
Vischer, Friedrich Theodor
   Aesthetics or Theory of the Beautiful, 157
Vollmer, Hans
   Nietzsches Zarathustra und die Bibel, 64n.
Voltaire (François Marie Arouet), 154, 346, 362, 366
   Essai sur les moeurs et l'esprit des nations, 155n.

Wagner, Cosima, 286
Wagner, Richard, 21, 98n., 144, 146, 147, 148, 150, 151, 156, 276, 286, 357, 358
   Gesammelte Schriften und Dichtungen, 148n.
Wallraff, Charles F. (trans.), 70n.
Weger, Karl von
   Religionskritik von der Aufklärung bis zur Gegenwart (ed.), 23n.
Wein, Hermann
   Positives Antichristentum: Nietzsches Christusbild im Brennpunkt nachchristlicher Anthropologie, 180n., 206n.
Weinberg, Kurt

Index 391

"The Impact of Ancient Greece and of French Classicism on Nietzsche's Concept of Tragedy," 291n.
Wellhausen, Julius, 101n., 106
Wenzel, Fritz
"Das Paulusbild bei Lagarde, Nietzsche und Rosenberg," 102n.
Werner, Martin, 370
Wessell, Leonard
G. E. Lessing's Theology: A Reinterpretation, 178n.
"G. F. Meier and the Genesis of Philosophical Theodicies of History in 18th-Century Germany," 178n.
Wettley, Annemarie
"Zur Problemgeschichte der 'dégénérescence,'" 209n.
White, William Hale (trans.), 133
"Wie klein mancher Große ist . . . " (anon.), 207n.
Wilcox, John T.
Truth and Value in Nietzsche, 181n., 275n.
Wilhelm I (Kaiser), 153
Winckelmann, Johann Joachim, 146, 150, 189
Witkowsky, Gustav
"Nietzsches Stellung zum Zionismus," 207n.

Wittgenstein, Ludwig, 271n.
Tractatus Logico-Philosophicus, 271
Wolff, Hans M.
Friedrich Nietzsche. Der Weg zum Nichts, 17n., 22
Wolff, Paul, 323
Denken und Glauben. Reden und Aufsätze, 111n.
Dionysus oder der Gekreuzigte, 111n., 323n.
Wright, G. Ernest
"The Faith of Israel," 77n.

Yahweh (Jehovah), 49, 51, 56, 57, 58, 60, 70, 94, 192, 206, 238

Zarathustra, 16, 17, 18, 19, 21, 45, 46, 51, 63, 65, 67, 68, 81, 87, 93, 94, 96, 98, 111, 115, 137, 138, 139, 140, 141, 190n., 204, 241, 307, 312, 313, 321, 324, 332, 334, 338, 340, 347, 359, 361, 367, 368, 370, 371, 372, 373
Zeus, 369
Ziesemer, Walther (ed.), 277n.
Zopyrus, 118n.
Zoroaster, 286
Zunz, Leopold, 217